Achievement behavior in schools can be understood best in terms of students' attempts to maintain a positive self-image. For many students, expending effort is scary because a combination of effort and failure implies low ability. Students have a variety of techniques for avoiding failure, ranging from cheating to setting goals that are so easily achieved that no risk is involved. Although teachers usually reward achievement and punish lack of effort, for many students risking the sense of defeat that comes from trying hard and not succeeding is too daunting. In *Making the grade,* Martin Covington extracts powerful educational implications from self-worth theory and other contemporary views that will be useful for educators, parents, and all people concerned with the educational dilemmas we face.

MAKING THE GRADE

Making the grade

A SELF-WORTH PERSPECTIVE ON MOTIVATION AND SCHOOL REFORM

Martin V. Covington
University of California, Berkeley

CAMBRIDGE
UNIVERSITY PRESS

Published by the Press Syndicate of the University of Cambridge
The Pitt Building, Trumpington Street, Cambridge CB2 1RP
40 West 20th Street, New York, NY 10011-4211, USA
10 Stamford Road, Oakleigh, Victoria 3166, Australia

First published 1992

Printed in the United States of America

Library of Congress Cataloging-in-Publication Data
Covington, Martin V., 1938–
Making the grade : A self worth perspective on motivation and school reform / Martin V. Covington.
p.   cm.
ISBN 0-521-34261-9. – ISBN 0521-34803-X (pbk)
1. Motivation in education   2. Self-respect in children.
I. Title.
LB1065.C65   1992
370.15′4–dc20   91-34323
                                                                      CIP

A catalog record for this book is available from the British Library

ISBN 0-521-34261-9 hardback
ISBN 0-521-34803-X paperback

To
Bette, my wife, and
Matt and Mark, our sons –
with love and gratitude

How can we provide opportunities and rewards for individuals of every degree of ability so that individuals at every level will realize their full potentialities, perform at their best and harbor no resentment toward any other level?

JOHN GARDNER

Contents

1

The future and its discontents

We know nothing about motivation. All we can do is write books about it.
PETER DRUCKER

Certainly much has been written about motivation. To this extent Drucker's observation is correct. The *Reader's Guide Index* lists scores of books on motivation written in the last decade alone, and these do not include the hundreds of research articles and technical reports churned out each year. What is less clear, however – and this is Drucker's concern – is the *nature* of our understanding. Actually, we do know a good deal about motivation, but on closer inspection our knowledge is quite uneven. We know *how* to arouse people to greater effort, especially for short periods of time: how, for example, to arrange incentives for factory workers so that production improves and absenteeism falls; and even how to rearrange the social organization of schools so that students are more willing to pursue learning for its own sake. But knowing *how* to motivate is not the same as knowing *what* is motivation. Here Drucker makes his point. Whatever is being aroused by the clever use of rewards and incentives, namely, motivation itself, remains mysterious and elusive. Motivation, like the concept of gravity, is easier to describe (in terms of its outward, observable effects) than it is to define. Of course, this has not stopped researchers from trying. The history of various attempts to grasp the essence of motivation is the first main theme of this book.

We will find that some observers believe motivation resides in human emotions. To them, positive motivation is synonymous with the feelings of pride and exhilaration that accompany success; and the darker side of motivation – despair, anger and resistance – is thought to be amplified by the feelings of shame and humiliation that accompany failure. There is much to recommend this position. Clearly, feelings can both arouse and inhibit action. Other investigators argue with equal conviction that motivation is fundamentally the property of thoughts, or cognitions, as we will call them – those faint musings, memories, and self-reflections that preoccupy humans much of the time. This basic proposition also is above debate. Clearly, thoughts also trigger, sustain, and inhibit action. Still other researchers look to physiological arousal – those momentary changes in body and brain functioning – as the telltale footprints of motivation. Here, too, the arguments are reasonable, even persuasive, but like the other positions they are also incomplete.

Finally, there is the contrarian point of view: Internal, subjective states like motivation or self-awareness are useless as scientific concepts, and are merely excess baggage when it comes to explaining behavior. To these *behaviorists,* motivation is simply a way of talking, metaphorically, about the effects of rewards and punishments that cause people to act with more or less energy or to pay more attention to some aspects of their environment than others. According to this argument, if researchers could describe reinforcement schedules in enough detail, then they would have access to all the information necessary to make accurate predictions about human behavior without the need to invoke the concept of motivation. Consider, for instance, the fact that Duncan's weekly allowance depends on keeping up with his homework. A casual observer might pronounce Duncan keen on school, and motivated to a fault, although we know that a more accurate, revealing interpretation is that Duncan's behavior is under the control of positive reinforcers.

A second theme of this book involves picking through this definitional maze and the various controversies created by these different perspectives. We will sift and weigh the evidence and eventually conclude that each position shares some portion of the truth. But how should these seemingly disparate claims and approaches to motivation be integrated into a larger, meaningful whole? Our rallying point is a self-worth perspective, and the arena of inquiry the schools and classrooms of America in the last decade of the 20th century. In the course of these inquiries we will encounter most of the major players, events, and lines of investigation that make up the history of research on achievement motivation over the last half century. The accumulated work of hundreds of scholars is reviewed here and woven (hopefully) as individual threads into a larger tapestry of understanding.

First of all, then, this book is meant to serve as an introduction to the topic of achievement motivation. But there is more. I will also deal with the future, and the possibility of reshaping American education to meet the challenges of the future. Clearly, these two topics – motivation and the future – are closely linked. As Harry Lauder once remarked, "The future is not a gift, it is an achievement," and it might be added, an achievement built in equal measure on discipline, realism, and joyful dreaming. I will arrange the research on achievement motivation in ways that lead to several recommendations for restructuring the educational experience of millions of schoolchildren today and many millions more tomorrow. This gathering together of current scientific knowledge, then refracting it through the lens of practical concern is the third main theme.

In effect, this book is intended to function variously as a treatise on achievement motivation, as a bridge between educational theory and practice, and as a blueprint for responsible change. In this first chapter we will see how the concept of achievement motivation and the demands of the future are inseparable aspects of any informed effort to recast the mission of schools. We will also unveil the broad outlines of what it means to undertake a motivational analysis of classroom life, and introduce the general psychological arguments to be pursued. I begin with a brief exposition of the future and of the desperate need for education to face constructively the challenges that a changing future will certainly bring.

Prospects for building the future

My interest is in the future because I am going to spend the rest of my life there.
CHARLES KETTERING

If the future is an achievement, as Lauder argues, then teachers are futurists along with politicians, filmmakers, and journalists – those individuals who according to J. McClellan (1978) "make other people's futures more real to them." Indeed, at its best, education should provide students with a sense of empowerment that makes the future "real" by moving beyond merely offering children plausible alternatives to indicating how their preferred dreams can actually be attained. By this reckoning teaching can be thought of as the ultimate, if only the second oldest, service profession.

But of what should this future-building legacy consist, especially since no one can know the future, at least in any detail? First, we can suggest that in preparing for the future, students develop viable occupational skills. Learning a discipline – whether it means becoming a plumber, a rodeo performer, or a writer – and doing it well provides the foundation for a sense of purpose, security, and confidence in adulthood. It is confidence that propels the future and, conversely, feelings of incompetency that cause us to fall short of what is best in us. This is true of individuals and also of societies and civilizing epochs. Perhaps Lord Kenneth Clark (1969) put it best when he remarked that

> civilisation requires a modicum of material prosperity – enough to provide a little leisure. But, far more, it requires confidence – confidence in the society in which one lives, belief in its philosophy, belief in its laws, and confidence in one's own mental powers. . . . Vigor, energy, vitality: All the great civilisations . . . have had the weight of energy behind them. (p. 4)

Second, students should prepare for change. Change, to recall a cliché, is the future's only constant. There is a need to accept with grace the inevitability of change – to be part of the process of change whether this means facing up to evershifting personal relationships, accepting change in the prevailing social order, or understanding changing global economics. As we shall see, change is best handled, and even welcomed, when individuals possess a well-developed arsenal of mental skills associated with original, creative, and independent thinking. This suggests that schoolchildren should cultivate the capacity to deal thoughtfully with future circumstances that they and even we, their mentors, cannot fully imagine. This capacity involves a continual readiness to find problems everywhere, to be puzzled by the obvious, to see the extraordinary in the ordinary, and a willingness to think about the seemingly impossible. Naturally, of course, change should not be accepted uncritically. It must first be evaluated in the light of both potential benefits and inevitable costs, an observation that calls to mind the *cliff-hanger theorem:* "Each problem solved introduces a new unsolved problem" (O'Brien in Dickson, 1978). Avoiding the pitfalls of expediency requires careful problem analysis, critical thinking, and the ability to anticipate the results of change.

Third, and perhaps above all, the greatest legacy of education is to encourage a will to learn and to continue learning as personal circumstances change – in short, to promote a capacity for resiliency and self-renewal. This point was anticipated over a half century ago when John Dewey (1938/1963) remarked that "the most important attitude that can be formed is that of the desire to go on learning" (p. 48).

These are brave sentiments and some would say hopelessly romantic and unattainable: a sense of commitment, self-confidence, and resiliency in the face of change. No one can be against these values, yet who among us is immodest enough to say precisely how to achieve them? As a result, these values are honored more in the breach than in the observance. Today too many students graduate or drop out of school without a single achievement for which they can feel uniquely responsible or justly proud. Moreover, the majority of our students understand neither the history of change nor the forces that shape their own individual lives; and their loyalties often run to self-indulgence and near-term gratification.

Also, there is little that is new about these values. There have been repeated calls for encouraging them, with a long history of failure to do so dating back at least as far as Greco-Roman times, when an anonymous observer lamented that "our students have grown lazy and are disrespectful of authority. They slight their tutors, mislead their teachers, and fail to attend to their lessons" (Covington & Beery, 1976, p. 1). These same troubling themes have echoed down through the ages and find their most recent embodiment in American ghetto youngsters who according to Shelby Steele (1989a), "see studying as a sucker's game and school itself as a waste of time. One sees in many of these children almost a determination not to learn, a suppression of the natural impulse to understand, that cannot be entirely explained by the determinism of poverty" (p. 506). The educational enterprise has been in deep trouble for a long time, and the problems continue to mount.

But now there is something *new,* not the values themselves but a fuller understanding of how to shape the educational experience of youngsters in order to encourage these values. Today we have a reasonably good grasp of why schools so often fail to achieve these broad humanizing goals, despite a consensus view among parents and teachers alike of their importance (Reasoner, 1973). We also understand, noble sentiments aside, why we often fall short of teaching even the barest essentials: reading with understanding, writing with clarity, and computing with accuracy.

The vision of the teacher as futurist prompts the one question central to all strategic institutional planning: "In the long run, in what business will this institution be?" (Keller, 1983). If this question is ignored, educators run the risk of being continually diverted by immediate crises and satisfied with stop-gap measures. But how do we establish the necessary perspective? To begin we must take note of the reasoning of Isaac Asimov, when he proposes that "the important thing to forecast is not the automobile, but the parking problem; . . . not the television but the soap opera" (Dede, 1988, p. 15). And extending this reasoning to education – to estimate, for instance, not the number of microcomputers in classrooms by the year 2020, but how these devices will alter the relationship between teacher and student, school and society. Similarly, by adopting a motivational perspective, we must ask, not so much what subject matter content will be most appropriate in the year 2020, but what kinds of reasons students will have for learning at all!

I concur with the wry observation that forecasting is very difficult, especially if it's about the future. This is the predicament faced by meteorologists. It is said that forecasting the intermediate future, say, weather patterns from 3 weeks to 6 months distant, is the riskiest. By comparison, there is more agreement about long-term global trends in the weather, years or even decades into the future, and about forecasting for today: Just stick your hand outside; if it's wet, it's raining!

In education, too, we know it's raining, not to say blustering. In fact, the storm warnings have been up for years, which prompted Louis Gerstner, President of American Express, to remark impatiently, "No more prizes for predicting rain. Prizes only for building arks." But what kinds of arks? And what is likely to happen if we do not go into the ark-building business? Before meddling with the future we must be convinced that alternative visions of education are likely to fare better than "business as usual" or, stated differently, that future prospects are so horrifying that virtually any change in the current ways of schooling will be welcome. Enough is now known for us to develop plausible scenarios of future events if trends continue. These trends project a dismal, downward course. If things are going to get worse, how bad are they now?

The class of 2001

The high school graduating class of the year 2001 just recently entered kindergarten. Like so many other students before them, they, too, approached the future with enthusiasm. Yet unless things change, their enthusiasm will also dwindle and soon evaporate. Kati Haycock and M. Susan Navarro (1988) describe it this way:

> For many, this process will begin very early in their school careers. Even in first grade, some youngsters will get the sense that something is wrong with them; that somehow they're just not doing things right. . . . By the sixth or seventh grade, many will not be proficient in the basic skills. . . . Though still in school, they will have dropped out mentally. Before high school graduation, they, and many of their peers, will drop out altogether." (p. 1)

In California, 3 out of 10 students entering the ninth grade today will not graduate from high school, a rate that has doubled since 1970 (Haycock & Navarro, 1988). Moreover, these figures are conservative when considering Latinos and blacks whose comparable dropout rates in California are now close to 50%!

For many of those who remain in school, the prospects for learning are shocking. For instance, the nationwide reading achievement scores for recent graduating high school seniors reflect a ninth-grade level of proficiency, which likely explains a U.S. Navy report that one-quarter of its recent recruits could not read well enough to understand basic safety instructions (reported in Wurman, 1989, p. 54). Writing skills are no better. According to Albert Shanker (1988), President of the American Federation of Teachers, only 20% of those youngsters still in high school can write a minimally acceptable letter applying for a job in a local supermarket. Shanker also reports that only 5% of all 17-year-olds can read a railroad timetable or a bus schedule well enough to get to a given destination on a certain day. Additionally, 88% of graduating high school seniors cannot correctly place six common fractions in order from smallest to largest. It makes little difference that the 20-year decline in SAT scores has recently been reversed, at least temporarily (Haycock & Navarro, 1988). The absolute level of intellectual functioning – the yield factor, as it is called by the Educational Testing Service – is still abysmally low by any standard. A majority of junior-high school students can name more brands of whiskey than they can past presidents of the United States. And in a recent ABC-TV sponsored survey of 200 teenagers, two-thirds could not identify Chernobyl (one youngster guessed it was Cher's real name).

Current events may not be their strong suit, but American schoolchildren show even less aptitude for problem solving, if that seems possible. For example, one group of first- and second-grade children blithely solved the following word problem, mostly by manipulating the integers 10 and 26: "There are 26 sheep and 10 goats on a ship. How old is the captain?" (Reusser, 1987). None of these students saw anything odd about this question. Unfortunately, immaturity is not the explanation. A group of 100 fourth- and fifth-grade students attacked a similar nonproblem with equal diligence, unperturbed (with the exception of only one child) by the fact that as presented the task could not be solved: "Yesterday 33 boats sailed into port and 54 boats left it. Yesterday at noon there were 40 boats still in port. How many boats were still in port yesterday evening?" Only after considerable prompting did five of the students describe the problem as "strange" or "different." These are examples of students calculating but not thinking, trapped by the mindless rote application of rules that unfold automatically, irrespective of their relevance to the problem. And, what is worse by far is that our children are unaware of these deficiencies or at least seem unperturbed by them. They know less about mathematics, less about their world, yet ironically they feel better about themselves than do students in China and Japan (Stevenson & Flanagan, 1990). Mary McCaslin and Thomas Good (1990) ruefully observe that "our students are like Buick, who advertises that its car is fifth-rated but is still the best in America" (p. 9).

The typical school environment for the class of 2001 is hardly conducive to academic learning of any kind. Many schools are literally armed camps. Nationwide, 135,000 children take a gun to school each day (Haycock, 1990) and thousands more must report to probation officers for past offenses. In Los Angeles County alone at least 600 rival gangs have been identified with a total of some 70,000 members (State Task Force on Gangs and Drugs, 1989). Gang-involved youth play a disproportionate role in acts of violence including rape, robbery, extortion, and vandalism, and in many cities they represent a serious threat to teachers and other students. Perhaps most distressing of all is the increased involvement of gangs as a primary network for drug trafficking. The money-making potential of drug dealing has turned many gangs into organized crime units. In some cities eight-year-olds are being used as drug runners for dealers, as weapons carriers, and when they have grown a little older they may become gang enforcers and hit men. Schools are rapidly becoming the main center of drug distribution in America.

Today in the 1990s bombing, arson, extortion, and injurious assault have replaced running in the halls, chewing gum, and getting out of line as the leading school discipline problems. In some ghetto schools, the rate of student deaths caused by peer violence and drug overdose approaches the rate of American combat fatalities in the Viet Nam War. Things have become so desperate in some urban areas that black teenage males have literally become an endangered group. And speaking of violence, consider suicide. Estimates of unsuccessful suicide attempts among our youth run as high as 600,000 per year nationwide with 6,000 actual deaths reported in 1986 (President's Newsletter, 1986).

Overall, this dismal scene can be put in stark relief by a single statistic: Thirteen million students – or nearly one-half of all school age youngsters – are at serious risk for failing academically ("Bringing Children Out," 1988). Also, more often than not, school failure clusters with delinquency, substance abuse, and teenage pregnancy. A recent study sponsored by the Carnegie Corporation (Dryfoos, 1990) estimates that at least three million adolescents, ages 10–17, have fallen prey to all or most of these high-risk behaviors, and that another four million are at substantial risk of destroying their life chances. These seven million youngsters represent one out of every four adolescents in the United States. Moreover, by this same accounting, an additional seven million adolescents are at "moderate" risk, "moderate" being defined as precocious, but at least protected, sexual activity, and by only *occasional* drug use! These statistics make grim reading. But what is even worse is the enormous future downstream costs they represent – more housing subsidies and health care, more police and prisons, and more welfare for adults who cannot qualify for jobs that would otherwise enable them to support themselves and their families.

These social costs are also reflected in disquieting statistics. Consider, as only one example, school dropouts and the burden to be borne by a poorly educated underclass. In California, girls who leave school – pregnant or not, married or unmarried – are nine times more likely to go on welfare than those who graduate from high school (Haycock & Navarro, 1988). Nationwide, the estimates are comparable (*Carnegie Quarterly*, 1988). For boys who drop out, the unemployment rate 2 years later is three times higher than that experienced by high school graduates. Moreover dropouts are four times more likely to commit a crime within 2 years of leaving school compared to their counterparts who graduate. The annual cost of housing a prison inmate in 1984 was $15,000 per year, roughly the annual undergraduate tuition fee and living expenses for Harvard, Yale, or Stanford at that time (Haycock & Navarro, 1988).

Finally, consider the dislocation and waste of talent created by under-achievement in school. In the technologically sophisticated society of the late 20th century, the need for unskilled labor has plummeted, and is likely to continue downward at least in the near-term. Over the next two decades, the majority of new job openings will require some form of education beyond high school. Yet, at present less than 40% of our youth enter any form of postsecondary education, including technical trade schools, and far fewer than half of these individuals complete their course of study. Among those blacks and Hispanics admitted to college, the rate of degree completion is under 20%.

This educational shortfall is largely responsible for the present employment problems of teenagers. For example, although the number of job openings in the period 1986–1988 was relatively plentiful, the unemployment rate among youth seeking work was five times higher than that found among adults. Many undereducated youngsters simply could not qualify for the available jobs. Nor is there much relief in sight. The national job market is characterized by rapid shifts in opportunities across economic sectors and by a diversity of employer needs. Automation, international competition, and seasonal fluctuations add to this instability.

Change is the watchword. For instance, when the graduating class of the year 2001 enters the permanent work force, it is estimated that they will change careers – not just jobs, but careers – an average of five times before they retire. Yet given what can be deduced from all of the statistics just cited, a near majority of our youth will face an unknown world utterly unprepared – compromised by neglect, bewilderment, and anger. Without the capacity to participate and learn from change, and from occasional upheaval, these youngsters will become crippled, confused, and then overwhelmed by a vastly changed future society in which they will no longer know how to participate. Such observations take on a special imperative in light of America's shrinking role as the economic engine and prime mover of the world economy. Clearly, we cannot hope to compete in a technologically advanced world game when many of our players are illiterate or underprepared. For example, one Tokyo firm uses high school graduates from Japanese schools to conduct statistical quality control on its semiconductor products. In the United States, the same firm had to hire individuals with graduate school degrees to carry out the same work because neither American high school nor college graduates could be taught the technology involved (reported in Wurman, 1989, p. 151).

Clearly much is amiss. For many children growing up in America has become a perilous, dispirited business. And unless things change, the over-whelming likelihood is that the situation will worsen. Before we rethink the mission of education, however, several additional observations are in order.

Issues of responsibility

The first observation concerns the matter of assigning blame. Who is respon-sible for the mess? The present crisis in learning cannot be attributed solely, or even largely, to the failure of any particular educational policy. Many other factors outside the reach of schools are also involved in this decline – poverty, the loosening of public morals, broken homes, and the drug epidemic, to name only a few. In fact, it can be argued that without the steadying presence of schools, for all their limitations, things would be even worse.

Be that as it may, finger pointing is of little value because in this maelstrom of abuse, abandonment, and failure, what is *cause* and what is *effect* become blurred. Take just one example. There can be no doubt that the failure of schools to teach contributes directly to youngsters dropping out of school; but then so does becoming pregnant. Teenage pregnancy is a leading cause of leaving school in America. Nationwide, more than one million girls in the class of 1986 became pregnant before high school graduation (Riessman, 1988). This translates into a teenage pregnancy rate twice that found in Great Britain and Canada, three times that of France, and more than four times the rates in Sweden and Holland ("Bringing Children Out," 1988). Although these rates are somewhat higher for black than white teenagers, the birthrate for whites alone still exceeds that for teenagers in all other western industrialized countries. It is these babies born to mere children, raised in unrelenting poverty and frequently abused, neglected, and drug exposed, who will in turn become handicapped in *their* social, cognitive, and emotional development, so that yet another generation becomes failure prone (Patterson, 1987; Schorr, 1988). And the deprivation can be elemental. Some children enter kindergarten never having held a pencil, others never having used silverware!

Here one can glimpse something of the multiheaded, interlocking nature of the problems that beset the efforts of teachers to teach, and of students to learn. Little wonder that teachers are so prone to disillusionment and burnout. Events simply overwhelm them. As one veteran teacher remarked, "When you've given your all and there is no hope – that's too much." There are fewer villains than victims in this scenario.

Not only are the causes of school failure many, but the burden imposed on schools grows daily. Increasingly schools are expected to act as custodians for a growing assortment of youthful misfits and incorrigibles. Schools also are expected to stem the tide of rising teenage promiscuity through instruction in a secular version of morality training, and to act as the first line of defense against public health dangers of truly catastrophic proportions, including epidemic drug use.

It would be foolish to argue that issues of drugs, sex, and violence are not part of growing up educated in America today. Nor can schools easily abandon their responsibilities in these areas. But their resources are limited. To these burdens we can add other responsibilities that in part represent failures of wider social policy, and public indifference. These additional demands involve the legitimate need for everyone to succeed – ethnic minorities, the economically disadvantaged, learning-handicapped pupils, and the burgeoning populations of immigrants from non-English-speaking homes. The enormity of this challenge is reflected by the fact that at last count some 91 non-English languages and dialects are spoken in the Los Angeles County

schools! And then there is the pressing need to teach children how to cooperate with peoples of diverse political, cultural, and religious backgrounds in
the face of a potentially hostile world whose boundaries shrink daily.

In the waning years of the 20th century, there is altogether too much evidence that American schools have become a dumping ground for the unwanted, the unacceptable, and for the seemingly unsolvable problem; a place
of failed individuals and of failed social policy. It is an enterprise for which
too much has been demanded, with too few resources made available. As a
consequence, schools do too few things well, and when they do achieve excellence, too few students benefit. This situation has occurred, despite the
Herculean efforts of dedicated, hardworking teachers, administrators and staff.
If energy and devotion alone could solve our educational problems, then solutions would be far more advanced than is now the case. We will argue that
teachers can do little to shorten the terrible odds arrayed against them and
their students unless there is a fundamental reconsideration of the motivational dynamics of learning, and of *what* should be taught as well as *how*.
Actually, teachers are victims, too, ensnared by the same outmoded views of
motivation and learning that hold students hostage.

Issues and answers

A second observation concerns the matter of solutions. If many of the causes
of academic failure lie outside the reach of schools to correct, then solutions
become just that much more difficult. More than schools must change. Everywhere today we find evidence of a struggle among scholars, policymakers,
and public officials to draw together into a more meaningful, coherent whole
a kaleidoscope of isolated facts, tantalizing but untried theories, and commonsense answers, which in the words of Ernest Becker (1981) are "strewn
all over the place, spoken in 1,000 competitive voices . . . insignificant frag-
ments magnified out of all proportion while major insights lie around begging
for attention. There is no throbbing vital center." Becker is correct. Inter-
twined problems are divided up into more manageable but essentially meaningless pieces that correspond to traditional academic, political, and bureaucratic boundaries. Drug abuse remains the province of rehabilitation programs,
and poverty the responsibility of welfare programs. This is a piecemeal approach to a problem that deserves a unified response. If we are ever to find
adequate answers these artificial distinctions must be abandoned. For example, an analysis of health-care delivery by David Hamburg (1986), President of the Carnegie Corporation, suggests that sustained health benefits are
most likely to occur when the target group, say, school-aged children in a
single community, are immersed in a circle of positive, interlocking influences in the form of parental health education programs, community clinics,
service organizations, and church-based outreach groups. Likewise, studies
of effective schools reveal that only the total school environment can have a
positive impact on student achievement. No single element − such as intensive parental involvement or reduced class size − is enough in itself to make
the difference, but none can be ignored. Effective schooling involves a shared

sense of commitment by students, staff, parents, and community alike (Levin, 1986; Tyack & Hansot, 1982; Bossert, 1979).

Within the last decade a series of blue-ribbon committees has attempted to rally the kinds of consensus of which Becker speaks, beginning in 1983 with the landmark report, *A Nation at Risk,* which warned ominously of a ''rising tide of mediocrity'' (National Commission on Excellence in Education, 1983), and most recently, the State of California Task Force on Self-esteem and Social Responsibility, which urges the incorporation of self-worth goals into the educational mission (Covington, 1989; Mecca, Smelser, & Vasconcellos, 1989). Yet, despite this national focus on reform, things remain largely fragmented, if we can judge from a recent poll of some 150 policymakers asked to predict those trends and issues that will mark education in the 1990s (''A Look Ahead,'' 1990). A number of these individuals mentioned *accountability* as the most important theme and stressed the need for higher, uniform national standards of performance for both teachers and students. Many others focused on the question of who should control school policy, with the local community, the several states, and the individual classroom teacher being nominated about equally. Still other respondents emphasized the need for more teachers – two million new teachers will be needed by 1995, but less than one million young people are expected to enter the profession before then. Incidently, only a handful of the 150 respondents pointed to the need for curriculum reform, and fewer still raised questions about the present quality of student motivation.

It is not that any one of these issues is right and the others wrong. Nor is it necessarily a question of their relative importance. Rather one wonders where Becker's ''throbbing vital center'' is to be found. Our particular search for this elusive center starts with a motivational analysis of the single most important, irreducible component in the equation of schooling – the individual learner.

Now, a few words about the kinds and scope of remedies to be offered in this book. First, my recommendations will focus on those that follow uniquely from a motivational perspective. In effect, I will ask if there is any special contribution that research on achievement motivation can make to our understanding of the exceedingly complex phenomena of school learning and school failure.

Second, these recommendations are intended to be compatible, insofar as possible, with other analyses of the school crisis that come from quite different starting points: from the business community, from minority neighborhoods, and from Main Street.

Third, recommendations will be restricted to those that are eminently practical and capable of implementation by schools within a relatively short period of time, say, within 5 years. This implies that these recommendations are not particularly new, but largely untried, yet familiar enough to be implemented without a massive overhaul of the system. Indeed, all the ingredients are well known to educators, but they are often overlooked and underappreciated – until now ''strewn all over the place.''

Fourth, there must be a reasonable prospect that these changes, if initiated even in modest ways, can influence youngsters here and now – those who will graduate in the year 2001 – and not be delayed in their impact until some distant, future time. This caveat is not meant to imply that a total reformation can occur within such a brief span, but only that hints of positive payback should emerge soon, portending greater dividends to come. Actually, any changes in schools of the magnitude ultimately needed must be worked out in terms of generations, not just decades, time enough to reshape public beliefs about the mission of schooling and to revitalize teacher training.

Finally, we must remain mindful of the classic predicament of all reform efforts captured in the picturesque lament, Who can think about draining the swamp when we are up to our asses in alligators? The answer, it appears, involves a little swimming, then a little draining, and an occasional hop up on the bank to gain the perspective (and safety) of distance. Hopefully, modern views of motivation can provide this perspective.

But does a motivational perspective admit to such possibilities, even in theory? And, seriously, what is the hope for any practical successes, especially given the fact that student indifference, truancy, and poor achievement often go hand in hand with classroom violence, drug dealing in the school yard, and other deplorable forms of abuse and exploitation? Obviously, academic failure is as much, if not more, the result of the inevitable pressures and risks of growing up in a dangerous, unforgiving environment as it is the fault of any misguided educational policy. Perhaps in the end there is little that schools can do to reverse the horrific statistics of failure and despair cited earlier. We must be prepared for the possibility that in the final analysis the massive failure to learn is merely the end result, and not the cause, of a steady accumulation of various social ills. But to abandon the search for school-related solutions now is to admit defeat prematurely. Basically, I will argue that even if schools were drug free, uncompromised by hatred and fear, and not a dumping ground for the rebellious and the unwanted, certain aspects of schooling would still be a threat to the future of our children. It is these dangers, no matter how modest they may be compared to the larger circle of threat, that will drive our recommendations for educational change.

It is important that I now introduce the topic of achievement motivation and reconnoiter the psychological landscape over which we will travel. It is one thing to pronounce that educational failure is best understood in motivational terms, but quite another to marshal convincing scientific evidence, especially around a concept like motivation that is so complex and far-reaching.

The failure to learn: A motivational analysis

People compose for many reasons: To become immortal; because the piano forte happens to be open; because they want to become a millionaire; because of the praise of friends; because they have looked into a pair of beautiful eyes; for no reason whatsoever.
ROBERT SCHUMANN

Just what is a motivational analysis of classroom life? Simply put, motivation deals with the *why* of behavior: *Why,* for example, do individuals choose to work on a certain task and not on others; *why* do they exhibit more or less energy in the pursuit of these tasks; and *why* do some people persist until the task is completed, whereas others give up before they really start, or in some cases pursue more elegant solutions long after perfectly sensible answers have presented themselves?

In essence, the answer to all these questions is that, like Schumann's composers, different persons have different reasons to achieve. In school, some students learn to earn gold stars and may stop when these reinforcers are no longer forthcoming. Other students strive to develop new skills for the sake of self-mastery, and will not stop until they are acquired. Still others seek to demonstrate superior ability either by outperforming others or by achieving notable successes with little or no effort. From these few examples, it is not difficult to appreciate that what students learn, how much they remember, and how engaged they become depends largely on which reasons dominate.

Over the past several decades, two broadly different conceptions of achievement motivation have emerged. One perspective views motivation as a *drive,* that is, an internal state, need, or condition that impels individuals toward action. In short, the need is the reason. In this tradition the reasons for action are thought to reside largely within the individual, a point nicely illustrated by Joan, a young corporate executive, who attempts to outperform all her colleagues in order to become indispensable. The behaviors associated with such a drive can be so all-consuming, insistent, and predictable that we often talk about them as being traitlike, hence the notion of something residing *within* the person. In Joan's case descriptors such as *ambitious, willful,* and *compulsive* readily come to mind: If anyone is first to use the in-flight phone during a cross-country business trip, it is Joan; if anyone is working after hours, Joan is sure to be there, too, so as not to be outdone.

The *motives-as-drive* approach typically views motivation as an *enabling* factor – a means to an end, with the end being improved status, better performance, or, in Joan's case, an increased sense of security. This drive perspective dominates popular thinking whenever schools are admonished by politicians or newspaper editors to motivate (drive) students to do better as the answer to those horrifying achievement statistics cited earlier. A particularly crude but unmistakable expression of this reasoning was recently overheard by education professor Michael Kirst (1990), "One legislator told me, 'I just want the little buggers to work harder.' " The underlying assumption is that if we can provide the right rewards and enough of them, or threaten sufficient punishments, we can arouse (drive) otherwise dispirited, lazy students to higher levels of achievement. Then there is the corollary: that arousal is maximized when these rewards are distributed on a competitive basis, that is, the greater number of rewards going to those who perform best.

A second perspective considers motivation in terms of *goals* or *incentives* that draw, not drive, individuals toward action (Bolles, 1967; Elliott & Dweck, 1988). Researchers in this tradition assume that all actions are given meaning, direction, and purpose by the goals that individuals seek out, and that the quality and intensity of behavior will change as their goals change. Considered from this perspective, motivation is a unique human resource to be encouraged for its own sake, not simply a means to increased school performance. Indeed, by this analysis fostering meaningful, goal-directed behavior and the right reasons for learning becomes the ultimate purpose of schooling. Many *motive-as-goal* theorists focus on noncompetitive, intrinsic reasons for learning, goals that by their very nature beguile and entice individuals into action rather than push or drive them, and generally for ennobling reasons – for the sake of "a pair of beautiful eyes," to recall Schumann, or "for no reason whatsoever," save perhaps curiosity. And, finally, because goals are always the creature of future thinking, the motives-as-goal tradition is heavily future oriented.

Obviously, this drive/goal distinction is somewhat arbitrary (Hyland, 1988). For example, although we can justly describe Joan as being *driven* to outperform others, she is also pursuing a goal of sorts, albeit potentially destructive – masking feelings of inadequacy by making herself indispensable to others. These are two sides of the same behavioral coin. Neither view discounts the validity of the other; rather they are complementary. In fact, this complementary quality is essential to our story. The research that draws its inspiration from the drive-theory tradition helps clarify the basic causes of school failure and their motivational roots. For example, whenever students are driven by competition as a means to encourage learning, they react in ways that characterize the current educational crisis. Students become defensive, resistant, angry, and may even doubt themselves despite doing well. This drive-theory analysis of school achievement and failure will occupy us for the first six chapters. By contrast, the motive-as-goal approach provides a broad perspective on the kinds of *solutions* we seek. Whenever students are drawn to learning out of curiosity, for reasons of self-improvement, to understand the world in which they live, or for the sake of valued personal goals, they act in ways we admire and wish all students might emulate: They become absorbed, committed, and oblivious to the passage of time.

We will now consider each of these two traditions in somewhat more detail, but still only briefly, and outline the basic arguments to be elaborated later.

Motives as drives

Many of our current notions about achievement motivation evolved from earlier theories that emphasized the satisfaction of basic tissue needs such as hunger and thirst. However, because of the limitations of applying a strictly physiological approach to understanding human behavior, researchers eventually broadened their focus to include *learned* drives or *psychological* motives such as the needs for approval, power, and achievement.

ATKINSON'S NEED ACHIEVEMENT THEORY
The most sophisticated view of achievement motivation as a learned drive was developed initially in the 1950s and early 1960s by John Atkinson (Atkinson, 1957, 1964, 1987; Atkinson & Raynor, 1974) and David McClelland (1965). This theory holds that human achievement is the result of an emo-

tional conflict between striving for success and the fear of failure. These two motivational dispositions are characterized largely in emotional terms. For example, *hope* for success and the anticipation of *pride* at winning or prevailing over others is said to encourage success-oriented individuals to strive for excellence. On the other hand, a capacity for experiencing *shame* and *humiliation* is thought to drive failure-oriented persons to avoid situations where they believe themselves likely to fail. It is this difference in emotional reactions (pride vs. shame) that was thought to answer the *why* questions: *Why* some individuals approach learning with enthusiasm and others only with reluctance, and *why* some choose easy tasks for which success is assured, whereas others tackle problems for which the likelihood of failure is exquisitely balanced against the chances for success.

Atkinson's portrayal of achievement motivation as the expression of an emotional conflict holds enormous implications for educational theory and practice. If conflict is the best way to characterize the achievement process, then questions arise as to whether conflict is inevitable or whether it can be moderated, and if so, by what means? For example, research in the need achievement tradition demonstrates a clear association between early child-rearing practices and the quality of subsequent achievement behavior, thus raising the possibility of altering the quality of motivation through relearning.

Atkinson's learned-drive theory has undergone several significant modifications over the years. From an educational perspective, two of these changes are the most important: the challenge posed by cognitive attribution theory and the advent of self-worth theory.

ATTRIBUTION THEORY

Beginning in the early 1970s researchers led primarily by Bernard Weiner and his colleagues (Weiner et al., 1971) posed a radical reinterpretation of Atkinson's theory. Weiner reasoned that cognitive (thought) processes rather than emotional anticipation were the agents primarily responsible for the quality of achievement. In effect, what people *think* was given priority over how people *feel* as the prime mover of achievement behavior.

More specifically, Weiner proposed that *how* individuals perceive the causes of their prior successes and failures was the more likely determinant for choosing or not choosing to work on a particular task, and also for deciding how long to persist once work began. The study of people's beliefs about the causes of their behavior is the domain of attribution theory. For instance, persons who attribute their past successes to high ability are more likely to undertake similar challenges in the future because they anticipate doing well. By contrast, people are less likely to be optimistic about the future if they attribute their prior successes to good luck, or if they judge themselves powerless to succeed again owing to insufficient ability.

From a theoretical perspective, a subtle change occurred as the result of this cognitive reinterpretation. The classic question of *why* individuals achieve or not, which was answered originally in terms of feeling states, is now treated more as a question of *how* – how people interpret events and attribute meaning to their feelings. Although this shift is admittedly subtle, it is immensely important, especially for its educational implications. For example, if the rational, cognitive side of our nature truly controls motivated behavior, then educators would be well advised to put a premium on teaching students to analyze the causes of their successes and failures in the most constructive, yet realistic ways possible.

One of the most important features of attribution theory is its focus on the role of effort in achievement. This emphasis is justified for several reasons. For one thing, if students believe their failures occur for a lack of trying, then they are more likely to remain optimistic about succeeding in the future. For another thing, trying hard is known to increase pride in success and to offset feelings of guilt at having failed. And, perhaps most important of all, the emphasis on the role of effort in achievement is justified because it is widely believed that student effort is modifiable through the actions of teachers. Whether this premise is true or not, at least teachers act on it: Students whom teachers perceive as having tried hard are rewarded more in success and punished less in failure than students who do not try. From these patterns of teacher reinforcement, attribution theorists have concluded that students should value effort as the main source of personal worth.

But if this is true, why is it so many students do not try in school? Recall Shelby Steele's depressing observation that "one sees in many of these children almost a determination not to learn, a suppression of the natural impulse to understand." And why do other children hide their effort or refuse to admit that they study hard? The answer to these questions lies in the domain of self-worth theory.

SELF-WORTH THEORY
In our society human value is measured largely in terms of one's ability to achieve competitively. For example, researchers have found that nothing contributes more to a student's sense of esteem than good grades, nor shatters it so completely as do poor grades (Rosenberg, 1965). It is achievement, then – and its handmaiden, ability – that dominates as the ultimate value in the minds of many schoolchildren. Given this reality, it is not surprising that the student's sense of esteem often becomes equated with ability – to be able is to be valued as a human being but to do poorly in school is evidence of inability, and reason to despair of one's worth (Covington, 1984e).

Here we have the makings of a profound conflict in values. On the one hand, cognitive theory stresses those sources of worth that come from complying with a work ethic, whereas on the other, self-worth theory emphasizes those sources that follow from feeling smart. But why should there be any conflict at all? Cannot students become competent through hard work? Yes, in theory – and sometimes even in practice – but all too often schools are arranged so that learning becomes an ability game. In this special game, the amount of effort students expend provides clear information about their ability status. For instance, if students succeed without much effort, especially if the task is difficult, then estimates of their ability increase; but should they try hard and fail anyway, especially if the task is easy, attributions to low ability are likely to follow. Thus effort becomes what Martin Covington and Carol Omelich (1979b) have called a ''double-edged sword'' – valued by students because teachers reward it, yet also feared given its potential threat to their worth.

Self-worth theory contends that the protection of a sense of ability is the student's highest priority – higher sometimes even than good grades – so that students may handicap themselves by *not* studying because to try hard and fail anyway reflects poorly on their ability. A number of strategies for avoiding failure, or at least avoiding the implications of failure, have been identified and documented by researchers (e.g., Birney, Burdick, & Teevan, 1969). We will soon discover an almost endless variety of defensive tactics, some favored by middle-class white students and others by impoverished youngsters and ethnic minorities, all of which – no matter who employs them or what form they take – undercut the will to learn and compromise school achievement in the process.

This self-worth analysis is useful because it helps us understand what are *not* the causes of the massive default to learn in America today. Two noncauses can be mentioned in advance.

1. First, we must be wary of blaming the failure of students to learn simply on a *lack* of motivation. The absence of behavior – docility, passivity, and listlessness – is surely just as motivated a condition as is a lively abundance of behavior. According to a self-worth analysis, the reluctant learner is already motivated, driven by circumstances to protect his or her self-esteem. Thus the failure to achieve is just as likely the result of being *overmotivated,* but for the wrong reasons, as it is of not being motivated at all. This suggests that educators must alter the reasons that make for truancy, poor achievement, and belligerency rather than simply raise the stakes in what is already a losing game.

2. Second, self-worth arguments make clear that the present educational crisis is not merely a matter of poor performance. Slumping achievement scores are only symptoms. Rather, schools face a crisis in motivation. Once teachers alter the reasons that students learn, the symptoms should coincidentally disappear, like the breaking of a fever.

This is not to say that many current proposals for reform that derive from drive-theory notions are irrelevant. But they are surely incomplete and certainly lacking in imagination—''*More* academic courses, *more* hours in school, *more* homework, *more* tests, *more* hurdles for prospective teachers, *more* units for graduation . . .'' [italics added] (Russell, 1988, p. 4). Basically, these recommendations follow a strategy of *intensification,* or what we might call ''tinkering'' – simply continuing to do what has been done for years, but more of it and hopefully better. This strategy assumes that the present mode of schooling is fundamentally sound, and that no basic changes are needed. However, I will argue that, although there may be much to recommend some of these specific proposals if considered in a larger self-worth context, taken by themselves they are at best insufficient, if not too tame, and at worst counterproductive.

The potential dangers inherent in following a policy of intensification are particularly great for the failure-prone child, the underprepared, and those disenfranchised youngsters from underclass ghettos and barrios. As things stand, simply adding days to the school calendar will condemn many of these youngsters to waste more time, often in depressing, dilapidated, and abrasive environments. Nor is the solution as easy as adding new course requirements or raising academic standards, as has been done recently by many states and local school districts. If students cannot now measure up to old, presumably less demanding requirements, or pass the courses already on the books, then these increased demands would seem rather pointless. Effective solutions lie elsewhere – elsewhere being in a paradigm shift of thinking about schools. Timothy Dyer, Superintendent of the Phoenix High School District, put the challenge well when he remarked that "the restructuring of American education is going to be the debate of the 90s. . . . Are we talking about tinkering, or are we talking about whole new approaches" ("A Look Ahead," 1990, p. 30)?

Motives as goals

The last four chapters in this book deal with the search for solutions to the educational crisis in America. John Gardner's provocative question sets the challenge in ways that are consistent with our motivational approach: "How can we provide opportunities and rewards for individuals of every degree of ability so that individuals at every level will realize their full potentialities, perform at their best and harbor no resentment toward any other level" (Gardner, 1961, p. 115)? As Gardner himself recognized, the answer lies not so much in increasing motivation, that is, arousing existing drive levels, as in encouraging different kinds of motives altogether.

However, if motivation as a concept is so elusive (recall Drucker's remark about how little we know), then how can educators change that which is not yet fully understood? One answer is to consider motives as goals. Goal-setting stands as a practical surrogate for motives. By rewarding some goals and not others, teachers can change the reasons students learn, which is to say, change their motives. Thus we need not await final, all-encompassing definitions or ultimate clarification before taking steps to solve more immediate, pressing problems that are basically motivational in nature. We know that goal-setting controls behavior, especially the individual's future actions (Locke & Latham, 1984; Locke, 1968), and it is this applied knowledge that allows reform to proceed.

If motives are sometimes best described in traitlike terms, as something embedded in the individual, then just how malleable are achievement styles? The answer is that depending on the particular individual and on specific circumstances, behavior can be either quite flexible or extremely rigid. How can we represent the inherent duality in the concept of motivation as something at once fixed yet potentially changeable? Abraham Maslow's (1970) hierarchical model provides one answer.

MASLOW'S THEORY

Maslow proposed a five-fold *hierarchy* of human needs: (1) a basic level of physiological needs that includes the need for food and water; (2) the need for personal safety; (3) social needs including the desire to belong; (4) esteem needs that include feelings of self-respect and positive recognition from others; and, finally, (5) self-actualization, the need for a sense of personal fulfillment or, stated differently, the realization that one is achieving fully what he or she is capable of becoming. Maslow suggested that before the needs at one level can be satisfied, all other lower-order needs subsumed beneath them must first be satisfied. Additionally, as the needs at one level become satisfied, their importance in motivating individuals decrease, and the next higher level of needs becomes the strongest source of goal-directed behavior.

Although Maslow's theory has been criticized as unscientific (e.g., Wahba & Bridwell, 1976), it provides a useful way of thinking about the factors that activate normal human beings. Moreover, commonsense observations generally support his claim, at least for the more primitive survival needs. For instance, if we are starving, the goals of self-actualization will certainly not be paramount. We may even risk our physical safety in order to obtain food, and probably would not care what people think of our table manners. But, once our hunger is satisfied, we will be less likely to compromise our desire for safety. By the same token, as long as individuals are preoccupied with concerns over self-esteem, say, protecting a reputation for ability, they will not be fully free to use their talents constructively. Indeed, they may even forfeit forever the pursuit of excellence.

According to Maslow, what is fixed about human motivation is its stepwise, hierarchical ordering. But it is the environment, represented by various rewards and punishments, presses and opportunities, that determines what sources of satisfaction prevail at a given moment. The challenge to educators posed by Maslow's theory is to arrange schooling so that students can focus on becoming fully human or self-actualized, not merely winning over others with the ever-present danger of losing.

EXTRINSIC VERSUS INTRINSIC MOTIVATION

Another way of talking about preferred goals is to consider a distinction stressed by many researchers in the *motive-as-goal* tradition between extrinsic and intrinsic motivation.

The pursuit of some goals, such as satisfying Maslow's need for approval, depends closely on external payoffs, which in this particular instance involves seeking out applause, kudos, and praise, or at worst avoiding disapproval. For example, one student may study to please his father, whereas another studies to avoid the wrath of her father. Both youngsters are in the thrall of external rewards, the first responding to positive payoffs (fatherly admiration), and the second controlled by negative reinforcers, in this case the relief that comes from *avoiding* punishment. These rewards are considered extrinsic because they are basically irrelevant to the act of learning. Once the need for recognition is satisfied or the threat of failure removed there is no longer any particular reason for these students to learn.

By contrast, intrinsic motivation can be defined as the desire (or goal) to become more effective as a person – in Maslow's terms, to self-actualize. For instance, when a student willingly completes a reading assignment on nutrition because he believes a proper diet will help him remain fit, we say he is intrinsically motivated. So, too, is the student who pays close attention to a lecture on how to write persuasively so she can convince others, through her writing, not to do drugs. In these cases learning becomes valued for what it can do to benefit the individual or to enhance one's effectiveness. Additionally, individuals may seek out answers or information simply to satisfy their curiosity – to find out why, for example, some shoes squeak and others do not.

Naturally, like the distinction between drives and goals, the difference between intrinsic and extrinsic motivation is never plain or absolute. And, they often work in unison. Take the young man who avidly reads about nutrition. Although he appears to be acting intrinsically, as far as the example went, things get more complicated when we learn that his interest in staying healthy is also prompted by the larger goal of earning fame and fortune as a professional basketball star. Also consider the college professor whose search for knowledge for its own sake is sustained in part by the accolades she receives from her colleagues at the annual research conference.

Typically, human beings pursue a number of higher-order goals at once – Maslow's theory notwithstanding – as well as single goals for several interlocking reasons that sometimes reflect an amalgam of altruism, selfishness, and expediency. Even so, where education is concerned things go better with intrinsic goals. One reason for this is the close correspondence between what students perceive to be the purpose of schools and the quality of their own motivation. John Nicholls and his colleagues (Nicholls, 1984; Nicholls, Patashnick, & Nolen, 1985) found that high school students who believed schools should develop a commitment to solving society's problems or encourage a search for personal excellence were more satisfied with their school experiences, had better grades, and held stronger beliefs about the value of hard work than did students who viewed the primary function of schools to promote status, prestige, and economic security. The personal goals of this latter group tended to focus on the avoidance of work, on a desire for easy academic successes, and on self-aggrandizement (e.g., ''to show people I'm smart''). These goals were associated with the belief that success in school depends largely on manipulating others and on good luck. Perhaps most striking, and certainly ironic, was the fact that this group also expressed less interest in attending college – ironic, because the very reasons that serve to justify school in the minds of many as a way to get ahead, actually count against continuing in school once students are no longer required to do so (Kroll, 1988). These data give little encouragement to those who would advocate education principally as a means to power and financial security.

FOSTERING MOTIVATIONAL EQUITY

Two main themes are addressed in the last half of this book. The first concerns how schools can create a condition of what I will call *motivational equity*. Obviously, not everyone is equally bright, nor can all children compete on an equal footing intellectually. But at least schools can provide all students with a common heritage in the *reasons* they learn. Everyone can experience feelings of resolve and a commitment to think more, and to dare more; feelings of being caught up in the drama of problem solving, and of being poised to learn and ready to take the next step. Low ability is no barrier to this kind of excellence.

Encouraging motivational equity is not easy. Several questions arise whenever the notion of fostering intrinsic involvement is proposed. The first issue concerns the sheer frequency of rewards. If learning becomes its own reward with the happy prospect that, as Alice put it during her Wonderland adventures, "everyone has won and all must have prizes," will not the value of these freely available rewards be cheapened? In short, who wants to play games in which everyone wins?

Second, sometimes it becomes necessary to reward students extrinsically (with praise or grades) in order to involve them long enough so that what they learn will eventually become valued for its own sake. This most often occurs in the early stages of learning, especially for tasks that are seen as chores (e.g., learning the multiplication tables). But how can students become truly involved if they are originally paid to learn? Will not students conform just long enough to win the prize, and then disengage once these rewards are removed?

Third, the goal of motivational equity confronts educators with a potential dilemma. The more we equate students motivationally, then the more salient their differences in ability become in determining who performs best. Herein lies the dilemma. Students who believe themselves most capable are more likely to approach success and those who believe themselves least capable will strive to avoid failure. Thus if differences in ability are magnified, how can an equality of motivation be sustained? Is not the goal of motivational equity beyond the capability of schools to achieve?

FOSTERING GOAL-ORIENTED COGNITIONS

Establishing motivational equity is but one step toward resolving the current crisis. Another is fostering goal-oriented cognitions. The second main theme concerns the matter of *what* to teach; in effect, what is worth knowing as students begin to create their own futures? Two kinds of knowledge stand out: (1) knowing *how to learn,* that is, how to acquire specific facts, information, and vocabulary – what can be called the raw material of thought; and (2) knowing *how to think,* that is, how to arrange facts and information in ways that permit solutions to significant problems. This emphasis on thinking is important for at least three reasons.

Self-discipline and freedom. First, encouraging intrinsic goals means allowing students considerable freedom – freedom to set their own learning objectives and then to decide how best to achieve them. Such freedom requires self-discipline, the ability to make plans, and the capacity to monitor one's progress toward these self-selected goals. These qualities are rare enough, and they are particularly in short supply among children who see learning as a threat. It is failure-oriented students who need autonomy and independence the most, yet often are the least able to handle it. To them success is an unexpected event, and as a consequence they are unable to accept success, let alone plan for it. They misjudge their capacities and aspire after irrational goals for defensive purposes, and they are crippled by anxiety and self-doubt. For these youngsters something more is needed than simply providing an opportunity for unlimited rewards. They must also be trained in the skills of intellectual self-discipline that form the essential complement to freedom.

Ability as a resource. Second, improving one's ability to solve problems fosters the will to learn. The key to this relationship is the notion of ability as a resource. Many contemporary psychologists distinguish between stable, underlying abilities such as verbal, spatial, and mathematical aptitudes and the trainable mental skills or strategies by which these basic abilities are mobilized into effective thought and action. These mental strategies or resources include planning skills, techniques for asking good questions, and rules for making sound judgments. Although the fundamental intellectual capacity of individuals may not be subject to improvement, it is nonetheless widely held that teachers can help increase that which Alfred Binet (1909), the father of the mental test movement, said constitutes intelligence: "Comprehension, planfulness, invention and judgment – in these four words lies the essence of intelligence" (p. 54). Binet goes on to suggest that

> a child's mind is like a field for which an expert farmer has advised a change in the method of cultivating, with the result that in place of desert land, we now have a harvest. It is in this particular sense, the one which is significant, that we say that the intelligence of children may be increased. One increases that which constitutes the intelligence of a school child, namely, the capacity to learn, to improve with instruction. (1909, pp. 54–55)

Today many cognitive theorists agree with Binet. They are not so much interested in *intelligence* per se, as measured by traditional IQ tests, as in understanding the ingredients of *intelligent behavior,* that is, effective planning and judging in everyday, real-world situations. This emphasis on human intelligence as a resource, not so much as a limiting capacity, has a close parallel in a child's belief that ability is perfectible. In the last analysis, it is one's beliefs – not necessarily their truth or falsity – that counts the most from a motivational perspective. For example, students who believe that ability is expandable through experience and practice – the so-called *incremental* view of intelligence (Dweck, 1986; Dweck & Bempechat, 1983) – tend to tackle more difficult problems, for longer periods of time, and with greater resolve and confidence than do students who hold an *entity* view of ability. An entity belief presumes that intelligence is a stable, immutable factor that does not yield to effort or improve through the accumulation of knowledge.

Not surprisingly, this limiting belief flourishes in competitive environments – the very place where ability is seen by students as a necessary and sufficient cause of success. Thus entity beliefs add a touch of fatalism to an already deadly situation. Not only is ability seen as absolutely necessary for success, but if one lacks ability, then there is little that can be done.

Future survival. Third, instruction in the skills of thinking is also critical to future survival. We can no longer safely assume that what is presently taught in schools will satisfy future job and civic responsibilities or help children adapt to radically different life-styles and to a myriad of other changes that can only be dimly perceived today. The future is overtaking our children at a rapidly accelerating pace. At the center of these changes is the knowledge explosion with its growing glut of facts. Robert Hilliard of the Federal Communications Commission estimates that "at the rate at which knowledge is growing, by the time a child born today graduates from college, the amount of knowledge in the world will be four times as great. By the time that child is 50 years old, it will be 32 times as great and 97% of everything known in the world will have been learned since the time he was born."

This observation and the sense of bewilderment and dislocation it prompts embodies the phenomenon of *future shock* (Toffler, 1970). Hilliard is serving notice that more information than ever before is needed to remain functional, literate, and adaptive, and that the range and breadth of such knowledge will continue to expand at a staggering pace. Worse yet, information itself is subject to increasing obsolescence at an astonishing rate. As Alvin Toffler explains it, "We are creating and using up ideas and images at a faster and faster pace. Knowledge, like people, places, things and organizational forms, is becoming disposable." Indeed, the half-life of facts today can be measured in terms of months or weeks, even days.

Today schools grapple with only the first aspect of future shock, that of mastering the sheer volume of information resulting from the knowledge explosion, by trying to make learning more efficient (sometimes through computer-based instruction) or by simply requiring students to spend more time at their studies. These solutions are easily recognized as part of the intensification mentality.

However, by far the more important challenge is the rapid turnover of information, an issue that has gone largely unaddressed by schools. Clearly, schools must do more than merely dispense facts to be memorized and reproduced later, so-called *reproductive* thinking (Covington, 1986b). Schools must also instruct in broader, future-oriented skills that include *productive* and *strategic* forms of thinking and problem solving. According to Lauren Resnick and Robert Glaser (1976), problem solving is required whenever individuals (1) encounter tasks never before seen in exactly that same form, and (2) for which the information necessary for a solution is inadequate. Given this definition, school instruction should proceed in two directions simultaneously. First, given the unknown quality of future problems, students must be taught to apply well-rehearsed thinking strategies to novel situations and in unprecedented ways. This means the transfer of problem-solving knowledge. Second, given the inadequate description of most complex problems, students must also learn how to determine what additional information is needed and how to access it. Being knowledgeable in the 21st century – or in any age, for that matter – means having a keen sense for which information is relevant and which is not. As Krates, the elder, remarked some 20 centuries ago, "One part of knowledge consists in being ignorant of such things as are not worthy of being known." Today as the computer age hits its stride, individuals will be confronted more and more with virtually infinite amounts of information, only a fraction of which will be relevant to any given problem. Students must learn to cope with this information glut so that they, and not the machine, will be the master.

A moral tale

Only a tiny minority of us ever are involved in inventing our present, let alone our future.
HARVEY RUBIN

The children of Fidel Castro's Cuban revolution of the 1960s provide a provocative view of the problems facing American education today. When asked to describe the study of history, these young Cubans hotly proclaimed that *they* were history in the making, the wave of the future. When American schoolchildren were also asked, it seems that history is something that happened in the past. Cubans: 1, Americans: 0.

Prolonged social upheaval was the price paid by these young Cubans for their forward-reaching, charismatic view of change. We must find other less tumultuous means to instill the belief in our children that it is *they* who are the architects of the future, and not for just a short, frenzied time, but for years to come. Fortunately, according to Lawrence Cremin, former President of the Spencer Foundation, a uniquely American solution is available. "Education," Cremin noted, "is the characteristic mode of American reform. In other countries they stage revolutions. In the United States we devise new curricula." It is to this task that we now turn.

2

Motives as emotions

Emotions are feelings with thoughts incidentally attached.
DAVID HUME

There are many individuals and events in this century that can lay claim to the beginnings of the scientific investigation of achievement motivation. We begin with a little known drama of relatively recent origin.

THE PLAYERS: Professor Kurt Lewin and his laboratory assistant, Ferdinand Hoppe
THE TIME: 1930–1931
THE PLACE: A small laboratory at the University of Berlin

Ironically, Professor Lewin's laboratory was only a 5-minute tram ride from another better-remembered laboratory whose mission threatened to send the world, in Winston Churchill's (1940) words, "into the abyss of a new dark age made more sinister, and perhaps more protracted, by the lights of a perverted science." In the early 1930s Nazi physicists were hard at work there on the development of the world's first atomic device. These were the twilight years of a golden age of science that had witnessed a revolution in the concept of energy in the fields of physics, chemistry, and biology, capped off by Sigmund Freud's sweeping proposal of a previously overlooked energy source – *psychic energy*. In Freud's schema psychic energy activates a dynamic system responsible for psychological work – the progenitor of all human thoughts, feelings, and actions.

Professor Lewin's laboratory was crowded with the research paraphernalia of his time, including an odd conveyor-belt contraption that allowed a series of pegs to move on circular rollers at a uniform rate of speed, much like a row of ducks in a shooting gallery. This unlikely apparatus would provide the key to the question of how, psychologically, humans define success and failure. There are few consistent yardsticks when it comes to judging whether or not a particular achievement is successful – certainly not in the same sense that we can objectively measure height, weight, or temperature. Success and failure mean different things to different people. The same accomplishment can elicit pride in one person and self-rebuke in another, giving rise to the truism that "one man's success is another man's failure." However, for all the subjectivity involved, these judgments do proceed in lawful ways, as Hoppe was to discover.

Hoppe (1930) invited an assortment of local tradespeople and university students to practice tossing rings on the moving pegs at various distances from the target. He found that some subjects felt satisfied after placing, say, 8 rings, whereas others expressed extreme frustration at only 12 correct tosses. Additionally, Hoppe found that the performance level needed to arouse feelings of success changed over time for each individual. A score that was initially judged a success might well be considered unacceptable on a later practice trial.

These curious behaviors make sense only in light of the individual's personal expectations or, as they eventually came to be known, *levels of aspiration* (for a review, see Diggory, 1966). Hoppe found that judgments of success or failure depended less on the actual goals achieved by his subjects than on the relationship between performance level and the individual's aspirations. Thus when Hoppe's subjects achieved their personal goals, say, placing 10 rings correctly, they felt successful. By the same token, when their performances fell below these permissible self-imposed minimums, they experienced feelings of failure. As we shall see, these same mechanisms operate in schools where success and failure are real, not artificial creations of the laboratory.

Hoppe's revelation prompted a cascade of crucial insights. For instance it was now possible to give meaning to the concept of *self-confidence,* another psychological state of mind like success and failure. There is no accounting for self-confidence in objective terms. Some individuals may discern a gleam of hope in a situation that seems hopeless to everyone but themselves. At the same time, others may express a vote of no confidence despite the fact that they have everything going for them. Basically, self-confidence reflects the extent to which the individual believes himself or herself able to win the prize, to turn back the foe, or in Hoppe's experiment to toss enough rings correctly.

The notion of expectancy also comes into play here. In its current usage, the term *expectancy* generally refers to subjective estimates of eventual success – how confident individuals are of the final outcome, but not necessarily how confident they are that they will be the cause of success. Thus *expectations* and *confidence* are not merely interchangeable concepts. For instance, individuals may remain optimistic, not necessarily because they judge themselves equal to the task, but because the assignment may be seen as quite easy – something anyone could do – or because they may be counting on help from others. From this example we can deduce that depending on its perceived causes, success may or may not act to increase self-confidence.

Hoppe was amazed at the cleverness with which individuals maintained a balance between success and failure experiences. By raising or lowering their aspirations, his subjects created a check-and-balance mechanism involving what researchers have subsequently called a "typical shift" (e.g., Atkinson & Raynor, 1974). After a success Hoppe's subjects tended to raise their aspirations and, conversely, after failure they tended to lower them. In this way they protected themselves against the possibility of repeated failure, and at the same time, insured that their successes were gratifying (Schönpflug, 1982). So pervasive were these self-correcting manuevers that subjects would often unconsciously lean in closer toward the pegs following a failure or two or after committing themselves to a particularly high performance goal, thereby making the task easier without necessarily having to change their stated objectives. In fact, the distance that individual subjects stood from the target, when given a choice, became recognized by later researchers as an important measure of the person's willingness to take risks (e.g., McClelland, 1958a).

Hoppe's subjects understood intuitively what researchers would later confirm empirically. The key to sustained involvement in learning requires that a reasonable match be established between the individual's present capabilities and the demands of the achievement task. This point is well illustrated in an experiment conducted by Charles Woodson (1975), who created varying degrees of match and mismatch between student ability levels and the difficulty of a learning task. Those students who experienced a close match (i.e., high ability–demanding task; or low ability–easy task) learned the most, and this was true for both bright and less bright students. On the other hand, a mismatch interfered with learning at all ability levels, but for different reasons. Those more able students who competed against easy standards became bored, whereas those less able students from whom too much was required quit when they failed to deliver.

Perhaps the most enduring legacy of Hoppe's research is the recognition today that judgments about success and failure, as well as feelings of confidence or despair and optimism versus pessimism are all creatures of a subjective world of the individual's own making (Carver & Gaines, 1987; Carver & Scheier, 1986). Truth and falsity aside, reality has little standing here. What counts are beliefs and appearances. For instance, by shifting our aspirations, even slightly, we can create a new round of successes or plunge ourselves into a downward spiral of failure. Naturally, the expectations of others, including parents and teachers, set limits on our freedom to maneuver. The finely tuned balance of successes offsetting failures enjoyed by Hoppe's subjects can quickly be overturned if individuals accept as their own the inappropriate standards imposed by others. But, then, there may be little choice. In a competitive environment there is continual pressure on students to raise their aspirations, irrespective of their ability and past performance, and often severe sanctions against lowering them.

The insights inspired by Hoppe's research provided most of the essential principles necessary for the development of modern theories of achievement motivation. Basically, all that was lacking were assumptions about the *why* of achievement – the reasons that arouse people to action. And, even here, Hoppe (as reported in Barker, 1942) came close with the speculation that aspirations represent a compromise between two opposing tendencies, one involving the need to strive for something better and the other the need to avoid repeated failures.

But what more precisely is the essence of this activation? Many of our current ideas about the basic wellspring of achievement motivation have evolved from earlier theories that stressed basic tissue needs such as thirst and hunger as among the most powerful organizers of behavior (Bolles, 1967; Weiner, 1972; Woodworth, 1918). Here the notion of drive was linked originally to a state of physical deprivation. This view held that bodily needs create tension and that motivated behavior is an effort to reduce this unpleasant tension and return the body to a state of *homeostasis,* or equilibrium ("equal state"). For example, when we are thirsty we search for water to reduce the need for moisture and reestablish a proper physical tissue balance.

Basically, such drive-reduction theories portrayed humans as passive organisms that act merely to reduce stimulation. This view of motivation is severely limited, however, at least in its application to humans. For example, humans sometimes seek out activities that actually increase tension, not decrease it. People ride roller coasters, go to horror movies, and sky dive – all for the thrill of it. Clearly, we value imbalance as well as balance. The purpose of these so-called *stimulus motives* – those involving activity, manipulation, and curiosity – extends beyond bare survival and involves investigating one's environment and sometimes changing it (Harlow, 1953; Hebb, 1961). These motives, like basic tissue needs, are probably largely unlearned, but their particular form of expression is conditioned by social convention and custom. It is not difficult to appreciate that the ultimate social expression of the need to manipulate, explore, and control is reflected in the process of becoming a top corporate executive, of risking danger to explore an undersea fault zone, or of making the dean's list in college.

These achievement behaviors involve *learned drives* or motives for approval, power, and achievement – *drives,* so called, because they impel individuals toward action, and *learned* because they are thought to develop over time through the slow accumulation of lessons gleaned from success and failure experiences starting in the earliest years. It is this inner world populated by aspirations, thoughts, and expectations as well as fantasies and fears that makes up the essence of learned drives. Just which of these various ingredients forms the essential character of motives – say, thoughts versus feelings – has been the subject of intensive debate since Hoppe's time. We will now follow the most significant developments in this debate from the 1950s to the present, starting with the view of motives as *emotions* and then in the next chapter turning to the arguments for motives as *cognitions*.

Need achievement

To overcome obstacles, to exercise power, to strive to do something well and as quickly as possible
HENRY MURRAY

John Atkinson's theory of achievement motivation (1957, 1964) assumes that all individuals can be characterized by two learned drives, a motive to approach success and a motive to avoid failure. These two opposing motives are viewed as relatively stable personality dispositions. Psychologically speaking, the approach mode is defined by a *hope* for success or, as Atkinson (1964) has put it, "a capacity to experience pride in accomplishment" (p. 214). The anticipation of success and its emotional correlates of pride and exhilaration combine to produce a trust in the future and in life generally.

By contrast, the motive to avoid failure is described as the capacity for experiencing humiliation and shame when one fails. According to Atkinson, this emotional anticipation produces a tendency *not* to undertake achievement activities. In fact, given a free choice among tasks that vary from easy to hard, failure-avoiding individuals should choose none of them – not even the easiest – unless extrinsic incentives such as money or the threat of punishment are introduced to overcome their resistance. Moreover, even if these persons are forced or enticed to participate, the anticipation of failure will likely disrupt their performance.

This brief description underscores the first of two basic features of Atkinson's need achievement model, namely the assumption that the driving force behind all noteworthy accomplishments is emotional anticipation. Simply put, persons with a high need to achieve anticipate pride, a feeling that propels them toward further successes. On the other hand, persons with low need achievement anticipate shame (caused by failure) and attempt to avoid its noxious effects by withdrawing or not trying.

The second basic feature of the model is captured by Atkinson's long-time associate and collaborator, David McClelland, who describes the need for achievement as "competing with standards of excellence." Others have defined it as the impulse to do better than one's rivals (Combs, 1957; Greenberg, 1932). As to the winners, McClelland (1955) had in mind individuals imbued with an entrepreneurial spirit – persons driven to produce change, relentlessly, often without consideration for others, and typically for personal gain. McClelland's notion (1955) neatly captures an unmistakable Protestant work ethic – the haunting fear that someone, somewhere, may be standing idle and the stoic virtues of independent thought, dedication, and autonomy.

The spirit of Hermes

Just so there was no mistaking his point, McClelland (1961) likened the essence of achievement motivation to the mythological figure of Hermes. Recall the precociously gifted and ruthless Hermes – born in the morning, inventing and performing upon a lyre at noonday, and yet with enough energy left over to steal cattle from his older brother, Apollo, in the evening. Hermes conveys perfectly a tense, dynamic restlessness, an energy source always on the move, in a hurry, for the purposes of material and intellectual self-advancement, even at the expense of his own family. Subsequent research confirms the broad outlines of this description. For instance, upwardly mobile boys appear more willing than those rated low in mobility to leave home in search of jobs, even though such a move might threaten family unity (Rosen, 1959; Strodtbeck, 1958). Moreover, persons high in need achievement tend to view time as a commodity – to be bought, sold, or saved – and perceive time as passing so rapidly that the future is "always here before we know it" (Knapp, 1960; Knapp & Green, 1961).

But the Hermes myth also reveals a darker, brazen, more troublesome side of the motive to achieve that McClelland (1961) not only recognizes but appears to savor:

> Above all else Hermes was dishonest. He lied outrageously to his brother Apollo and his father Zeus; he stole his brother's cattle; he wore special sandals backwards to try and conceal the way he had really gone; he boasted untruthfully of his exploits. And in all he was a pretty unethical trickster and thief. (p. 329)

Thus, according to McClelland, the achievement archetype is not above flattery, trickery, and bluffing. Given these parameters, we can imagine an updated schoolboy counterpart of the ancient Hermes – the ruthless student who gains competitive advantage by stealing assigned readings on reserve in the library or who studies secretly hoping his intense effort will go unnoticed in the event of failure so that his reputation for brilliance will remain intact.

Actually, more recent research softens considerably McClelland's harsh portrayal of the success-oriented individual (Roberts & Covington, 1991). Although it is true that some success strivers are fiercely competitive, what emerges as the dominant characteristics of this group are a capacity for intrinsic involvement, a restless curiosity, and an unquenchable desire to learn and improve, and not always as a means to demonstrate superiority over others.

Losa Wu, a high school junior, neatly fits this description. The immigrant Asian culture stresses upward mobility and self-improvment through hard work, a heritage that began for Losa's family three generations earlier when her great-grandparents emigrated from China. Losa's parents expected her to excel and she was groomed for high achievement right from the beginning, almost before she could walk. After school and on Saturdays her "free" time was filled with various extracurricular activities – dancing and music lessons and family outings to museums or concerts. As Losa grew older she was permitted greater freedom in deciding what activities to pursue – music, photography, and biology became her favorites – but the high expectations remained and any success was quickly acknowledged. As the years passed Losa developed into a self-sufficient, resourceful, and self-assured young woman who now stands on the threshold of a highly promising college career.

McClelland and Atkinson believed that the motive structure of individuals is best revealed through fantasy. For this reason the motive to approach success has traditionally been measured using projective techniques, principally the Thematic Apperception Test (TAT) (Atkinson, 1958; Murray, 1943). For the reader unfamiliar with them, projective techniques (which include the Rorschach inkblots) require individuals to make sense of ambiguous, unstructured situations. In the case of the TAT, the subject is shown a series of pictures, one at a time, and asked to create an imaginative story that explains: (1) what events led up to the scene; (2) what is happening at the moment; (3) what the characters are thinking and feeling; and (4) how the situation will end. The assumption is that in the process of imparting meaning to the pictures, individuals unwittingly reveal or "project" their own basic and largely unconscious needs, motives, and characteristic ways of viewing the world.

One such picture depicts a boy in late adolescence sitting at a desk. A book lies open before him, and he gazes off into the distance. The picture is regarded as a stimulus that arouses achievement imagery, imagery that in turn is taken as indirect evidence for the strength of an underlying motive to approach success. Consider the following stories (Table 2.1), one generated by Losa and the other by John, a high school senior.

Scoring for need achievement is based on the frequency with which certain themes are found in the individual's stories. (A full description of the scoring procedures is found in Atkinson, 1958). One theme involves long-term com-

Table 2.1. *Examples of need achievement imagery*

Losa's story	John's story
1. This chap is doing some heavy meditating. He is a sophomore and has reached an intellectual crisis. He cannot make up his mind. He is troubled; worried. 2. He is trying to reconcile the philosophies of Descartes and Thomas Aquinas – and at his tender age of 18. He has read several books on philosophy and feels the weight of the world on his shoulders. 3. He wants to present a clear synthesis of these two conflicting philosophies, to satisfy his ego and to gain academic recognition from his professor.	1. The boy in the checkered shirt whose name is Ed is in a classroom. His is supposed to be listening to the teachers. 2. Ed has been troubled by his father's drunkenness and his maltreatment of Ed's mother. He thinks of this often and worries about it. 3. Ed is thinking of leaving home for a while in the hope that this might shock his parents into leaving him alone. 4. He will leave home but will only meet further disillusionment away from home.

Source: Adapted from *Educational Psychology: A Contemporary View* (1973). Del Mar, CA: CRM Books (p. 186).

mitments to achieving valued goals over extended periods of time. Another part of the scoring system gives credit for anticipating achievement obstacles in advance and outlining the steps by which they can be overcome or avoided.

Individuals who have high scores on achievement imagery, as does Losa, are expected to persist more in situations where long-term goals are at stake (such as getting a college degree) and also to do better on brief school tasks when the reason for doing well involves competing with others or with some exacting standard of excellence (McClelland, 1961, 1965). High scorers also are known to delay gratification longer than low scorers and tend to do better in college courses related to their chosen careers (Mischel, 1960; Raynor, 1970).

Avoiding failure

By contrast, the fantasies of John are important not because he appears merely unambitious – the exact opposite of Losa – but deeper still, because his indifference likely masks a fear of failing (as reported in Beery, 1975). Although John is only a hypothetical figure, many students will nonetheless identify with at least some of his reactions to school. John can be characterized by a single phrase – able but apathetic. He describes his feelings toward school as a sense of continual boredom. Not that John was ever in academic trouble; in fact, to all outward appearances his academic record proclaims John to be a good, if not an outstanding student. He has always figured out the easiest way to get a good grade and relies heavily on a last minute surge of studying to make up for weeks of neglect and disinterest in his classes. In this way John can blame any failures on a lack of preparation. Considering how little interest John shows in school, these strategies have worked well – well enough, in fact, to earn him a place in the freshman class at a prestigious four-year college beginning next September.

Not surprisingly, John feels somewhat guilty and anxious about his accomplishments, worrying secretly that he is somehow a fraud, not really as knowledgeable as his grades reflect and bothered that someday he will be found out. As was said, John's behavior stems not so much from indifference, a relative absence of the motive to achieve, but rather from excessive worry about failure and its implications that he is not able enough. John shares much in common with those individuals described as *anxious-defensive* (Wieland-Eckelmann, Bösel, & Badorrek, 1987) who repress and deny threatening messages and react to stressful events by withdrawing.

In chapter 5 we will follow John's exploits as he settles into college, a perilous time during which the coping strategies that worked well enough in high school begin to unravel under the increased pressures of college life.

Traditionally, the motive to avoid failure has been measured by various paper-pencil questionnaires designed to assess anxiety, especially test-taking anxiety. One measure that conveys well the notion of anxiety as possessing drivelike properties is the Taylor *Manifest Anxiety Scale* (Taylor, 1953) (e.g., "I cry easily." or "I work under a great deal of tension."). Using test-anxiety scales as an index of failure avoidance was originally justified on the grounds that as a convenient emotional barometer anxiety reveals the strength of the individual's *resistance* to achievement. Atkinson and his colleagues (e.g., Atkinson & Raynor, 1974) argued that resistance as a disposition cannot easily be measured by projective techniques because they are more suitable for revealing what the individual will *do* – that is, for example, what he or she will likely choose to achieve – than what the individual will *not* do, which is to say, avoid the situation altogether.

The model: $B = M \times P \times I$

Every achievement situation, whether it be taking a school test, mastering the game of tennis, or competing for a job, implies the promise of success as well as the threat of failure. This means that all achievement situations involve an approach–avoidance conflict to one degree or another. For those persons like Losa, whose optimism heavily outweighs any thoughts of failure, the conflict is minimal. Losa readily approaches success, and for her any momentary anxiety usually gives way to a sense of challenge. We will refer to such individuals as *success oriented* (high approach–low avoidance).

For others like John, avoidance tendencies outweigh the anticipation of success. Their tension is most typically reduced by escape, either actual or psychological. In the psychological realm, the implications of failure can be avoided through the use of defensive, magical thinking that denies the meaning of failure or minimizes the importance of the failed task to the individual. We will refer to these individuals as *failure avoiders* (low approach–high avoidance).

These twin approach–avoidance motives can best be understood in terms of the classic formula, $B = M \times P \times I$. *B* refers to actual, observable *behavior*, say, Losa's curiosity or John's indifference. These behaviors are said to be the product of three factors, the first of which is *M*, or *motivation*, which represents a combination of the approach–avoidance motives. Atkinson assumed that these two opposing motives combine algebraically (with the avoidance motive being negative in sign) to yield a *resultant* tendency that is either predominantly avoidant or approach in character.

But this resultant tendency (*M*) cannot be the sole determinant of achievement behavior. Sometimes failure-oriented students perform just as well or are just as willing to perform as success-oriented students. Why should this be? Something more must be taken into account. The motives to approach and to avoid achievement are only *potential* – potential in that they lie dormant until activated by cues from a specific achievement situation. For example, if the circumstances of achievement are highly competitive, that is, if there are potentially more losers than winners, then fear or flight is likely, especially if the individual in question is already failure-avoidant. If, on the other hand, neither approach nor avoidance motives are aroused by the situation – perhaps not much is at stake – then performance will be desultory and uninspired, no matter what the individual's dominant motive (Lens & DeVolder, 1980).

According to the formula, two additional factors are especially critical to this process of selective arousal. First, motives will be aroused depending on the *attractiveness* of the goal, that is, its incentive value (*I*). Second, motives will be aroused depending on the *probability* of attaining the goal (*P*). Taken jointly, these two elements ($P \times I$) lead to the commonsense observation that individuals will be stirred to action if there is a reasonable chance (*P*) that they will get something they want (*I*). Likewise, as the probability of achieving a desired goal decreases, so will the individual's efforts to attain it, even though the goal may actually become more attractive because of its elusiveness. This observation reminds us once again that inaction does not necessarily mean an individual is unmotivated. In fact, motive strength can remain high, but there may simply be no opportunity to satisfy it. And, finally, it does not matter how available a goal may be. If it holds no attraction, it will be ignored.

Recognition of these dynamics qualifies Atkinson's model for what is referred to as an *expectancy* $\times$ *value* theory. Over the years many researchers, working independently of the need achievement tradition, have also stressed the role that expectancies and values play in the regulation of behavior, quite apart from motives (Edwards, 1953; Heckhausen, 1977; Pekrun, 1984; Tolman, 1932; Vroom, 1964).

$P_S \times I_S$: *success*

How does the expectancy $\times$ value portion of Atkinson's model operate in the case of success-oriented individuals? Simply stated, the greater the subjective probability of success (P_S), the more the approach motive will be aroused. Yet, surely, this too is an oversimplification. Although we rarely tire of success, it is not the "easy victory" that fully motivates us; as human beings we quickly become bored with a sure thing. Hence although an approach motive may be activated by the prospects of a foregone conclusion, actual behavior (B) may not necessarily follow. Atkinson makes allowances for this important reality by taking into account the attractiveness of the task. He assumes that the incentive value of success (I_S) increases as the probability of success diminishes. Therefore if the individual does succeed at solving a very difficult problem, then the rewards (pride) are greatest. For instance, George Litwin (reported in Atkinson & Feather, 1966) found that the farther back subjects stand from the peg in ring-toss experiments, the greater the subjective value of success when it occurs. Similarly, occupations that require the greatest preparation and for which only a few eventually qualify are accorded the greater prestige and salary (Strodtbeck, McDonald, & Rosen, 1957).

Now we see how the motivational elements of P_S and I_S interact in their influence on behavior. To the extent that the task is perceived as difficult, the rewards of success become more enticing, yet as the task becomes harder, the chances of success diminish. Given this offsetting dynamic, we would expect that the optimal level of task difficulty for those motivated to approach success is in the intermediate range – just hard enough to provide some satisfaction should they succeed, but not so difficult that success is improbable. Also we would expect success-oriented individuals to lose interest quickly in exceedingly difficult tasks and to reject altogether a simple assignment as unworthy.

$P_f \times I_f$: failure

Now consider the risk-taking preferences of failure-avoiding individuals. In the context of fear, task attractiveness is defined in negative terms – how noxious failure will be if it occurs. From this perspective, the easy task is preferred because the chances of failure are low and the anticipation of shame is thereby minimized. Hence in theory, at least, it appears that failure-avoiding individuals are the exception to our observation that humans shun the certainty of a sure thing. By similar reasoning, very difficult tasks should also prove attractive to failure-avoiding individuals because they can't feel very bad when they fail at a task for which the odds against them are exceedingly high. Thus the noxious quality of failure (or its negative attractiveness, I_f) depends on how likely success is.

These predictions have received broad empirical support. The tendency for anxious individuals to set either extremely low or extremely high goals has been well documented (Atkinson & Litwin, 1960; Lewin, Dembo, Festinger, & Sears, 1944; Moulton, 1965; Sears, 1940). For example, in one ring-toss experiment McClelland (1958a) found that kindergarten children, as well as third graders rated high in achievement motivation, more often set their aspirations in the middle range of difficulty. They also pitched the rings from modest distances. On the other hand, children low in achievement motivation tended to make extreme choices, either standing right on top of the pegs or so far away that success was virtually impossible.

Typical shifts

The general reasoning behind the $B = M \times P \times I$ formula also accounts for the phenomena of typical shifts. When individuals undertake an activity and succeed, it is only reasonable that their aspirations will increase; and, conversely, when they fail, their aspirations should correspondingly decrease (Diggory, Riley, & Blumenfeld, 1960; Zajonc & Brickman, 1969). This pattern describes the most frequent or typical shift in aspirations following success and failure, and is precisely what Hoppe found years before. By being free to alter one's aspirations as circumstances dictate, the individual can balance the likelihood of success against failure (Schönpflug, 1985, 1986). At least this appears to be true for success-oriented persons. Success at a task in the intermediate range of difficulty leads to a reappraisal of its difficulty; if one succeeds, the task is probably easier than was originally thought. At the next opportunity, then, success-oriented persons will seek out a slightly more difficult task for which the likelihood of success and failure is now thought to be equally balanced. Conversely, when these individuals fail at a challenging task, it is judged as more difficult than originally thought and, as a result, a slightly easier task is selected the next time.

Atypical shifts

The less frequently observed pattern of aspiration change, the *atypical shift,* involves lowering one's aspirations after having succeeded and raising them after failure. This paradoxical behavior excites our interest because at first glance it appears so bizarre, even self-destructive. Atypical shifts literally ensure failure and herald the breakdown of self-regulated learning. As Atkinson anticipated, these patterns are associated with failure-avoiding individuals. For instance, Robert Moulton (1965) supplied success or failure feedback to individuals following their performance on a task of intermediate difficulty. Following this feedback, subjects were then given the choice of working next on either an easy or a very difficult problem. Moulton found that success-oriented subjects chose the more difficult task after success and the easier one following failure – the typical shift pattern – whereas anxious, failure-avoiding subjects reflected the opposite pattern.

This atypical anomaly can be explained by extending the previous reasoning. For failure avoiders, any failure is threatening; however, failure at difficult tasks is less threatening, and hence preferred. This is why failure avoiders often choose the more difficult task after having failed the preceding simpler one. But what happens when the improbable occurs, and these individuals succeed at a difficult task? Following Atkinson's earlier logic, failure avoiders now see the task as less difficult than originally thought. As a result, the task now approximates the intermediate level of difficulty that is to be avoided, so they choose an easier task next time around.

Multiple motives

Another important focus of need achievement theory concerns the relationship of achievement motives, both approach and avoidance, to other learned drives, and their joint influence on performance. According to Atkinson, the quality of performance in a given situation depends on the total strength of all motivational sources combined. The need to achieve is only one possible source. The need for affiliation, or social approval, is another and has also been the subject of considerable research, although far less extensive than the motive to achieve. In laboratory settings the need for approval (e.g., the desire to please the experimenter) is typically aroused and then satisfied by introducing extrinsic incentives (e.g., monetary rewards for doing well).

The available evidence suggests that although the total motive strength from all sources is important, *more* arousal is not necessarily *better*. For example, when both achievement and affiliation needs are stimulated, success-oriented students perform no better than do failure-avoiding students (Atkinson & Reitman, 1958). And in some cases, failure avoiders actually do best (Smith, 1963). Presumably, the presence of extraneous incentives (for approval and recognition) disrupts the intrinsic need to better oneself that is the forte of success-oriented individuals. At the same time, the presence of social incentives may compensate failure-avoiding students who would otherwise avoid the activity.

This overall pattern of data is compatible with the notion that for all individuals there is an optimal level of total motivation, and that to exceed this level – in effect, to *overmotivate* the individual – leads to decreases in performance (Atkinson & O'Connor, 1966; Lens, 1983). As we will see, a similar *curvilinear* relationship also exists between anxiety and performance (chapter 5). A moderate degree of arousal (fear) may improve performance, whereas too much anxiety interferes with performance, and too little leaves the individual unmoved.

Dynamics of action

Recognition that motives can interact and combine had led Atkinson and McClelland to infuse the need achievement model with even more dynamic qualities than were originally envisioned. The *dynamics of action model* (Atkinson, 1981; McClelland, 1980, 1985) reflects the fact that many motives, not just one, operate in any achievement setting and that the individual's behavior is best understood in terms of the moment-to-moment changes in the relative strength of these motives. For example, a person strongly driven to approach success will not always act solely in accord with this disposition, but will at times, depending on circumstances, respond principally to the need for social approval or for power (Veroff & Veroff, 1972; Winter, 1973). Given this more dynamic perspective, earlier static predictions about the performance superiority of success-oriented over failure-threatened individuals become outmoded. They give way to predictions that reflect a more dynamic, ongoing process measured in terms of, say, the percentage of time success-oriented individuals spend on various activities rather than all-or-nothing choices among tasks.

The perspective afforded by the dynamics of action model is useful because it portrays achievement behavior in its full richness and complexity.

But at this point, its practical value is more potential than real. For the time being, more than anything else, the model stands as a challenge to the present limits of our theory building and taxes our ingenuity to develop ways to measure instability as well as stability in human behavior.

Future time perspectives

While Atkinson and McClelland were elaborating the dynamics of action, other investigators were giving a future-oriented twist to Atkinson's original concepts (for a review, see Gjesme, 1981). J. R. Nuttin and Willy Lens (Nuttin, 1984; Nuttin & Lens, 1985) argued that one's perceptions of the future, and especially subjective notions of time, form the basic motivational space within which humans operate. Kurt Lewin (1948) anticipated this same point years earlier when he remarked that "the setting of goals is closely related to time perspective. The goal of an individual includes his expectations for the future, his wishes, and his daydreams" (p. 113).

In effect, people translate their needs and desires into specific goals. This process involves the recognition that goals are time bound. Some goals involve satisfaction in the near term, say, anticipating the taste of a candy bar as the wrapper is being removed; other goals involve planning within an intermediate time frame as when, for example, a child begins saving a weekly allowance for ice skates next winter; and yet other goals like becoming a physician can preoccupy one's attention for years, even decades. In addition to this *time hierarchy,* goal striving can be distinguished by the number of intervening subtasks or steps that must be completed successfully on the way to a goal – a kind of *task hierarchy* (Raynor, 1969; Raynor & Entin, 1982). Thus future time perspective can be characterized by its extension or length, its density (the number of steps in a certain future time interval), its degree of structure, and its level of realism.

According to Lens, success-oriented individuals aspire to more complicated, distant goals than do failure-threatened individuals (DeVolder & Lens, 1982), and they are highly adept at arranging small steps of intermediate difficulty so that the chances of moving from one to another, like stepping stones, is maximized. A special characteristic of such plans, what Joel Raynor (1982) calls *partially contingent paths,* is also the province of success-oriented persons. Here success in a step guarantees the opportunity to continue, but failure has no direct bearing on future striving. This is because success-oriented persons are forever hedging their bets by having backup plans. They also entertain alternative goals should the original objective prove impossible to reach.

According to this reinterpretation, the motive to excel will be aroused most strongly when there are many steps in the plan and the time to fulfillment is short. Thus *time* and *task hierarchies* have opposite motivational effects. As the time required to achieve a goal increases, motivation is correspondingly reduced. But for success-oriented individuals this decreased arousal is offset by their ability to establish additional intervening steps that provide more opportunities for partial reinforcement along the way.

This extension of Atkinson's model holds powerful implications for educational practice. For one thing, it suggests that the ability to plan is a necessary, perhaps even a sufficient condition for motivation. In fact, later we will consider the possibility that *motives* are actually just *plans* by a different name. For another thing, believing oneself to be an *Origin* (De Charms, 1968) – that is, in personal control of events (as contrasted to feeling like a *Pawn*) – is the key to all noteworthy achievement (Findley & Cooper, 1983; Stipek & Weisz, 1981). Ellen Skinner and her colleagues (Skinner, Wellborn, & Connell, 1990) explain the bidirectional, cyclical relationship between a sense of perceived control and school achievement in the following terms:

> When children believe that they can exert control over success in school, they perform better on cognitive tasks. And, when children succeed in school, they are more likely to view school performance as a controllable outcome. . . . Children who are not doing well in school will perceive themselves as having no control over academic successes and failures and that these beliefs will subsequently generate performances that serve to confirm their beliefs. (p. 22)

The legacy of Atkinson's model is clearly evident in these comments as well as in other recent attempts to conceptualize student achievement motivation. For example, Paul Pintrich (1988, 1989) and his colleagues (Eccles, 1983; Pintrich & De Groot, 1990) propose three factors essential to task involvement that are also linked to realistic goal setting and to the effective regulation of plans: (1) an expectancy factor that includes beliefs about one's ability to perform successfully ("Can I do this task?") – what James Connell (1985) calls *capacity* beliefs; (2) a value component that includes the reasons for being involved – in other words, "Why am I doing this?"; and (3) an emotional component, "How do I feel about this task?"

Analysis and critique

What about an evaluation of the original need achievement model? To what degree have its various predictions been supported by research? What are the limitations of the theory? And what special contributions has it made to the understanding of achievement motivation, particularly as they might relate to our broader educational concerns?

In addressing these questions I cannot possibly do justice to the avalanche of research that has been inspired by the need achievement model; the references literally run into the hundreds. Nor can I fully reflect on all the various controversies sparked by the theory, many of which continue to this day largely undiminished (for a review, see Heckhausen, 1986).

As to the accuracy of the various predictions, perhaps the most succinct and balanced appraisal comes from Heinz Heckhausen, Heing-Dieter Schmalt, and Klaus Schneider (1985). Based on their encyclopedic review of the literature, these researchers concluded that Atkinson's predictions regarding greater *persistence* among success-oriented persons are "surprisingly accurate," whereas those hypotheses regarding risk-taking *preferences* are "satisfactory," but "quite unsatisfactory" for *predicting performance*.

This allegedly poor record for predicting actual performance, say, school grades, calls for a brief comment in advance of a more detailed treatment later. Need achievement scores do, in fact, bear little direct relationship to GPA. But this is less a criticism of Atkinson's model than a reflection on the nature of the achievement process itself. More specifically, just within the last few years researchers have begun to demonstrate empirically what was originally only conjecture by Atkinson. Atkinson and his colleagues viewed the role of motives basically as a trigger, an instigator of a multitude of other psychological events that in turn determine actual performance. They have now been proven correct. As only one example, it is poor study habits, not failure-avoiding tendencies per se, that lead directly to poor test performance (Covington & Omelich, 1988a). But poor study habits are also a property of failure avoiders. This causal chain of events can be written as: failure avoidance → poor study → poor performance. The more adept that researchers become at identifying the various intermediate steps in the achievement process that lead up to actual test taking, the less direct bearing underlying motives will have on final achievement. This is not to say that motives do not influence behavior, but only that their influence is largely *indirect*. By analogy, we would not dismiss as unimportant the nudge that sends a boulder crashing down the hill simply because later events proved to be so much more dramatic.

However, even if we accept this explanation for the general failure of the need achievement model to predict actual school performance, there is no doubt that the theory is also limited in certain other important respects as well. We will consider four potential shortcomings here.

Likelihood versus value

One potential limitation is that two of the main elements in Atkinson's model, the incentive value of a task (I) and the probability of success (P), are treated as reciprocal factors. As the probability of success decreases, the value of succeeding increases, and vice versa. But are likelihood and value merely two sides of the same coin? Not necessarily. For instance, the value of success as an incentive to learn often depends on more than the mere likelihood that it will occur. Deborah Stipek (1988) makes this clear in her example of the difference between solving an exceedingly difficult puzzle and winning a national merit scholarship. Although both accomplishments may be equally difficult, intuitively we would expect greater pride to be aroused in the latter case. Because the need achievement model does not allow for the possibility that the same task can reflect different intrinsic values for different learners an important reality is overlooked, one that not only leads to less accurate predictions but, as we will soon see, oversimplifies the task of teachers as well.

Bipolar versus quadripolar

Another shortcoming involves the subsequent failure of many researchers to maintain Atkinson's original view that the motives to approach success and

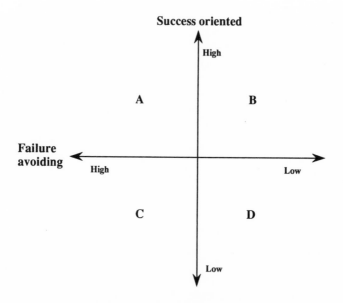

Figure 2.1. Quadripolar model of need achievement

to avoid failure are independent dimensions (Rand, Lens, & Decock, 1991). The notion of independence is important because it allows us to characterize the achievement process as a conflict of opposing forces. Common sense as well as the observations of many clinical investigators including Sigmund Freud suggest that individuals can be simultaneously attracted to and repelled by the same task.

Originally, Atkinson proposed a typology of individuals of the kind illustrated in Figure 2.1. We can easily place Losa and John in this schema as persons B and C, respectively, that is, predominantly success oriented and failure threatened. This taxonomy also allows us to represent persons as either high or low with respect to both approach–avoidance dimensions. For example, some individuals, like person A, are driven simultaneously by both excessive hope and fear (high approach–high avoidance). This reflects the classic approach–avoidance conflict, where opposing tendencies are both highly insistent yet exquisitely balanced. Stress is maximum in this case. By comparison, person D remains basically indifferent to achievement events, reflected by the relative absence of both hope and fear (low approach–low avoidance). In this case conflict (therefore arousal) is minimal and as a result so is the likelihood of learning anything.

Research has largely ignored the two potential configurations represented in persons A and D (for exceptions, see Atkinson & Litwin, 1960; Feather, 1965). Instead, investigators have concentrated almost exclusively on the two remaining combinations we have labeled *success oriented* (high approach–low avoidance) and *failure avoiding* (low approach–high avoidance). But by

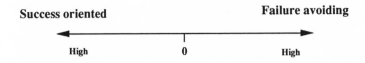

Figure 2.2. Bipolar model of need achievement

considering only these two latter combinations, we end up with a unidimensional, bipolar interpretation of achievement motivation (see Figure 2.2). This implies that approach and avoidance tendencies blend within the same individual so that everyone, not just extreme cases like Losa and John, can be placed somewhere on a single continuum, ranging from high approach to high avoidance.

However, if achievement motivation is best conceived of as a *quadripolar* phenomenon with four different achievement types, as suggested by Figure 2.1, then collapsing everyone into two groups (bipolar) not only loses information about people, but it also misrepresents the processes we wish to understand. For example, what are we to make of the zero point in Figure 2.2? Is a total absence of caring or commitment best represented as the resultant canceling of extreme motives? Probably not. The bipolar model leaves no room for genuine indifference, only *apparent* indifference in which some individuals are unable to act because they are held temporarily in check between two opposite and implacable forces, much like the two adjacent planes of an earthquake fault. This predicament can scarcely be considered a matter of indifference or passivity.

Research favors the quadripolar model. Covington and Omelich (1991) analyzed the learning styles and achievement characteristics of some 400 college students. Not only did the classic success-oriented and failure-avoiding profiles emerge from the data, but so did two other groups that coincided with individuals A and B in Figure 2.1. We will label these individuals as *overstrivers* and *failure accepters,* respectively, and consider them in more detail later. For the moment, suffice it to say that as a hybrid group, overstrivers are at once drawn to and repelled by the prospects of achievement. In self-worth terms, these individuals attempt to avoid failure by succeeding! This reason for achieving is eventually self-defeating because its purpose is basically defensive, even though in the short run it may lead to extraordinary successes.

Amy, a black sixth-grade student, typifies the plight of the overstriver. Amy is a teacher's joy – bright, hard working, compliant – and seems especially mature for her young years. Whenever possible she does more than her assignments require and when school work is not challenging enough – which is usually the case – she sets additional goals for herself by negotiating extra credit assignments with her teacher. Amy's parents have high expectations for their only child, perhaps too high, and they are willing to sacrifice everything – their time, attention, and meager resources – in the hope that she will become a ''somebody'' in the mainstream world of white America.

To all appearances Amy is an exemplary student, but as with John, with whom she shares an intense apprehension about her adequacy, things are far from well. Amy's slavish commitment to work often drives her to the edge of exhaustion. And, for the last month she has been battling a painful case of the hives. There are also ominous signs of a pre-ulcerous condition that has been diagnosed as psychosomatic.

Compared to the other students' types, *failure-accepting* pupils are indifferent to school achievement. But *this* lack of involvement is open to several interpretations. We have already considered John's passivity as a kind of motivated inaction that allows him to avoid making mistakes. But indifference can also mean genuinely not caring, or may even reflect anger and passive resistance, as when the idea of conforming to middle-class values holds no attraction. This kind of indifference has often been attributed to minorities and poor white children. Finally, indifference may reflect resignation. In self-worth terms this means giving up the struggle to avoid the implications of failure and in the process concluding that one is not bright enough to succeed in school (Covington & Omelich, 1985).

This slide into self-despair and resentment is illustrated by Ralph, a displaced eighth-grade youngster from Appalachia. There was never any doubt in Ralph's mind that he would become a coal miner like his father – no doubt, that is, until his father's job was lost to automation. To make ends meet, Ralph and his three older brothers and sisters were sent to live with relatives. Sadly, Ralph never felt welcome in his new school. He was an instant outsider, a dumb "hillbilly" to hear malicious classmates describe him. Although Ralph tried hard at first, he could not keep up with the assignments. His name began to appear more frequently on the list of homework delinquents on the chalkboard. Ralph was angry at himself for feeling stupid and resented his classmates for making him feel that way. Ralph's frustration was often expressed in a wild, impetuous flurry of attention getting that also had the effect of keeping others from learning – throwing erasers during silent reading or making armpit farts when the teacher's back was turned. Ralph's dreams were quickly evaporating. To work in mining, Ralph's generation will need to operate computers and other highly sophisticated equipment. Unless Ralph acquires the basics, he will only carry a shovel, what his father referred to derisively as "an ignorance stick."

By including both overstrivers and failure-accepters like Amy and Ralph in our analyses, we restore Atkinson's original vision of an interplay of independent motives. Doing this will help explain several puzzling classroom behaviors that might otherwise remain a mystery, including the fact that some highly successful students cannot endure even a single minor setback without feeling devastated.

Task- versus ego-involvement

Another limitation of Atkinson's theory concerns a preoccupation with achievement as a competitive phenomenon. Although competition can, and at times does, mean striving to overcome one's own inexperience and ignorance, more often than not the experimental pardigms employed by researchers in the need achievement tradition have pitted one subject against another as the preferred way to arouse achievement striving. Also, as Nicholls (1989) observes, attempts to define task difficulty in this literature reflect a confusion as to what kinds of excellence are worth pursuing. Some researchers (e.g., Hamilton, 1974; Moulton, 1965) measure task difficulty against a yardstick of personal probability of success, that is, "hard or easy for *me*," a self-reference that, according to Nicholls, implies the opportunity for an individual to exercise and extend his or her competency, irrespective of how well or poorly others are doing. However, other researchers (e.g., Meyer, Folkes, & Weiner, 1976; Trope & Brickman, 1975) have employed a normative definition of task difficulty – "hard for me compared to others" – that is an open invitation to become preoccupied with one's ability status. Here students are faced with the prospect that their best performance may still leave them feeling dissatisfied and incompetent.

Although it is true that much achievement, especially in our society, involves winners and losers, not all accomplishments are driven by the competitive spirit of Hermes. Even McClelland occasionally questioned the universality of his own competitive metaphor. Further doubts were eventually raised by researchers who more recently have distinguished between task-involved and ego-involved motivation (Deci, 1975; Deci & Ryan, 1980; Nicholls, 1989). The grasping, self-absorbed image of Hermes as the archetypal achiever seems quite consistent with the concept of ego-involvement with its emphasis on immediate payoffs for work done and achievement for personal gain. For this mentality, learning becomes a way to enhance one's status, often at the expense of others, rather than a way to satisfy curiosity or to create personal meaning. These latter intrinsic goals are largely missing from the need achievement tradition.

The larger point is that much of what can go wrong with achievement – as reflected by atypical shifts, irrational goal setting, and overweening anxiety – is the product of ego-involvement brought on by normative comparisons. This is why those who doubt their ability but still hope to salvage a reputation for competency, like John, prefer difficult tasks because most others will fail at them, too. This also is why those who are convinced of their incompetency, like Ralph, are likely to content themselves with the easy, low-risk assignment. Obviously, neither of these behaviors is desirable from the standpoint of making the most of one's talent; fortunately, as we shall see, neither of them is inevitable.

Diversity versus deficit

If the concept of need achievement was tied originally to the dynamics of competition, then its validity is necessarily limited to that citadel of the competitive spirit, middle-class America. Indeed, the model portrayed in Figure 2.1 easily accommodates Amy, John, and Losa – all of whom, despite differences in age, ethnicity, and social background, share an allegiance to middle-class values. This makes Ralph the odd-person-out. For Ralph the spirit of

Hermes is a foreign country, as it is for countless other youngsters in America today.

Initially, investigators paid little attention to social class and ethnic differences in achievement motivation, perhaps because the early research found evidence of the entrepreneurial spirit among a wide diversity of groups, including the Japanese, Israelis, Europeans, and East Indians (Biaggio, 1978; Hayashi, Rim, & Lynn, 1970; Murlidharan & Topa, 1970; Singh, 1977). But what was not fully appreciated at the time was that most of these groups were either native to cultures that held values similar to middle-class America or represented recent immigrants to America – the so-called immigrant minorities. These two groups share little in common with American born *castelike* minorities who, according to John Ogbu (1978), were incorporated originally into our society against their will: Mexican-Americans through colonization of the Southwest Territories, Puerto Ricans following the American takeover from Spain, blacks through slavery, and the American Indians through the dispossession of their tribal lands. These groups were relegated by virtue of birth to the lower rungs of the economic ladder and were traditionally exploited as cheap labor.

What about the need achievement patterns of these so-called castelike groups? Black Americans typically score lower on traditional need achievement measures than do white Americans (Adkins, Payne, & Ballif, 1972; Cooper & Tom, 1984; Graham, 1984a; Mussen, 1953; Rosen, 1959). Native Americans and Hispanics also exhibit these same depressed patterns (Ramirez & Price-Williams, 1976; Sanders, Scholz, & Kagan, 1976). Does this mean that black and Hispanic minorities lack the drive to achieve? No, at least not according to McClelland, who believed that the motive to achieve is merely depressed among minorities because of inadequate socializing (McClelland, Atkinson, Clark, & Lowell, 1953). What was missing in McClelland's view was a home environment that placed a premium on independence, individualism, and the ability to delay gratification – all attributes of children from middle-class America. As Benjamin Bloom, Allison Davis, and Robert Hess (1965) explained it, the root of the problem of underachievement can be traced to "experiences in the home which do not transmit the cultural patterns necessary for the types of learning characteristic of the schools and the larger society" (p. 4).

Although there is much to be said for this cultural deprivation argument, as far as it goes, more recent research points to another and potentially more important source of cultural differences, namely, kinds of achievement goals (Maehr, 1974; Maehr & Nicholls, 1980). According to this view, achievement differences among ethnic groups are reflected in the various goals to which they aspire, not in different levels of achievement fantasy or even in the quality of their environments, because many impoverished immigrants, like Central American refugees, thrive in American schools despite cultural alienation (Suarez-Orozco, 1989). This emphasis on differential goals explains why only Westerners are so intent on climbing Mt. Everest. As an achievement goal this conquest is irrelevant to the Tibetans and Nepalese who live around Everest (Maehr & Nicholls, 1980).

Different goals also explain the remarkable academic accomplishments of Ernestino, a recent refugee from Nicaragua (as reported in Suarez-Orozco, 1989). On the face of it Ernestino should have become just another nameless statistic in America's sad litany of crime, poverty, and personal failure. By fleeing to America, Ernestino barely escaped the random draft and military service that had left two of his brothers dead and his father crippled. But Ernestino's escape had left him both traumatized and broken-hearted; not only had he left his mother behind, but his cultural heritage as well. Moreover, Ernestino's adopted American high school was hardly conducive to the middle-class socialization process of which McClelland spoke. Pushers regularly peddled drugs within a two-block radius of the school, violence and petty theft was rampant on campus, and prostitutes routinely paraded their wares nearby. Additionally, Ernestino worked 40 hours a week as a dishwasher in order to support himself and other members of his extended family in America. But despite it all, Ernestino graduated from high school with an overall GPA of 3.8 and now attends a four-year college.

By any commonsense reckoning, Ernestino is a highly ambitious achiever. Yet, according to Marcelo Suarez-Orozco, who interviewed dozens of similar Hispanic refugees, need achievement concepts are inadequate to explain Ernestino's unique motivational dynamics. Obviously, like traditional white entrepreneurs, Ernestino's basic purpose was to "better himself" – to become a doctor, an attorney, or an engineer, but not (in the spirit of Hermes) for the purpose of self-indulgence or personal gain. Ernestino's achievement fantasies revealed a different ethos, one of nurturing and cooperation. He was driven first to rescue his mother left behind in Nicaragua who had sacrificed so much for his sake, and then more generally to convert his successes into help for others of his people who had been devastated by war. Nor do Ernestino's fantasy themes suggest that he will become a "somebody" at the expense of breaking family ties or denying his heritage in a search for liberation and new freedoms.

Ernestino's fantasy themes would certainly receive high marks for *affiliation* and *nurturance,* but not necessarily on the *need achievement* scale. In effect, Ernestino is not easily accommodated by the taxonomy presented in Figure 2.1. The original need achievement construct misses a rich set of achievement values that lie beyond the narrow constraints of the white middle class. Incidentally, from this perspective we see just how meaningless it is to control for racial and ethnic bias in the TAT simply by changing the ethnicity of the characters depicted on the story cards as a way to make them more representative of the populations being tested (Lefkowitz & Fraser, 1980).

Recent research indicates that, like Hispanic-American children, black Americans also favor achievement goals that benefit their families (as opposed to individual benefits) and from which they would gain family recognition (Castenell, 1983, 1984; Ramirez & Price-Williams, 1976). As one example, researchers assessed the meaning of some 600 concepts among adolescent males from some 30 language groups worldwide (Fyans, Maehr, Salili, & Desai, 1983). Terms like *independence, competition,* and *hard work* were most closely associated with notions of success among white Americans, prerevolutionary Iranians, and West Germans. These same terms were least salient for East Europeans and black Americans. Instead, for many of these black Americans who clearly had parted company with the dominant Protestant work ethic, the most prominent associations with feelings of success were *family, cooperation,* and *tradition.* Finally, not only were terms like *competition* and *champion* less salient in the minds of these black youngsters – words that represent major preoccupations among most middle-class whites – but worst yet for blacks, they were associated with feelings of failure and defeat, and even images of death!

These findings suggest why some minority groups are placed at particular risk in school. First, for many youngsters the primary goals to which they aspire – assuming adult work roles, caring for others, becoming self-reliant – lie outside the more traditional realm of academics. As a result, these goals are not particularly honored or encouraged in many schools. Second, given the mainstream emphasis on competitive values, independence, and on the scramble for improved social status, minority students are being deprived of preferred means to achieve their objectives, which is to say through cooperation, sharing, and close social cohesion. Finally, to make things even worse, these youngsters must play by competitive rules, if they are to play at all, rules that are often alien, frightening, and confusing. Given these handicaps, we should not be surprised by the shocking number of school dropouts found in the ghettos and barrios of America.

Just why academic competition represents a special threat to minorities, especially black youngsters, is a topic for later discussion (chapter 4). In the meantime, the larger policy implications of this research seem clear. We must arrange school learning so that it encourages more varied achievement goals than the narrow set of values often associated with competitive excellence and high standardized test scores for their own sake. We must also learn to respect alternative reasons for attaining excellence, for the sake of the group, for tradition, and for honor. Finally, these changes must be made without doing violence to the fundamental mission of all schooling, that of providing students with the subject-matter skills necessary for survival.

The history of research on need achievement concepts provides an important perspective on this challenge. Scholars have moved from initially viewing ethnic differences in achievement motivation as a matter of *inferiority* for some groups and *superiority* for others, to seeing the issue in terms of *diversity.* Deficiency explanations are generally unsatisfactory because they divert attention from one constant feature of underachievement among ethnic minorities, that is, the inability of the educational system to recognize the particular needs of these children. As Dennis McInerney (1988) points out,

When educators place the blame for minority children's poor achievement on factors for which the school cannot be held responsible, particularly such factors as children's innate lack of ability, or inappropriate cognitive style, then there is little perceived need for major alterations in the organizational structure or policies in school. (p. 33)

Further educational implications

One final observation rounds out my analysis of the need achievement model. It concerns the fundamental nature of achievement motivation and whether or not changes in what is often thought to be a basic, traitlike personality dimension are possible through relearning and instruction. According to Mc-Clelland, the characteristic way in which individuals resolve the inherent approach–avoidance conflict posed by achievement situations depends largely on childhood experiences. Subsequent research has borne out this expectation (for a review, see Smith, 1969). Several aspects of child rearing appear especially relevant to later achievement striving.

Parental expectations and guidance

First, parents of success-oriented children expect their youngsters to achieve notable successes. As a result they encourage their children at an early age to try new things, explore options, and exercise independence compared to parents whose children are relatively low in the need to achieve (Winterbottom, 1953).

Second, these same parents also provide an uncommon amount of nurturing so that their children will also acquire the skills necessary for independence. Bernard Rosen and Roy D'Andrade (1959) administered problem-solving tasks to two groups of young boys, one of which was rated high and the other low in achievement motivation. In one test the boys were blindfolded and asked to build a tower using oddly shaped blocks. Parents could encourage their sons in any way they wished as long as they themselves did not touch the blocks. The parents of the high-striving boys provided far more encouragement, usually in the form of task-oriented tips about how to proceed (e.g., "Put the larger blocks on the bottom") and expressed more praise when the task was finished. Moreover, as in the Winterbottom study cited, these parents also expected more of their children and were also more optimistic that their sons would not disappoint them. These same findings have been confirmed more recently for both boys and girls in The Netherlands (Hermans, ter Laak, & Maes, 1972).

A third line of research initiated originally by Virginia Crandall and her colleagues (Crandall, Katkovsky, & Crandall, 1965; Crandall, Preston, & Rabson, 1960) suggests that patterns of parental rewards and reprimands are also critical to the development of attitudes toward achievement. The parents of high-achieving youngsters tend to reward praiseworthy accomplishments, yet ignore disappointing performances, a pattern well illustrated by Losa's parents. This pattern is essentially reversed when it comes to the parents of failure-avoiding youngsters like John (Teevan & Fischer, 1967). Here disappointing performances are seen as violations of adult expectations and punished accordingly – usually severely – whereas success is met with faint praise and even indifference.

More recently, researchers have isolated another devastating parental reaction to failure, one of inconsistency – a tendency to punish failure sometimes and at other times to disregard or even reward poor performance (Kohl-mann, Schumacher, & Streit, 1988). These reactions have been implicated in the development of *learned helplessness,* a topic to be considered in the next chapter. These learners give up trying because they come to believe, often rightly so, that they have no control over their destiny (Mineka & Henderson, 1985; Mineka & Kihlstrom, 1978). Eventually profound depression, anger, and overwhelming feelings of anxiety can result. This description fits Ralph in most respects.

Research conducted by Walter Krohne at Mainz University (Krohne, 1980, 1985, 1990; Krohne, Kohlmann, & Leidig, 1986) suggests that such gener-alized anxiety reactions can also be triggered by another different combination of child-rearing strategies. In this particular case, parents provide neither con-stant standards by which children can judge performance nor the intellectual support necessary to develop effective coping skills.

Another disastrous pattern involves aggressive, often overbearing parental demands for excellence, but with little or no guidance for how to achieve it (Chapin & Vito, 1988; Davids & Hainsworth, 1967). In this case the child hopelessly outclasses himself or herself by maintaining unrealistically high self-standards with no way to attain them. This discrepancy between *hoped-for* and *expected* outcomes has been associated with the phenomenon of *un-derachieving* (Bricklin & Bricklin, 1967). Underachievers perform at levels far below their capacity because, as the prevailing argument runs, if they were to try hard and fail anyway – a virtual certainty given such high standards – their self-esteem would suffer. By refusing to try at all, these individuals deftly sidestep any test of their worth.

The overstriver also shares this same ideal–actual discrepancy (Martire, 1956). However, rather than avoiding a test of their worth, these students, like Amy, are driven to avoid failure by actually living up to their overly demanding ideals. The parents of overstrivers demand excellence, and typi-cally nurture the proper intellectual tools to ensure success, but in the process overzealously pressure the child by also punishing failure.

Not surprisingly, child-rearing practices also have an ethnic dimension. Consider the case of black ghetto dwellers. In order to survive in the face of marginal economic resources, many black households organize themselves into cooperative, mutual exchange groups based on kinship (Stack, 1974). Extended family members band together in order to share limited goods and services – money, clothes, food, and shelter. Even children are shuttled back and forth between households depending on who is in the best position to help, with the result that a number of women may become "mothers" to the same child, including aunts, grandmothers, and cousins (Ladner, 1978). Dur-ing infancy black youngsters receive a great deal of warmth and affection (Rainwater, 1966, 1975), but in the postinfancy period, the onset of which often coincides with the birth of a new child, this emphasis on nurturing is replaced by a kind of contest between the child and adults that is typically initiated by the biological mother (Young, 1974). The purpose of this com-petition is to teach self-reliance and prepare children for the harsh, often dan-gerous realities of the street culture. Sometimes this training takes the form of physical punishment designed to discourage emotional dependency on adults (Silverstein & Krate, 1975). Other times children are taught to be aggressive and fight back when their interests are being threatened (Foster, 1974). In the process many black youngsters learn that formal schooling is but one alternative survival strategy and that being streetwise is another (Nobles & Traver, 1976).

Motivation training

If the quality of child rearing contributes to later achievement styles in such straightforward, discernible ways, then cannot negative dispositions be changed and positive ones reinforced through systematic instruction in schools? Research with adults does suggest that intense skill training can increase the quality of entrepreneurial activities, and for at least several years after instruction (Aronoff & Litwin, 1966; Lasker, 1966; McClelland & Winter, 1969). Typically such training involves using problem-solving games to teach realistic risk appraisal. For example, in the "business game" (Litwin & Ciarlo, 1961) players calculate how many toy rockets they can assemble in a given amount of time. If players overestimate how much they can accomplish and buy too many parts, they will lose money. But if too few parts are requisitioned, players will end up with time on their hands.

If realistic goal setting can be encouraged in adults, then why not in children? Given the importance of this question, it is surprising that more is not known about the answer. However, what little evidence we do have is promising (McClelland, 1972). It suggests that positive changes are possible, not only in those behaviors associated with a success orientation such as realistic goal setting and independence of judgment, but also in improved school grades and reductions in absenteeism and dropout rates (DeCharms, 1968, 1972; Kolb, 1965; Ryals, 1969). We will consider the wider educational implications of this kind of research in chapter 8.

The literature on child rearing also suggests at least two other potentially effective classroom approaches to encouraging excellence. The first is to establish incentive systems that reward successful performance on the one hand, and that minimize the likelihood of failure on the other, or at least alter the meaning of failure. We will consider this strategy more fully in chapter 7. A second approach is to teach children to analyze the causes of their successes and failures in constructive ways. This is the realm of "attribution retraining," a topic considered next.

3

Motives as thoughts

I would say only that if some of my judgments were wrong . . . they were
made in what I believed at the time to be the best interest of the nation.
RICHARD NIXON (resignation speech as President of the United States, August,
1974)

According to Fritz Heider (1958), each of us, including ex-presidents, searches
ceaselessly for ways to create meaning in our lives. Heider proposed that this
process is guided by the principles of attribution theory, which involve ascribing causes to our actions and to the actions of others. Clearly this is what
Richard Nixon was doing, trying to make comprehensible his questionable
actions during the Watergate scandal. These same dynamics are also illustrated by the self-searching of aeronautics pioneer, Samuel Langley, who an-
guished over why his flying machine crashed into the Potomac River on take-
off (incidently, just nine days before the Wright brothers' first successful flight).
Was it his fault? Did the crash result from a design flaw in the steam-launch
catapult, or were erratic wind currents to blame? A TV commentator who
attributes the success of a college basketball team to brilliant preseason re-
cruiting is playing the attribution game as well. A schoolchild who frets over
a failing grade also is trying to ascribe causes. Was failure the result of incompetency, or the fault of the teacher for not better explaining the assignment?

As all these examples show, meaning is a construction of reality, not reality itself, and a variety of constructions are possible. Perhaps the schoolchild
is in fact intellectually backward. This is a difficult reality to accept. So, too,
was the revelation for Richard Nixon that others believed his actions involved
criminal intent. Such disclosures threaten to diminish the individual and, if
possible, are to be avoided. Thus the search for causes can serve the goal of
self-justification as well as a need for objective self-appraisal.

In this chapter we will explore the latter proposition that attributions serve
to create relatively accurate, unvarnished appraisals of one's actions and resources. The next chapter provides a discussion of attributions as *motivated
cognitions* (Covington, 1984b), that is, explanations for one's actions that are
designed to protect a sense of personal worth and excuse one's shortcomings.

Attribution theory is central to the topic of achievement motivation because
in the early 1970s cognitive psychologists led by Bernard Weiner proposed a
radical reinterpretation of Atkinson's need achievement model (Weiner et al.,
1971; Weiner, 1972, 1974). Recall that Atkinson postulated emotional anticipation as the basic driving force behind all achievement behavior and defined
the motive to approach success as "a capacity to experience pride in accomplishment." Weiner transformed Atkinson's definition with an intriguing substitute: "a capacity for perceiving success as caused by internal factors, particularly effort" (Weiner et al., 1971, p. 18).

This is a fascinating assertion. Can it really be that all noteworthy accomplishments depend on the meaning individuals ascribe to their successes and failures? For instance, was Nixon's slow, painful rise out of gentile poverty to world prominence basically a matter of a lifetime habit of positive self-talk that extolled the virtues of hard work? It is certainly true that Nixon's career embodied the spirit of Hermes to an extraordinary degree – his concern for the unique accomplishment, the restless energy, his entrepreneurial activities (in his early years Nixon pioneered the marketing of frozen orange juice), and his now-famous opportunistic style of leadership, which at times involved (allegedly) breaking rules and even illegal activities. According to psychologists David Winter and Leslie Carlson (1988; also see Winter, 1987), who analyzed the content of the first inaugural addresses of all U.S. presidents, Nixon scored near the top on achievement striving (trailing only Herbert Hoover and Jimmy Carter). It is also the case that Nixon's autobiographical statements are filled with references to hard work, persistence, and renewed effort as the reasons for turning potential crises to his advantage (Nixon, 1962). Even at the level of the mundane, Nixon was known to take extraordinary care. H. R. Haldeman, Nixon's chief of staff, confided that "he'd check every item of the [formal dinner] menu and each facet of the evening program adjusting this or that detail until he got it right. The next day Nixon would treat the dinner as if it had been a major military battle. Every detail was commented upon" (Haldeman, 1978, p. 73).

Although we must leave Nixon's motives as well as his cognitions to the verdict of history, there can be little doubt that the way individuals perceive the causes of their actions plays an important part in their lives, whether these perceptions be accurate or distorted.

What then is attribution theory? How successful has it been in altering the dominant view of achievement motivation as a matter of emotional conflict? And what are the implications of attribution theory for educational practice and reform?

Cognitions versus emotions
Emotions are thoughts with feelings attached.
SPINOZA

Weiner proposed that it is the naturally occurring attribution process that controls achievement behavior, not emotional anticipation. In making this declaration, Weiner and other cognitive theorists are not denying the fact of emotions. Our daily experience confirms that emotions happen and that they can be vivid, intense, and sometimes inescapable. But cognitive theorists doubt whether emotions – which besides being intense are also vague and often diffuse – are specific enough to guide behavior in the precise ways proscribed by Atkinson's model. It is one thing to become aroused, but then, once aroused, quite another to direct one's actions in finely orchestrated ways toward specific goals.

As with so many debates, the issue at stake here is more a matter of emphasis than of substance. Today few cognitive scientists would maintain that once emotions are activated they no longer play a part in the achievement process. On the other hand, motivational theorists rarely deny the importance of cognitions in controlling behavior. In fact, we will soon discover (chapter 5) that the relative importance of the roles played by cognitions and emotions depends largely on where in the achievement process researchers choose to begin their observations and where they stop. At certain points emotions prevail, and at other points cognitions assume a dominant causal presence.

For our purposes we may leave aside as basically unprofitable the long-standing debate over whether emotions or cognitions are the ultimate prime movers of human behavior. The kinds of evidence it would take to prove that emotions are independent of or even precede cognitions in the earliest stages of human development are not presently available, nor are they likely to be any time soon if we can judge from the most recent debate on this topic (see Lazarus, 1982, 1984; Zajonc, 1984).

Although I will argue, as have others (see Clark & Fiske, 1982), that emotions and cognitions share a basic compatibility, we must not lose sight of the fact that ultimately the sources of motivational power assumed by Atkinson and Weiner are quite different. In Atkinson's original schema emotional anticipation provides the ultimate stimulus for future actions. By contrast, the cognitive view asserts that emotions provide the impulse for action only to the extent that they have informational value, that is, when emotions convey some knowledge about one's world. It is in this reasoning that cognitive theorists come close to embracing the idea of motives. When they do speak directly of motivation, which is seldom, they talk about the need to gain a measure of predictability and control over one's surroundings (Weiner, 1985). For example, as Harold Kelley (1971a) sees it, ''The attributor is not simply an attributor, a seeker after knowledge; his latent goal in attaining knowledge is that of effective management of himself and his environment'' (p. 22).

Social comparison theory, another related cognitive tradition, also stresses the need for individuals to create accurate appraisals of their ability and talents by comparing their performances to those of others (Festinger, 1957; Schachter & Singer, 1962). According to our working definition, these tendencies amount to motives. The need to assert control, to predict future events, and to provide an accurate self-assessment are yet additional reasons for *why* students strive, right along with the desire to improve, to succeed, and to avoid failure.

In the cognitive tradition, emotions can serve the goal of self-understanding but only to the extent that they push individuals toward self-appraisal, as when, for instance, feelings of shame trigger heightened self-awareness, which in turn leads to the discovery of the causes of one's disappointing performance. Perhaps the Roman poet Virgil best captured the essence of feelings as sources of information when he observed that ''*happy* is he who has been able to perceive the causes of things.''

By this cognitive interpretation, the motives to avoid failure and to approach success are regarded, respectively, as the tendency to resist or to seek out definitive information about one's abilities and to use this information in

Table 3.1. *Perceived determinants of achievement behavior*

Stability	Locus of causality	
	Internal	External
stable	ability	task ease or difficulty
unstable	effort	luck

order to improve (Trope, 1975). Clearly, motivational theorists would agree with much in this statement (see especially White, 1959). Indeed, one gets the impression sometimes that only differences in terminology separate these positions. Despite the clear overlap, however, and even after we discount confusions caused by imprecise language, each position does in fact start from a different perspective. If we begin with attributions as the basic building blocks of achievement behavior, new prospects arise for educational theory and practice that do not readily flow from Atkinson's model. For this reason, it is important that we become more fully acquainted with the details of Weiner's attribution model and with the research inspired by his proposed reformulation.

Heider's causal matrix

Following the earlier, seminal work of Fritz Heider (1958), Weiner proposed ability, effort, task difficulty, and luck as the major perceived causes of achievement performance (Weiner, 1972, 1977, 1979). These four basic causal elements can be classified along three dimensions, two of which are portrayed in Table 3.1. The first is referred to as the *locus of causality* dimension that specifies the causes of an event as either *internal* (within the person) or *external* (outside the person). *Ability* and *effort* attributions are designated as internal elements because they reflect inherent characteristics of the individual. Likewise, *task difficulty* and *luck* are portrayed as external factors because they are beyond the individual's immediate capacity to control.

The second dimension, that of *stability,* classifies the four causes as either constant or transient. *Task difficulty* and *ability* are taken to be relatively stable causes of achievement outcomes, whereas *luck* and *effort* are clearly subject to change.

A third dimension (not shown in Table 3.1) reflects the *controllability* of events (Rosenbaum, 1972). This extra dimension helps differentiate between some perceived causes that would be classified identically in the locus × stability scheme in Table 3.1, but are, in fact, treated differently in the real world. Consider effort and illness. Both are classified as unstable and internal causes. Yet when students fail a test simply for lack of trying they are reprimanded more by teachers than if illness kept them from studying (Covington & Omelich, 1979b). The difference in treatment occurs because presumably students can control their effort, but not the flu bug.

Basically, the distinguishing property of this third dimension is *intentionality,* that is, whether or not a cause is subject to deliberate control by the individual. The controllability dimension introduces a moral tone into the attribution scheme. In our society accountability for one's actions depends as much on one's intentions as on the gravity of the actions themselves. For example, if a person harms another without intending to do so, then he or she will likely be judged less culpable than if intentional harm had been done. These same dynamics apply to school achievement, especially as they relate to the virtues of hard work. Since effort is widely believed to be under conscious, intentional control, persons are generally held responsible when they do not try hard, thereby engendering feelings of guilt and remorse in the offender.

Weiner (1983) rightly observes that this three-dimensional structure is largely the product of rational theory building, and may not always capture the essence of real-life thought patterns. For example, we might ask, are there other important perceived causes of achievement besides the basic elements portrayed in Table 3.1? Also, does this three-dimensional model really reflect the way human beings think about causality outside the research laboratory? Might there not be more dimensions, psychologically speaking? or fewer dimensions? or some entirely different way of portraying these realities?

As to the first question – whether the model exhausts all reasonable causes – we know it does not. When people are asked to generate spontaneously their own lists of causes for academic success and failure, a whole host of additional reasons emerge (Cooper & Burger, 1980; Frieze, 1976; Bar-Tel & Darom, 1979; Whitley & Frieze, 1985; Wimer & Kelley, 1982; Wong & Weiner, 1981). Most of these newcomers are treated as miscellaneous factors under the original category of *luck.* They include fatigue, mood, teacher bias, and help from others. Even so, the original four basic attributes – ability, effort, task, and luck – predominate in the minds of most individuals. Also, as we shall see, three of these four elements (sans luck) have been repeatedly shown to influence actual achievement events. Thus although other perceived causes are possible and have even been studied extensively, as in the case of *help from others* (e.g., Graham, 1990; Newman, 1990), the four original attributes appear reasonably exhaustive.

Now consider the second question – whether or not Weiner's three-dimensional structure reflects psychological reality. Some researchers have found that individuals think about causal attributes in ways that suggest other basic dimensions may also be operating (e.g., Falbo & Beck, 1979). Among the several alternative dimensions suggested, that of *motivation* (either high or low) is an especially attractive candidate (Wimer & Kelley, 1982). It captures the idea of "willful," purposeful striving, qualities not adequately reflected in the original structure. By and large, however, the present model, especially the stability and locus dimensions, appears well justified on empirical grounds (Day, 1982; Meyer, 1980; Stern, 1983). In effect, these dimensions have proved to be a useful, durable schema for describing the way human beings organize their subjective world of causality.

What is not so clear, however, is the proper placement of the individual causal elements within Weiner's model. It turns out that not all persons classify the same causal element, say, ability, in the same ways. For example, if an individual believes that ability is the result of hard work, as do young children (Blumenfeld, Pintrich, Meece, & Wessels, 1981; Harari & Covington, 1981), then ability will likely be classified as a transitory, unstable element. On the other hand, by the time students reach the high school and college years, they generally believe that ability is a relatively fixed, immutable capacity, and as a consequence tend to rate it as a stable element (Chandler & Spies, 1983). As another example, low effort may be classified as a stable element – contrary to its original placement in the model – if chronic inaction is believed to reflect traitlike dispositions such as laziness (Covington, Spratt, & Omelich, 1980). Moreover, there is evidence that under some circumstances task difficulty is perceived as an unstable element, particularly if the problem is novel or not likely to be encountered again (Wimer & Kelley, 1982). Also, judgments of task difficulty are likely to change over time even for the same task because individuals get better with practice (Weiner, 1983).

All these observations suggest that subjective reality is invariably far more complex than can be accommodated by our conceptual models. But to the extent these models do approximate reality, they can be useful. Just how useful, we are about to see.

The attribution model

How do these attributional elements relate to Atkinson's theory? Basically, attribution theorists contend that success-oriented persons, like Losa, and failure-prone individuals, like John and Ralph, harbor different explanations about their successes and failures, and it is precisely these differences that are taken to be the essence of individual differences in achievement motivation. Generally speaking, persons motivated to approach success are thought to attribute their failures to internal factors – chiefly to a lack of effort (unstable, internal) – and their successes to a combination of high ability and effort. By contrast, failure-threatened persons are said to ascribe their failures to a lack of ability (stable, internal) rather than to insufficient effort. Additionally, they attribute their successes, should any occur, to unstable, external factors such as luck or the help provided by others. This pattern is especially characteristic of those students like Ralph, who we have designated as failure-accepting (Schmalt, 1982).

Generally, the evidence supports these predictions (Arkin, Detchon, & Maruyama, 1982; Leppin, Schwarzer, Belz, Jerusalem, and Quast, 1987; Meyer, 1970; Weiner & Kukla, 1970, Exp. 4; Weiner et al., 1971; Weiner, Heckhausen, Meyer, & Cook, 1972). The findings are especially strong when it comes to verifying the predominance of low-ability explanations among failure-threatened students (see Covington & Omelich, 1979a).

Clearly, the attribution pattern associated with success-oriented individuals is positive. Because success-oriented individuals, like Losa, believe themselves capable of success, failure when it occurs (which is rare) means they

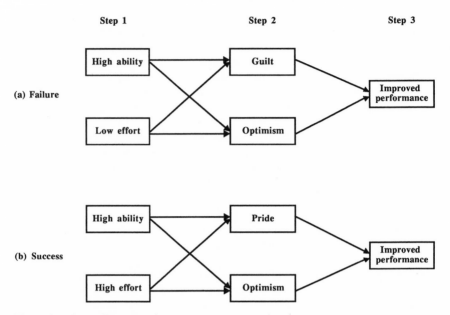

Figure 3.1. Losa: Success striver

have not tried hard enough nor taken the right path. Notice this interpretation robs failure of its threat. Failure no longer implies incompetency, but rather ignorance – simply not knowing or understanding – something that can be corrected by redoubling one's efforts (Man & Hrabal, 1988). On the other hand, failure-prone individuals, like Ralph, find themselves caught up in a catastrophic situation. They take little credit for success (which is rare enough anyway) because they don't feel worthy of it, and they blame themselves for failure by reason of stupidity.

Now, how do these attribution patterns fit into the larger achievement process? Figure 3.1 portrays what happens step-by-step to Losa following both a success and a failure experience.

SUCCESS STRIVER: LOSA

Recall that Losa is a high school junior on a college preparatory track. Yesterday she took a sample geometry test for advanced placement on the college entrance boards. This was the first of several practice tests scheduled over the next few weeks, an arrangement that suits Losa fine. She relishes the opportunity to demonstrate her intellectual prowess, and the possibility of doing well always excites her. In fact, Losa's enthusiasm for this particular contest carried her along despite her having scored at the 85th percentile, a clear failure in her mind. Why isn't Losa's ardor dampened by this setback, and why is she likely to do better the next time?

The answers depend initially on Losa's explanations for failure. Losa attributes her allegedly substandard performance to inadequate study (Step 1, Figure 3.1a), a conclusion that arouses feelings of self-reproach for not having attended all the review sessions provided by the geometry teacher (Step 2: low effort → guilt). Chagrin at not having studied enough the first time around ensures that Losa will now take things more seriously, feelings that eventually lead to more study and improved performance (Step 3: low effort → guilt → improvement) (Hoffman, 1982; Wicker, Payne, & Morgan, 1983). For Losa, then, effort-linked emotions such as guilt or remorse, although clearly unpleasant, can ultimately work to her advantage. So emotions do in fact mobilize actions.

Meanwhile, we note that Losa's explanation of inadequate study (back to Step 1) also helps her maintain high expectations for eventual success (Step 2: low effort → optimism) because effort, being an unstable, internal element, can always be increased the next time around (Fontaine, 1974; McMahan, 1973; Meyer, 1970; Rosenbaum, 1972; Valle, 1974; Weiner et al., 1972). High expectations in turn exert a powerful influence on future achievement (Step 3: low effort → high expectations (optimism) → improvement). Indeed, individuals who believe they will excel in the future do, in fact, perform better than those who remain pessimistic, even when both groups are equated for ability. This is because those youngsters who are more certain of attaining the grades to which they aspire work harder and spend more time on class assignments (Battle, 1965).

To complete our example, Losa believes she possesses the ability to achieve a top score, so her initial disappointment represents no particular threat because failure is seen as caused by factors within her control. Undiminished ability perceptions are important for several reasons. First, like attributions to low effort, they also lead to high expectations for future success (Step 2: high ability → optimism). Second, when able individuals perform below their expectations, guilt drives them to redouble their efforts.

A somewhat different scenario applies if Losa's initial score on the practice test had placed her at the 98th percentile – an unqualified success even for Losa. In this case she would likely attribute this extraordinary performance to a blend of skillful effort and ability (Step 1: Figure 3.1b), a conclusion that leads both to pride and to increased future expectations (Step 2). Both these factors – one cognitive (high expectations) and the other emotional (pride) – combine in turn to ensure a continued record of excellence. In fact, one success begets another. Losa is likely to find herself on the crest of an upward cycle of attribution-triggered triumphs.

FAILURE AVOIDER: JOHN

Now consider the same attribution model as it applies to failure-threatened individuals like John, the self-doubting, apathetic high school senior (Figure 3.2). Last year John also took the same advanced geometry course and went through the same gauntlet of practice tests. As luck would have it, John's initial performance was identical to that of Losa's. He, too, scored at the 85th percentile and his sense of disappointment was equally keen. But the meanings that John and Losa attributed to these identical outcomes were worlds apart. For John, this disappointing performance raised anew lingering doubts about his ability (Step 1: Figure 3.2a). Whenever John does worse than antic-

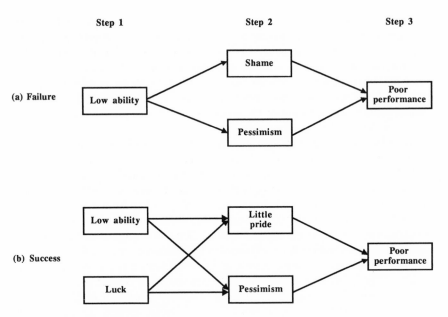

Figure 3.2. John: Failure avoider

ipated, his first reaction is that he is not bright enough. These doubts elicit feelings of shame (Step 2), an emotion that leads in turn to impaired performance the next time around (Step 3: inability → shame → poor achievement), largely because shame and humiliation block effective study. These same perceptions of incompetency (back to Step 1) also lead John to view his future prospects pessimistically, a judgment that also undercuts his next performance (inability → pessimism → poor achievement). Thus we see how easy it is for John to become trapped in a reverberating cycle of downward expectations, diminishing resolve, and increasing self-doubt, test after test.

Even if John is able to defy the odds and perform better on the next practice test – recall that he excels at turning defeat into victory at the last moment – he will nonetheless continue to doubt himself and worry about being found out as a kind of high-achieving imposter (Figure 3.2b). So even high grades offer John little reassurance, because success, when it does occur, is discounted by failure-threatened students, and their pride is dampened because success is attributed to factors they feel helpless to control. John might believe he simply had the good fortune to study the right questions (luck). John's future prospects remain dim because he does not believe himself capable of repeated excellence.

Note, once again, that all this aggravation can occur despite a perfectly reasonable record of achievement. The same good grades carry different messages and burdens for different people. From this perspective, the gravest danger to American education is not necessarily slumping achievement scores. John and other white students like him can always be coaxed, cajoled, or otherwise pressured into performing just a little bit better, or so the advocates of an intensification policy would have us believe. Actually, the greatest danger concerns the matter of *choice*, which according to the need achievement model is controlled by motives and expectations (Meece, Wigfield, & Eccles, 1990). One choice always available to students is whether to continue in school or not. John is at far greater risk for quitting school or dropping out mentally than for literally failing geometry. Moreover, academic potential is not as critical to this choice as many believe. In fact, contrary to the popular view, dropouts are not always the worst students. According to one estimate (Fetterman, 1990) nearly 30% of all school dropouts in America would test out as gifted.

For the moment, John will continue to cope marginally, even though he is performing well above average. In the words of Richard Beery (1975), John is "afloat but drifting" (p. 192). John hovers between hope and despair – a precarious balance that unfortunately will soon be destroyed by the added stresses and dislocation of college life. Increased fears of being discovered as incompetent and mounting anxiety will soon exhaust, then overwhelm John's natural resiliency and erode his notable academic talents until finally he will accept even top grades as evidence of a failed cause.

Analysis and critique
The causes of events always interest us more than the events themselves.
CICERO

Weiner's cognitive attribution model represents an important step in the evolution of thinking about achievement dynamics. There is the implicit recognition that achievement behavior, whatever else might be said, is best seen as an ongoing historic event that unfolds for individuals over time. When persons, like Losa or John, move step-by-step through Weiner's model, the causal focus shifts sequentially from attributions (cognitions), to emotions, back to more cognitions (expectations), and then to the interplay of emotions and cognitions as they determine the quality of achievement.

The explanatory value of such a model depends largely on our ability to conceptualize emotions and cognitions as being both interactive and independent. In real life, thoughts and feelings are inseparable; indeed, they become fused. Yet they are not the same thing. This much is clear from the fact that under conditions of extraordinary stress, thoughts can be dissociated from feelings and become compartmentalized. Moreover, compared to thoughts, emotions often seem unforgettable, difficult to verbalize, yet easy to communicate to others (Zajonc, 1984).

Weiner has provided the conceptual means for disentangling feelings and thoughts long enough to chart the course of their individual contributions without doing violence to the larger truth that ultimately emotions and cognitions share a basic compatibility as joint movers of behavior. Now what about the evidence for the general attribution model, and for the many specific pathways portrayed in Figures 3.1 and 3.2? A number of studies that confirm specific linkages in Weiner's model have already been cited as we followed the fortunes of Losa and John. However, the diversity of this literature makes an overall appraisal difficult. Basically, these studies do not always map onto the model in comparable or uniform ways. For one thing, attribution research draws on many different student populations, ranging from the elementary grades through the college level. For another thing, many research methodologies are represented. For instance, some researchers artificially induce feelings of success and failure in the laboratory (e.g., Weiner & Sierad, 1975), whereas other investigators monitor actual classroom events during test taking (e.g., Bernstein, Stephen, & Davis, 1979). Furthermore, researchers often measure the same concepts in different ways, a practice that inevitably leads to confusion and to a dilution of results (for a critique, see Covington & Omelich, 1984d). Finally, most researchers typically examine only one linkage in the model at a time, to the exclusion of all others. In short, the general approach to testing the attribution model has been a rather piecemeal affair.

However, having said this, when individual studies are aggregated within the kind of framework provided by Figures 3.1 and 3.2, there emerges a strong case favoring the fundamental proposition that attributions play a significant role in the achievement process. Although some of the specific predictions that flowed from Weiner's original model have been modified over the years and various ambiguities clarified (for a debate see Brown & Weiner, 1984; Covington & Omelich, 1984a, 1984b, 1984d; Weiner & Brown, 1984), the overall attributional interpretation of achievement dynamics has withstood well the tests of time and empirical scrutiny.

Now that the main features of the attribution model have been presented, how do sex and ethnic differences fit in? For example, do males exhibit attribution patterns uniquely different from those of females? Do minority groups differ among themselves and from the white majority in their causal perceptions of the world?

Sex differences

Although the evidence on sex differences is far from complete and the findings occasionally mixed, it appears that on balance women and girls are more likely to express negative, failure-prone attributions than are men and boys (Croxton & Klonsky, 1982; Dweck & Reppucci, 1973; Frieze, 1975; Frieze, Fisher, Hanusa, McHugh, & Valle, 1978; Levine, Reis, Sue, & Turner, 1976; Nicholls, 1975; Rosenfield & Stephen, 1978). For example, females are more prone than males to cite inability as the cause of their failures. And, compared to boys, girls see ability as less important to their successes (Parsons, Meece, Adler, & Kaczala, 1982).

Several explanations for these differences have been offered. One is that girls and women simply mirror a dominant perception in our society, erroneous as it is, that females are less able and therefore their successes are rightly attributed to hard work and compliance (Etaugh & Brown, 1975; Hellman & Kram, 1978; Heilman & Stopeck, 1985; Taynor & Deaux, 1973). It has also been suggested that the exercise of intellectual ability may be seen by many females as less role appropriate (Nicholls, 1975). In this connection, it has been found that women readily express failure-prone attributions but only when the partner with whom they were in competition was a male (Stephen, Rosenfield, & Stephen, 1976). Likewise, young girls often exhibit greater evidence of helplessness, but mostly in the company of teachers (Dweck, Davidson, Nelson, & Enna, 1978) – not surprisingly, because teachers are more apt to interpret the failures of girls as a matter of inadequate ability while attributing the failures of boys to a lack of effort and discipline. A third explanation is that males privately make the same attributions for their successes and failures as do females for theirs, but males are simply more defensive in their public statements owing to societal pressures to maintain an image of assertiveness and competency (Covington & Omelich, 1978; Snyder, Stephen, & Rosenfeld, 1976; Wolosin, Sherman, & Till, 1973; Zuckerman, 1979). Whatever the causes of these sex differences, attempts at educational reform must be sensitive to the possibility that females may be more prone than males to discount themselves as agents of their own achievement.

Ethnic differences

For the moment interest in ethnic differences has far outrun the available evidence. We do know, of course, that many minorities, especially blacks and Hispanics, hold achievement goals that are not always shared by the white middle-class majority. The achievement fantasies of Ernestino and other Central American refugees attest to this (Suarez-Orozco, 1989). It is also well established that many minority group members doubt that they will ever achieve satisfactorily in school. But the question is, Are the attributions these students make to effort, ability, and chance or luck responsible for this pessimism? And, if so, do effort and ability attributions mean the same thing to minorities? Regarding the latter question, probably not. For example, compared to black college students, Asian students view effort, especially doing homework, as more of a social event involving cooperation and sharing than as an opportunity for solitary accomplishment (Treisman, 1985). Thus not only do the achievement goals of minorities typically differ from those of the white majority, but the preferred *means* to these ends may also differ from those of whites, and among various minority groups as well. These are tantalizing possibilities with obvious implications for individualizing instruction, but for the moment they remain only that, tantalizing and largely unproven.

If any consistent finding does emerge from this literature, it is that most castelike minorities tend to exhibit an external locus of control. They feel like pawns of fate, buffeted by forces beyond their control. The evidence for blacks is especially strong (Battle & Rotter, 1963; Phase, 1976; Zytkoskee & Strickland, 1971), although more recent studies suggest that black–white differences in locus of control may be less than originally thought (Graham, 1988). The prevailing responses of native Americans, including the Plains and Pueblo Indians, are also consistent with an external orientation, likely because these cultural traditions emphasize mankind's dependency on nature rather than dominance over it. The tendency toward fatalism and a tradition of noncompetitiveness in the Hispanic culture can also be accounted for by this same reasoning (for a review, see McInerney, 1988).

More specifically, as to attribution patterns, the bulk of the evidence suggests that Asian youngsters – Japanese, Chinese, Filipinos, and Koreans – act more success oriented compared to the white majority, as evidenced by their greater tendency to attribute academic success to effort (Holloway, 1988; Mizokawa & Ryckman, 1988; Hess, Chang, & McDevitt, 1987). On the other hand, when compared to whites, black students behave in more failure-oriented ways. For example, in one study white elementary school students rate ability and effort as the most important causes of school performance compared to luck and task difficulty, whereas blacks tend to reverse these ratings (Friend & Neale, 1972). The tendency among blacks to discount themselves as agents of their own achievement is thought to occur in part because white America has long held low academic expectations for blacks and because blacks, as a result, have come to doubt their intellectual potential (Fordham & Ogbu, 1986). These are essentially the same arguments as those used to explain the low self-regard suffered by many females. Presumably, then, black females would be most vulnerable to the kinds of failure dynamics portrayed in Figure 3.2.

Educational implications

The educational implications of attribution theory are central to our analysis of the current educational crisis. Four points are pivotal: the meaning of failure, the role of effort, learned helplessness, and attribution retraining.

The meaning of failure

Attribution theory provides an answer to the question, Why can failure, which elicits shame and leads to lowered esteem among so many students, mobilize other students to greater effort? Attribution theory teaches us that it is not so much the event of failure, or even its frequency, that disrupts performance as it is the *meaning* of failure. For students like Losa, who steadfastly interpret failure as the result of improper or insufficient effort, failure acts as a challenge – a goad to renewed striving. But for other students like Ralph, who see failure as confirming suspicions of incompetency, it can only be paralyzing. Likewise, it is now understandable why success does not always reinforce self-confidence. If individuals believe their victories are the product of forces beyond their control – luck, chance, or the humanitarian impulse of a teacher – then there is little assurance that success can be repeated. This reasoning also accounts for why failure-prone students often prefer to explain their successes, infrequent as they may be, as simply lucky breaks (Marecek & Mettee, 1972). Doing so releases them from the obligation to repeat their successes, something they are doubtful of doing anyway.

The wide policy implications of these observations seem clear. One often-heard refrain in the chorus of reform proposals is the suggestion that teachers should arrange classroom learning so that students experience either no failure or as little failure as possible (e.g., Glasser, 1969). This view assumes that failure per se causes loss of esteem and self-respect. Quite to the contrary, failure can act as a positive force so long as it is properly interpreted by the learner. Rather than focusing on failure as the culprit, educators should arrange learning so that falling short of one's goals, which inevitably happens to everyone, will be interpreted in ways that promote the will to persist.

The role of effort

Cognitive theory also draws attention to the critical role that effort attributions play in achievement dynamics. As we have seen, this emphasis is not misplaced. For one thing, effort cognitions control expectancies for future success. If individuals can honestly attribute their failures to a lack of trying, then they are more likely to remain optimistic about succeeding later on. For another thing, effort cognitions shape emotional reactions to events. High effort increases pride in success and low effort elicits guilt in failure, emotions that in turn mobilize future effort. And, perhaps most important of all, according to reinforcement principles, student effort – being an internal but unstable element – can in theory at least be aroused and then controlled by the actions of teachers.

The virtues of hard work have long been extolled in America. Nowhere is this more true than in schools, where it is widely held among teachers and parents alike that whereas not all children are equally bright, at least everyone can try. The paramount importance of this work ethic in the teacher's scheme of values has been convincingly demonstrated by Weiner and others (e.g., Covington & Omelich, 1979b; Eswara, 1972; Rest, Nierenberg, Weiner, & Heckhausen, 1973). In the typical study (Weiner & Kukla, 1970), teachers receive information about several hypothetical students including how well each did on a school test (either excellent, fair, borderline, moderate failure, or clear failure), amount of study time (either lots or little), and the student's ability level (either high or low). Teachers then judged the performance of each student by providing varying amounts of rewards (in the form of gold stars) or reprimands (red marks). The results of the Weiner and Kukla study (1970) are presented in Figure 3.3. The subjects were student teachers.

To start, it is obvious that test outcome is the major determinant of teacher evaluation. Whether the student is bright or dull, motivated or not, teachers reward good performances and reprimand poor ones. At the same time, however, it is also clear that teachers reinforce effort. Students who studied diligently (those groups with solid black circles and squares) were rewarded more in success and punished less in failure than those who studied little. Interestingly, information about ability level alone does not exert much influence on these evaluations. Everyone who tries is rewarded, irrespective of ability, although there is a slight tendency for teachers to reward less able students more than bright ones. This finding may reflect a disposition among teachers to compensate poorer pupils by focusing on their occasional successes (see chapter 6). In fact, those low-ability students who work hard (black circles) are evaluated more favorably than all others, even more than high-ability students who also try!

This pattern of teacher rewards and punishments varies for different kinds

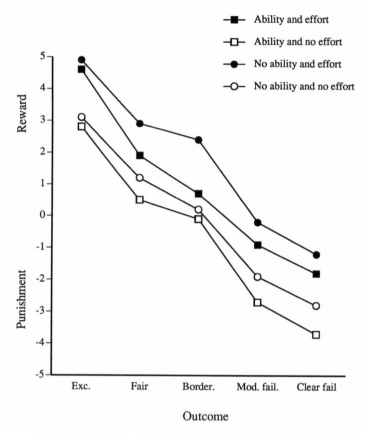

Figure 3.3. Evaluation (reward and punishment) as a function of pupil ability, motivation, and examination outcome (From B. Weiner & A. Kukla. (1970). An attributional analysis of achievement motivation. *Journal of Personality and Social Psychology,* 15(1), 1–20. Copyright 1970 by the American Psychological Association. Adapted by permission of the publisher.)

of students. For example, note in Figure 3.3 the decidedly positive teacher reaction to high effort–high ability students, basically those youngsters we refer to as success oriented. Students who succeed through a combination of high ability and hard work are rewarded generously, an action that reinforces their willingness to keep on trying. At the same time, in the rare event of a clear failure, these same students are among the least punished because they tried hard (Rest et al., 1973). Such a reinforcement pattern – praise for success and leniency in failure – reminds us of those parental patterns that encourage achievement motivation at home (Teevan & Fisher, 1967).

A far less positive reinforcement pattern applies to failure-avoiding students, nominally, those youngsters represented in Figure 3.3 who are less likely to try, especially when they are judged by teachers to be able. This latter group includes underachievers who are known to be capable but unwilling to work hard (Bricklin & Bricklin, 1967). Such students (ability–no effort) are accorded less praise in success and subjected to more punishment in failure than any other type of student represented in Figure 3.3. Whether these teacher policies are helpful in reversing the negative dynamics of underachievement will be discussed later. Meanwhile, there is no denying that teachers as well as adults in general believe that the most effective way to promote learning is to provide rewards for increased effort, and that the greater the rewards the more children will be willing to comply (Boggiano, Barrett, Weiher, McClelland, & Lusk, 1987).

Learned helplessness

One of the most important potential contributions of attribution theory to educational practice concerns the phenomenon of *learned helplessness*. Learned helplessness has been described as a state of depression or loss of hope that accompanies a belief that no matter how hard or how well one tries, failure is the evitable outcome (Coyne & Lazarus, 1980; Miller & Norman, 1979).

Learned helplessness was first studied in research laboratories on the conditioning of fear in animals (Seligman, Maier, & Geer, 1968). In the first phase of these experiments, dogs were subjected to electric shock from which there was no escape. In a second phase, the dogs could avoid the shock by performing a simple routine that under other circumstances they would have easily learned. Yet many of the dogs continued to endure the shock and exhibited symptoms of extreme withdrawal, passivity, and even yawning – reactions that had they occurred in humans would be construed as indifference or boredom. On the basis of these results, it was suggested that being exposed to an uncontrollable, aversive outcome in the first phase of the experiment rendered these animals helpless to act in their own behalf later on (Seligman, 1975; Seligman, Maier, & Solomon, 1971). Once punishment was accepted as beyond their ability to control, positive coping strategies were inhibited. In short, it was not the aversiveness of the shock, but rather its uncontrollability that caused helplessness.

This same experiment paradigm (minus the shock, of course) has been used in research with human subjects (Abramson, Seligman, & Teasdale, 1978; Dweck & Reppucci, 1973; Klein, Fencil-Morse, & Seligman, 1976; Tennen & Eller, 1977). These procedures often form an uncomfortably close parallel to regular classroom learning. As a first step, students are given a series of problem-solving tasks that unbeknownst to them are unsolvable. Next, once a pattern of failure is well established despite the best efforts of the children to succeed, they are given simpler solvable versions of the same failed tasks. In this second phase subjects often fail to solve problems known to be well within their capabilities. Such impotence is often accompanied by feelings of despair, frustration, and hopelessness, and in some cases even anger and hostility (Gatchel, Paulus, & Maples, 1975).

From the cognitive perspective such outcomes are quite understandable. If I believe studying will influence my grade, them I'm more apt to study. But if I believe my grade is the result of uncontrollable factors such as a teacher's compassion, an easy test, or just plain luck, then there is really no point in studying at all. As just noted, the logic of this position suggests that despair is a reaction to the uncontrollable nature of the situation. If true, the culprit would seem to be the vagaries of school achievement, including unfair tests, teacher bias, or institutional indifference, but not necessarily personal limitations. However, this argument appears to violate common sense. Why, as Lyn Abramson and Harold Sackeim (1977) ask, should people feel responsible for events beyond their control, especially if they have tried their best? The answer is found in the fact that the main trigger for a sense of despair is not the fact that the individual tried hard and failed anyway – that is, of not being in control – but rather the implication that one is incompetent (Covington, 1985a). This is a perfect description of Ralph, the displaced Appalachian child.

This finding suggests the need to maintain a distinction between *universal* helplessness (where *no one* can be expected to succeed) and *personal* helplessness, where events are perceived as more controllable by some individuals than by others. Accordingly, we conclude that a sense of personal helplessness occurs when one repeatedly ascribes failure to internal, stable causes – in attributional terms, to low ability, not high effort (Sweeney, Anderson, & Bailey, 1986).

Helpless children differ from success-oriented youngsters not only in the attributions they make, but also in the kinds of strategies they employ when confronted with failure. In a study by Carol Diener and Carol Dweck (1978), both helpless and successful children were trained to solve a series of visual discrimination tasks. By the end of training both groups were equally proficient. In a second phase of the experiment, similar but unsolvable discrimination problems were introduced, and students were then asked to verbalize their thoughts as they worked. As soon as the failure phase began, helpless children behaved as though their prior successes had never occurred. They showed a progressive decrease in the use of reasonable strategies such as hypothesis checking and began engaging in irrelevant, stereotyped activities. Classic statements of helplessness were much in evidence (e.g., "nothing I do matters"). By contrast, during this failure phase, success-oriented children employed the same and on occasion even more sophisticated strategies than they had learned in the initial training session. They also tended to attribute failure variously to a lack of personal effort or to increasingly difficult problems. But, most important, they were less concerned about dwelling on the causes of failure than they were with discovering remedies for failure.

The true insidiousness of this helplessness dynamic and its pervasive, negative influence on all aspects of achievement was demonstrated in a companion study by Diener and Dweck (1980). After helpless students had experienced repeated failure, they were asked to reflect back on their earlier successes during the training phase. These youngsters revised their earlier attributions, which initially had been quite positive, so that in retrospect they no longer recalled feeling competent. On the other hand, success-oriented youngsters remained steadfast in their positive recollections. Finally, the helpless children systematically underestimated the number of problems they had solved correctly in the first phase and recalled more failures than had, in fact, occurred. We know that the meaning individuals attribute to their past successes and failures can influence the future. In addition, we now observe that for some individuals the present can also reach back and distort the past, to the detriment of the future.

Attribution retraining

The practical implications of the learned helplessness paradigm have not been lost on researchers. If it is true that the essence of learned helplessness, or what might be called a "motivational deficit," is the belief that one is unable to control events, then perhaps teachers can promote a renewed sense of hope by encouraging students to change their explanations for failure from low ability to a lack of effort.

This reasoning has given rise to a body of research referred to collectively as *attribution retraining*. These retraining procedures generally involve giving failure-threatened students repeated practice in verbalizing effort-oriented explanations for their failure (e.g., "I failed because I did not try hard enough"). For example, Gregory Andrews and Ray Debus (1978) worked with sixth-grade boys who routinely attributed their failures to low ability. Some of these youngsters were randomly assigned to a control group that received no training, and the remainder were assigned to one of two training conditions in which the experimenters either reinforced the boys with tokens or with verbal praise whenever they gave a low-effort explanation after failing to solve various geometric puzzles. High-effort explanations were likewise reinforced whenever the boys succeeded.

The findings from this study form part of a consistent pattern of results shared by several similar studies (Chapin & Dyck, 1976; Dweck, 1975; Wilson & Linville, 1985; Zoeller, Mahoney, & Weiner, 1983). Following attribution retraining, otherwise demoralized individuals tend to persist longer in their work on school-related tasks, and in some cases there is evidence that the quality of persistence also improves, that is, students display more effective thinking strategies that lead, in turn, to actual gains in performance.

Although the evidence for performance gains is clear and is generally undisputed (for an exception, see Block & Lanning, 1984), the mechanisms by which these changes occur are still a matter of conjecture. Some investigators assume that emphasizing effort acts to enhance the individual's *expectation* that he or she will eventually succeed, whereas others stress increased feelings of *personal control* over events as the primary mediator of improved performance (Dweck, 1975; Dweck & Wortman, 1982). It is also possible that improvements in *emotional climate*, such as reduced shame, may also promote a willingness to persist. All these explanations are plausible within the causal networks portrayed in Figures 3.1 and 3.2.

Whatever mechanisms are involved, the effectiveness of attribution retraining will likely depend on where in the downward spiral of demoralization students find themselves. If, for example, students are already convinced of their incompetency (failure accepters, like Ralph), then they may be unable to accept success as caused by their own efforts (Marecek & Mettee, 1972). Success implies an obligation to succeed again in the future, something for which these self-doubters do not feel capable. By contrast, other students may not yet have completely internalized their failures, and hence remain uncertain about their ability status. These failure avoiders, like John, are more likely to embrace success as evidence that their self-doubts are unfounded after all (Coopersmith, 1967).

The effectiveness of attributional retraining may also be greatest among younger children, and for several reasons. For one thing, trying hard is consistent with adult values, and it is the young child who is most willing to accept adult authority. For another thing, effort is associated in the young child's mind with increasing competency. On the other hand, adolescents have reason to doubt the benefits of effort, but not only because they are more likely to reject adult values. There is also the dawning recognition, beginning in late childhood, that effort and ability are separate, essentially independent contributors to achievement, and that trying hard can compensate only so much for a lack of ability (see chapter 4). For these reasons, admonishments by teachers to try harder (or even by researchers in the laboratory) may do little to improve the performance of older students if they already feel themselves incompetent.

In chapter 8 we will explore more recent approaches to attribution retraining that largely avoid this problem. They involve ascribing failure to inadequate learning strategies – in short, to the poor *quality* of one's effort, not just the small *amount* of effort. The concept of learning strategies bridges the domains of effort and ability, so that trying hard in sophisticated, strategic ways is tantamount to increasing one's ability to learn. In this sense, the beliefs of young children about ability as perfectible through effort may be less naive than might be first thought. When students are taught *how* to think, effort and ability become mutually reinforcing dimensions. As we will see, this perspective ushers in quite different ways of thinking about the educational enterprise.

Conclusions

We have now reached an important juncture in our analysis of achievement motivation. We are familiar with the broad historic perspective that envisions motivation as a learned drive, whether it be thought of as unresolved emotional conflicts arising from early childhood or the result of attributional mediators. We have also discovered much that will be useful in crafting our recommendations for educational change, among which are the following critical points: the importance of early child-rearing practices; the notion of multiple, often conflicting motives acting simultaneously; and a recognition that the meaning individuals attribute to life events – like failure – is often more important, motivationally speaking, than the event itself.

Yet despite these potentially valuable observations, there is an important sense in which, if we are not careful, the lessons of the learned-drive tradition can thwart effective reforms and, worse yet, even perpetuate wrong-headed proposals for change. If motivation is thought of largely as a matter of internal arousal, whether such arousal is characterized variously as needs, feelings, or effort cognitions, it then becomes all the more reasonable to assume that the current crisis in schooling can be overcome by pressuring (arousing) students (and teachers) to greater effort through "*more* hours in school, *more* homework, *more* tests." In effect, the learned-drive tradition lends plausibility, and even a measure of scientific justification, to a policy of intensification. Support for such a policy is growing nationwide and has been endorsed at the highest levels of government. At least this seems to be what George Bush, our "education" president, had in mind when he remarked during the 1989 Education Summit of Governors that "educators should not worry about *resources*, but rather *results*" (italics mine). If it is results America wants, then one sure way to get them, the argument runs, is to increase student motivation – arouse youngsters to greater effort through the judicious application of positive rewards like good grades and the withholding of negative reinforcers, like poor grades. And then there is the additional, typically unspoken assumption that these grades should be distributed on a competitive basis, with the best performers receiving the most rewards.

Intensification policy also implies the need to raise academic standards. But this solution is by itself incomplete and also too facile. Veteran poker players know what is likely to happen when the table stakes are increased. Far from clarifying one's mind, increased pressure is likely as not to encourage irrational risk-taking and even cheating. Because we will soon liken school achievement to a special kind of competitive game (chapter 6), this poker analogy becomes quite compelling. The counterproductive aspects of an intensification policy are not limited to poker play, nor are its potential ironies lost on the business community. A leading industrialist was recently overheard to say, "If I had a situation in which one-third of my products [students] fell off the assembly line along the way [referring to the national dropout rate prior to high school graduation] and two-thirds of those remaining did not work right in the end, the last thing I would do is speed up the conveyor belt!"

Not only is the ultimate goal of intensification policy misplaced, but the means are inappropriate as well. Every time a crisis occurs, there are renewed calls for higher standards. But the basic issue is not really a matter of increasing academic standards (Levin, 1988). Nor can we any longer afford the kind of cheap rhetoric that reinvents higher standards from time to time for political gain. Actually, standards of excellence have never really been forgotten. For years teachers have struggled to maintain high academic standards and also to lament, often alone and unheeded, the slow erosion of the quality of academic life in our schools.

The proper question now is how to revitalize a commitment to excellence, and learned-drive formulations do not provide the key to this process. If merely intensifying student effort were the answer, then the current crisis should never have occurred. Teachers already reinforce effort. Moreover, when elementary grade school children are placed in the role of "proxy" teachers, they dispense and withhold rewards in essentially the same ways as do adults

(Weiner et al., 1972). This means that students get the message starting early on: America values achievement through effort. Youngsters quickly become aware, often painfully so, of the consequences of not trying. On the basis of these pervasive reinforcement patterns, cognitive theorists have concluded that students should come to value effort as a major source of personal worth, and to the extent that students do not comply with this work ethic, they will experience guilt and remorse.

There is little doubt that students experience guilt when they do not try (Covington et al., 1980). But do they also come to value effort? Not always. Why not? If teachers are so generous in their praise of effort, then why is it that so many students do not try, often giving themselves up to inaction and failure? And, why do others hide their effort or refuse to admit that they have studied at all? On the basis of cognitive reinforcement principles alone, we might expect that the systematic application of appropriate patterns of teacher rewards and punishment, beginning in the earliest years, would encourage a will to learn and would provide the optimal conditions for fostering achievement motivation. For some students this prescription seems to work and work well; but for others, perhaps a majority, it clearly does not. Why should this be?

To this question we can add several other puzzles that also seem to defy the logic of the cognitive position. First, why is there little relationship between a sense of personal satisfaction in school and GPA (Jackson, 1968)? Again, assuming that high grades are an important source of positive reinforcement, then an outstanding academic record should lead to feelings of pride – but apparently not always. Second, why should it be that many failure-prone students perform at their best when the odds against succeeding are at their worst? Should not a hopeless cause intimidate these students even more? And, third, if, as is generally assumed, high self-regard is the result of numerous successes accumulated over the years, then why is it that for some seemingly capable students a sense of confidence can be devastated after only *one* failure? Should not all those past successes count for something?

These questions indicate that something more is going on than can be accounted for easily by cognitive reinforcement principles. Basically, we need to know more about achievement dynamics than cognitive attributions alone can tell us. In order to get to the heart of the matter we must understand the *reasons* students study or not, not just *how much* they study or their retrospective causal explanations for success and failure. For example, merely attributing a prior failure to inadequate effort is no guarantee that a student will remain optimistic about the future, despite all the evidence cited. Inaction may also reflect the fact that the student has become demoralized and given up. Likewise, consider the fact that failure-threatened students are just as likely to study a great deal as to study little or not at all (Goldman, Hudson, & Daharsh, 1973). Why should anyone continue to try, especially if these students typically attribute inadequate performance to low ability? The answer is that some failure-prone students like *overstrivers* try hard because they are attempting to avoid failure by succeeding. This suggests that the quality and amount of study is not so much a matter of attributions as the motives that drive individuals.

In summary, for all the conceptual benefits of the attribution approach – and we have seen they are substantial – it is nonetheless important to relocate our search for a fuller understanding of school dynamics elsewhere. Attributions are no substitute for the concept of motivation.

4

Self-worth and the fear of failure

> *Your soul is oftentimes a battlefield upon which your reason and judgment wage war against your passion and your appetite. Your reason and your passion are the rudder and the sails of your seafaring soul.*
> KAHLIL GIBRAN

Kahlil Gibran, the contemporary Syrian poet, describes human behavior as a unitary process in which passion and reason act in tandem – sometimes as coconspirators and at other times as adversaries. Human beings are caught up constantly in the struggle for a blending and reconciliation of these factors, or at least a truce.

In the last chapter we explored the proposition that passion – or put more sedately, motivation – is the by-product of cognitive (rational) processes, and that emotions such as shame and pride depend on the meaning (cognitions) that individuals attach to their successes and failures. The guiding metaphor of this cognitive view is that of the *intuitive scientist* (Kelley, 1971a) who ceaselessly searches for and analyzes data in order to master himself and his environment. The principal values associated with this quest are rationality, consistency of action, and accurate self-knowledge. Obviously, these attributes are critical to survival. Accurate self-knowledge enables individuals to credit their talents fairly as well as to recognize their shortcomings so they can avoid those tasks that exceed their present skills, yet when possible seize the moment and take advantage of unexpected opportunities that fall within the scope of their abilities. The use of attribution principles to explain achievement motivation has resulted in considerable, even historic, strides in the precision with which researchers have come to think about this topic. However, the *intuitive scientist* metaphor does little to encourage an understanding of how attributions themselves may be influenced by the very impulses that cognitive theory attempts to explain.

In this chapter we will examine the alternative view that it is motives that sometimes drive thoughts and alter, even distort, the meaning of success and failure. The essence of this complementary argument is reflected in another metaphor, that of the *intuitive politician* (Tetlock, 1985). This metaphor implies that life, like politics, requires the reconciliation of contradictory demands, a process that involves compromise and concession. What are these demands? First, as just noted, there is the need for accurate *self-knowledge*. Second, there is the need for *self-validation* – the need to gain the approval, love, and respect of others and, when necessary, to disassociate oneself from those events that might cause disapproval or rejection. This disposition to establish and defend a positive self-image is the self-worth motive (Wylie, 1979).

Speculation about the relationship of motives and feelings to thought and action is nothing new. For instance, consider Sigmund Freud's classic assertion: "Thought is not the slave of impulse to do its bidding. . . . What intelligence has to do in the service of impulse is to act, not as its obedient servant, but as its clarifier and liberator. . . . Intelligence converts desire into plans." Despite Freud's hopes for the ascendancy of reason, we will see that intelligence (cognitions) does not always act as a clarifier, but rather more often as not as a servant of emotions.

Before proceeding, it is important that we preview the broad theoretical context in which motivation and cognitions will be treated here. A *constructionist* view of humankind suits our purpose best (Haan, 1977; Paris & Byrnes, 1989). This position holds that individuals construct their own subjective realities and then act on them. When individuals are free to pursue legitimate developmental needs such as becoming competent or gaining control over their environment, cognitive processes act both as the clarifier and servant of self-expression. These constructions of reality are essentially veridical and lead to flexible, realistic coping. Recall Hoppe's pioneering ring-toss experiments. When Hoppe's subjects set their *own* targets, they aspired to goals slightly higher than their last performance, but not much higher. If the subjects fell short on a given trial, they typically readjusted their aspirations downward. This dynamic interplay between a growing sense of competency, self-monitoring, and realistic goal-setting has been described elsewhere by James Diggory (1966):

> If [the individual] chooses an activity which he never attempted before, his first attempts will be purely exploratory. . . . [But] once this exploration ends and he begins a more or less systematic attempt to produce something, he very likely will set implicit or explicit aspirations for his successive attempts; then he can define success or failure. He seldom needs anyone to tell him when he succeeds or fails because he sets his own standards of performance. At first these standards are likely to be modest, relatively easy to achieve, but he moves always towards standards more difficult to achieve. The standards he uses are quite varied and may change from one attempt to the next.

> To the casual uninterested observer this may all seem repetitive and dull, but the operator, the worker, may be intensely interested because he never has exacted the same goal on two successive trials. . . . By this process of gentle spurring himself to successively higher achievements, he approaches mastery of himself and his environment. (pp. 125 – 126).

Here we see the positive side of human nature at its finest with motives (in this case, self-mastery) and logic acting together. Fundamental to this harmonious process is the conviction that everyone creates his or her own purposes and determines his or her own fate, at least in part. When the belief in personal efficacy flourishes, so does imagination, flexibility, and compassion; and when this belief is compromised, so is a major share of our humanity.

The downside of this constructionist process is also illustrated in Hoppe's ring-toss example by the phenomenon of the *atypical shift* by which subjects raise rather than lower their expectations after failure as a way to maintain a sense of worth. By merely stating a worthy goal, say, doing better the next time – even if it is unlikely – individuals attempt to compensate for failure with an alternative source of gratification (Sears, 1940). In this case, however, the person has substituted fantasies for actual accomplishments. From the vantage point of self-protective dynamics, such irrational goal setting becomes a reasonable, even logical and entirely self-justified response to situations in which one is required to perform but in which the likelihood of succeeding is low and failure abrasive.

By this analysis, rationality per se is not the primary goal of human beings (except perhaps among logicians!). Rather the goal is to achieve a sense of competency, respect, and self-acceptance. Sometimes rationality prevails in this quest, whereas at other times – principally when self-worth motives are frustrated or threatened – the same logical capacity is diverted in the service of self-deception, a process in which persons come to trade dexterously on excuses, sly fabrications, and denial, all cloaked in an illusion of credibility. Potentially threatening information may be wished away by primitive, magical thinking, or conveniently forgotten, denied, or even repressed. In such situations, far from being a clarifier, the purpose of logic and reason is to obscure the implications of failure. Here cognitions act in the service of impulse.

Self-worth theory of achievement motivation

Rationality, even now, is a promise waiting for fulfillment.
REUVEN BAR-LEVAV

Self-worth theory (Covington, 1984d, 1985c, 1987; Covington & Beery, 1976) assumes that the search for self-acceptance is the highest human priority, and that in schools self-acceptance comes to depend on one's ability to achieve competitively. In our society there is a pervasive tendency to equate accomplishment with human value, or put simply, individuals are thought to be only as worthy as their achievements. Because of this, it is understandable that students often confuse ability with worth. For those students who are already insecure, tying a sense of worth to ability is a risky step because schools can threaten their belief in their ability. This is true because schools typically provide insufficient rewards for all students to strive for success. Instead, too many children must struggle simply to avoid failure.

There are many failure-avoiding strategies available to students. Students can simply not try – Nothing ventured, nothing lost. And, whenever there is no escaping failure, then at least students can try to avoid the *implications* of failing: that they are stupid and hence unworthy. This means that sometimes students may actually sacrifice their chances for success and settle for failure, if by doing so they can salvage a reputation for ability. For instance, a child may strive for unattainable goals that literally invite failure, but "failure with honor" because so few others can be expected to succeed against these odds.

In essence, then, self-worth theory holds that school achievement is best understood in terms of attempts by students to maintain a positive self-image of competency, particularly when risking competitive failure. There is compelling evidence that students value ability, sometimes above all else. For instance, Covington and Omelich (1984b) found that at the college level a reputation for sheer brilliance was the most important contributor to feelings of personal well-being in school, far more important than the individual's overall GPA. This suggests that for older students it is ability alone, even in the absence of solid accomplishments, that defines worth! By contrast, being a hard worker contributed only marginally to positive feelings among college students. Research on student preferences confirm these findings. After reviewing the relevant literature, Jonathan Brown and Bernard Weiner (1984) concluded that in the event of failure, students prefer low-effort explanations to low-ability explanations. This makes sense not only because low ability is predictive of future failure, but also because failure does not necessarily imply low ability, if one does not try. Correspondingly, in the case of success it is not just that high-ability explanations are preferred; of even greater value are those successes achieved without much effort, indicating once again that it is a reputation for brillance that is most important to self-definition (Covington & Omelich, 1979b).

But why should students be concerned with ability at all, given the universal pattern of teacher reinforcement that favors a work ethic? Basically, the answer is that the importance of effort in the teachers' value scheme is limited to the instructional context. When the job is to instruct, teachers recognize the importance of hard work and reward pluck and energy accordingly. However, when the focus shifts from learning per se to predicting those students who will most likely succeed in prestigious occupations, teachers weigh ability as the more important factor (Kaplan & Swant, 1973) – equal, in fact, to the heavy weight accorded ability by students. This distinction between ability as a predictor of future occupational success and effort as a necessary ingredient for learning is not lost on students and places them in a cruel bind. Despite the undeniable benefits of trying hard, self-worth theory postulates a competing need for students: the protection of a sense of competency. From this perspective, ironically enough, trying hard puts students at risk because a combination of studying hard and eventual failure is compelling evidence for low ability (Covington & Omelich, 1979b; Kun, 1977; Kun & Weiner, 1973). There is also the obvious corollary: By not studying, the causes of failure become obscured. These propositions are consistent with the principles of attribution theory as reflected in Harold Kelley's (1971a) notion of "multiple sufficient schema," which states that achievement outcomes can be explained by any number of factors, each of which is sufficient in itself to produce the outcome. So, for instance, a person might speak of a classmate's failure as being caused either by low ability or by inadequate preparation. However, if the classmate were to study diligently, lack of effort would be eliminated as a probably cause of failure, leaving low ability as a sufficient explanation.

Several points have been made so far in outlining the broader self-worth position. First, it has been suggested that ability estimates, either high or low, depend on the circumstances of failure. For example, a combination of high effort/failure implies *low* ability. Second, self-perceptions of incompetency trigger feelings of shame and humiliation. Third, by not trying, individuals are able to minimize information about their ability should they fail, and thereby avoid these mischievous ability-linked emotions. Fourth, the presence of excuses – for either why one did *not* try or why one *did* try but to no avail – can also deflect suspicions of inability following failure. And fifth, student preoccupation with ability status and the teacher's understandable tendency to reward effort set the stage for a conflict of classroom values.

Each of these five assertions can be demonstrated in a single experiment.

Failure dynamics

Covington and Omelich (1979b) asked college undergraduates to imagine how much shame they would experience if they failed a test that most of their classmates passed. The students could fail in each of four ways: little study without an excuse (e−); little study with an excuse (e−/x); intense study without an excuse (e+); and intense study with an excuse (e+/x). Little effort in failure was excused by reason of illness. The excuse accompanying high effort was that by chance the student studied different parts of the assignment than those emphasized on the test. Besides introspecting their feelings of shame, these subjects also indicated how much they would attribute failure to incompetency. Finally, the subjects were asked to assume the role of teachers and administer reprimands (low grades) to hypothetical students under the same four failure conditions. The results of this study are presented in Figure 4.1.

STUDENT PERSPECTIVE

Let's consider things from the student's perspective. First, consistent with all the research cited, the students judged themselves to be most incompetent when they studied hard and failed anyway (e+) and far less stupid when they did not try at all (e−). As already noted, in making these ability inferences, the students were acting in accord with the principle of "multiple sufficient schema." Low effort is a sufficient reason to explain failure, but when students study hard, ascriptions to inability increase dramatically. Excuses played an important role in moderating these harsh judgments. Following Kelley's (1973) "discounting principle," the students discounted low ability as the cause of failure even when their effort was great, as long as other plausible causes (excuses) were available (e+/x). There can be little doubt that ability estimates depend on the circumstances of failure.

Second, the intensity of shame depended on the degree of ability demotion – the greater one's perceived incompetency, the greater the shame. And since ability estimates depend in turn on the conditions of failure, the students experienced the greatest shame under conditions of high effort (e+) and far less shame under low-effort conditions (e−). Additionally, shame was reduced even more when low-effort excuses were available (e−/x).

TEACHER PERSPECTIVE

Now we'll consider things from the teacher's perspective. The data on teacher punishment are entirely consistent with research previously cited in chapter

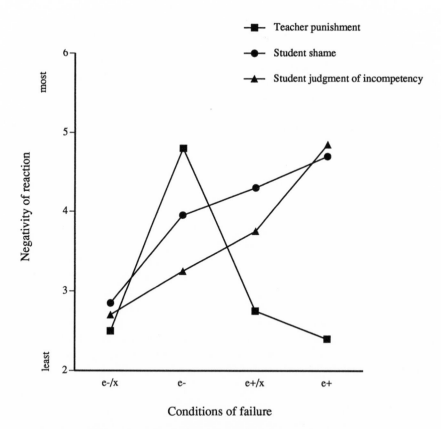

Figure 4.1. Student and teacher reactions to failure (From M. V. Covington & C. L. Omelich. (1979). Effort: The double-edged sword in school achievement. *Journal of Educational Psychology*, p. 177. Copyright 1979 by the American Psychological Association. Reprinted by permission of the publisher.)

3. Individuals who studied hard and failed anyway (e+) were less severely punished than those who simply did not try (e−). Effort is critical for students, too, but in an opposite way as we have seen. This incompatibility is best seen by juxtaposing the teacher data with student self-estimates of ability and their shame reactions. The contrast is most striking under conditions of high effort–failure (e+). Although students were reprimanded the least by teachers under this condition, they nonetheless felt the most incompetent and experienced the greatest personal dissatisfaction of any of the four conditions. Students can reduce this discomfort substantially by not trying (e−), but they do so at the risk of increased teacher punishment. In fact, this condition (e−) elicited the most severe teacher sanctions of all. Yet despite this pattern of teacher disapproval, students (as we know) still prefer low-effort explanations for failure!

We have seen that excuses can moderate student shame. But can excuses also minimize teacher punishment? The answer is also found in Figure 4.1.

Teachers made allowances for low effort if students had a reasonable excuse for not studying (e−/x). Without an excuse, however, low effort (e−) was severely punished. Indeed, the data suggest that students may achieve roughly the same protection from teacher displeasure by providing plausible excuses for not working (e−/x) as they can be trying hard in the first place (e+)! Naturally, of course, teachers are unlikely to withhold disapproval of a particular student indefinitely in the wake of continued excuse making. Nonetheless, these data point to the enormous survival value of excuses and the likelihood that they can work to the student's advantage on a given occasion.

Covington and Beery (1976) summarized this entire situation in the following terms:

> Thus there emerges from this complex interplay among students, peers, and teacher a "winning" formula in the anticipation of failure that is designed to avoid personal humiliation and shame on the one hand and to minimize teacher punishment on the other: Try, or at least *appear* to try, but not too energetically and with excuses handy. It is difficult to imagine a strategy better calculated to sabotage the pursuit of personal excellence. (p. 84)

These data indicate why simply increasing the pressure on students to try harder in the face of failure is to invite disaster. The basic premise of the policy of intensification is flawed. It is assumed that teachers can control student effort by rewarding hard workers and punishing the indifferent. Clearly this is a dicey proposition because what is most meaningful to students is not necessarily effort-based rewards but ways to avoid the implications of *too much* effort when risking failure.

Success dynamics

Do things change when success is the outcome? Yes, naturally. Everything goes better with success. Just how much better − or at least different from failure − is indicated by a companion study of success dynamics also conducted by Covington and Omelich (1979c). College students estimated how much ability others would attribute to them given various test successes, including those for which they had studied very hard or barely at all. These students also introspected the degree of *pride* they would likely experience following each successful test performance. Finally, as in the previous study, students also adopted the role of teachers, but in this case administered varying degrees of *praise*, not reprimands, to hypothetical students.

The results can be easily summarized. In success, pride depends on trying hard; the harder individuals studied the more pleased they were with their success. And, happily, teacher approval was also greatest when success was the result of hard work. At last, it appears that teachers and students are in agreement about the value of effort. Not quite, however. Things are not so simple, because the harder individuals worked for their successes, the more limited they perceived their intellectual gifts to be. But if high effort in success implies lesser ability, then why do successful students find so much that is admirable about effort? The answer is that self-estimates of ability typically remain relatively high given any successful outcome, no matter how hard the individual had to study. This is because success at a hard task is in itself convincing evidence of ability (Fontaine, 1974; Harvey & Kelley, 1974; Kun & Weiner, 1973). This finding is consistent with attribution theory as reflected in Kelley's (1971a) notion of "multiple necessary schema," which asserts that succeeding at a complex task requires a combination of high effort and ability; neither ability nor effort alone is sufficient. Thus, from a self-worth perspective, successful effort should represent little personal threat. In effect, a hard-won success allows students to share the best of two possible worlds: They are seen as *virtuous* by reason of their diligence and *capable* by the fact of their success.

Still, we cannot assume that all is well. Even here teacher–student compatibility is subject to considerable strain. Ultimately, it is ability, not effort, that commands the highest loyalty of students even in success. As part of the same experiment, students also rank-ordered their preferences for ways to succeed. Not surprisingly, high ability was preferred to low ability as an explanation for success, with high-effort explanations correspondingly preferred over low-effort explanations. However, when a choice between high-effort and high-ability explanations was given – and push came to shove – students preferred being perceived as able, a finding replicated by others (Brown & Weiner, 1984, Exp. 1; Sohn, 1977; Nicholls, 1976a). In fact, for some students ability status is so important that they go to great lengths to disguise the role of effort in their successes. Consider the student who complains about not having had enough time to study for a test but who, in reality, secretly spent the weekend in an isolated part of the library. This "closet" achiever will appear unusually capable if successful, and also has protected a reputation for brilliance if he or she should fail.

To be *able* is to be *worthy*, but to do poorly is evidence of inability and is reason to despair. The essence of achievement motivation according to self-worth theory resides in this formula. This proposition can be applied far beyond the confines of formal schooling whenever ability, in whatever form, is equated with worth. For instance, sports psychologists Damon Burton and Raynor Martens (1986) have demonstrated that those high school boys who drop out of wrestling competition do so primarily when their win–loss record no longer supports a reputation for physical strength, another kind of ability that defines the world for many adolescent males. Likewise, in the field of music individuals who have given up an instrument despite a history of early musical training react to the prospects of failing to play well in a public recital in exactly the same ways as do failure-avoiding students when confronted with academic failure (Covington, 1982) (see Figure 4.1). Feelings of shame were greatest when these ex-musicians imagined themselves as having worked hard to prepare for the recital. By contrast, for still-active amateur musicians, it was *low* effort, not *high* effort, that caused the greatest distress, but distress (guilt) at not having practices more. Because this latter group was more secure in the knowledge of their musical ability, one isolated failure held little threat to their sense of worth as musicians.

Developmental trends

The self-worth dynamics just described have a clear developmental history. The relationships portrayed in Figure 4.1 apply to only older students and adults. For younger, primary-grade children the situation is quite different.

Recall that attribution theorists originally argued that because teachers encourage effort, students should internalize a work ethic. We now know that at least among older students self-worth factors can override these otherwise straightforward reinforcement mechanisms. For young children, however, this prediction about effort is essentially correct. Primary-grade youngsters accord a far greater role to effort as a source of well-being than do college adults or even high school students. This work-ethic mentality embraces a number of behaviors, all related to being well thought of – complying with authority, behaving oneself, and generally staying out of trouble. In short, young children believe that hard-working, compliant pupils will succeed and, as a result, are worthy of praise and admiration. Thus early in the developmental sweep of events, teachers and students find themselves truly in agreement – effort reigns as the supreme classroom virtue. But, obviously, this alliance is only temporary. Somewhere along the way a discontinuity sets in. For example, teacher praise for trying hard, which in the primary grades conveys competence (Meyer et al., 1979), just a few years hence in junior high comes to imply the opposite – a lack of ability. Indeed, among these older students praise for effort is seen as one way teachers encourage pupils of low ability (Graham, 1984b). What do we know about this shift? How and why do these changes occur, and over what period of time? The answers require that we start at the very beginning.

PRECURSORS OF ACHIEVEMENT
The precursors of achievement motivation are thought to emerge starting around two years of age (Harter, 1981; Lutkenhaus, Bullock, & Geppert, 1984). These beginnings are truly humble by adult standards. For example, they involve only the rudimentary discovery that one's actions can produce an outcome (Geppert & Kuster, 1982). If we can judge from the open body stance and the triumphant facial expression of mere toddlers, there is great pleasure in self-produced effects like building a tower of blocks. Likewise, temper tantrums are the result of finding that anticipated outcomes do not always occur.

However, despite the intensity of these reactions, there is as yet no developed sense of personal agency, no recognition that outcomes are influenced by how hard or how well one tries (Blumenfeld et al., 1981). These more subtle revelations must await the development of a distinction between effort and ability, something that is beyond the capabilities of the preschool child. As a result, much of what adults take for granted about the dynamics of achievement is still missing in these early years.

For one thing, success and failure as subjective states of mind remain ill-defined. Children younger than two-and-one-half years take pleasure in outcomes, regardless of whether they are successful or not (Heckhausen, 1982, 1984). When the distinction does first dawn, it is initially reflected only at the most primitive emotional level. Success elicits diffuse excitement and, at first, the failure to achieve may elicit scarcely any reaction at all.

For another thing, preschoolers do not realize that more difficult tasks may require more ability (Karabenick & Heller, 1976; Kun, Parsons, & Ruble, 1974; Stipek, 1981). For them it only takes trying harder. To the preschooler everything is possible with effort; nothing is beyond their capacity, which seems limitless. For instance, Nicholls (1975, 1978) reports that most five- and six-year-olds rank themselves relatively higher than their classmates in ability. (And we thought such smugness existed only in Garrison Keillor's hometown, Lake Wobegone, where, as he tells it, "the men are rich, the women good looking, and all the children above average.") Moreover, in these early years it is unlikely that youngsters can be convinced otherwise (Parsons & Ruble, 1977). Even failure does not impose much of a limit on ability perceptions. For example, Steven Yussen and Victor Levy (1975) found that when young children fail to memorize a list of several items, they still estimate that they will succeed easily at a similar task in the future. Clearly, the adultlike compensatory goal-setting mechanisms described by Hoppe in his ring-toss experiments are nowhere in evidence at this young age.

In sum, preschoolers are confined to a highly limited, aboriginal view of themselves as prime movers of events. They see themselves as capable of anything and blatantly disregard past information in making future predictions. Researchers have offered various explanations for why this should be.

First, very young children may simply lack the capacity to recall from one time to another how hard they tried or how well they did in the past (Clifford, 1978). Until children can reconstruct the past accurately, they will remain unable to make realistic judgments about the future. Second, young children cannot always distinguish between actual and desirable outcomes (Stipek, 1984). In effect, children may be the victims of their own magical thinking. They believe that what they *want* to happen *will* happen no matter how well or poorly they might have performed in the past. Clearly, hope springs eternal, staring at a young age. A third possibility is that children do, in fact, use information about effort and ability when they think about likely outcomes, but that the rules they employ to make these judgments are quite different than those used by older children and adults. We will explore this latter possibility in some detail.

CONCEPTIONS OF ABILITY

The development of individuals is marked by predictable, systematic changes in their beliefs about the structure of intelligence and in the relative importance they accord ability and effort as causes of achievement. The developmental schema proposed by Nicholls (1978, 1984) provides us with a way to track these changes. Basically, Nicholls argues that the reason young children cannot accurately predict future performance is that their conception of ability is inadequately developed. Nicholls divides the slow march from primitive to sophisticated reasoning into four stages.

Stage one. In the first, most primitive stage – corresponding roughly to the preschool and kindergarten years – children have not yet differentiated between ability and effort (Blumenfeld, Pintrich, & Hamilton, 1986). As a result, trying hard is thought to be clear evidence for ability (Kun, 1977); as one first-grader slyly confided, "Smart students try, dumb ones don't" (Harari & Covington, 1981). Youngsters also believe that by trying harder they can actually increase their ability, or, as another first-grader remarked, "Studying hard makes your brain bigger" (Harari & Covington, 1981). This latter kind of reasoning is basic to the *incremental* theory of intelligence in which individuals believe ability is a process that is expandable through hard work and experience (Dweck & Bempechat, 1983).

In this first stage, then, young children achieve only the most global, diffused view of competency and its causes. According to Anna Kun (1977), for these youngsters "all good things go together" – high ability, effort, and outcome. Even behaving oneself in class is taken as evidence of ability (Anderson, 1981; Rohrkemper & Bershon, 1984). Little wonder that most children believe themselves capable of any feat and disregard failure feedback.

Stage two. Stage 2 corresponds roughly to the early and middle elementary years. Ability and effort are still largely undifferentiated, but it is now effort that begins to prevail as the most salient cause of success. Youngsters also begin to assume a one-to-one correspondence between effort and outcome – the harder one tries the better one's performance is likely to be. Children in this stage believe that by increasing effort even the dullest student will be successful (Harari & Covington, 1981).

Stage three. By Stage 3 (the late elementary years) youngsters begin to view ability as an independent factor, separate from effort in its impact on achievement. As a result, 10- to 12-year-olds begin to think in terms of compensatory schema. Students are able to understand that increased effort can make up for low ability and that high ability permits a relaxation of effort. Yet, for all this emerging sophistication, the naive sense of optimism that effort will conquer all remains largely intact. Many of these students still insist that as a task becomes more difficult one need only increase effort to succeed.

Such compensatory thinking involves a complex bit of mental gymnastics unavailable to the younger child. Here the learner must hold in mind and coordinate several factors when predicting future performance, including past outcomes and task difficulty. Such sophistication is welcome. It ushers in the world of abstract and scientific reasoning. For example, recognition that increased effort compensates for low ability is akin to understanding that in the area of physical causality, a balance beam can be brought to equilibrium by placing different combinations of weights at different distances from the fulcrum (Piaget, 1950). There is a potential price to pay, however. Compensatory schema depend on viewing ability not only as independent of effort, but also as a fixed, stable factor. This development corresponds to the onset of *entity* beliefs about ability (Dweck & Bempechat, 1983).

Stage four. With the rise of entity beliefs, beginning at about 13 years of age the perceived importance of effort wanes as coequal partner in success, and is replaced by the conviction that ability alone is a necessary condition for success and that lack of ability is a sufficient explanation for failure. In short, ability becomes the limiting factor in achievement, or, as stated emphatically by an 11th-grader, "When people who are not smart study, they do not do very well" (Harari & Covington, 1981). Without ability, the benefits of effort are now seen only at the margins. This pessimistic assessment stands in stark contrast to the buoyant, optimistic view of ability held by the young child as knowledge well and wisely used.

Having established this series of developmental anchor points, we can now answer the earlier question of why a work-ethic value declines as students grow older. It is not merely that effort is seen as progressively less important to success – which is true – but also because the child's conception of intelligence changes so that trying hard and failing anyway comes to signify low ability. But if young students value ability as much as the evidence suggests (Harari & Covington, 1981), then why should they, too, not experience the same threat from trying hard that besets older students? The answer is that for the young child, effort, ability, and outcome are basically indistinguishable and that, if anything, trying hard actually increases ability. Thus a work-ethic mentality allows these children to enjoy a double bonus. By working hard – and, in the bargain, being diligent and well behaved – they can appear not only able, but virtuous as well. Note that the young child's predictions about who is bright and who is not depend on effort cues just as much as do adult estimates. But the direction of the relationship is reversed: Children believe that high effort rather than low effort is indicative of ability. In time, however, through a combination of social comparisons, competition, and the advent of adultlike reasoning, ability status emerges as the dominant value over effort. And with this change comes a reversal in the cue value of effort. It is now high effort, not low effort, that leads to suspicions about one's ability. Not surprisingly, the self-serving advantages of low effort also become increasingly clear. Low effort in success enhances a reputation for brilliance and low effort also obscures the causes of failure (12th-grader: "If he does not try, you don't know how smart he is." Harari & Covington, 1981).

As the child grows older, protecting a sense of worth defined by the ability to achieve competitively becomes increasingly more important. Some of the many self-aggrandizing strategies available for this purpose are discussed next.

An arsenal of excuses

We have good reasons for our bad performances; other people give excuses.
C. R. SNYDER

Excuses have been a part of the human scene ever since Adam first blamed Eve and Eve blamed the serpent (Snyder, 1984). In school, as we have seen, excuses moderate the conflict of classroom values. They allow students to repackage otherwise questionable actions, like not trying, in a more flattering, less blameworthy form.

Getting along, going along

Actually, many of the ploys used in this self-protective drama are not excuses at all, but simply ways to avoid revealing one's ignorance, because students don't always do every homework assignment nor do they always listen when directions are being given. At their most innocent, these tactics form a cherished part of childhood lore. Everyone recalls those desperate classmates who scrunched down in their seats, trying hard to become the smallest possible target as the teacher scanned a sea of anxious faces searching for a victim in the game of "question and answer." Above all, eye contact with the teacher was to be avoided. There also was the outrageous business of waving one's hand wildly in response to the teacher's question – *not* knowing the answer, of course, but hoping against hope that he or she would call on someone else who appeared less well prepared. Then there was, and still is, the universal strategy of responding to the teacher's questions in as vague a manner as possible, vague enough to hedge against exposing a mistake or revealing that one simply does not know the answer. The student who hesitates in answering or gives only a provisional answer can often count on the teacher for help (Dillon & Searle, 1981). This cat-and-mouse game often involves what Ulf Lundgren (1977) has called "piloting." Here the teacher unwittingly leads the student toward an answer until the correct response is virtually assured. The teacher may derive considerable satisfaction from such an exercise, assuming that the student knows something, but is simply too nervous to express it. Obviously, the student *has* learned a lot, but likely more about how to control and "pilot" the teacher toward the right answer than anything about the topic in question.

There is also the strategy of simply not trying, of avoiding work that is not absolutely required, or of doing as little as possible and assuming somehow, magically, that this lack of participation would be overlooked or forgiven. By remaining silent or at least uncommitted, the student is operating on the principle that it is better to be thought a fool than to open one's mouth and remove all doubt. Yet blatant noninvolvement is risky because teachers *do* expect students to try. For this reason, students often combine outright refusal with other more subtle ploys, including the ruse of *false effort*, or what Donald Hansen (1989) refers to as *lesson dissembling*. This involves appearing to be interested in one's schoolwork, but in reality using a cloak of apparent commitment to dodge the teacher's wrath. Here the gambits are almost endless: giving the appearances of understanding, while not really understanding at all; posing a pensive, quizzical look – too busy thinking to be interrupted; asking questions whose answers are already known; or copying from a neighbor's paper, and perhaps adding a unique touch. This drama admits to many other subtle variations as well. For instance, indifferent students can sometimes redeem themselves in the eyes of teachers and generate considerable sympathy if they occasionally undergo a flurry of work activity at the last moment just before an assignment is due. Teachers judge these erratic performers to be more prone to discouragement than diligent students, because when they do try, their reward is often another failing mark. As a result teachers tend to reward these marginal workers, hoping to encourage more effort next time (Covington et al., 1980). They often do try harder, but largely in the interests of perfecting their strategies for dissembling with scarcely any attention given to the assignments themselves.

Unfortunately, all too often not trying takes a more ominous turn. Instead of merely avoiding being seen as unprepared – for instance, not knowing a

particular answer – the struggle is to escape being labeled as stupid. Ignorance and stupidity are not the same. Ignorance can be corrected but, presumably, not stupidity. Certainly this is what older youngsters believe. As a result, riskier defenses are called for, riskier because they are more likely to
undermine the will to learn by causing the very failures that students are
attempting to avoid. These tactics can be divided into two broad categories:
self-handicapping strategies and techniques designed to guarantee success.

Self-handicapping strategies

Self-handicapping involves the creation of some impediment to one's performance – either imagined or real – so that the individual has a ready excuse
for potential failure. For instance, Steven Berglas and Edward Jones (1978)
as well as others (e.g., Tucker, Vuchinich, & Sobell, 1981) have proposed
that some people may use alcohol or other drugs to protect their self-image.
If one is drunk, success may be seen by others as quite remarkable, whereas
failure is more readily explained, if not always excused. In a similar fashion,
some students may use excuses like a narcotic, addictively, and to excess, in
order to defend against the pain of academic failure. Unfortunately, although
the pain may be relieved, relief is only temporary, and in the process, the
likelihood of chronic failure increases.

PROCRASTINATION

One of the most universal self-handicapping strategies involves procrastination, universal and decidedly contemptible as well if Thomas DeQuincy's
famous 17th century epigram is any indication: "If once a man indulges himself in murder, very soon he comes to think little of robbing; and from robbing
he next comes to drinking and sabbath-breaking, and from that to incivility
and procrastination." Today some experts believe that at the college level a
near majority of students procrastinate as a way of life (Rothblum, Solomon,
& Murakami, 1986; Solomon & Rothblum, 1984). Other more pessimistic
estimates range as high as 95% (Ellis & Knaus, 1977).

Putting things off – postponing until tomorrow what one might do today –
is sometimes entirely justified. But when it cannot be, postponement becomes
stalling and a way to sidestep failure. It is not always easy, however, to detect
the difference. According to Maury Silver and John Sabini (1981, 1982), two
psychologists who have studied this topic extensively, postponing things must
have an element of irrationality in order to qualify as procrastination. For
instance, it is not necessarily irrational to put off a difficult decision if there
is a good chance that the issue will eventually be resolved of its own accord.
Many politicians and bureaucrats have built successful careers on little more
than the clever application of this wait-and-see strategy. But what about the
student who postpones writing a term paper for which there is a firm deadline
with no escape? Is this procrastination? Not necessarily. It all depends on how
long a postponement is involved and for what reasons. Consider an example
provided by Silver and Sabini. Judy has only the weekend to complete a term
paper that she has not yet started, but she accepts a Saturday night movie date

with Tom anyway, explaining to herself, "I'll just work very hard on Sunday." Is she procrastinating? No, not if in the past Judy has been able to write similar papers in the space of one day.

Likewise, consider Silver and Sabini's example of Dave. If Dave's domestic priorities truly require that he keep a clean house, then his decision to put off studying until after spring cleaning would not necessarily imply irrationality. But suppose Dave's concerns about cleanliness emerge only when a test looms? In this case we would suspect postponement is driven by a fear of failure. Silver and Sabini point out that the irrational aspects of procrastination are rooted in a firm grasp of rationality – for example, everything depends on Dave knowing what he should do and doing something else that is counterproductive to his main goal, which presumably is getting a college degree.

These examples are meant to convey the elusive quality of excuses and how they are fitted unwittingly and often undetected by perpetrators into a landscape of apparent coping. Yet despite these subtleties, it is abundantly clear that postponement – whether reasonably justified or only marginally so – can readily serve the goals of self-justification whenever one risks failure. By studying only at the last minute, procrastinators can hardly be blamed for failure – they simply had too much to do, and not enough time. Moreover, if these individuals are successful, a reputation for brilliance will be assured because they will have succeeded with so little effort (Beery, 1975). Thus, in one sense at least, procrastinators have little to lose and much to gain. Indeed, the temptation of succeeding with little apparent effort is often too much for some students, who become what we have called closet achievers.

A subtle variation on the procrastination theme involves apparently genuine attempts to keep busy – very busy – in fact, too busy and with little to show for it. The student who can never get beyond rewriting the introduction to her term paper in an endless succession of polishing and tinkering illustrates this point. So does the behavior of the student who spends endless hours collecting references for his paper so that in the end nothing ever gets written. This illogical use of one's time and resources allows a variety of explanations for eventual failure, including the often-heard refrain, "I ran out of time," and its implied corollary, "Given enough time, I could have done much better." Then there are those students who take on many jobs so that they can never devote enough time to any one project. The resulting work may be uniformly mediocre, but at least they score big on being involved and energetic. Busyness also has the added advantage of making one feel important. If these individuals can't do everything they should, then, the implied argument runs, they must be doing something significant.

UNATTAINABLE GOALS

The trauma caused by failure can also be minimized by pegging one's achievement goals so high that failure is virtually assured – for instance, aspiring to a straight A average while carrying a double major and two part-time jobs. This apparently irrational behavior makes perfectly logical sense when viewed from a self-worth perspective. Failure at an exceedingly difficult task reveals little about one's ability because success is beyond all but the most capable or energetic of students. If virtually everyone else fails, too, then the problem resides not in us, but rather in the goal. Even if the failed task is in reality not very hard, we can still easily convince ourselves of its inherent difficulty. Just how this neat trick is accomplished is illustrated by the research of David Bennett and David Holmes (reported in Snyder, 1984). These investigators informed one group of students, falsely, that they had failed a vocabulary test, and another group was provided no test feedback at all. The first group estimated that a near majority of their friends would also fail the same test, whereas the second group estimated that most of their friends would pass. As Snyder points out, "misery loves company," which is what the alleged failure group arranged – lots of company – and now we understand why. It is because the collective failure of the many obscures the individual failure of the few.

This reasoning also explains why low self-confident individuals sometimes actually *perform* better when the odds are hopelessly against success (Feather, 1961, 1963; Karabenick & Youssef, 1968; Sarason, 1961). Simply put, these students now have the "freedom" to fail, and can work up to their capacities openly because failure no longer necessarily implies low ability. Such "risk-free" failure also provides secondary benefits. We all admire the individual who struggles stoically for a worthy cause against overwhelming odds, no matter what the outcome.

UNDERACHIEVERS

Chronic underachievers avoid any test of their ability by refusing to work, thereby maintaining an inflated opinion of themselves. In order to justify this deceptive cover, underachievers often make a virtue out of not trying. They may take a perverse pride in their unwillingness to achieve by downgrading the importance of the work they refuse to do, or by attacking others who do try as hypocritical, foolish, or stupid. Underachievers may convince themselves that failure is a mark of nonconformity and evidence of their individuality. Naturally, this kind of uniqueness is more piteous than admirable, originating as it does out of a fear of inadequacy rather than out of any high moral conviction. Experts agree that underachievers not only believe that their worth depends on succeeding, but on succeeding perfectly and against virtually unattainable standards of excellence (Bricklin & Bricklin, 1967). For underachievers, this gap between their *ideal self* (as they think they *ought* to be) and *actual self* (as they perceive themselves to be) produces an intolerable situation (Higgins, 1987). Often the result is self-rage for not achieving perfection, and anger toward others who would insist on perfection. These "others" are typically parents who expect too much, too early, without the guidance necessary for such idealistic performances (Davids & Hainsworth, 1967). From this perspective, there are also many other advantages to be gained by not trying. Underachieving students can punish their parents by attacking parental pride in their prior accomplishments.

THE ACADEMIC WOODEN LEG

The final example of self-handicapping involves a kind of self-worth plea bargaining. Here the individual admits publicly to a minor personal weakness or handicap – the proverbial wooden leg – in order to avoid disclosing a far greater imagined weakness, in this case, being intellectually inadequate and hence unworthy. One of the most convincing of these handicaps is anxiety. By arguing that their poor performance is the result of test-taking anxiety, individuals reason that it is better to appear anxious than stupid, and, in the process, they can convert ridicule and scorn instantly into sympathetic, solicitous concern.

Actually, test anxiety is far more than a convenient excuse; it is real enough, and its disruptive effects on school performance are well documented (see chapter 5). Still, from a self-worth perspective, anxiety is the near perfect alibi. Test anxiety is not a reprehensible shortcoming, and everyone has experienced it enough to know that anxiety is legitimate, unlikely to be feigned, and often beyond the control of the individual. The text-anxious student is the perfect blameless victim.

For these reasons, we would be surprised if students did not occasionally use symptoms of anxiety to self-serving advantage. In fact, the evidence suggests that they do. For example, researchers told both high and low test-anxious college students that they had performed poorly on the first half of an achievement test (Smith, Snyder, & Handelsman, 1982). One-third of these students were also told that performance on this kind of test was highly subject to interference from anxiety. Another third was informed that anxiety had no effect on such performance, and the final third was told nothing. Before taking the second half of the test, students were asked to report any anxiety symptoms that they may have experienced on the first half. Those high test-anxious students who were given reason to report symptoms did so to a greater degree than those test-anxious students who were not given the provocation. At the same time, students with low levels of anxiety reported an equally small number of anxiety symptoms whether or not they had been given permission to do so. This pattern of results suggests that the symptoms of highly anxious individuals may or may not appear, depending on their potential for excuse making. Also of interest is the fact that when anxiety was not allowed as a viable explanation for poor performance, high test-anxious subjects reported lower levels of study in preparation for the test. This attempt to minimize one's effort is easily recognized as an alternative form of self-protection.

In summary, the pervasiveness of self-handicapping tendencies lends support to our contention that for humans self-justification is the highest priority, even at the risk of sacrificing achievement. However, this is not to suggest that excuse-makers are free of conflict. Even when students believe they have convinced others that their poor performance does not reflect on their ability but rather is due to insufficient effort, they nonetheless describe themselves in self-deprecatory terms as "lazy" and "shiftless" (Covington et al., 1980). The willingness of students to endure such social and personal stigma indicates something of the strength of these self-worth needs. Humans stop at little; lying, cheating, even failure are not too high a price to pay to protect their self-image. Yet, in the process failure-threatened students become their own worst enemies. No matter how adroitly they maneuver, they still harbor doubts about their ability because they are unwilling to test the limits by trying their hardest. They fear that they *might* be inadequate, but what they fear even more is finding out (Covington & Beery, 1976).

Guaranteeing success

Another group of self-serving ploys involves a frontal assault on failure – avoiding failure by succeeding! These fear-driven successes can be extraordinary. Many failure-threatened students are merit scholar finalists, class valedictorians, and National Science Fair winners. Despite such outward signs of success, however, being driven to succeed out of fear may be the ultimate academic ordeal. The individual's sense of worth comes to depend to an increasingly perilous degree on always succeeding, relentlessly, and against lengthening odds. Moreover, because such successes are essentially defensive in nature, they do little to help individuals shake their suspicions of worthlessness. The textbook example of this predicament is the *overstriver*.

OVERSTRIVERS

According to our analysis of Atkinson's need achievement model (chapter 2), overstrivers reflect an intense desire both to succeed and to avoid failure (high approach–high avoidance). On the hopeful side, overstrivers, like Amy, describe themselves as being highly qualified academically; but on the fearful side, they worry that they are not really as smart (and worthy) as their outstanding record would seem to indicate.

It is this hybrid quality of hope and fear that conspires to drive overstrivers to greater and greater accomplishments through a combination of high ability, meticulous attention to detail, and effective study strategies (Covington & Omelich, 1991). Indeed, ironically, overstrivers are *too* effective because in the long run their successes become an intolerable burden. No one can avoid failing forever, despite Herculean efforts. Eventually, failure is assured because human beings cannot remain satisfied for long; the next obstacle must be more difficult, more of a challenge than the last if success is to retain its allure. We know that raising one's aspirations after success is a perfectly natural reaction, part of the typical-shift phenomenon. But for the overstriver, setting one's sights higher and higher, success after success, becomes an obsessive ritual. Overstrivers cannot moderate their self-demands because perfection is their goal; they experience no grace and exercise no self-forgiveness. This predicament is analogous to the tightrope walker who must perform increasingly more daring feats, at ever greater dizzying heights, to ensure that the circus crowds will return. But the drop can be a long way down for overstrivers. Just how far down, and how devastating the fall, is reflected by the fact that overstrivers are risking failure under the most threatening circumstance of all: failure after having tried hard. Slavish preparation strips the overstriver of most potential excuses. Overstrivers rarely procrastinate; in fact, they are among the first to begin studying and among the last to stop, often just as the test is being passed out in class. Nor do overstrivers settle for utterly unattainable goals, because they are betting on success, not excused failure as the way to prove their worth.

The dynamics of overstriving offer the key to the two remaining puzzles mentioned at the end of chapter 3. First, I have argued that for overstrivers, success masks but does not resolve lingering doubts about their ability. It is for this reason that a single isolated failure can be so devastating despite a long history of academic success. Failure simply acts to confirm what these students have always feared, that they are less capable than perfection demands. Once again, we see it is largely the psychological meaning of success and failure – not necessarily their occurrence or frequency – that controls the quality of achievement striving.

Second, it is now quite understandable why there is so little relationship between GPA in school and one's satisfaction as a student. Personal satisfaction depends less on high grades than on the kinds of motives that drive achievement. As pointed out in chapter 1, students learn for many different reasons, not all of which are positive: Some strive mistakenly to gain prestige at the expense of their peers; others achieve as a means to ingratiate themselves with authority; and still others, like the overstriver, succeed to avoid the humiliation of defeat. For this reason, there is no direct one-to-one correspondence between satisfaction in school and GPA because this linkage depends on a third factor: the reasons, or motives, for achieving.

LOW-GOAL SETTING

Another success-ensuring strategy involves setting one's academic goals so low that there is little or no chance of failing. In its most sophisticated form this tactic involves the manipulation of what Robert Birney, Harvey Burdick, and Richard Teevan (1969) call the *confirming interval*. This is the interval between the lowest performance an individual can attain without experiencing discomfort and the best he or she can hope for. Performances that fall within this range are acceptable. By extending this interval – for example, by dropping the lower bounds of what one will accept – students can continue to evade feelings of failure, sometimes indefinitely. The student who publicly announces before each examination that he or she will be satisfied with just a passing grade is taking crafty advantage of this strategy.

Naturally, however, there are tradeoffs. Low-goal setting eventually leads to both inadequate performance and boredom. Students do only as much as they expect of themselves. When they expect more, they deliver more; when they expect less, they deliver that, too (Locke, 1968; Locke & Latham, 1984). At the same time, success that is virtually assured becomes predictable and loses any intrinsic value associated with challenge and uncertainty. Because there is no real challenge, there can be no pride in accomplishment and boredom is the result.

Chronically low aspirations create a dull, protracted mediocrity where success is defined only by *not* losing. Students may occasionally find some thin satisfaction in such marginal successes because, as has been observed, at least mediocre people are *always* at their best. Still, they have constructed an illusion for self-respect based on a life of underachievement.

ACADEMIC CHEATING

Cheating in school has long been a topic of concern and sometimes moral outrage. Some investigators have interpreted chronic cheating as a sign of stress and misplaced coping, whereas others see cheating as further evidence of a general ethical decline. And there are those who believe cheating to be the result of bankrupt educational policies that encourage deception and fraud. Whatever the validity of these several interpretations, it is abundantly clear that cheating also qualifies as a highly tempting way to avoid failure by appearing to succeed (Aronson & Mettee, 1968; Monte & Fish, 1989; Shelton & Hill, 1969).

From the self-worth perspective, cheating qualifies as part of the unhealthy legacy that results from having tied one's sense of worth to achieving competitively. Students themselves contribute poignantly to our understanding of the stakes involved. In one informal study youngsters who were caught cheating wrote an essay explaining why. Several of their replies follow (as reported in Covington & Beery, 1976, p. 55):

Kids don't cheat because they are bad. They are afraid that they aren't smart and what will happen if they don't do good. People will call them dumb or stupid.

If you cheat you will not know how to do the lesson right. You just put off flunking until later. It is scary.

Sometimes teachers don't see cheating. But something terrible will happen to cheaters anyway. They will pay for it. Maybe they will get sick. Or maybe they will have to explain their right answers in class.

I know someone who studies hard for tests and cheats too. They feel really bad but it is better than being yelled at for bad grades.

People cheat because they are afraid of doing poorer than other kids and feeling miserable for being different and behind. Some do it to be the best in class or move to the next group.

Naturally, we must view these confessions with caution. Whatever they may reveal about the stresses of school life, they are also self-serving. No one likes to cheat, but being caught is even more hateful, and it is important to cast such wrongdoing in as positive a light as possible. Nonetheless, the intensity of these confessions, their emotionally charged content, and, above all, their expressions of fear, self-loathing, and anger indicate something of the extent to which students are haunted by the fear of falling behind, of being compared unfavorably to others, and of the persistent, often overbearing demands of others. Also, there is a rueful awareness of the true horror of cheating that has all the classic elements of a Faustian bargain. By trading on their integrity, cheaters may gain some measure of relief from the prospect of failing. The respite is short-lived, however, because this ill-starred postponement creates a new and greater fear: being unable to repeat one's successes, and of being found out.

Minority dynamics

The failure-avoiding strategies described so far are largely the property of middle-class white students and of those minority youngsters – represented by Amy, our young black overstriver – who accept traditional schooling in the competitive spirit of Hermes. If Hermes is the archetype of achievement motivation, as McClelland (1961) argued, then he is solidly middle class, as reflected in his impatience to get ahead and the lengths to which he will go to stay ahead or at least not fall behind.

But as we have seen, thanks largely to the research of Suarez-Orozco (1989), Hermes is a stranger in the barrios and urban ghettos of America. Castelike minorities often strive for different goals and prefer different means to those goals. They eschew competitive advantage, strive for honor, and prefer the cooperation that comes from tightknit family or neighborhood traditions. However, these youngsters must still operate in schools dominated by middle-class values and ways of doing things. What does the self-worth perspective reveal about the special problems that face minority youngsters who choose for the moment to play the school game, or at least pretend to play?

ESTEEM AND SCHOOL PERFORMANCE

To start with, we are now in a position to explain yet another puzzle of long standing. Although the academic performance of black and Hispanic students is lower on average than that of whites, these minority youngsters nonetheless often exhibit relatively high self-ratings on scales of well-being and even on indices of self-perceived ability (e.g., Cervantes & Bernal, 1976; Franco, 1983; Hare, 1985; Healey, 1970; Rosenberg & Simmons, 1973). In fact, sometimes when socioeconomic level is controlled, blacks exhibit higher self-estimates of ability than do whites (Clark, 1983). But if poor performance in school is associated with low levels of self-esteem among middle-class whites, which it is, then why should minorities buck this trend and hold themselves in higher self-regard than their grades would indicate?

The answer is that feelings of well-being among many castelike minorities have little to do with performing well in school. Rather, these youngsters find strength and recognition in peer acceptance, nurturance, and cooperation (Hare, 1985). Also, minority youth tend to view ability differently. In the contemporary black community, ability is typically measured in a broader, more practical, everyday context than in the narrow academic sense in which being bright means getting good grades. Ramah Commanday (1992) found that black family members judge the ability of children with reference to concrete actions: "My boy is so smart he can help me fill out job application forms," or "My granddaughter is able to go to the pharmacy for me all on her own." Being able also means mastering the rules and facts of survival: knowing, for example, whose turf is whose and who is likely to back up demands with violence. In such an earnest, sometimes dangerous world, aggrandizing ability as an academic credential scarcely seems relevant. As one of Commanday's exceptionally bright fifth-grade ghetto informants explained, "I know

I'm smart so I don't have to prove it in school.'' If ability is equated with effective coping and survival in the ghettos and barrios of America, then the reports of high self-perceived ability among minority children are neither puzzling nor inaccurate.

At the same time, minority children often reject the dominant academic values of middle-class schools, especially competitiveness, thereby distancing themselves from what they see to be a losing battle. Recall from chapter 2 that many black adolescent males associate concepts like *champion* and *competition* with failure and death (Fyans et al., 1983). This self-distancing process has been referred to as "disidentification" by Claude Steele (1988). Simply put, individuals devalue that which threatens their sense of well-being. We have already met the white version of this conflict-management technique as practiced by John, our college-bound high school senior. John routinely minimizes the importance of his occasional academic disappointments, thereby becoming less vulnerable to personal devaluation.

For minorities, it is only a small step from rejecting mainstream American values to attributing one's failures to discrimination and institutional indifference (Crocker & Major, 1988). Whether teachers are in fact biased and discriminatory is often less the issue than what students believe to be the truth. However, there is plenty of reason to justify the suspicions of minorities when it comes to teacher indifference, even brutality; certainly enough to make charges of ethnic bias more than just an ill-founded excuse for failure.

These same disidentification dynamics also operate in the case of poor white youth – withdrawal, separation, and suspiciousness of out-group members. But the problem for blacks is compounded and their predicament intensified by the burden of stigmatization (Steele, 1989a). Stigmas arise when a person's actions violate social expectations. For example, a student's blackness may be stigmatized and the child held up to ridicule if he or she does well in school, since many whites refuse to acknowledge that black Americans are capable of significant intellectual accomplishments. Such biases are well illustrated by the black fifth-grade student described by Dorothy Gilliam who was questioned about whether he had really written an outstanding essay without help, an episode that "ended when the teacher gave him a grade that clearly showed that she did not believe the boy's outraged denials of plagiarism" (reported in Fordham & Ogbu, 1986, p. 176). It is the accusation, tacitly implied by this example, that black Americans are inferior – inferior simply because they are black – that has helped relegate them to the sidelines of American life. All children worry about not being good enough, but it is principally blacks who, in the words of Shelby Steele (1989b), "come wearing a color that is still, in the minds of some, a sign of inferiority" (p. 50).

Under the circumstances it is easy to see why many young blacks and Hispanics are driven into such potentially destructive pursuits as ganging, which, although it may provide a means for self-affirmation and peer acceptance, nonetheless places children on the wrong side of the law at increasingly early ages and at risk for drugs, violence, and death. Yet withdraw as they might, minority youngsters must eventually come to terms with traditional, mainstream American values in order to make a living, even a marginal one. The fact that less than 20% of all black families in America have incomes above the poverty line attests to the difficulty of this task.

This need for survival places castelike minorities in a tortuous bind. On the one hand, they must function at least minimally in the larger society to make ends meet, yet on the other, they must hold the values of this same society at arm's length to protect their sense of group identity. Here, once again, we are reminded of dilemmas. We have considered the effort-avoiding dilemma facing many white students who struggle to maintain a balance between too much effort, at the risk of being judged incompetent should they fail, and too little effort, at the risk of incurring teacher displeasure. Now I suggest a special dilemma for minorities that can best be described as an allegiance-avoiding dilemma: accepting dominant white values just enough to get along, but not enough to incur the wrath of one's friends and family. This dilemma is brought to an exquisite level of torment for those minority students like Amy, who struggle at least in the beginning to succeed in a white world.

ACTING WHITE

According to Signithia Fordham and John Ogbu (1986) this struggle inevitably involves blacks taking up the burden of "acting white," which means, among other things, speaking standard English, working hard to get good grades, going to museums, and having parties with no music. These behaviors invite anger and resentment from both blacks and whites. On the one hand, by doing well academically – a domain of excellence long forbidden to blacks – the black child is often met with hostility and mistrust from a large cross-section of the white community. On the other hand, upward-striving blacks risk rejection from their own peer group and sometimes even their families, as betrayers of their cultural heritage.

From this perspective, then, black underachievers may be thought of as youngsters who have the ability to do well in school but choose, consciously or unconsciously, to avoid the costs of acting white. And the pressures to give up on school are enormous. For example, there is the fear that performing well will bring on additional responsibilities and problems. Shelvy, an underachieving black girl in the eleventh grade, expresses it this way:

> because if you let . . . all your friends know how smart you are, then when you take a test or something, then they are going to know you know the answer and they are going to want the answers. And, if you don't give them to them, then they're going to get upset with you. (Fordham & Ogbu, p. 191)

Also, those minority students who persist in attempts to better themselves academically become a *target* in the experience of Kareem Abdul-Jabbar, one of the great black athletes of this century:

> When the nuns found this out [being able to read with proper inflection] they paid me a lot of attention, once even asking me, a fourth grader, to read to the seventh grade. When the kids found this out I became a target. . . . I got all A's and was hated for it; I spoke correctly and was called a

punk. I had to learn a new language simply to be able to deal with the threats. I had good manners and was a good little boy and paid for it with my hide. (Abdul-Jabbar & Knobles, 1983, p. 16).

The key to academic survival for gifted minorities in such a climate is to conceal their ability from peers – ironically, exactly the opposite tack taken by many middle-class whites who typically seek to aggrandize and flaunt their ability as a mark of superiority. Concealing means drawing as little attention to one's achievements as possible – in effect, cloaking one's ability or sabotaging one's successes in order to remain part of the group. Kaela, a brilliant black teenager, carried this later strategy to perfection by doing well on all her course examinations, but by not attending classes on a regular basis, she forced her teachers to give her F's. By putting "the brakes on," according to Kaela, she was also able to avoid the eventual frustrations of being overqualified for the low-status job for which she believed herself destined (Fordham & Ogbu, 1986).

Another strategy for maintaining a low academic profile, one especially favored by young, aspiring black males, is called *lunching* (Fordham & Ogbu, 1986), that is, becoming a clown or buffoon who achieves well despite his bungling, often manic, ways – feigning surprise at receiving high grades, disrupting the class with jokes, or making strange facial grimaces during silent reading. Yet behind this facade of apparent disinterest and ineptitude stands a serious student who often attends classes faithfully and completes most homework assignments. Other bright students survive by choosing friends – sometimes hoodlums and bullies – who will protect them from hallway violence and fights in exchange for favors, like helping with homework or taking tests for them.

Although bright black males are more likely to draw attention to themselves as a way to disguise their ability, high-achieving black females typically work to maintain a low profile. Fordham & Ogbu (1986, p. 196) describe the plight of Katrina, a brilliant straight-A math student, who arranged with her physics teacher not to be chosen as one of three students to represent her school in a television competition, even if she qualified for the team. As things turned out, Katrina was the top qualifier, but because of the prior arrangement she was made an alternate member of the team.

Given the burdens of acting white, we can only worry at the future prospects for Amy, our young black overstriver, who for the moment is uncritical in her acceptance of middle-class values. However, in time this loyalty may bring her into increasing conflict with the countervailing values of many youngsters in her immediate peer group.

Motivated cognitions and coping

Those who know they are profound strive for clarity. Those who would like to seem profound to the crowd strive for obscurity.
FRIEDRICH NIETZSCHE

If individuals feel compelled to convince others of their competency – a difficult *enough* task in itself – they must also satisfy a second, interlocking demand: They must convince *themselves* as well! This Byzantine drama is reminiscent of Abraham Lincoln's famous remark regarding democracy, "You can fool some of the people all the time, and all the people some of the time, but never all the people all the time." Because the human mind is neither very democratic nor particularly rational – actually more like a tyranny, to press our earlier political metaphor – the goal becomes that of fooling "all of the people (and one's self in the process) all the time." We are about to see how this trick is attempted, how difficult it is to sustain, and what happens when the necessary fictions begin to unravel.

Self-worth theory holds that the need for personal justification is primary and universal, and that it is the strategic use of self-serving tactics – their frequency, timing, and the sense of proportion involved, rather than their mere presence or absence – that differentiates successful and unsuccessful achievers (Lazarus, 1983). Even successful students have their deceits. For example, Meryl Botkin (1990) found that when elementary school pupils who were expected to do well did not deliver, they offered logical-sounding rationalizations for their failures. Granted, rationalizing is a far more sophisticated expression of defensive posturing than the angry striking out exhibited by some of Botkin's failing, low-expectancy students, but sophisticated or not, rationalizations are still self-aggrandizing. In effect, the line between rationality and deception is typically blurred and continuous, with our lives played out mostly in the vast middle ground between these polar opposites.

Does this mean that all behavior is necessarily defensive to one degree or another? Probably not. For instance, consider the matter of student inaction. I have argued that indifference is, in fact, often evidence of highly motivated behavior, an attempt by youngsters to avoid failure and its implications. Alternatively, however, not trying can also be interpreted as a deliberate, wholly rational decision simply to avoid tasks where the chances of success are low (Jagacinski & Nicholls, 1990). In fact, there is a large body of research that confirms the basic rationality of human beings when it comes to expending effort. Individuals typically try harder as tasks become more difficult, they also slack off once a task is mastered, and they may disengage entirely from assignments that prove too difficult. No motivational assumptions are needed to account for these actions. They simply follow the dictates of common sense (Schönpflug, 1985).

Moreover, we must not assume that behavior is always defensively motivated merely because it seems contrary to the individual's best interest. For example, consider Richard, a fourth grader, who has completed fewer and fewer homework assignments in recent weeks. Some might interpret Richard's behavior as reflecting a motivational deficit. However, if Richard stopped doing homework because studying no longer led to better test scores, then his actions are best thought of as the result of a logically sound, albeit maladaptive, conclusion and not necessarily the result of a motivational shortfall. Richard's reasoning may be correct as far as it goes, if in fact after having studied hard he continues to fail. Thus his decision may be less a matter of defensiveness than a misreading of the true nature of academic study. Richard may not realize that studying *hard* is not always the same as studying *well*.

The distinction between defensiveness and rationality also depends on de-velopment factors. Young children may possess all the necessary facts, but the meaning of these facts and their relevance to more rational, adultlike thinking may be distorted through the imperfect lens of childhood perceptions. Recall that young children interpret the meaning of effort in a manner precisely op-posite that of adults, by concluding that trying hard in school implies high ability and is an occasion for pride. For older persons trying hard implies *low* ability, a revelation that often leads to shame and self-doubt. These young children are not putting a good face on a bad prospect through denial or dis-tortion; they are acting rationally within the limits of their worldview.

These points illustrate the need to maintain a distinction between devel-opmentally immature cognitions, logically derived yet maladaptive attribu-tions, and defensively driven or motivated cognitions (Covington, 1984b). Although the issue is still in flux (e.g., Frankel & Snyder, 1978; Miller, 1978; Miller & Ross, 1975; Tetlock & Levi, 1982), we can reasonably assume that *defensiveness* occurs whenever individuals construct personal realities that cast themselves in either a better or a poorer light than the external evidence warrants (Skaalvik, 1990). To continue our previous example, defensive ex-planations would seem more appropriate if Richard continued doggedly to hold high expectations for himself despite repeated failure or imprudently sought out tasks more difficult than those he had previously failed. By stub-bornly maintaining that he will eventually succeed – a most laudable senti-ment – Richard is engaging in a forlorn attempt to maintain a sense of respect-ability.

But assuming that the tendencies for self-acceptance and self-accuracy are constant companions, how then, more precisely, does rationality come into play in the service of self-interests? And under what circumstances does de-ception prevail? One of the most useful approaches for answering these ques-tions comes from a distinction proposed by Dale Miller (1978) between biases in one's *private* beliefs about self and distortions about one's *public* image of self.

Private versus public selves

According to Miller, privately held beliefs may involve an unconscious dis-tortion of the meaning of events designed to promote a positive self identity. For instance, John, our failure avoider, finds it quite reasonable to blame a mediocre grade on his being overworked, without recognizing that he unwit-tingly takes on more than he can possibly accomplish in order to have this excuse available. The second kind of bias involves a more conscious and, at times, quite deliberate manipulation of the impression that one makes on oth-ers. Here John may hedge his bets by bemoaning his lack of preparation for an upcoming exam within earshot of all to hear but, in fact, studies very hard.

This private–public distinction suggests a two-step process: Individuals first unwittingly create a private, self-serving belief system that can then undergo a second round of distortions for public consumption. Thus, failure-threatened students who are plagued by doubts that cannot be entirely reconciled within themselves may attempt to mask the conflict by presenting a public facade of bravado. This example reminds us once again that failure-avoidance can take on many faces, even the appearance of confidence.

Although the first step in Miller's model, that of unconscious image making, has proven the more difficult to document given its private, often unconscious character (see Covington, 1984d), there is little doubt about the second step. Individuals do construct *public* images that are favorable to themselves. How, in this process of impression management, do rational considerations fit in, and in turn constrain egotistic tendencies? The basic answer is that self-flattery is limited by the need to maintain credibility in the eyes of others (Schlenker, 1975; Frey, 1978), or as Heider (1958) put it, excuses maintain their self-serving value only for as long as they "fit the constraints of reason." This balancing act is illustrated by the fact that individuals constantly alter their public image depending on circumstances. For instance, the degree to which individuals present a positively skewed self-image depends on how much information others have about them (Hendricks & Brickman, 1974; Schneider, 1969). It is harder to fool a friend than a stranger and we adjust our self-portrayals accordingly. This is why self-flattering half-truths and even outright lies are traded with such ease at cocktail parties and in other casual, anonymous surroundings. Also, people describe themselves in far more modest terms if they think they might have to live up to these claims later. This is of course why cheating is so perilous. Such ill-gotten successes can create a reputation that may be impossible to sustain.

Yet even with the demands for modesty, the urgencies of self-bolstering are ever present. For example, Roy Baumeister and Edward Jones (1978) report that when individuals were forced by circumstances to accept an unfavorable description of themselves, they bolstered their self-descriptions on positive traits for which the observer had no knowledge. Such actions are all part of the balancing act implied in our political metaphor, and of the need to fool ourselves and others as circumstances permit.

Covington and Omelich (1978) have explored these self-protective mechanisms as they relate specifically to classroom achievement. These researchers hypothesized that in the event of a test failure, college students would act egotistically to enhance their ability status, but only when plausible explanations for failure other than low ability were available. Egotism was defined experimentally as the extent to which students would attribute lower levels of ability to others rather than to themselves under identical circumstances of failure. Besides judging their own ability status, students also estimated how much they expected others to agree with their own self-perceptions of ability. This rating provided a measure of what Edward Jones and Richard Nisbett (1971) call *egocentrism*. Egocentrism implies that the efforts of individuals to sustain an inflated view of their ability beyond what is logically reasonable depends on the expectation that others will also agree. If image-makers begin to wonder whether or not others also share their inflated view of themselves, then doubts about their credibility will likely arise and may require a readjustment or even the temporary abandonment of egotistical tendencies.

As expected, the students took advantage of any uncertainty to aggrandize their ability status. They illogically ascribed higher levels of ability to themselves than to hypothetical others whenever alternative excuses for their failures were available, such as illness, even though everyone had exactly the same alibis! Moreover, not only did these students act egotistically, but they also believed that outside observers would accept these inflated self-serving views (egocentrism). In effect, the circle of self-deception was complete – these individuals fooled themselves, and in the process, believed that they had fooled everyone else as well. In contrast, whenever low ability was a sufficient and compelling explanation for failure, say, when the students tried hard and failed anyway, they judged their ability equal to that of other failing students, and at a level substantially lower than their earlier egotistic self-ratings. Also, these students perceived others as agreeing with this pessimistic view. In this instance both egotistic and egocentric tendencies were held in check by compelling evidence of low ability that could not be easily explained away.

This study demonstrates how rational considerations control the degree and expression of egotism. It also supports the contention that individuals tend to aggrandize their ability status whenever reason permits. It is in this sense that the need for self-justification is the primary psychological reality and rational considerations secondary and derivative. As Reuven Bar-Levav asserts, "In general, people are led by their feelings, and then they unknowingly invent rationalizations to explain their actions or decisions to themselves and to justify them to others."

However, the ascendancy of egotism must be qualified. Not everyone appears equally prone to self-aggrandizing tendencies. In the study just described (Covington & Omelich, 1978), degree of egotism also depended on whether subjects were male or female and on initial levels of self-confidence. Among males, both those high and low in self-perceived ability, and for high self-confident females, the findings were just as reported – a pervasive tendency to bolster one's reputation whenever circumstances permit. But low self-confident females acted in an entirely opposite way. These women *understated* their ability status in all conditions of failure and believed that others would agree with this excessively pessimistic self-appraisal. In short, they denigrated their ability beyond what was rationally indicated by the available evidence. It appears that many of these women had abandoned the struggle to maintain a positive self-image of ability, and had become failure accepting. By contrast, low self-confident males consistently aggrandized their ability status despite their private doubts. This latter finding is not surprising if we are to judge from the many accounts suggesting that males in general are more likely than females to act defensively, owing to social pressures to maintain a self-image of competency (Snyder et al., 1976; Streufert & Streufert, 1969; Wolosin et al., 1973).

This same pattern of sex differences has been found among junior high school youngsters. Arden Miller (1986) reports that boys are more likely to avoid revealing low ability by withdrawing from difficult tasks or by not trying. On the other hand, girls appeared more willing to accept low-ability status and to give up sooner on attempts to demonstrate high ability (also see Dweck

& Reppucci, 1973). These findings are consistent with data already reviewed in chapter 3 that suggests that girls may see the struggle for intellectual status as less role appropriate. For these reasons women and girls are likely more vulnerable to the dynamics of learned helplessness.

Certainty and uncertainty

As the credibility of self-serving excuses fades, suspicions of incompetency can crystallize to a certainty; and with certainty comes despair and loss of hope. Conversely, it is *uncertainty* about one's ability status that permits continued striving and may even drive individuals to extraordinary achievements. The research of Stanley Coopersmith (1967) illustrates this point. Coopersmith identified two groups of boys, both of whom rated themselves equally low in ability. However, one group not only doubted themselves but also were convinced of their judgments to a certainty because they were also held in low regard by their teachers and friends. The other boys were less certain about their low self-ratings because *their* peers and teachers believed them to be bright. The boys in this latter group were far more successful in school because, according to Coopersmith, they sought to reduce their feelings of uncertainty by proving their worth through succeeding.

The research of Jeanne Marecek and David Mettee (1972) provides further insights into the dynamics surrounding this certainty–uncertainty distinction. Low self-confident college women were divided into two groups depending on how certain (or uncertain) they were about these self-judgments. One-half of each group was convinced (falsely) that doing well on an upcoming task was strictly a matter of chance, whereas the other half was led to believe that success was largely a matter of skill. Midway through their work, all the subjects were told that so far their performances were highly successful. Following this unexpected success, the subsequent performance of women in the *low self-confidence–uncertain* group improved under both luck and skill conditions. This finding suggests that students who are not yet completely convinced of their inability may still accept success and, indeed, may even benefit from it by increasing future achievement. However, the performance of the women in the two *low self-confidence–certain* groups were quite different. For those women whose unexpected successes were alleged to have occurred because of skill, performance fell dramatically during the second half of the experiment. These women appeared to have suppressed their performances unwittingly to offset their earlier success, presumably because they could not handle the obligation it implied. On the other hand, those low self-confident–certain women whose unexpected successes were attributed to luck *increased* their performances to such an extent that, in fact, they surpassed the performances of all the other three groups. It appears that success *can* motivate low self-confident students to higher achievement, but only if they attribute success to a lucky break or chance.

These findings hold the proverbial good news–bad news message. First, the good news: Not all low-esteem students are unresponsive to success. As long as individuals remain unclear about their ability status, there is a reasonable prospect for reducing uncertainty in a positive direction. The potential bad news is that if other low-esteem students can perform well only when they feel no obligation to repeat their successes, then meaningful learning becomes impossible.

The Marecek and Mettee experiment underscores the critical importance of intervening as early as possible before failure becomes a chronic way of life. Once the seeds of self-doubt are planted, other factors also conspire to discount success. For example, pressure increases on the individual to act in ways that are more congruent with prevailing self-doubts. According to this *consistency-theory* position (Festinger, 1957; Secord & Backman, 1961, 1965), individuals are driven to reduce inconsistencies in their beliefs by creating a congruent view of themselves, even if this means accepting themselves as failures. In effect, there is comfort in knowing things to a certainty, even bad things; at least then there are no surprises. By this reasoning it follows that in order to maintain self-consistency, failing students ought to seek out unfavorable negative evaluations from others (Deutsch & Solomon, 1959) and, as we have just seen from the Marecek and Mettee experiment, even handicap their successful efforts (also see Aronson & Carlsmith, 1962; Berglas & Jones, 1978; Taylor and Huesmann, 1974). Although these predictions have found broad support in the research literature, they are also clearly challenged, as we know, by contrary evidence that attests to the fact that individuals are anything but consistent when it comes to manipulating their public image.

The seemingly contradictory nature of the consistency-theory and egotism literatures may be resolved if we assume that both self-consistency and self-presentational needs operate simultaneously but that the ascendancy of one over the other depends on where on a continuum, from effective coping to disfunctioning, individuals find themselves. For example, as long as an individual is coping successfully with only periodic failures, the maintenance of a public image of competence may provide the necessary resiliency to continue achieving. But what happens when students finally forfeit the struggle to avoid the implications of failure and embrace a permanent image of low ability? Here we enter the realm of the *failure accepter*.

Failure-accepting students

Even though one's failures may be well defended for a time by a bodyguard of alibis and excuses, these self-serving explanations eventually lose their credibility, and vague doubts about one's worth become virtual certainties. This collapse of defenses has been studied in classroom settings where unremitting failure is a natural, albeit unfortunate occurrence. In one study researchers tracked college students who fell short of their grade goals on each of several successive tests, thereby enduring repeated feelings of failure (Covington & Omelich, 1981). Following each test, these disheartened students were asked to judge their ability to handle the course material, indicate the degree of shame they experienced, and estimate their chances for success on the next test. An analysis of these data indicated that the degree of shame endured following a first failure depended largely on the individual's initial self-concept of ability – the lower the student's self-estimate, the more he or she experienced shame and feelings of hopelessness. And as one failure followed another, these feelings intensified, driven by two interlocking processes. First, as nonability explanations for failure became increasingly implausible, self-estimates of ability steadily deteriorated. Second, failures were increasingly attributed to a lack of ability. In other words, as failures mounted, these students rated themselves lower and lower on the very factor – ability – that was emerging in their minds as the most important ingredient to success. This dual process – akin to a kind of double jeopardy – was most pronounced among those students who initially held the lowest self-concepts of ability (also see Feather, 1969; Feather & Simon, 1971; Markus, 1977).

The conceptual formulations of Ralf Schwarzer and his colleagues (Schwarzer, Jerusalem, & Schwarzer, 1983; Schwarzer, Jerusalem, & Stiksrud, 1984) are consistent with this double jeopardy interpretation. They proposed that a first failure, especially if unexpected, represents a *challenge* to be overcome. However, subsequent failures, particularly as they become anticipated, elicit anxiety caused by increasing implications for low ability, until finally – after repeated failures – individuals may experience feelings of a total loss of personal control over events. In order to test these predictions, Schwarzer tracked the relationship among test anxiety, feelings of helplessness, and school grades for German high school students over a two-year period. Of special interest was the identification of a substantial subsample of these students whose level of anxiety progressively decreased over time only to be replaced by an increasing sense of hopelessness. This process appears akin to a state of resignation that may share much in common with the flat, restricted affect and unresponsivenesss of those individuals identified as *failure accepters* in American samples (Covington & Omelich, 1985).

Having given up the struggle for approval via high achievement, failure-accepting students naturally search for alternative sources of worth. The evidence suggests that at least some of these low ability–certain individuals come to embrace the socially rewarding values of diligence, punctuality, and hard work, a strategy that is especially favored by women and girls (Covington & Omelich, 1985). For other students, most likely men and boys, failure acceptance means the rejection of both effort and ability as sources of worth, which may lead to dropping out of school or simply refusing to cooperate.

Conclusions

In this chapter we have explored the dynamics of classroom achievement from a self-worth perspective. School learning has been described as involving a profound conflict of values between ability and effort. By this analysis, failure-prone students, especially middle-class white youngsters, are condemned to thread their way between the threatening extremes of trying too hard (for fear of being revealed as incompetent should they fail) and of exerting too little effort (for fear of teacher reprimand). For those minority students who struggle to succeed in a white world, the situation is further complicated by the need to maintain an ethnic identity that may not share mainstream values.

We have also cataloged many of the ruses and artful dodges employed by students in their struggle to preserve a sense of dignity in school and, in the process, accounted for a number of puzzling classroom behaviors, including the fact that some pupils actually perform at their best when the odds against success are the greatest and that a single failure can be extremely damaging to otherwise apparently successful students. Despite the many complexities involved, these dynamics reflect in one way or another a primordial struggle for self-protection that is so elemental that many students are prepared to sacrifice even good grades for the sake of appearances.

The vision of school life conjured up by self-worth theory is disturbing. The kinds of motivational dynamics revealed here portray a far more troubling picture than the idealized account of schools in which "teachers gladly teach, and students gladly learn." All too often, classrooms are, in reality, battle-grounds where the rules of engagement favor deception, sabotage, and lack-luster effort.

This self-worth analysis gives further reason to doubt the wisdom of implementing a policy of intensification as the best way to meet the current crisis in education. Increasing the pressures on students to work harder may prove effective for a time, especially in the earliest years of school when students value effort and respond eagerly to effort-based rewards. According to the evidence presented here, however, this policy becomes progressively bankrupt as students grow older, until eventually intensification becomes part of the problem, not part of the solution.

Needless to say, motivating students to try harder is critical if we are ever to reverse the shameful statistics that place American students last in the academic sweepstakes among all leading industrial nations. But our attempts to mobilize student involvement will be counterproductive and effort will remain an undiminished threat, as long as effort is viewed as a commodity to be aroused, managed, and manipulated through competitive incentives.

5

Achievement anxiety

I wrote my name at the top of the page. . . . But thereafter I could not think of anything connected with it that was either relevant or true. Incidentally there arrived from nowhere in particular a blot and several smudges. I gazed for two whole hours at this sad spectacle; and then merciful ushers collected up my piece of foolscap and carried it up to the Headmaster's table.
WINSTON CHURCHILL

Thus Winston Churchill described one of the most celebrated anxiety attacks ever recorded. Churchill was not, as some have assumed, dyslexic. Nor in his youth was he as stupid as he appeared. It was simply that when confronted by the testing ritual Churchill became stricken. And so it is with millions of schoolchildren today. Kennedy Hill (1984) estimates that as many as 10 million elementary and secondary pupils in America, or roughly one-third to one-half of all students, suffer from achievement anxiety. This means that the test scores for a near majority of children may provide an invalid estimate of what they have learned or of what they are capable of learning. Fear has misclassified these students; they likely know more than they are able to tell us through conventional testing. Nor is the problem limited only to depressed test performance. Anxiety interferes with learning as well. In fact, it detracts from everything students do, say, remember, and hope to achieve.

The extent of the corrosive effects of anxiety on school performance is reflected in the generally negative correlation between measures of test anxiety, on the one hand, and achievement test scores on the other (Seipp, 1991; Schwarzer, Seipp, & Schwarzer, 1989). These correlations are essentially zero in the first and second grades, but increase to between $-.20$ and $-.30$ in the third and fourth grades, depending on the particular study consulted (e.g., Hill & Sarason, 1966; Payne, Smith, & Payne, 1983; Zimmerman, 1970), and can reach a staggering magnitude of $-.60$ by the high school years (Fyans, 1979; Hill, 1984). Stated differently, by the sixth grade 10% of the least anxious students score approximately one year ahead of the average on achievement tests, whereas the 10% who suffer anxiety the most score one year below the average (Hill & Horton, 1985). Not only are these debilitating effects massive, they are also widespread. Test anxiety is found among both boys and girls (Schwarzer et al., 1989), at every socioeconomic level, and among all ethnic groups. For example, in one junior high school study the correlations between anxiety and performance were $-.48$ for Hispanic students, $-.27$ for whites, and $-.35$ for black students (Willig, Harnisch, Hill, & Maehr, 1983).

The fact that anxiety is such an all-consuming event, encompassing as it does both physical upset and mental worry as well as disruptive feelings and emotions, makes it particularly difficult for researchers to sort out all these components and identify their respective roles as causes of poor performance. The earliest explanations were based on the view of anxiety as a *drive* that arouses people. When there is too much arousal, however, a racing heart and heightened blood pressure may compromise performance. It was this "butterflies-in-the-stomach" theory that dominated the thinking of researchers well into the 1950s. A second, more recent variation on the arousal theme focused on emotional factors such as feelings of stress and tension as the culprit. This view prevailed until the early 1970s, when cognitive theorists proposed a third possibility, that the causes of poor performance are not so much excessive emotional or physical arousal as the troublesome, self-defeating thoughts that often accompany test taking. This development marked the advent of the cognitive *interference* tradition of anxiety that predominates today. According to this view, anxious students become trapped in what Jeri Wine (1971, 1973, 1980) calls a "reverberating circuit of worry": They worry that they will not have enough time to finish the test and then can't think of anything to say, they worry that others might be watching so they appear to be busy, and they recall other similar situations that ended disastrously.

Finally, and most recently, some researchers have raised the provocative possibility that anxiety is not responsible for poor performance at all, and that the real problem is improper or insufficient study. From this perspective, emotional and physical arousal and even self-defeating thoughts may merely reflect recognition by the student that he or she is ill-prepared for an upcoming exam and is likely to fail. Or, as Dean Inge has remarked, "Anxiety is the interest paid on trouble before it is due."

This chapter is divided into three sections. In the first section we will review these successive theories in more detail and the research inspired by them. In the second section we will explore how these various manifestations of anxiety – distressing feelings, worry, and physical upset – combine and enter into the process of school achievement. Additionally, we will consider what anxiety shares in common with motivation and offer an interpretation of both the arousal (motivation) and interference (cognition) traditions from a self-worth perspective. I will argue that achievement anxiety in its many forms is basically a reaction to the threat of failure – an event that implies incompetency, hence, worthlessness.

Finally, in the third section we will explore the practical question of how to relieve achievement anxiety, especially as it relates to the issue of school reform. This question has become all the more urgent given the widely held belief that anxiety does not necessarily indicate a maladaptive or flawed personality. Rather, it is more likely a temporary condition that compromises an otherwise perfectly adequate or even a superior capacity for learning.

A brief history
The greatest of all inventors – Fear.
FRENCH PROVERB

Anxiety as arousal

DRIVE THEORY
The earliest explanations for poor performance were based on an assumption that anxiety is a *drive*. Anxiety was said to have motivating properties; it

arouses people to action. But when there is too much arousal, performance is compromised. This implies that anxiety need not always disrupt learning, but might even facilitate learning under some circumstances (Alpert & Haber, 1960). This point was first made at the turn of the century by Robert Yerkes and John Dodson (1908) who proposed that arousal would benefit the learning of simple responses but would compromise performance on more complex tasks. This proposition has since been verified so thoroughly for all age levels (e.g., Farber & Spence, 1953; Palermo, Castaneda, & McCandless, 1956) that it is widely referred to as a *law*. The Yerkes-Dodson law is well illustrated by the various demands placed on students in the course of problem solving. High-anxious students excel at simply generating a large volume of ideas, presumably triggered by a high state of arousal or readiness, but usually ideas of poor quality (Covington, 1967, 1983). By contrast, it is the low-anxious student who is most likely to produce the single *best* solution idea.

Although Yerkes and Dodson set the stage for a drive theory of anxiety, it remained for Clark Hull (1943) to propose the specific mechanisms by which excessive arousal compromises achievement. Hull's version of drive theory alleged that the chances of a correct response (R) occurring depend on the joint influence of two hypothetical factors: habit strength (H) and drive state (D). This relationship can be expressed as: $R = (H \times D)$. Habit strength refers to the strength of the "correct" response compared to that of all other possible, but wrong, responses. Hull believed that the strength of a correct response depends largely on the number of times it had been practiced. For example, as adults we overlearned the alphabet long ago. But habit strength is sufficient only for reciting the alphabet in the A to Z order. Attempts to recite the alphabet backwards result in much hesitancy, sheepish grins, and numerous errors. These backward connections have yet to attain enough habit strength for a smooth, automatic performance.

The concept of drive in Hull's system referred to various physiological need states (e.g., hunger, thirst) that combine to determine the organism's total level of activation or arousal. One especially human source of noxious, aversive arousal is anxiety. Anxiety was taken to be an index of the individual's readiness to respond, or level of excitability (Spence & Spence, 1966; Taylor, 1956).

By this complex Hullian analysis, we can deduce that the appearance of a "correct" response, say, recalling that the state capital of California is Sacramento, depends on whether or not the response is aroused at all and then, once aroused, how distinctive it is compared to other competing but erroneous answers such as Akron or Philadelphia. Practice makes the right answer more distinctive, but then excessive anxiety can offset the benefits of practice. More specifically, anxiety enters the equation by increasing overall drive level, which heightens competition among all the possible responses, thereby leading to errors. Everyone knows how being under pressure can disrupt even the most automatic routines, and the distraction need not be great – sometimes simply being made suddenly self-conscious, for example, when we trip on the next stair after being reminded to "be careful."

Hull's general reasoning suggests that the effects of anxiety will likely depend on the stage of learning. For instance, early in the process of memorizing the multiplication table, anxiety will interfere with learning until the correct responses are of sufficient strength to compete successfully with error tendencies. Thereafter, anxiety may actually aid recall of the fact that $8 \times 4 = 32$. The drive model also takes into account the intelligence of the learner. Highly anxious students of superior ability are presumably at a handicap during the early stages of complex learning compared to low-anxious students of equal ability. By contrast, students of lower ability will likely experience difficulty at all points in the learning curve, but especially if they are anxious (see Man, Blahus, & Spielberger, 1989).

In its day, Hull's drive theory covered most of the facts known about human performance and anxiety. It also provided a coherent, relatively precise explanation for why anxiety interferes with performance – heightened response competition. For all its value, however, the promise of drive theory was ultimately limited by the fact that it applies best to those kinds of learning that are of least interest to educators, namely, relatively simple tasks whose respective habit strengths and competing response tendencies could be well specified. For example, one favorite laboratory demonstration involved the conditioning of human eyelid blinks to a puff of air. Because blinking is usually dominant in the individual's response repertoire and simple as well, it was hypothesized that highly anxious subjects would become conditioned faster than less anxious ones. Although this proved true (Spence, 1964; Spence & Taylor, 1951; Taylor, 1951), it is scarcely useful information for teachers. Also, of concern from a motivational perspective is the fact that drive theory formulations neglected important prior matters, particularly the question of why individuals should experience anxiety in the first place.

TRAIT–STATE THEORY

It remained for Charles Spielberger and his colleagues to place drive theory in the larger dynamic context of stress and coping behavior (Gaudry & Spielberger, 1971; Heinrich & Spielberger, 1982; Spielberger, 1966, 1972). According to Spielberger, anxiety represents a reaction to real (physical) or perceived (psychological) threats. Among the most important sources of psychological threat is an anticipated loss of self-esteem caused by failure. It was speculation about the nature of these potential threats to one's worth that transcended traditional drive theory.

These revelations gave rise to questions about whether anxiety is a stable personality characteristic residing within the person – as Atkinson originally assumed – or whether anxiety is merely the creature of situations, only a transitory reaction to various threats that come and go. The answer appears to be both. At times anxiety acts like a general, relatively permanent condition and at other times like a specific, situation-bound reaction, and *which* is *which* depends on a distinction proposed by Spielberger between trait and state anxiety (Spielberger, 1972; Spielberger, Anton, & Bedell, 1976).

Some individuals, more so than others, seem prone to negative arousal much of the time. They are typically vigilant, even hypervigilant, and quick to react with suspicion and doubt (Eysenck, 1988). Such chronic proneness to anxiety is indicative of *trait* anxiety (A-trait). Yet, even the most hypersensitive persons are not always on guard. The degree of arousal experienced by high A-trait individuals depends on immediate circumstances. Thus A-trait anxiety, as an underlying condition, becomes manifest on the surface as temporary *states* of anxiety (A-state), but only when the environment is sufficiently threatening. If the environment poses no obvious threat, then even high A-trait individuals may feel relatively secure. In effect, the degree of arousal experienced by individuals depends on an interaction between personality dispositions (either high or low A-trait) and the transitory features of the environment.

In general, the accumulated evidence has confirmed predictions flowing from the trait–state distinction (Gaudry & Poole, 1975). As one might expect, high A-trait persons tend to perceive a greater number of situations as dangerous and threatening (Eysenck, 1989; Spielberger, Gorsuch, & Lushene, 1970). Not only do these persons overestimate the degree of threat, but they also underestimate their ability to cope (Beck & Clark, 1988). Also, assuming that high A-trait persons are more sensitive to threat, it follows that their performance should improve if threat is reduced. A number of studies confirm this prediction. Conditions that have proven especially reassuring for anxious individuals include providing them with frequent feedback as to their progress and providing memory aids that help recall information (Campeau, 1968; Morris & Fulmer, 1976; Noll, 1955) as well as suggesting ways to stay task-focused (Brockner, 1979; Brockner & Hulton, 1978). Allowing students more time during testing is another helpful strategy (Hill & Eaton, 1977). Conversely, when the conditions of learning are made threatening – the most diabolical procedure is to falsely describe tests as measures of ability – then the performance of highly anxious individuals invariably deteriorates (Barnard, Zimbardo, & Sarason, 1968; Lekarczyk & Hill, 1969).

By any measure, the introduction of a trait–state distinction was highly successful. Not only did it stimulate an enormous volume of research in the 1960s and 1970s, but most predictions have been broadly supported. This is not to suggest that trait–state theory has an infinite conceptual reach. Actually, more recent research has qualified this view in several important respects, leading to a third wave of alternative theory building. Trait–state theory views anxiety basically as a process of emotional arousal (drive), and assumes that feelings of excessive tension are the primary cause of poor performance. However, beginning in the late 1960s this assumption came under increasing attack. First, a number of studies showed little if any relationship between indices of emotional or physiological arousal, on the one hand, and decreases in the quality of performance, on the other (e.g., Doctor & Altman, 1969; Morris & Fulmer, 1976; Morris & Perez, 1972; Spiegler, Morris, & Liebert, 1968). Second, other studies demonstrated that both high-anxious and low-anxious persons display similar patterns of physical and emotional arousal when either anticipating tests or actually taking them (Deffenbacher

& Hazaleus, 1985; Hollandsworth, Glazeski, Kirkland, Jones, & Van Norman, 1979; Holroyd, Westbrook, Wolff, & Badhorn, 1978).

Until the late 1960s the study of anxiety and motivation was essentially the same; both concepts were part of the larger drive-theory tradition. But then a new tradition was born. The emphasis shifted to the search for cognitive mechanisms.

Anxiety as worry

The stage had been set for this departure from classic drive theory some years earlier by George Mandler and Seymour Sarason (1952). These investigators proposed that anxiety-impaired performance results from intrusive throughts that are irrelevant to the task at hand, mainly a mental preoccupation with failure and with one's own personal shortcomings. Over the intervening years, evidence has steadily accumulated in support of the proposition that high test-anxious persons engage in more irrelevant thoughts and behaviors during test taking than do low test-anxious individuals (Borkovec, Robinson, Pruzinsky, & DePree, 1983; Bruch, 1978; Galassi, Frierson, & Sharer, 1981; Galassi, Frierson, & Siegal, 1981; Ganzer, 1968; Sarason, 1988; Zatz & Chassin, 1983).

However, it remained for Robert Liebert and Larry Morris (1967) to introduce the critical distinction that has provided the main focus of contemporary research: worry versus emotionality. *Worry* reflects the cognitive aspects of anxiety – negative beliefs, troubling thoughts, and poor judgment. *Emotionality* refers to unpleasant affective reactions including feelings of tension and nervousness. By this reckoning, emotionality is treated not as arousal itself, but as the subjective perception of internal physiological events. Two broad empirical generalizations have emerged from research on this worry–emotionality distinction.

WORRY VERSUS EMOTIONALITY

A number of studies have demonstrated the relative independence of worry and emotionality responses. These two anxiety components are triggered and maintained by different circumstances. For example, Morris and Liebert (1973) demonstrated that the threat of electric shock during work on an intellectual task aroused only emotionality, whereas failure feedback on this same task aroused only worry. Based on these results and a host of similar findings, we can conclude that worry is aroused in situations that threaten the individual's sense of adequacy and worth (Morris, Harris, & Rovins, 1981; Morris, Brown, & Halbert, 1977; Spiegler et al., 1968).

By contrast, the arousal of emotional responses depends on cues that are largely incidental to test taking itself but that signify the immediate onset of a test, such as merely walking into an examination room. In essence, emotionality is best characterized as a set of autonomic (if not automatic) responses that become conditioned to specific testing situations and that may quickly lose their importance once the student begins a test (Morris, Davis, & Hutchings, 1981). In fact, emotionality typically wanes as work on a test progresses (Doctor & Altman, 1969; Morris & Engle, 1981; Smith & Morris, 1976). Not so, however, with worry. Worrisome thoughts are known to maintain themselves over the entire period of test taking, and may be aroused days or even weeks in advance of an examination (Becker, 1982, 1983).

This is not to say that the worry–emotionality distinction is absolute but, rather, only relative. There is some overlap in these dynamics that may explain why some laboratory attempts to arouse emotionality and worry components separately have succeeded either in activating both together or neither of them (Holroyd et al., 1978; Morris & Fulmer, 1976).

WORRY AND PERFORMANCE

Be that as it may, emotionality and worry components remain sufficiently unique, one from the other, to permit a second generalization. Worry during test taking is strongly associated with declines in academic performance – the greater the worry, the poorer one's performance. This relationship has been demonstrated so often that it has assumed the status of a truism (e.g., Deffenbacher, 1977; Doctor & Altman, 1969; Morris, Finkelstein, & Fisher, 1976; Morris, Kellaway, & Smith, 1978). Emotionality also usually bears a negative relationship to performance. But, compared to that of worry and performance, this association is typically weaker (Deffenbacher, 1980; Morris & Liebert, 1973; Seipp & Schwarzer, 1990). For example, in a series of studies Jerry Deffenbacher (Deffenbacher, 1978, 1986; Deffenbacher & Hazaleus, 1985) examined the separate but simultaneous influence on performance of several anxiety factors: physiological arousal (pulse rate), emotionality, worry, and task-generated interference. Task interference is illustrated by the student who continues to perseverate obsessively about test items left unsolved in earlier parts of an examination. Of all these potential sources of disruption, worry scores were the best predictor of decreases in performance followed by task interference and emotionality, in that order, with physiological arousal only minimally related to performance.

Taken together, these various studies imply the existence of a *retrieval deficit* among anxious individuals. In effect, achievement suffers because attention is misdirected during test taking when students must remember, or retrieve, what was learned previously.

Anxiety as skill deficit

Most recently the retrieval deficit theory has been challenged by a competing position: the *skill deficit* theory. This alternative model proposes that poor performance is largely the result of inadequate study (Culler & Holahan, 1980; Topman & Janson, 1984). In effect, anxious students do poorly on tests because they did not learn the material properly in the first place. Thus rather than being a cause of poor performance, anxiety is viewed merely as an emotional reaction that accompanies the realization that the person is inadequately prepared and will probably do poorly. By this account feelings of anxiety play

no significant causal role in the achievement process apart from being corre-
lated with poor study habits.

Evidence for the skill deficit position can be inferred from a series of studies that report negative relationships between study habits and anxiety (Benjamin, McKeachie, Lin, & Holinger, 1981; Desiderato & Koskinen, 1969;
Lin & McKeachie, 1970; Wittmaier, 1972). There also is the frequently reported finding that efforts to reduce test anxiety are largely ineffectual unless
poor study habits are remediated (Allen, 1971; McCordick, Kaplan, Finn, &
Smith, 1979; Mitchell & Eng, 1972). Finally, reducing anxiety (emotionality)
has little impact on the academic performance of students with poor study
habits (Gonzalez, 1987a, 1987b; Spielberger, 1980).

The study habits of anxious students appear most deficient at the level of
self-monitoring. They are particularly handicapped when it comes to judging
whether or not they understand something well enough to pass a test, or what
to do when one learning strategy that has worked well in the past is no longer
appropriate (Covington, 1984b). They also have difficulty organizing information into larger patterns of meaning (Cromer & Wiener, 1966; Lefevre,
1964; Steiner, Wiener, & Cromer, 1971). Moreover, anxious students appear
particularly distractible, not only by their own worries and preoccupations,
but also by external stimuli such as classroom disruptions (Eysenck, 1988).
Finally, anxious individuals restrict their attention unduly, thereby ignoring
peripheral features of a problem that might otherwise be important to its solution.

Sigmund Tobias (1980, 1985, 1986) has proposed a way to conceptualize
these assorted findings using a ''limited capacity'' model of human performance (also see Craik & Lockhart, 1972; Eysenck, 1988; Hamilton, 1975).
Tobias argues that the already limited capacity of human beings to process
information may be further eroded by emotional preoccupations. High-anxious
individuals are placed at a considerable disadvantage because, in Tobias's
(1985) words, ''the cognitive representation of test anxiety must absorb some
of the student's processing capacity, leaving a reduced portion for task solution'' (p. 138). This handicap becomes progressively more burdensome as
tasks demand more attention and processing capacity (Everson & Millsap,
1987; Paulman & Kennelly, 1984) – shades of Yerkes and Dodson, almost a
century later! It follows from Tobias's model that instruction in study skills
will help students to organize tasks better so that less cognitive capacity is
required than before, thus profiting anxious students more than less anxious
ones.

In summary, the past half century has witnessed a progressive dismantling
of the concept of achievement anxiety into a number of competing theories
and distinctive lines of research. At first, an arousal interpretation of anxiety
held center stage with its emphasis on motivational, drivelike properties. Then,
beginning some 25 years ago, this notion came under increasing criticism,
opening the way for a cognitive interference, or retrieval deficit, interpretation. Now, most recently, evidence has come to light favoring a rival, skill
deficit view.

Integration

Anxiety is fear of one's self.
WILHELM STEKEL

Achievement anxiety is a concept under scientific siege but hopefully not in disarray. It is now time that we attempt to integrate these various theories – skill deficit, arousal, and interference – into a higher-order understanding of anxiety and of its place in the dynamics of school achievement. In effect, we ask: How do these various elements fit together, and is the fit invariably the same for all individuals?

From what we have learned so far, it seems clearly an oversimplification to assume that achievement anxiety represents a single process. Rather the notion of anxiety as a set of interrelated elements seems closer to the mark. But what is their deeper source of interconnectedness? Our answer comes from a self-worth perspective and centers on the notion of anxiety as a failure-of-self.

Anxiety as failure-of-self

As already noted, many researchers view anxiety as a multifaceted reaction to the threat of failure (e.g., Becker, 1982; Hagtvet, 1984; Hobfoll, Anson, & Bernstein, 1983; Lazarus, 1966; Pekrun, 1984, 1988; Schwarzer & Cherkes-Julkowski, 1982; Spielberger, 1972). But what can be so devastating about failure that its occurrence can result in prolonged, even paralyzing anxiety attacks? Our earlier analysis leaves little doubt as to the answer. In attributional terms failure, especially following heightened effort, implies low ability, and suspicions of incompetency represent a major threat to a sense of worth in our society. Thus whatever specific form anxiety may take – a worrisome thought, an uncomfortable emotion, or an erratic pulse rate – it is basically a reaction to failure triggered by the implication of low ability. What is the basis for this sweeping claim? The answer comes in three parts.

First, consider the *emotional* component of anxiety. When viewed as a feeling, anxiety is best thought of as an *ability-linked* reaction to failure. Recall the series of role-playing studies in which college students estimated levels of shame under various conditions of failure that included the presence and absence of excuses (chapter 4). In one of those studies students also estimated the degree of anxiety (emotional upset) they would probably experience (Covington et al., 1980). Like shame, emotional tension was also greatest after students imagined themselves having studied hard and failing anyway, the very condition that casts the gravest doubts on one's ability. Also, like shame, tension diminished whenever ability-protecting excuses were available. These same relationships were also found in actual classroom settings where failure was real, not contrived (Covington & Omelich, 1981). We conclude that emotional tension follows from failure, and the degree of emotional upset experienced depends on the extent to which failure implies low ability.

Second, consider the *cognitive* component of anxiety. Here, too, the evidence supports an interpretation of anxiety as a reaction to implied low ability. For one thing, those worries that have proven most disruptive to learning and performance typically concern fears about public disclosure of incompetency (Carver & Scheier, 1988; Helmke, 1988; Salamé, 1984). For another thing, several studies designed to establish cause-and-effect relationships support the idea that decreases in self-perceived ability precede the occurrence of test anxiety in school and are causal for its development (Hodapp, 1989; Jerusalem, 1985).

Third, there is a growing suspicion that the power of many test-anxiety measures to predict school performance depends on a self-perception-of-ability component. For example, Nicholls (1976b) divided the items from the *Test Anxiety Scale for Children* (TASC) (Sarason, Lighthall, Davidson, Waite, & Ruebush, 1960) into two groups. One set of items reflected self-perceived ability and the other reflected emotional arousal. The perceived-ability subscale was the better predictor of those behaviors originally taken as evidence for the validity of the TASC as a measure of anxiety, such as the negative attributional patterns of failure-prone children. Nicholls concluded that self-concept of ability is likely the more important organizing construct, whereas emotional upset is but one of a number of possible results of perceiving oneself as incompetent. Similar conclusions have been reached by other investigators (Dunn, 1964, 1965; Feld & Lewis, 1969; Morris, Davis, & Hutchings, 1981).

Other researchers led by Knut Hagtvet (1974, 1980, 1983a, 1985) have also explored the internal structure of various test-anxiety measures. These measures appear to assess a general factor that reflects a negative sensitivity to being evaluated – a fear-of-failure owing to insufficient ability (Schmalt, 1982) – as well as several other more specific factors that Hagtvet (1983b) labels as worry and emotionality. Not only do these findings underscore the central role played by ability perceptions in anxiety, but they also link two otherwise separate and historically distinct research traditions: arousal theory associated with Atkinson's fear-of-failure construct, and interference (cognitive) interpretations.

Taken together, all these converging lines of evidence forge a powerful argument for viewing anxiety in its many forms as a manifestation of perceived incompetency. But if the arousal (motivation), skill deficit, and cognitive interference traditions represent different aspects of the same overarching self-worth process, how more precisely do these disparate elements combine in a dynamic whole, as individual pieces of a larger mosaic? And, what relevance might such an assemblage have for understanding the achievement process in classrooms and for educational change? The answers cannot be found solely in the results of laboratory-based, experimental studies conducted under contrived circumstances. Nor can we rely only on isolated correlational studies that establish simple associations between variables, taken two at a time. As important as such procedures are for theory building, in the last analysis they provide only a limited glimpse of the larger perspective we seek. Rather, we must consider the interactions among a number of factors operat-

Figure 5.1. An interaction model of achievement anxiety

ing simultaneously as they jointly influence school achievement for the same persons and over extended periods.

A proposed model

Such an understanding requires a model or blueprint for how such interactions occur. One organizing model is presented in Figure 5.1 (Covington, 1985d). It portrays several sequential steps involved in the typical study–test cycle as it unfolds over time. First comes the motivational or arousal (drive) component of anxiety represented by Atkinson's need achievement construct. Whether individuals are disposed to approach success or to avoid failure will largely determine if in the *test appraisal* stage they judge the upcoming test to be a challenge or a threat. In the *test preparation* stage students begin studying while harboring various feelings, expectancies, and thoughts regarding the futility or wisdom of their study. Students threatened by failure may indulge in defensive behaviors such as irrational goal setting or procrastination that will further erode their study effectiveness. This stage is a major focus of self-worth theory and of the skill deficit view of anxiety. Finally, in the *test-taking* stage students attempt to retrieve what they have learned, sometimes in the face of great tension, worry, and physical turmoil. This stage is the focus of retrieval deficit theories of anxiety.

The free-running cycle portrayed in Figure 5.1 can vary in duration from only a few hours, at the briefest, to weeks or even months. Moreover, the entire sequence is recursive. It repeats itself every time there is a test or evaluation. More specifically, the meaning one attributes to feedback on a first test – either success or failure – largely dictates how well one will perform on the next test (Covington & Omelich, 1990). For example, if an initial failure is attributed to low ability, then shame results, an emotion that in turn disrupts study the second time around. It is this feedback, or test reaction stage (not shown in Figure 5.1), that occupies the attention of attribution theorists.

In recent years researchers from the United States and Europe have begun to trace out and verify the kinds of dynamics portrayed in Figure 5.1 (e.g., Covington, Omelich, & Schwarzer, 1986; Folkman & Lazarus, 1985; Hagtvet & Min, 1990; Helmke, 1987; Hodapp, 1989; Jerusalem, Liepmann, & Herrmann, 1985; Meece et al., 1990). These studies share a common methodology called multivariate prediction analysis. Simply put, researchers predict scores on an achievement test using many (multiple) kinds of information gathered from students at each stage of the model. Typically students are asked to rate how much anxiety (tension) they felt during a test, indicate how often various kinds of thoughts intruded on their study, and attribute reasons to their successes and failures. This approach has several important features. First, because data is gathered for the same students over time, a longitudinal perspective is created. Second, researchers can establish the relative importance of various factors as predictors of test performance, say, worries versus emotions, at any point in the cycle. Third, under special circumstances the use of multiple-prediction models allows researchers to assume causality. For example, the arrows in Figure 5.1 imply that one event, say, a fear-evoking thought arising in the appraisal stage, can disrupt study in the preparation stage (i.e., fear → inadequate study). Because it seems natural to speak of such causal relationships as pathways of influence, we will use the generic term *path analysis* to describe these multiple-prediction techniques (Anderson & Evans, 1974; Pedhazur, 1982).

What, then, are the findings that emerge from these various studies? Do the cognitive, motivational, and emotional dimensions of anxiety combine in meaningful and lawful ways to influence real-life achievement? And what are the respective roles of skill deficit and retrieval deficit theories in this process? We will address these questions with reference to a single multivariate study involving some 400 Berkeley undergraduates enrolled in an introductory psychology course who were tracked over several successive midterm examinations (Covington & Omelich, 1988a).

JOHN, THE FAILURE AVOIDER

In order to simplify this complex study the results will be presented through the eyes (and mind) of John, our eager young college freshman. John's misadventures are presented in path-analytic terms in Figure 5.2. Only the strongest predictors of test performance are presented. The arrows imply cause and effect, and the direction of influence.

In the summer following high school graduation, John decided to become a physician, a career choice that pleased his parents and impressed his friends. Unfortunately, John had not taken the advanced high school courses needed to prepare him for the rigors of the premed major. As a result, he started his college course work in chemistry, physics, and biology at a disadvantage. Also, just to complicate things, John was in the habit of procrastinating. Recall that in high school John put off whatever he could until the last moment and then relied on his superior intellect to save him. But because studying science is typically a cumulative affair, not something to be put off, John began to do poorly for the first time in his academic career. But he did not give up. John's pride was now on the line; he would still show everyone that he could succeed. He vowed to work twice as hard next semester. Besides, even if he should fail, it is better, he reasoned – in the style of failure avoidance – to flunk premed than a less prestigious major!

Previous research makes clear that failure-avoiding students, like John, describe themselves as doubting their ability (Laux & Glanzmann, 1987; Sal-

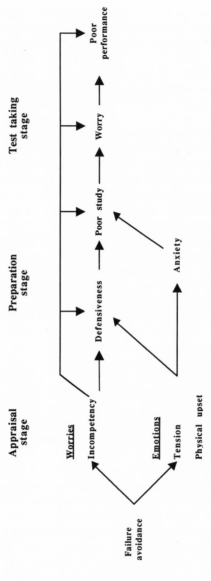

Figure 5.2. Achievement dynamics: Interaction of motives, thoughts, and emotions over time

amé, 1984; Schmalt, 1982), as feeling inadequately prepared (Covington & Omelich, 1988b), and as being riddled with anxiety (Carver & Scheirer, 1988; Hagtvet, 1984). This dismal picture was confirmed in every detail by the Berkeley data. Failure avoiders enter the achievement arena reluctantly, largely out of necessity – emotionally aroused, vigilant, and, above all, preoccupied with fearsome thoughts. Now, as John stands on the brink of his next college ordeal – the beginning psychology course – he, too, shares this legacy.

Appraisal stage. As John listens to the instructor explain the course require-ments, a sense of dread washes over him. These formless emotions are given specific meaning by exaggerated worries (cognitions) that he will not do well enough to stay in school, that he will not have enough time to study, but mostly that he will be found out as incompetent. Try as he might to rid himself of these worries, John remains preoccupied.

Preparation stage. The test is the day after tomorrow. Time to start studying! But John's study will prove largely ineffective, not only because time is so short, but also for the several reasons portrayed in Figure 5.2. John's plight recalls to mind the anonymous definition of *worry:* ineffectual thought revolv-ing around a pivot of fear. For John the pivot point is recurring self-doubts of ability that, for one thing, break his concentration (incompetency → poor study). Whenever he fails to grasp a point quickly, John wonders if others might not be right about him: Perhaps he isn't smart enough to become a physician. For another thing, these mounting self-doubts of ability also trigger a host of defensive thoughts – all of which, according to the Berkeley data, act to disrupt John's study even further (incompetency → defensiveness → poor study). John indulges in blame projection ("If I had a better teacher, I might do better.") and in wishful thinking ("I wish the test would somehow go away."). John also experiences considerable relief by minimizing the im-portance of the course ("This course is less important than I originally thought."). And, finally, just to close the ring of fear, feelings of tension and occasional nausea further disrupt John's attempts to concentrate (emotions → poor study).

Not surprisingly, John never really settles into study; he quits as soon as he starts, but promises himself to begin again when he feels better. Yet some-how he never makes it back to the study cubicle until the very last moment. In the meantime, John busies himself idly, drifting from one activity to an-other – listening to records, watching daytime TV, and once to the secret delight of his roommates, talking *them* out of studying in order to play cards.

John's struggle in the recesses of the library is compounded by not know-ing how best to study. The Berkeley data suggests that good study habits serve to offset disruptive worries about one's ability. Unfortunately, for John and others like him, there is no relief from this quarter. John is completely at the mercy of his fears and self-doubts. Here, then, is clear evidence for a *skill deficit* interpretation of anxiety. In short, John approaches the test wholly unprepared.

Test-taking stage. Now as John sits in the examination room nervously awaiting the test, he is assaulted by another wave of worry. During the test itself he continually glances around wondering why so many students are leaving early

– perhaps the test is easier than he thinks. He really must be dumb! These worries interfere with John's ability to recall whatever he did learn or thought he had learned (worry → poor performance). John finds himself unable to think, forgetting the most basic facts, and sometimes not even understanding the questions. In the words of William Manchester (1983), it is as if ". . . the mind seems fathoms down, like some poor land creature entangled in the weeds of the sea" (p. 150). Here also is evidence for a *retrieval deficit* view of anxiety.

Incidentally, we can now see why researchers have typically found that the relationship between emotionality (tension) and performance is weaker than the linkage between cognitive worry and performance. According to Figure 5.2, worries during test taking, especially those associated with incompetency, act *directly* to interfere with performance (test-taking worry → poor performance). By contrast, although emotional arousal also contributes to poor performance, it does so only *indirectly* through a circuitous route by first interfering with the quality of study (anxiety → poor study → poor performance). The preeminence of cognitions over emotions at this stage in the model is consistent with other similar multivariate studies (Corcoran, Mac-Dougall, & Scarbrough, 1985; Everson, Millsap, & Browne, 1989; Hodapp, 1989; Hodapp & Henneberger, 1983), including one in mathematics achievement among middle school children from Norway (Hagtvet, 1984).

By viewing Figure 5.2 as a whole, we can also see just how invasive the effects of low-ability perceptions are as they reverberate throughout the entire model. First, John's initial self-doubts of ability set up a cascade of defensive thoughts that eventually disrupted his study weeks later; second, these same self-doubts triggered delayed worry reactions during test taking; and, third, in addition to everything else, these self-doubts also exerted a direct, forward-reaching and chilling effect on performance itself (incompetency → performance). The *direct* nature of this latter linkage is important. Being direct means that self-doubts of ability bypass all other mediators and influence performance in an undiminished way. Not only is this a strong influence – so strong in fact that among failure-avoiding students self-doubt was the single most important contributor to poor performance – but whenever self-doubts are aroused they are invariably deadly, no matter what kinds of compensatory mechanisms are available.

Overall, John's plight can be summarized quite simply: He is doubly handicapped. Like other failure-avoiders, John learned less to begin with due to a massive skill deficit rendered more deadly by defensive posturing. Then what little he did learn was recalled later only imperfectly (retrieval deficit) because of intrusive worry during testing.

The two other types of failure-prone students, overstrivers and failure accepters, present intriguing variations on this pattern, as revealed in the Berkeley study.

OVERSTRIVERS

As we know, overstrivers represent a unique combination of approach and avoidance tendencies. On the avoidance side, overstrivers experienced great emotional tension in the appraisal stage, equal to that of failure avoiders. But for overstrivers, the direction of the causal impact of tension on study preparation was reversed. Instead of impairing study, as it did for failure avoiders, the presence of emotional tension actually mobilized the enormous capacity of overstrivers for study, which typically took the form of slavish overpreparation (arousal → intense study). There is no evidence here of a skill deficit and certainly no lack of involvement. Overstrivers begin work immediately after assignments are made and continue studying right down to the wire. In fact, overstrivers spent more time studying than did even success-oriented students (Covington & Omelich, 1988a, 1991).

Unfortunately for overstrivers, however, learning and performance are not the same thing. Although anxiety may arouse their considerable intellectual gifts for learning, eventually they pay a heavy price. As tension mounted during the test-taking session, overstrivers suffered a massive failure to recall what they learned originally. In fact, the Berkeley data indicate that the presence of worry cognitions at this point was far more devastating to overstrivers than for either failure avoiders or failure accepters. Worry about falling short of perfection could not have surfaced at a worse moment. There can be no greater frustration for students than to know they know something but can't remember it until it is too late. The student who justifiably laments, "But I knew it cold before the exam," is most likely an overstriver (Covington & Omelich, 1987a).

FAILURE-ACCEPTING STUDENTS
Eventually, many students are forced to accept the implications of repeated failure. These failure-accepting students are likely to withdraw from academic competition and simply give up. As a consequence, they prepare for tests in only the most marginal ways. In the Berkeley study, failure accepters spent less time studying than any other group, even failure avoiders. This suggests that the immediate cause of poor performance is inadequate preparation, not disruptive emotions, because failure accepters also reported relatively low levels of tension and worry during test taking (Covington & Omelich, 1988a). In fact, inadequate emotions seem to be a general pattern. Failure accepters express neither much pride in success nor much shame in failure (Covington & Omelich, 1985). From all this, we deduce that for failure accepters the main cause of poor performance is inadequate study, which reflects a sense of resignation and perhaps heralds the advent of learned helplessness.

Implications

The findings of the Berkeley study and other similar multivariate research hold several broad implications for understanding the nature of the achievement process and of anxiety in particular:

1. Our assumption about the complex nature of anxiety appears justified. Anxiety is not a single, unified reaction to perceived threat. Rather it is more properly viewed as a clustering of factors – cognitions, self-protective mech-

anisms, and emotions – whose relationships to one another and to test performance change as students progress from one stage of the achievement cycle to the next. Moreover, these linkages differ from one student to another.

This interactive analysis places both the skill deficit and retrieval deficit theories of anxiety in a larger dynamic context, to the advantage of both positions. First, the addition of a self-worth assumption explains an otherwise potential embarrassment for the skill deficit theory. If this theory is correct, then adequately prepared students should have little to be anxious about. Yet we know that some students are anxious despite the fact that they possess good study strategies and typically perform quite well (Naveh-Benjamin, 1985; Naveh-Benjamin, McKeachie, & Lin, 1987; Paulman & Kennelly, 1984). From a self-worth perspective there is no mystery here. These individuals are *overstrivers*. Overstrivers know how to get good grades, but this knowledge does little to forestall their fears. For overstrivers the capacity to do well intensifies their anxiety rather than reducing it because they have tied their worth to the nearly impossible dream of academic perfection.

Second, the skill deficit and retrieval deficit theories have sometimes been treated as incompatible propositions (e.g., Kirkland & Hollandsworth, 1980), that is, to the extent one position is proven correct the other must be false. Now we know better. Both kinds of deficits can be operating in tandem for the same individual in the case of failure avoiders, like John. Also, each deficit may operate singly depending on whether the individual is an overstriver (retrieval deficit) or a failure accepter (skill deficit).

Clearly, then, from the standpoint of helping students, no single intervention will be equally effective for all. Different types of students suffer different deficits and require different kinds of treatment, a point neatly demonstrated by Moshe Naveh-Benjamin (1985). He administered relaxation therapy to one group of highly anxious students with good study strategies, akin to overstrivers. Another group of equally anxious students who possessed *poor* study habits was instructed in how to improve their organizing skills. These same treatments were also administered to two other identical groups, but in the reverse order to provide a control comparison. The benefits of therapy were minimal for these latter two groups because the intervention did not compensate them for their particular weaknesses. But when the match was proper, improvements occurred. Relaxation training reduced anxiety during test taking for those students who already possessed good study habits and, conversely, skill training was effective in reducing anxiety for those students with initially poor study habits.

2. We have also learned something about the relative roles of cognitions and emotions as they enter into the achievement process. The findings from the Berkeley study as well as those from a number of similar multivariate investigations implicate cognitive worry, especially fears of incompetency, as the primary cause of disruption throughout the entire study–test cycle. Although feelings of tension are also present, emotionality per se is at best a secondary source of disruption. However, this does not mean that emotions play no role in the achievement process. Had John's story begun at the end of the first study–test cycle when he received failure feedback, we would have

found that his emotional reactions (largely shame) lead the way to a new round of defensive posturing (Covington & Omelich, 1990). There is an important lesson here. Whether cognitions appear ascendant over emotions as primary causal agents, or vice versa, depends to a great extent on where in the achievement cycle researchers choose to start and end their investigations.

3. We also have a better understanding of the unique role played by trait-like antecedents. Atkinson's motives to approach success and to avoid failure represent latent dispositions that lie dormant until circumstances trigger a flood of thoughts, actions, and feelings that in turn control the quality of achievement. Thus achievement motivation itself is not the critical event, but rather the instigator of critical events. This does not mean that traitlike factors are insignificant. Recall our earlier analogy. We would not dismiss as unimportant the nudge that sends the boulder crashing down the hill simply because subsequent events proved so much more arresting. The Berkeley study confirms this bit of wisdom and places in perspective the criticism that need achievement measures are of dubious value, because by themselves they do a relatively poor job of predicting achievement outcomes. We now see this is no criticism at all. Rather, this fact should be taken as a reminder that the influence of motives on final achievement is largely indirect and must be traced through a number of intervening pathways.

4. Finally, we can now also appreciate why investigators have often found little relationship between knowledge of proper study skills and academic performance (e.g., Schuman, Walsh, Olson, & Etheridge, 1985). Even when students know in theory how best to study, they cannot always take advantage of their understanding. If one is driven to learn out of fear, then the potential benefits of strategy knowledge may be neutralized by intrusive worry. Even when students do study efficiently and perform well, they still may not be able to avoid feelings of self-doubt. This predicament describes the over-striver. Here superior study skills simply reinforce a maladaptive achievement strategy: avoiding failure by succeeding. The possession of good study strategies is an important source of compensation for perceptions of low ability, but only if students can employ these skills in task-oriented, nonthreatening circumstances.

Reducing anxiety

Anxiety is a thin stream of fear trickling through the mind. If encouraged, it cuts a channel into which all other thoughts are drained.
ARTHUR SOMERS ROCHE

Therapeutic intervention

The most frequent attempts to reduce achievement anxiety involve various forms of therapeutic intervention that can be described in terms of an emotion-cognitive continuum (Spielberger & Vagg, 1987).

EMOTIONAL-ORIENTED THERAPIES
Consider the emotion end of the continuum where interventions are intended to reduce excessive stress and tension. Chief among these therapies are *relax-*

Table 5.1. *Sample hierarchy of anxiety-producing scenes for systematic desensitization*

Least anxiety producing

1. Noticing a newspaper advertisement for a computer.
2. Looking through a college catalog at the computer courses offered.
3. Hearing the beeping noises the computer at home makes when the children are playing.
4. Sitting in a computer class the first day and hearing about the assignments that must be completed.
5. Having a friend help you on a computer assignment.
6. Working in the computer room on a computer assignment that is due in two weeks.
7. Having your children ask you to help them figure out a computer homework problem.
8. Getting an error message while working on a computer assignment and not knowing where the problem lies.
9. Having a class assignment due in one hour and having no one to help you if you can't figure it out.

Most anxiety producing

From M. M. Weil, L. D. Rosen, and D. C. Sears (1987). The computerphobia reduction program: Year 1. Program development and preliminary results. *Behavior Research Methods, Instruments, and Computers, 19*(2), 1980–1984. Reprinted by permission of Psychonomic Society, Inc.

ation training and *systematic desensitization* (Wolpe, 1973). Desensitization therapy involves behavior modification and is accomplished in several steps. First, the client constructs a personal *anxiety hierarchy*. This is a list of fear-evoking situations arranged from least threatening to most threatening. One example of such a hierarchy involving computer anxiety is provided in Table 5.1 (Weil, Rosen, & Sears, 1987). As a second step, the therapist directs the client to imagine the least threatening items on the list while relaxing. Over a period of time the client practices relaxing in the presence of more and more threatening images, until finally he or she feels comfortable thinking about any item on the list. This procedure involves counterconditioning, a process in which relaxation becomes conditioned to the same stimuli (or images) that earlier elicited anxiety. Fear and relaxation represent incompatible physiological states. Therefore, through repeated exposure to the same threatening idea, feelings of calm replace feelings of fear.

If excessive emotional arousal contributes to poor test performance, then relieving feelings of stress during test taking should improve performance. But we now know from the Berkeley research and other studies that such arousal has little direct causal impact on performance – with the exception of overstrivers as already noted (Naveh-Benjamin, 1985). This explains why relaxation therapy does little to improve actual test performance, even though patients do typically report feeling less tension during examinations (for reviews see Allen, 1972; Allen, Elias, & Zlotlow, 1980; Tryon, 1980).

COGNITIVE-ORIENTED THERAPIES

At the other end of the therapeutic spectrum are various forms of cognitive-oriented therapy that attempt to reduce or eliminate worries believed to interfere with test taking (Beck, 1967; Beck & Clark, 1988; Beck & Emery, 1985). Consider *rational-emotive therapy* (Ellis, 1962, 1971; Ellis & Kraus, 1977). Here the therapist attempts to discover and then refute irrational or inappropriate beliefs held by the patient that would otherwise interfere with a rational assessment at the appraisal stage. For instance, students often attach more long-term significance to a particular test than it deserves ("If I don't do well I can kiss off law school!") or exaggerate the actual physical risks of not doing well ("I will never survive this test.").

Another somewhat different cognitive approach – actually involving more direct training than therapy and focusing on the test preparation stage – is to teach students how best to study (Doctor, Aponte, Burry, & Welch, 1970; Gonzalez, 1976; Mitchell & Eng, 1972; Mitchell, Hall, & Piatkowska, 1975). Typically, study-skill training includes instruction in effective note taking and how best to organize course material. Other kinds of training programs focus on improving test-taking skills ("testwiseness"), which include coaching for the optimal use of guessing and making the best use of one's time (Kalechstein, Kalechstein, & Doctor, 1981; Sarnacki, 1979; Zeidner, Klingman, & Papko, 1987).

Given the compensatory value of good study strategies, we would expect cognitively oriented interventions to be among the most effective techniques for increasing the test scores of anxious students. This expectation has generally been confirmed, especially in the case of study-skill training (Hill & Horton, 1985; Spielberger & Vagg, 1987; Weinstein & Mayer, 1986). Not surprisingly, becoming more testwise also produces gains in performance (Bangert-Drowns, Kulik, & Kulik, 1983; Benson, Urman, & Hocevar, 1986) and has been shown to reduce irrelevant cognitions at time of testing (Kalechstein, Hocevar, & Kalechstein, 1988).

Even so, the case for therapeutic intervention of any kind, including cognitive approaches, is not all that strong. Success is not uniform and for many studies the magnitude of improved scholastic performance is marginal in practical terms, small enough in fact that sometimes the results of a number of studies must be aggregated to establish a reliable, overall trend (Hembree, 1988).

Why should these benefits be so limited? Several reasons come to mind. First, as already noted, no one intervention is equally effective for all because some anxious students suffer from retrieval deficits, others from skill deficits, and still others from both. But this point is not yet widely appreciated. Until a closer match is created between type of deficit and the therapy of choice the record of successful treatment will be spotty.

Second, for some students reducing anxiety may actually result in poorer performance. Recall that for overstrivers fear mobilizes study and ensures heightened concentration. Thus, ironically, therapy may at times be counterproductive as far as improved test performance is concerned. This is not to say that relieving anxiety per se is not desirable. Clearly it is, especially in light of the fact that overstrivers, or those individuals Eric Depreeuw (1990a, 1990b) describes as *active avoiders,* often risk their health by taking excessive amounts of tranquilizers and other drugs before exams to control stress. Similarly, if students use anxiety as an excuse for performing badly, and we know that they sometimes do – recall the academic wooden leg ploy (chapter 4) – then robbing anxiety of its self-protective role could actually compromise student resiliency in the face of stress.

Third, and finally, the dynamics portrayed in Figure 5.2 suggest that so many things can go wrong for failure-prone students at so many different points in the study–test cycle that treating only one factor – any factor, whether it be poor study habits, irrational fears, or excessive arousal – may simply not be enough to make a meaningful difference. Even when cognitive procedures are combined with other techniques, say, pairing rational-emotive therapy with desensitization training, the record of success is not much improved (Spielberger & Vagg, 1987; Vagg & Papsdorf, 1987; van der Ploeg-Stapert & van der Ploeg, 1985, 1987).

From a self-worth view, the most formidable obstacle to effective intervention is the ego-threatening situation itself. Therapeutic interventions have traditionally focused on increasing the individual's capacity to *resist* the threat of failure, not necessarily *reducing* the threat itself. From this perspective we see how the benefits of even cognitive retraining can be limited. For example, failure avoiders may learn how to study better but not profit from this knowledge because it requires effort, and trying harder in the face of potential failure can be a highly threatening proposition. As long as the fear of failure dominates as the reason for striving, the goals of anxiety reduction will not be fully realized. If anxiety is basically a reaction to the threat of feeling worthless, we must act to remove this threat. Once this is done, anxiety itself will likely diminish with or without special intervention. This is not to suggest that direct attempts to ease test anxiety are irrelevant or unnecessary, but only that by themselves they will not create a positive climate for learning. Under the circumstances learning is likely always to remain, at best, a chore.

Reducing the threat

What happens if the conditions of learning and testing are altered to reduce the threat of failure? Will anxious students now do better even without therapeutic intervention? First, what about changing the conditions of test taking?

ALTERING CONDITIONS OF TESTING
Varying item order. One of the most intriguing suggestions for optimizing test performance is to arrange items within a given test so that easier items are presented first, followed by items of increasing difficulty (Hutt, 1947; Lafitte, 1984; Rocklin & O'Donnell, 1986). As Kaplan and Sacuzzo (1982, p. 146) put it, "a few easy items may help keep test anxiety in check." Presumably by the time more difficult items are encountered, the disruptive effects of anxiety will have dissipated.

Despite the intuitive appeal of this "initial-success" theory, the evidence is mixed. Some studies support the hypothesis (e.g., Hambleton & Traub, 1974), and others do not (see Hembree for review, 1988; Kestenbaum & Weiner, 1970; Lafitte, 1984). Such inconsistencies may occur because the item order that is best for one student is not necessarily best for another. For example, Covington and Omelich (1987b) found that overstrivers benefited most from having hard items presented first, presumably because failure at a difficult task holds fewer implications for ability, thereby freeing these conflicted students to perform at their best. On the other hand, failure-avoiding students were handicapped most by this ordering. They performed far better when easy items were presented first. Success-oriented students yielded a third pattern. Not only did they perform better than any other group, but they succeeded equally well under both item orders. Apparently success-oriented individuals can accommodate a wide range of achievement conditions.

Clearly, these findings hold more theoretical than immediate, practical significance. Teachers cannot be expected routinely to prepare and administer a variety of test forms depending on the achievement history of their students, although in theory such possibilities do exist through the advent of custom testing.

Custom testing. Custom testing involves presenting examinees with a test designed to fit their particular abilities, thus allowing them to perform closer to their potential (Weiss, 1983). Test items of known difficulty are administered sequentially to an individual, usually by computer. If the examinee fails a given item, a less difficult one is selected next until, through this matching process, a set of correctly answered items is identified that provides an estimate of the upper boundaries of the individual's ability. And because the goals of diagnosis can be served just as well by emphasizing the *successful* completion of items as focusing on *failed* items, as is typical of conventional testing, the disruptive effects of anxiety may well be mitigated. Winston Churchill (1923) spoke poignantly to this issue when he wryly observed:

> These examinations were a great trial to me. The subjects which were dearest to the examiners were almost invariably those I fancied least. . . . I should have liked to be asked to say what I knew. They always tried to ask what I did not know. When I would have willingly displayed my knowledge, they sought to expose my ignorance. This sort of treatment had only one result: I did not do well in examinations. (p. 156)

A promising variation on custom testing is self-adaptive testing. Here the examinee, not the computer, chooses the next test item from several levels of difficulty. As Thomas Rocklin and Angela O'Donnell (1986) explain, "Instead of being tailored to the examinee's estimated ability level, a self-adapted test is tailored to the examinee's *self-perceived* [italics added] ability as well as to his or her current motivation and affective characteristics" (p. 315). Obviously, it is the individual who is most fully aware of these internal states. When students are free to choose, they usually start with easy items and then select increasingly more difficult ones (Kuhl & Blankenship, 1979). This behavior suggests that anxiety level may control only the difficulty level of initial item choice. Rocklin and O'Donnell (1986) tested this proposition by permitting a group of college students to select their own ability items, one after another, from different pools of difficulty. These students demonstrated higher ability scores than did other students who encountered the same kinds of items in a standard test format, and the advantage held up even for the most test-anxious students. As predicted, anxiety expressed its influence only on the initial choice of items, with high-anxious individuals choosing the easier items. But anxiety status predicted neither the rate of progression toward more difficult items nor the average difficulty level of all items chosen. In effect, anxious students eventually worked on problems that were just as difficult as those attempted by low-anxious individuals. The Rocklin and O'Donnell study suggests that the use of self-adaptive testing may reduce the disruptive effects of anxiety on performance. If so, self-adaptive testing should lead to more accurate estimates of student ability.

Untimed testing. Another approach to optimizing test conditions is found in the work of Kennedy Hill and his colleagues. Hill (1977, 1980; Hill & Wigfield, 1984) argues that time pressure is likely to accentuate the debilitating effects of anxiety and hasten the use of maladaptive strategies such as slow, overly cautious work or its opposite – reckless abandon. Although in many work situations a cautious style is desirable, even critical, it is clearly dysfunctional when the premium is on speed, as is typical of traditional testing. Likewise, a rapid, impulsive work style is also dangerous, and it is the failure-prone individual who is just as likely to turn in a fast, but inaccurate performance (Williams, 1976). Working quickly has several advantages, although doing well is not one of them. By finishing ahead of everyone else, failure-prone students can at least appear to know what they are doing, and at the same time they can escape an aversive situation sooner.

Hill and Eaton (1977) first demonstrated the influence of time pressure on the quality of test performance in the laboratory. When high-anxious students were tested under a "time pressure" condition, they made three times as many errors as did low-anxious children. However, when tested without time limits, the performance of highly test-anxious students increased dramatically, reaching essentially the same level as that enjoyed by low-anxious students. The results of this laboratory based research were so striking that Hill was encouraged to extend his investigations to actual classroom settings. The findings of a number of field studies confirmed these earlier laboratory results (see Hill & Horton, 1985; Plass & Hill, 1986). By allowing about 50% more time to take a test, the performances of high-anxious students show marked improvement.

These studies provide convincing evidence that the poor performance of test-anxious students is due at least in part to retrieval deficits and is not solely the result of inadequate study. Yet, as we concluded earlier, skill limitations are almost certainly involved as well. This latter point is well illustrated by research on the use of take-home essays as a way to alleviate achievement stress. Not only should high-anxious students be subject to fewer retrieval problems – now they have only to look up the needed information – but there is the further advantage of avoiding disruptive emotions triggered by merely being in an examination room. Unfortunately, the evidence tells a different story. Allowing high-anxious students the option of take-home exams does little to improve their performance relative to that of low-anxious students (Benjamin, McKeachie, Lin, & Holinger, 1981). These anxious students report not knowing how to organize the essay or how to decide which aspects of the assignment to emphasize, which suggests deficits in planning skills.

ENHANCING OPTIMISM AND INVOLVEMENT

So far we have considered only ways to make test taking more user friendly. But there are possibilities for improving things in the appraisal and the test preparation stages as well. As for the appraisal stage, we know that expectations of future success can be influenced positively by altering a person's mood state (Bower, 1981; Clark & Fiske, 1982; Kendall & Hollon, 1981). Practically speaking, this means directing students to attend to the positive rather than to the negative aspects of a stressful event (Lewisohn & Libet, 1972). This intriguing premise was tested by Irwin Sarason and Earl Potter (1983), who encouraged one group of Coast Guard Academy recruits to record only positive experiences (e.g., learning new things) in a daily diary during boot camp. Compared to control cadets, who either recorded negative events or kept no diaries at all, the "positive-event" group experienced greater personal satisfaction, felt less tension during this stressful period, and were less likely to resign from the academy at the end of boot camp.

As for the test preparation stage, it has been shown that when students are required to teach others, they rehearse the material in more comprehensive ways and are more intrinsically motivated to do so (Benware & Deci, 1984). This research suggests that by merely altering the set under which students study, otherwise uninspired preparation may give way to previously unused but effective strategies for study. Greater intrinsic task involvement can also be induced by simply asking students to evaluate the usefulness of the material being studied, a technique that is particularly effective for overstrivers (Olsen, 1991). Finally, it has been demonstrated that studying over several work sessions compared to studying all at one time (distributed vs. massed practice) increases the test performance of high-anxious students (Zimmer, Meinke, & Hocevar, 1989).

The techniques reviewed in this section are intriguing because they hold promise for reducing the threatening aspects of the study–test cycle itself. Hopefully, such procedures would not only lead to less biased, more accurate ways of estimating what students are learning, but would do so in ways that actually enhance the will to continue learning.

Conclusions

We have covered much ground in this chapter. First, we reviewed the vast body of literature on achievement anxiety and considered the various mechanisms by which anxiety is thought variously to arouse, facilitate, or disrupt learning.

Second, we offered a self-worth interpretation of these dynamics, arguing that anxiety for all its complex manifestations is basically a reaction to the threat of being revealed as incompetent. This perspective permitted us to create a unifying description of how emotional, motivational, and cognitive factors enter jointly into the achievement process.

Third, we assessed the literature on intervention. I am hopeful that doing this has promoted a deeper appreciation of the many difficulties involved in reducing anxiety by therapeutic means. Basically, we are left wondering: Just how effective are remedial techniques likely to be by themselves as long as competitive, ability-focused values dominate in the classroom?

A postscript provides special insight into the role of competition as an instigator of anxiety. Multivariate achievement models of the kind portrayed in Figures 5.1 and 5.2 have proven quite useful in describing the dynamics of various types of failure-prone students. Not so, however, with success-oriented students. The data generated in the Berkeley study did a relatively poor job of predicting test scores for these students. For example, even self-perceptions of ability were only marginally related to the test scores of success-oriented students. Is it possible that these individuals have moved beyond concerns about ability status and the conventional meaning of success and failure defined competitively?

Certainly the positive attributional patterns of success-oriented students suggest as much (see chapter 3). Whatever factors describe the special psychology of this group, they are not being captured by a competitive portrayal of the achievement process. In fact, what appears to distinguish success-oriented students most is their single-minded devotion to the task at hand. This involvement seems to transcend even the most blatant competitive pressures, so that these students will do relatively well in most learning environments. In this connection, we know that the performance of intrinsically motivated youngsters is neither enhanced by tangible rewards – since presumably they are already performing at their best – nor lessened when such rewards are either removed or not available (Harackiewicz & Manderlink, 1984; Harackiewicz, Abrahams, & Wageman, 1987).

This line of inquiry raises a fundamental question about the proper choice of environments for failure-prone students. Social scientists may congratulate themselves on having learned a great deal about the dynamics of failure-prone youngsters, but only because they have been studied in environments that are peculiarly hostile to their particular vulnerabilities. In effect, competitive stress has magnified failure-prone dynamics sufficiently for researchers to uncover the dangers inherent in tying one's sense of worth to outperforming others. But now we must ask: What will be the consequences for failure-prone students if they are placed in less threatening achievement contexts? We know from the evidence presented earlier that they will likely perform better. But will the goal of learning for its own sake be enhanced or, ironically, will reduced stress actually rob some students of their will to achieve? This question is especially pertinent for overstrivers, whose reasons for succeeding may actually depend on the presence of a threat to their worth.

We ask such questions not only in the interest of clarifying the basic nature of achievement motivation, but also out of a concern for the well-being of students. Although researchers are in no position to answer these questions fully at present, at least they are the right questions to ask when it comes to reshaping the educational experience of our children.

6

The competitive learning game

Learning is an exciting adventure – unless, of course, we go out of our way to make it unpleasant.
JOHN KRUMBOLTZ

What is it about school life that drives the hurtful, destructive dynamics that subvert the joy of learning and create such a profound conflict between ability and effort as sources of worth? Many answers have been offered, but none comes as close to the mark as that implied by John Krumboltz's mocking challenge (1990):

> Imagine how we would go about designing an educational program if our purpose were to make students hate to learn. [First, he suggests,] we would not involve them in establishing the purposes of their class. [Second,] we would require them to perform some impossible tasks – for example, to be perfect in everything they do. Third, when we discovered that the students were failing to master the impossible tasks, we would ridicule them and report their mistakes, failures and shortcomings to their friends and relatives. Fourth, just to pour some salt into the wounds, we would identify one individual in the class who was doing the tasks better than any of the others, and say, ''If Frank can do it, why can't you?'' This would isolate Frank and make all the other children hate him. Finally, if we should happen to catch any students helping another trying to master these impossible tasks, we would punish such cooperative behavior unmercifully, insisting that each youngster work in silent solitude separated from the support and encouragement of fellow students. (p. 10)

It is hard to improve on this formula if the purpose is to make learning unpleasant, yet ironically – and, of course, this is Krumboltz's point – these are precisely the circumstances that prevail in many schools today and help explain why children become alienated from school, hate teachers and learning, vandalize school property, and drop out as soon as they can. Basically, this recipe involves forcing children to compete with one another in isolation, and under intense, unremitting scrutiny. But no one wants to make learning unpleasant, not deliberately anyway. So why do we treat children this way? According to George Leonard (1968), a prominent education critic, it is not for the purpose of helping ''students to learn other subjects, but to teach competition itself'' (p. 129).

Is the competitive spirit of Hermes so important that we must promote it directly in schools? Certainly there can be no mistaking the unique American commitment to competition, a commitment that is summed up perfectly by

Vince Lombardi: "Winning isn't everything, it's the only thing." In later years Lombardi regretted his comment: "I wish to hell I'd never said the damn thing. I meant having a goal." Misunderstood or not, Lombardi's remark neatly illuminates the highly competitive nature of American society that is perpetuated by a powerful set of claims. First, there is the assertion that teaching competition prepares students for the rigors of economic survival in later life, and that to downplay competition in school is to prepare children for a world that does not exist. Second, there is the argument that academic competition is the most efficient – some would say even the fairest – way for society to allocate talent proportionally across the available jobs, some of which are more prestigious and more sought after than others.

These powerful arguments must be addressed and unmasked for what they are – appealing but basically misleading articles of faith – before we can take seriously the kinds of changes to be proposed in coming chapters. These two particular arguments will be rebutted in chapter 10. Meanwhile, there are several other reasons thought to favor competition that are best examined now because they concern the mission of schools more directly. First, there is the widespread belief that competition motivates students to do their best, and that for the mass of dispirited, listless students competition is the only way to ensure a minimum level of competency. The second belief is that achieving under adversity (competition) builds character and enhances a sense of self-confidence. In this chapter I will present evidence to the contrary and document the enormous costs associated with arranging schools around a competitive ethos.

The structure of learning

The literature on school achievement makes clear that different kinds of incentives call out different student behavior. Every classroom reflects some type of reward structure within which all academic work is embedded. It is this structure that conveys information to students, explicitly or implicitly, about how they are to be evaluated and what they must do if they hope to be successful (Doyle, 1983; Dreeben, 1968). Alfred Alschuler (1969, 1973) likened these dynamics to a game, albeit a serious one. For instance, in what Alschuler called failure-oriented (competitive) classrooms, the rules of the learning game require that an inadequate supply of rewards (e.g., good grades) be distributed unequally with the greatest number going to the best performers. This arrangement amounts to a zero-sum scoring system. When one student (player) wins (or makes points), other students must lose (points). This dynamic is not limited just to schools. Take musical chairs, for example, that childhood staple in which a scarcity of rewards is introduced artificially; competitors scramble after one less chair than there are players in each round. Eventually, there is only one winner and the rest are losers, all of whom have been standing around for varying amounts of time excluded from play (Kohn, 1986). Musical chairs may be harmless enough when played sparingly, once or twice a year, and then only as a temporary diversion until the birthday candles are lit. But to use such zero-sum scoring as a way to encourage school learning, incessantly, for years, and always with publicly acknowledged outcomes is neither harmless nor particularly effective.

The formal properties of the zero-sum game are easily grasped, but what is exceedingly difficult to appreciate is the depth of turmoil and antagonism that can result. In fact, these feelings are almost impossible to comprehend unless one experiences a bitter foretaste firsthand, say, by playing games designed to simulate these inequities. In one such simulation, STARPOWER (Shirts, 1969), players create a multitiered society built up through the distribution of wealth in the form of poker chips. In the first round, winners and losers are arbitrarily determined by randomly distributing chips unequally among the players. Once established, the group with the most wealth has the power to make the rules for the remainder of the game, which includes the possibility of redistributing the wealth on each round in a more equitable fashion. However, almost invariably those in power attempt to maintain their superior position. And what seems fair to the powerful is unlikely to seem fair to those out of power. Even when the elite are willing to admit that their rules are biased, they cannot understand why the other players are so upset.

What is particularly chilling is the behavior of sophisticated adult players who can freely articulate exactly why they feel so angry and dispossessed; they understand fully that it is only a game and that they are being manipulated by its rules, yet they cannot escape their feelings. As things heat up, the powerful justify their actions by appealing to an implied superiority, something akin to the divine right of kings, while the powerless often acquiesce and even blame themselves for their predicament – all in the full knowledge of course that everyone owes their status initially to luck alone. What chance then do schoolchildren have who often play under similar rules, but in their turn assume that this is the way things are supposed to be?

Many parallels have been drawn between such inequities in school and society generally. In his controversial book, *Points of Rebellion* (1970), William O. Douglas warns that disadvantaged groups (including our youth) who feel victimized by an unresponsive society may rebel unless their needs are considered. Likewise, in the book *Student as Nigger*, Jerry Farber (1969) argues that young people are treated like slaves in schools – they work too hard for too few unfairly distributed rewards and are powerless to change the system. Novelist Mark Childress (1990) puts it this way: ''For a while, we thought we were all just alike. Then we began to compete among ourselves to see who could be the best slave. . . . They taught us about slavery, as if it happened only in the past'' (p. 25).

Although comparing schools to slavery is clearly farfetched, the parallel concerning dehumanization is not entirely fanciful, as can be judged by experimental attempts to reproduce various features of the competitive power game. Consider the research of Linden Nelson and Spencer Kagan (1972) who awarded young students prizes (attractive toys) if they cooperated in their work on a problem-solving game. The children did in fact cooperate as long as everyone received a reward. However, when fewer rewards were provided than players, the children became antagonistic. In fact, some even forfeited their own chances to win by sabotaging the game in order to deprive others! This research tracks in microcosm a vicious cycle: Inadequate rewards create competition that in turn discourages cooperation, and competitive pressure further diminishes the likelihood of rewards. Moreover, as scarcity increases, the more important these fewer rewards become as evidence of ability. Incidentally, of all the groups investigated by Nelson and Kagan, the most antagonistic were middle-class whites. Mexican-American youngsters from low-income families were far less competitive (Kagan, 1977; Kagan & Knight, 1981; Knight & Kagan, 1977; McClintock, 1974), but not necessarily because of their ethnic background. Middle-income Mexican-American youngsters also proved to be highly competitive, suggesting that competition is mainly a characteristic of the middle classes.

Student versus student

Aggression and resentment toward one another is the inevitable result of the kinds of competitive dynamics set in motion experimentally by Nelson and Kagan. These destructive impulses can take many forms, not all of which are immediately obvious or always directly related to academic achievement. In its milder forms, competitiveness involves outdoing others for the attention of the teacher, a game that teachers themselves often initiate unwittingly and promote to their own advantage. Consider the example of an observer who enters a fifth-grade classroom as reported by Jules Henry (1957):

> TEACHER: "Which one of you nice polite boys would like to take [observer's] coat and hang it up?"
>
> (Observer notes: From the waving hands it seemed that all would like to claim the title.)
>
> Teacher chooses one child . . . who takes observer's coat. . . .
>
> TEACHER: "Now children, who will tell [observer] what we have been doing?" Usual forest of hands . . . and a girl is chosen to tell. . . .
>
> Teacher conducted the arithmetic lesson mostly by asking, "Who would like to tell . . . the answer to the next problem?"
>
> This question was usually followed by the appearance of a large and *agitated* forest of hands; apparently *much competition* to answer. (pp. 122–123)

Here learning has been subverted for the purpose of gaining teacher recognition, a scramble set in motion by the teacher herself who in this instance hopes to create the appearance that her students are paying attention.

A less subtle, if not outright hostile, expression of competitiveness involves spying and tattling. For example, if Susan can get Heather into trouble, even though the transgression is minor and the purpose of the accusation transparent – "It hurts me to say this, but I saw Heather talking" – then Heather's status as a rival will be diminished. Also there is the merciless laughter at someone else's mistakes and those delicious opportunities to provide answers for other children who cannot get the problem right themselves.

Boris had trouble reducing 12/16 to lowest terms, and could get only as far as 6/8. . . . Much heaving up and down from the other children, all frantic to correct him. Boris pretty unhappy. Teacher, patient, quiet, ignoring others, and concentrating with look and voice on Boris. . . . After a minute or two she becomes more urgent. No response from Boris. She then turns to the class and says, ''Well, who can tell Boris what the number is?'' (Henry, 1957, p. 123)

Students versus teacher

In the competitive learning game teachers become the gatekeepers of success and approval. This puts a powerful weapon in their hands. Sometimes teachers use the dynamics of scarcity to ensure good behavior or at least to create the impression that classroom activities are organized around some kind of plan. Other times teachers may use competition to divide and then subdue students, a strategy born of the fear, often justified, that students will otherwise unite against them in open revolt and rebellion. It is easy for teachers to imagine that their particular students cannot be controlled and that they will always remain wild and undisciplined. Such fears hang over many ghetto schools like a shroud.

For some children, especially the young, the compliant, and the middle class, the use of competition by teachers for self-protection works well most of the time. Many of these students react docilely, giving teachers what they want for fear of offending them. Unfortunately, this scarcity of rewards also discourages intellectual risk taking by placing a premium on conformity and submissiveness. In its more extreme manifestations, submissiveness sets the stage for what Henry (1957) calls the ''witch-hunt syndrome'' – a devastating confection of student docility, boredom, feelings of vulnerability, and fear of punishment. Witch hunts allow teachers to mobilize and direct student anger inward toward themselves and each other in a perpetual search for wrongdoers. A critical part of this process, in fact, the culminating act, involves the confession by those who would violate the rules, however minor the infraction – whispering in line and the like. In this drama of total submission to teacher authority, the teacher decides what type of confession he or she wishes to hear and what the resolution should be. Children eagerly throw themselves into the role of both the hunter and the hunted in an effort to placate the teacher: First come the hunters, resolute in their defense of the realm, followed by the hunted with their confessions of weakness and statements of contrition.

The dynamics just described, including docility and submissiveness, are mostly found in white middle-class schools where respect for authority is the norm and children are well versed in the rigors, the techniques, and the importance of deciding who are the winners and losers. On the other hand, these controlling tactics are less effective among minority students, especially blacks and Hispanics, who, being more cooperative, are likely to band together to make life miserable for the teacher (Erickson & Mohatt, 1982; Foster, 1974; Philips, 1972).

Alschuler (1973; also see Alschuler & Shea, 1974) has identified some of the basic tactics involved in a game in which teachers are pitted against students.

For teachers:

1. *Waits, stares* (stops lesson)
2. *Tunnel vision:* ignores disruption or does not see it
3. *Making rules:* ordering student to "stop"
4. *Sarcasm, belittling:* "Do you think you can remember if I tell you a fifth time?"
5. *Minilecture on good and bad behavior and its consequences:* "She wouldn't be bothering you if you did not turn around."

For students:

1. *Getting up:* student gets up to sharpen pencil, . . . to throw something in wastebasket, . . . to get paper from desk . . .
2. *Noise making* (individual): tapping foot, drumming desk, playing imaginary harmonica, . . . banging teeth with pencil . . .
3. *Solitary escape:* daydreaming, combing hair, pretending to do work, sleeping
4. *Forgetting or not having materials:* "My mother tore it up by mistake."

Obviously students lose out because they fail to learn. The teacher is savaged, too, by having to spend an average of some 22,000 minutes per year (Alschuler's estimate) in reproaching, rebuking, nagging, and otherwise punishing students.

Even at the best of times, the relationship between students and teacher is remarkable for its complexity and potential dangers. As already noted, many students, especially white middle-class pupils, value ability and prefer to be seen as succeeding by reason of brilliance. But in a climate of scarcity, few students are consistent winners. And at the worst of times, teachers face sullen, suspicious groups of students – an "absent audience," as Herbert Kohl (1967) describes them – or children who chatter away, oblivious to the pleas of the teacher, all the result of a breakdown in the teacher–student relationship.

Scarcity of rewards

The game is on again. . . . The winner takes it all. The loser has to fall.
ABBA

What is it about the competitive learning game that sets up these conflicts? Basically it is a *scarcity* of rewards such as approval, recognition, and personal satisfaction caused by the fact that in competitive climates those students who perform best are rewarded most. In fact, ironically enough, it is this scarcity, the very factor thought by many to arouse student effort, that actually subverts it.

The devastating consequences of this competitive mentality have been demonstrated in a series of experimental laboratory studies conducted by Carole and Russell Ames (for a review, see Ames & Ames, 1984). These investigators observed elementary school students working in pairs on a common task (typically solving puzzles) under either a competitive condition (e.g.,

"The one who solves the most puzzles will be the winner.") or a condition of individual goal setting (e.g., "Solve as many puzzles as you can."). Under both conditions one student in each pair solved most of the puzzles (success) and the other solved only a few (failure). This success–failure manipulation was accomplished by assigning students to work on puzzles that unbeknownst to them were either easily solvable or completely unsolvable.

When conditions of scarcity prevailed, failure was more likely to be interpreted as a matter of personal incompetency (Ames, 1978, 1984; Ames, Ames, & Felker, 1977), whereas success was often seen as the result of chance or good fortune (Stephan, Kennedy, & Aronson, 1977). Scarcity also elicited different reactions to success and failure. When competing subjects succeeded, they were more likely to perceive themselves as smarter than their companion (adversary). As a result, the winners tended to engage in more self-praise at the expense of their failing competitor, who was seen as less deserving (Ames, Ames, & Felker, 1977; Ames & Felker, 1979). As for the losers, failure created self-loathing, especially among those students who were high in self-perceived ability (Ames, 1978). This suggests that under competitive goals, individuals are likely to continue striving only for as long as they remain successful. No one wants to continue if the result is shame and self-recrimination.

Finally, in one additional study Ames and Ames (1981) incorporated a special feature not found in their other work. Prior to assigning their young subjects to either competitive or individual goal-setting conditions, they administered an initial set of puzzles without stating a specific purpose. By design, half of the subjects were made to fail this initial task while the other half succeeded. This preliminary success–failure manipulation provided all subjects with a powerful context within which to interpret the meaning of their subsequent performances. Interestingly, those students who were later placed in the competitive condition tended to ignore their past record when vying with fellow students. For example, a prior record of success enjoyed by half of the competitive subjects did little to reassure them when they later lost. Nor, conversely, did winning over another person offset a prior history of failure. At first glance this latter finding may appear surprising. One might expect that a competitive win would compensate for previous failures by repairing an earlier sense of injured pride. Actually, this is unlikely under a goal (competition) that does little to encourage a belief in personal control even when one succeeds. Recall that competitive successes are likely to be interpreted as a matter of luck.

So it appears that competition drastically narrows the information base that individuals use in interpreting the meaning of their current successes and failures. Past memories have little standing. In competition there is only winning and losing, and only the results of the current contest appear to count.

School as an ability game

First and foremost, scarcity turns learning into an ability game. The fewer the rewards available, the more ability becomes a factor in attaining them. The fewer the rewards, the more valued they become, too, because if only a few can win, then success becomes all the more convincing as evidence of high ability; conversely, if many succeed, then, attributionally speaking, the task will be considered a relatively easy one, certainly not requiring any great talent. If success becomes inflated in its importance, the meaning of failure likewise becomes distorted. Not surprisingly, most students are unable to explain how failure might be useful in the process of learning (Covington & Beery, 1976). Children, it seems, rarely ascribe to Alexander Pope's observation that being wrong is but another way of saying that the individual is wiser today than yesterday.

This reluctance to appreciate mistakes goes deeper than simply not understanding that failure is an important part of all problem solving. In the minds of children, seeking help tacitly implies incompetence (Graham & Barker, 1990; Karabenick & Knapp, 1988). These youngsters have confused ignorance – for which help seeking is but one cure – with stupidity, with the likelihood that they will remain both ignorant *and* stupid. Interestingly, help seeking as a cue for low ability seems especially strong when children are working for extrinsic payoffs like praise or a grade compared to those times when they are pursuing some independent line of inquiry for no other reason than to satisfy their curiosity (Newman, 1990; Newman & Goldin, 1990; Nelson-Le Gall, 1985).

UNIDIMENSIONAL CLASSROOMS
All these sources of distortion are present in those classrooms defined by Susan Rosenholtz and her colleagues as *unidimensional* (Rosenholtz & Rosenholtz, 1981; Rosenholtz & Simpson, 1984a, 1984b). Unidimensional classrooms are those in which students perceive themselves as segregated mainly by ability, with a specific emphasis on *verbal* ability as the single most important dimension compared to visual, artistic, or spatial ability. Such a narrow focus can lead to a great inequity in feelings of worth beginning in the earliest grades. Susan Harter, a psychologist who studies social development in children, estimates that "by the second or third grade children know precisely where they stand on the 'smart' or 'dumb' continuum, and since most children at this age want to succeed in school, this knowledge profoundly affects their self-esteem" (quoted in Tobias, 1989, p. 57).

Rosenholtz argues that one of the main reasons for the drift toward unidimensional dynamics is the seemingly innocuous practice of assigning a single task to all students or assigning students in the same class to different reading and math groups based on ability. Such within-class grouping invites students to think of ability in narrow, fixed terms and encourages the view that ability or a lack of ability is the dominant cause of success or failure, respectively (Pepitone, 1972; Rosenholz & Wilson, 1980; Weinstein, 1981). By contrast, when students work individually on different tasks or participate in groups not defined by ability, then perceptions of ability become less salient to achievement. Another aspect of unidimensional dynamics involves the perceived boundary between academic and nonacademic work. Whenever this line becomes sharply contrasted and what counts as academic assignments narrows to only a few activities, then the potential for ability stratification increases. On the other hand, if students have some choice over what they learn, and when and how they learn it, the distinction between academic and nonacademic work will likely blur.

Ability stratification also controls the quality of classroom social relationships. Given its valued status, ability commands power and prestige far beyond academic matters (Botkin & Weinstein, 1987). For instance, good readers tend to be accorded positions of leadership in group decision making even when the problems under discussion are unrelated to reading (Morris, 1977; Stulac, 1975). As a result, many students experience feelings of powerlessness and isolation, and those who suffer from a low self-concept of ability are likely to rate themselves as lazy and mean, basically a moralistic self-censoring reaction to school (Simpson, 1981).

Another form of grouping – ability tracking – involves assigning students to whole classrooms on the basis of ability or achievement scores. For example, an elementary school might have a high fifth grade, an average fifth grade, and a low fifth grade, and at the high school level students might be tracked into either vocational, general, or college preparatory courses. Although this is the most frequent kind of grouping in American schools – by one estimate 25% of all first-grade classrooms are tracked – there is no evidence that doing so accelerates student achievement compared to what one would expect from students in mixed-ability classrooms (for reviews, see Esposito, 1973; Gamoran & Berends, 1987; Oakes, 1987; Slavin, 1987a). If anything, ability tracking actually seems to accentuate initial differences among students. Those students placed in the top tracks excel, partly because better teachers are attracted to more able students (Davis, 1986; Finley, 1984; Ball, 1981), while lower track students fall progressively behind (Calfee & Brown, 1979; Findley & Bryan, 1971; J. E. Rosenbaum, 1980). Moreover, the available evidence simply does not support the belief that slow students suffer emotional strains brought on by invidious comparisons when enrolled in mixed-ability classes. Actually, just the opposite has been found. Rather than helping students feel better about themselves, the tracking process seems to foster unreasonable aspirations, lowered self-esteem, and negative attitudes toward school (Alexander & McDill, 1976).

Ability tracking also leads inevitably to a watered-down curriculum for those students in the lowest groups that often simply reflects the school's minimal expectations for these youngsters (J. E. Rosenbaum, 1976, 1980). When teachers expect little from students, they are usually not disappointed – the minimum is what they get. And, typically, because these students are in the lower track to begin with, teachers attribute their unresponsiveness to a lack of ability. This reaction is understandable; no one wants to accept responsibility for the failure of others. Teachers tend to take credit for their successful students, but are reluctant to shoulder the blame for mediocre ones (Felsenthal, 1970; Johnson, Feigenbaum, & Weiby, 1964; Omelich, 1974). Better to attribute student failure to factors beyond one's ability to control such as indifference, idleness, and depravity.

Quite often, however, these explanations are without foundation. Take, for example, the experiences of those recent refugees from Central America described earlier in chapter 2 (Suarez-Orozco, 1989). Far from being marginal students, many of these youngsters came to America with outstanding academic backgrounds, having excelled in schools that in some cases were superior to those in which they now found themselves in America. Also, contrary to the conventional wisdom, the parents of these children *do* care about education and often made considerable sacrifices to see that their children stayed in school. They saw America as giving their children chances for advancement not available to them in their own homelands. But these parents were rarely consulted by schools because, according to Suarez-Orozco's convincing documentation, the school staff routinely presumed that these new arrivals lacked the intellectual potential necessary for college. Time and again, counselors saw their primary duty to enroll these Hispanic students in programs that would simply graduate them from high school with no thought of preparing them for college entrance. As one teacher, herself a Hispanic, told Suarez-Orozco, her primary job was to "housebreak the little immigrants who come down from the Central American mountains" (1989, p. 10). Another counselor dismissed a student's request for an advanced algebra course since he had already completed the beginning class back in Nicaragua by explaining that algebra in his country is "different from American algebra" (Suarez-Orozco, 1989, p. 5).

The expectation that few if any of these immigrants are "college material" is one form of inadvertent tracking, or, as Suarez-Orozco calls it, "gatekeeping." This process of segregation based on dubious ability rankings sets the stage for self-fulfilling prophecies.

SELF-FULFILLING PROPHECY

The concept of self-fulfilling prophecy has been a powerful conceptual tool for understanding classroom achievement dynamics ever since Robert Rosenthal and Lenore Jacobson (1968) first attempted to demonstrate that the expectations teachers hold for their students influence the students' future performance. These researchers informed teachers at the beginning of the school year that several of their students had shown potential for considerable academic growth based on the results of a written examination. In actual fact, these students were selected randomly. By the end of the school term those students for whom teachers held artificially high expectations enjoyed significantly greater IQ gains than did other students in the same classrooms. These findings were said to demonstrate the operation of a self-fulfilling prophecy that has been defined as a "false definition of a situation [that] evokes a new behavior which makes the original false conception come true" (Merton, 1949, p. 423).

The original Rosenthal and Jacobsen study came under immediate and intense criticism as being inadequately designed and unscientific in its conclusions (for a recent debate, see Rosenthal, 1987; Wineburg, 1987a, 1987b). The reaction to these challenges was swift and on the whole constructive. As a result a far more convincing case has now been established for the phenomenon of self-fulfilling prophecy, especially after researchers began uncovering the specific mechanisms involved (for recent reviews see Jussim, 1986; Jamieson, Lydon, Stewart, & Zanna, 1987).

In schools the process of self-fulfilling prophecy involves several steps (Brophy, 1983, 1985; Cooper & Good, 1983). First, teachers anticipate that certain students will succeed in school, whereas others will not (note the preceding Hispanic examples). Second, these expectations invariably influence the ways teachers relate to students. For example, teachers spend less time with students whom they believe are less likely to succeed (Allington, 1980; Felsenthal, 1970). And not only are these interchanges fewer, but they are of dubious educational value. Investigators report a tendency among teachers to supply answers impatiently to children of lesser ability, thereby depriving them of the chance to think through and formulate their own ideas (Brophy & Good, 1970, 1974; Jetter & Davis, 1973; Rowe, 1972). Given this kind of treatment, it is not surprising that students of whom little is expected and to whom little help is given will fall progressively behind, in effect completing the third step of the prophecy cycle by acting in ways that fulfill the teacher's initial predictions of incompetency.

Ray Rist (1970) provides a compelling example of how the dynamics of self-fulfilling prophecy can shape the lives of children, in this case a group of ghetto youngsters just entering kindergarten. Covington and Beery (1976) take up the story from its beginning:

> After the first eight days of school, the kindergarten teacher identified the "fast" and "slow" learners in the group and assigned them to different work tables. Rist convincingly demonstrates that these placements were made not so much on the grounds of academic potential – no test scores were available to the teacher – but, in reality, according to social class differences within the group. Children who best fit the teacher's middle-class "ideal" (e.g., neat appearance, courteous manner, and a facility with Standard American English) were seated at Table 1, while everybody else was relegated to an inferior status. Predictably the teacher spent the majority of her time and energy on the students at Table 1. Just as predictably, this led to a lack of interest and restlessness at Tables 2 and 3, so that when the teacher *did* attend to these students, it usually took the form of reprimands for misconduct ("sit down"). From the lack of attention and teaching, these students made little or no progress, which further convinced the teacher of the correctness of her original judgment that these were indeed nonlearners. Sensing the teacher's low regard for these children, the students at Table 1 began to ridicule them ("I'm smarter than you"; "The answer is easy, stupid"). The youngsters at Tables 2 and 3 reacted by withdrawal, self-blame, and hostility directed within their own group. In effect, these children were internalizing what the students at Table 1 were saying about them.
>
> The label of "fast" and "slow" learner was reinforced throughout the kindergarten year, first by the teacher and then by the students themselves, so that when it came time for first grade, these labels which were originally informal, took on an official character in the form of cumula-

tive records. Acting on these evaluations, the first grade teacher assigned the children to *new* reading groups but in predictable ways. No child who had sat at Tables 2 or 3 in kindergarten was placed in the top group; conversely, with the exception of one student, no one from Table 1 was placed in the middle or low reading groups. Later, when these same students entered second grade, the names of the reading groups changed once again, but the pattern of placement remained virtually the same. (p. 78–79)

Rist (1970) summarizes his three years of observation:

No matter how well a child in the lower reading groups might have read, he was destined to remain in the same reading group. This is, in a sense, another manifestation of the self-fulfilling prophecy in that a "slow learner" had no option but to continue to be a slow learner, regardless of performance or potential. . . . The child's journey through the early grades of school at one reading level and in one social grouping appeared to be pre-ordained from the eighth day of kindergarten. (p. 435)

More recently, Rhona Weinstein and her colleagues (Brattesani, Weinstein, & Marshall, 1984; Marshall & Weinstein, 1984; Weinstein, 1983, 1985, 1986; Weinstein, Marshall, Sharp, & Botkin, 1987) have focused on that part of the cycle described by Rist in which children who initially were bystanders eventually become active participants themselves. Sensing the teacher's low regard for children at Tables 2 and 3, the students at Table 1 began to ridicule these outcasts. Weinstein asks: How, besides the particular seating arrangements, do teachers convey the expectation to students that some of their peers will succeed while others will not (Weinstein, Marshall, Brattesani, & Middlestadt, 1982)? As it turns out, students are very attuned to the behavioral cues provided by teachers. For example, children believe that when teachers expect a lot of a particular student, especially if he is a male and is also given special privileges, then he must be bright. On the other hand, those students who are subject to the greatest teacher surveillance, often males as well, and receive fewer chances before being reprimanded are believed by other students to be among the least bright in class.

Twenty years have passed since Rist published his findings. One would hope that with the passage of time and with an increased sophisitication among teachers that Rist's observations would be a thing of the past. Unfortunately, not. Whole generations of new students continue to get the message that they are educational discards and untrainable. In fairness, many teachers are quite aware of the negative potential of self-fulfilling prophecy and attempt to compensate by consciously dispensing greater praise to students of lesser ability whenever they succeed and by downplaying their failures (Fischer, 1982; Smits & Meyer, 1985; Weinstein, 1976). There is some evidence that this is especially true for teachers of minority students (Kleinfeld, 1972).

Ironically, however, praising students for success on relatively simple tasks – those that are more easily solved by the less able – and withholding blame for failure can actually convey the impression that teachers expect little academically from these youngsters (Meyer et al., 1979; Graham, 1984a, 1984b;

Rustemeyer, 1984). This seeming paradox occurs because withholding comment in the case of failure suggests that the cause was not insufficient effort; otherwise the teacher would have reprimanded the student. Therefore, by the process of elimination, the cause must be low ability! This is the psychological basis for the so-called *paradoxical effect* of praise and blame. These compensatory efforts by the teacher may fail for other reasons as well. Although teachers praise hard work, effort alone may not be sufficiently rewarding for the failure-prone student who is just as likely to judge himself or herself inadequate when measured by the stringent, competitive standards of the peer group. When such discrepant evaluations occur, teacher praise is unlikely to increase student self-confidence (Covington & Beery, 1976).

At times it seems that teachers cannot win, no matter what they do. Once again, it must be noted that things go badly not because teachers are necessarily insensitive, but rather because in a competitive climate their actions are likely to be interpreted incorrectly.

SOCIAL COMPARISON THEORY
Competitive dynamics have also been studied from the vantage point of social comparison theory. Social comparison theory suggests that humans look to one another for information when they are in doubt about themselves (Festinger, 1957; Suls & Miller, 1977; Veroff, 1969). Our particular interest concerns how individuals form opinions about their ability. Primary-grade children typically make these judgments against a standard of self-improvement and express satisfaction at how much they are learning, irrespective of how well others are doing (Ruble, Parsons, & Ross, 1976). However, in time self-appraisal gives way to comparing one's rate of progress with that of others as the basis for judging ability (Frey & Ruble, 1985). This transition from self-comparison to social comparison roughly parallels the shift from incremental concepts to entity concepts of ability. For example, although upper-elementary youngsters may still believe they can become smarter by trying harder, they also begin to recognize that they may never be as smart as others.

The transition from elementary school to junior high is critical to these changes (Metz, 1978; Wigfield, Eccles, Midgley, Iver, & Reuman, 1987). In junior high school evaluation and instruction become more formal, controlling, and competitive. Gone is the earlier emphasis on generous rewards for everyone in the form of happy faces, stickers, and stamps. Also, children are no longer able to redo their work without penalty, nor can they succeed simply by behaving themselves or feigning interest in classroom activities. Moreover, the junior high school years usher in an increasing use of homogeneous ability grouping and tracking (Reuman, MacIver, Eccles, & Wigfield, 1987), with a corresponding decrease in opportunities for cooperation and student input to the process of learning (Midgley & Feldlaufer, 1987; Midgley, Feldlaufer, & Eccles, 1988).

The self-perceived ability of all students tends to decline over the junior high school years, but at an accelerated rate for those children who are doing less well to begin with (Entwistle & Hayduk, 1978; Stipek, 1981, 1984). Students also become more anxious about school (Fyans, 1979; Schulenberg,

Asp, & Petersen, 1984) and attach less value to all school subjects, including mathematics, English, and, surprisingly, physical education (Wigfield et al., 1987). Thus at a time – early adolescence – when ability is seen increasingly as the most important factor in success and low ability as the preeminent cause of failure, many youngsters have already come to doubt that they are sufficiently capable.

Learning to lose

A scarcity of rewards also fuels unrealistic aspirations. Once students realize that the prevailing standards of excellence are set by the performance of other students, many lose control over their own learning, and instead must scramble to keep pace with ever-accelerating demands that grow increasingly beyond their reach. In effect, scarcity causes a collapse of those self-protective mechanisms originally described by Hoppe. No longer are students free to lower their sights after failure or adjust their aspirations in ways that balance the likelihood of failure against the chances for success. The true insidiousness of this situation is revealed by the fact that not only is a pattern of atypical shifts encouraged, but raising rather than lowering one's expectations after failure actually becomes adaptive in the circumstance (Sears, 1940) because there are serious sanctions against lowering one's aspirations, mainly the threatened loss of social respectability.

Albert Bandura and his colleagues have studied the consequences of young children resolutely conforming to inappropriate goals (Bandura & Kupers, 1964; Bandura, 1971; Bandura, Grusec, & Menlove, 1967). In a typical experiment children watched adult models playing games of skill, including bowling in a miniature bowling alley. Whenever these adults did better than their publicly stated goals, they rewarded themselves generously with freely available toys and candy. But whenever they fell short – a deliberate part of the experimental design – the adults denied themselves these same rewards. After watching these proceedings, the young observers were then given a chance to play. Their behavior is troubling for several reasons.

First, these youngsters imposed upon themselves essentially the same standards they observed in the adult models, despite the fact that sometimes these expectations were so stringent that even the adults had difficulty achieving them! Second, the children clung rigidly to these inappropriate standards even after repeated failure, and they – like the adult models before them – denied themselves the otherwise freely available rewards. Third, once having adopted these self-defeating standards, children who rewarded themselves sparingly, if at all, transmitted these same unrealistic expectations to other children who had no part in the original experiment (Mischel & Liebert, 1966). Fourth, these unforgiving standards took on an existence of their own. These young subjects continued to punish themselves, days and even weeks later, for otherwise perfectly adequate performances and in the absence of the original cause, namely, the implied social pressure of an adult authority.

What is especially disturbing is the apparent ease with which these grievous dynamics can be established. Children, it appears, are especially vulnerable because they have little basis on which to make realistic judgments about their own capacity relative to the demands of the task. They rely heavily on adults to make these judgments for them, and, to make matters worse, they are subject to various kinds of magical thinking (chapter 4). All too often children believe that what they *want* to happen *will* happen, no matter how well or how poorly they might have performed in the past.

But why should these children continue to punish themselves needlessly, especially when there is no longer any reason to do so? One possibility is that self-criticism itself reinforces this illogical behavior because criticism is known to be followed by a sense of relief (Aronfreed, 1964). In effect, self-contempt provides a measure of relief by temporarily lifting the burden of failure, but – perversely – in order to experience relief again one must continue to be blameworthy! Thus the process is self-perpetuating, and worse yet, provides no real solution to the problem of failure. The basic causes of failure remain intact.

Jack Sandler and John Quagliano (as reported in Bandura, 1971, p. 34) demonstrated just how easily self-punishment can set up a debilitating cycle of needless pain and meaningless relief. These investigators trained monkeys to terminate a severe electric shock by pressing a bar. Pressing the bar triggered a second shock but of such low intensity that it did not really matter, at least not in the beginning. Eventually, however, as the experiment progressed, the intensity of this second self-administered shock was slowly increased until it was as great as that of the initial shock. Yet the monkeys continued to punish themselves, and needlessly because the first shock had long since been halted. Originally, the self-administered shock provided escape from a far greater danger, and as such became a source of relief that in the end the animals could not give up. The same mechanisms may be operating in human beings. Self-criticism may render unattainable standards more tolerable by temporarily relieving the anxiety they cause.

If such self-destructive behavior can be initiated so effortlessly in laboratory settings and sustained indefinitely, how much more dismal the prospects for youngsters in regular classrooms where a whole host of factors continue to promote inappropriate standards relentlessly, year after year, including teacher preferences for superior achievement and the tendency for students to model after other high-status pupils.

It is little wonder that a large proportion of children hold unrealistically high achievement expectations for themselves – unrealistic when compared with their actual records of past accomplishments. For instance, Esther Battle (1966) found that a majority of junior high school students set their *minimum* achievement standards (the lowest grade they could receive and still feel satisfied) higher than the grades they actually expected to get! It is likely that these unrealistic aspirations are partly the product of wishful thinking caused by an intense desire for acceptance and respectability (Sears, 1940).

Battle's research also indicated that such irrational goal setting is found among youngsters at all ability levels. Students tend to associate with other pupils of like ability and achievement. Within the context of their own particular group, then, even bright students can see themselves as relatively dull compared to their immediate peers. Moreover, when homogeneous peer groups are artificially created, as in the case of ability grouping and tracking, the evidence indicates that students tend to hold themselves to standards of performance exhibited by pupils in more advanced, prestigious groups (Weinstein, 1976, 1989). As a consequence, these aspirations remain unfulfilled and frustration leads to deteriorating performance (Reuman, 1988). And what is worse, teachers often mistakenly praise unrealistic aspirations as evidence of a student's willingness to try hard, and thereby unwittingly reinforce goals that are destined not to be realized.

All the arguments marshaled so far imply that learning itself is also a casualty when students compete for diminishing rewards. Granted, scarcity may set students to scrambling at least for a time and especially among those who believe they have a chance to win. But in their scramble most students do virtually everything *except* learn in their attempts to avoid having fewer points than others. The futility of this dynamic is driven home by Alfie Kohn (1986): "How can we do our best when we are spending our energies trying to make others lose – and fear that they will make us lose" (p. 9)?

With few exceptions, the available evidence supports Kohn's commonsense analysis. For instance, competition among individuals leads to a lower *average* performance than when individuals are encouraged to cooperate in their learning. This is especially true when the rewards for cooperation are interdependent, that is, when the success of the entire group depends on how well each individual performs. As only one example, each team member might be required by the teacher to master a spelling list and pass a test before all members receive a common reward. When each person's fate is tied to the performance of everyone else, then there are powerful incentives to help slower learners in the group and to discourage indifference and loafing.

This is not to suggest that noncompetitive learning is superior in all situations or for all tasks. Actually, when tasks are simple and mechanical or highly repetitive, as in the case of canceling letters in the alphabet as quickly as possible, then performance is best promoted by offering prizes to the fastest workers (DeCharms, 1957; Maller, 1929; Shaw, 1958). This competitive edge quickly disappears, however, when the task requires that students come up with the best ideas for solving novel or complex problems of the kind found in human relations and conflict management issues (Deutsch, 1949).

It must be especially galling to advocates of competition to find that competitive rewards are most effective in those situations that are of the least importance. The shift favoring cooperation over competition occurs because when individuals compete to solve complex problems, they are less willing to share information (Miller & Hamblin, 1963) and may even try to hinder others (Shaw, 1958). On the other hand, when students cooperate they are less prone to make errors precisely because they do share information and act as vigilant monitors. When working toward a common goal it is in the interest of everyone to correct errors. But when students are competing for that goal, it is best not to draw attention to their mistakes, at least not until it is too late.

Not surprisingly, then, cooperating individuals feel less hostile than do competing individuals, show greater personal concern for one another, and even express greater interest in the task at hand (Raven & Eachus, 1963).

Rewards as motivators

One final criticism can be leveled against competition as a means to promote learning. Competition threatens intrinsic task involvement. This is scarcely surprising. Whenever students are preoccupied with trying to make others lose for fear that they themselves will lose, the joy of learning quickly fades. It is not only the economics of scarcity that is at fault here. The problem is also the *kinds* of rewards teachers often use and their *role* in competitive dynamics. First, competitive rewards tend to be tangible – gold stars, stickers, and grades – and extraneous in that they are unrelated to the process of learning itself. Second, as to their role, competitive rewards are seen by many educators as providing the motive power for achievement. This is part of the myth of intensification: If we can only provide the right rewards and enough of them, so the argument goes, then we can arouse (drive) otherwise passive students.

OVERJUSTIFICATION EFFECT

Rewarding individuals unnecessarily for doing something they already enjoy can undermine their interest in the task. This happens because an already justifiable activity becomes suspect by the promise of additional rewards – hence the term *overjustification* – so that the individual reasons, in effect, if someone has to pay me to do this, then it must not be worth doing for its own sake.

This phenomenon was first noted by Mark Lepper, David Greene, and Richard Nisbett (1973). These investigators found that a group of nursery school children who were rewarded extraneously (given a "good player award") for drawing pictures – an activity they had previously enjoyed without rewards – were less likely to draw later during free play time compared to a group of youngsters who had not been rewarded for drawing. The overjustification effect has since been demonstrated in dozens of experiments with both adults and children (for a review, see Lepper & Greene, 1978).

It appears that rewarding an individual for what he or she might otherwise do freely can turn pleasure into drudgery. This phenomenon was used to advantage by an old gentleman (probably a retired psychology professor) who was bothered by the noisy play of boys in his neighborhood (Casady, 1974, as reported in Covington & Berry, 1976):

> How could he get the boys to stop? The old man called the boys together, told them he was quite deaf, and asked that they shout louder so that he might enjoy their fun. In return he was willing to pay each of them a quarter. Needless to say, the boys were delighted to combine business with pleasure, and on that first day the old man got more than his money's worth. On the second day he told the boys that owing to his small

pension, he could afford to pay only twenty cents. As the pay rate dwindled day by day, the boys became angry and finally told the old man they would not return. The sly old gentleman had turned play into work and then paid so little that making noise for five cents was not worth the effort. (pp. 24–25)

Although researchers still debate the exact nature of the mechanisms by which the old man was able to rid himself of the boys (for example, see Morgan, 1984; Reiss & Sunshinsky, 1975; Ross, Karniol, & Rothstein, 1976), there is general agreement on one point. Bribing, paying, or threatening individuals to perform creates an extrinsic set that discourages intrinsic involvement. These detrimental effects take many forms, all of which cut directly at the heart of the educational mission. For instance, offering tangible rewards as inducements to learn causes students to select easier assignments over more challenging ones (Harter, 1974). Also, students are less persistent in their studies (Fincham & Cain, 1986) and less creative and flexible in their problem-solving efforts (Amabile, 1979, 1982; Amabile & Hennessey, in press). Additionally, students appear more willing simply to "guess" at correct answers (Condry & Chambers, 1978) and are less likely to remember information learned earlier (Grolnick & Ryan, 1986). Poor recall likely occurs because extrinsic rewards tend to narrow the individual's attention during learning.

Perhaps most troublesome of all – from the longer motivational perspective – is the fact that the preference for easier assignments just mentioned generalizes so that later, when tangible inducements are no longer available, students show no renewed interest in more challenging problems. Equally alarming is the fact that children who adopt an extrinsic mentality take on many of the characteristics we have associated with learned helplessness. They come to doubt their ability to complete the very kinds of assignments that they undertook successfully for rewards just a short time before (Boggiano, Main, & Katz, 1988). Also, they may believe that powerful others control their academic destiny (Boggiano, Harackiewicz, Bessette, & Main, 1985). This belief makes sense when we realize that the availability of extrinsic rewards depends on factors that lie outside the control of students and that may be quite unpredictable and quixotic, such as the teacher's mood. Yet despite this unstable source of rewards, or perhaps because of it, externally oriented children become more rather than less dependent on teacher opinion about how to approach school work.

John Condry (1977) succinctly summarized the large body of research on extrinsic rewards when he observed that

subjects offered an extrinsic incentive choose easier tasks, are less efficient in using the information available to solve novel problems, and tend to be answer oriented and more illogical in their problem-solving strategies. They seem to work harder and produce more activity, but the activity is of a lower quality, contains more errors, and is more stereotyped and less creative than the work of comparable nonrewarded subjects working on the same problems. (p. 471–472)

MINI-MAX PRINCIPLE

Behind this complex pattern of deterioration lies a single process. When students are offered rewards for good behavior and adequate school work they operate expediently (Pittman, Boggiano, & Ruble, 1983). They attempt to maximize rewards for a minimum of effort, a work orientation referred to as the *mini-max* principle (Kruglanski, 1978). Learning becomes the way to obtain a reward, not a way to satisfy one's curiosity or to discover something of interest. The mini-max dictum may make a certain amount of economic sense in other contexts – why spend more time at a task than is necessary? But in school, coming to rely on extrinsic rewards creates impatience at best, and at worst induces instability in one's expectations, self-doubt, and eventual dependence on the judgment of others.

Research conducted by Ann Boggiano and her colleagues (Boggiano et al., 1987) suggests that most teachers and parents accept uncritically the notion that offering and withholding rewards produces good results – better, in fact, than any other teaching strategy, including punishing students for not trying, reasoning with the child, or just plain not interfering. Moreover, adults generally ascribe to the theory that the greater the reward, the more eagerly students will compete. This commonsense reasoning is correct, but only up to a point. Rewards do actually increase students' willingness to try, as Condry has pointed out, but only in the case of simple and therefore tedious, boring tasks (Calder & Staw, 1975a; Kruglanski, 1975; McGraw, 1978).

As already noted, rewards may optimize performance on easy tasks, but they do not work well in the case of more complex assignments that because of their complexity may be intrinsically interesting. Unfortunately, teachers do not always make the important distinction between high-interest and low-interest tasks. They appear to understand quite well what "turns students on" to certain kinds of learning, especially that involving low-interest tasks, yet they seem quite oblivious to the ways that students get "turned off" to higher-order thinking and discovery. But this is understandable. As adults we operate in a world dominated by extrinsic incentives: "If you sell enough items then you will receive a commission; if you succeed on the GRE then you will be admitted to graduate school; if you publish enough research then you will receive tenure" (Boggiano & Pittman, in press).

Little wonder that adult theories for improving achievement depend heavily on extrinsic rewards. Many teachers believe that short-term rewards *should* promote greater task involvement. As a result, when this formula does not work – and the desire to learn wavers – they blame other factors such as student fatigue or indifference, thereby missing the whole point. Parents, too, become frustrated when monetary bribes, cajoling, and threats fail to improve their children's report cards. Violence is often the result. In one study reports of child abuse doubled in the three days after grades were issued, and the problem intensified at the end of each academic year. David Elkind (in Toufexis, 1989) explains that report cards are an "emotional lightening rod" for parents who worry about their children's prospects for the future and sometimes equate good grades with good parenting skills.

GRADING POLICY

These observations provide an important perspective on grading policy and on how grades affect the reasons students learn, for good and ill. Grades are frequently defended on the grounds that they, like other tangible incentives, motivate learning even though the evidence is solidly against this proposition. But still, should not grades make a difference in how hard students try? If they do not, we should find out; and we should also know *why* not.

Some of the best evidence on this issue comes from the classic study by Louis Goldberg (1965) who attempted to alter student test performance by manipulating grading policy. One group of college students was graded severely – with only a few high grades awarded – on the theory that the group would be aroused, or driven, to try harder on the next exam. A second group was graded leniently on the theory that positive reinforcement would best motivate future achievement. Finally, for a third group, Goldberg gave a disproportionate number of A's and F's, thereby creating a discrepancy for many students between the grade they expected and what they actually received. Presumably those students who did unexpectedly well would work harder to keep their high grade. Likewise, those students who were surprised by a poor grade would also work harder, but in their case, to improve. Actually, no differences were found in test outcomes among the three groups; neither did the performances of these groups differ from that of a fourth, control group that was simply graded on a "normal" curve.

Although we know that a specific grade given to a particular student can influence his or her subsequent achievement, sometimes dramatically, there is no guarantee that blanket, institutionalized grading policies of the kind featured in Goldberg's research will affect all students in similar ways. One reason is that grades motivate students differently. This much is clear from our earlier attributional analysis of success and failure experiences. Recall that success-oriented individuals are driven to do better following failure because they attribute it to factors under their control. In contrast, failure-oriented persons are demoralized by failure because they feel inadequate to correct the situation. Similarly, an unexpected high grade – like some of those administered by Goldberg – may be met by failure-oriented students with disbelief because they may feel themselves incapable of achieving such a mark. In short, good grades tend to motivate those who need motivating the least, and further to discourage those who need motivating the most. No wonder that the effects of a single, uniform grading policy on individual students is so unpredictable, and for some may even be counterproductive. These include not only poorer students but successful ones as well. For example, Ruth Butler (1988) has shown that a narrow preoccupation with grades can interfere with the kinds of higher-order thinking often associated with students of superior intellect.

In sum, grades are apt to motivate marginal students, but for the wrong reasons and only temporarily, by arousing threat; at the same time they foreclose the most able students from using their capacities to the fullest. Tragically, the more students resist learning, the more grades are justified by educators as a necessary, often last-ditch way to motivate the unruly and the uncontrollable. It is in this sense that teachers refer somewhat apologetically to grades as a "necessary evil." The threat of a poor grade is thought of as a weapon to overcome apathy. But we know better. Indifference is already à motivated behavior. Therefore, when students compete for limited rewards, grading will likely intensify avoidant behaviors, not reduce them, and in the process exaggerate the value of ability as a source of worth.

Competition and minorities

Many minority students and disadvantaged white youngsters are put at special risk whenever pupils are stratified and rewarded according to ability level. In our zeal to magnify differences among students rather than to seek out the common ground shared by all in matters of curiosity, enthusiasm, and creativity, we unwittingly turn scores on achievement tests into self-fulfilling prophecies that favor some and damn others. Little wonder that many students quickly get the message that they are educational discards, untrainable, and, worst of all, unworthy.

The inevitable result of this sorting process is the "warehousing of children," a thoroughly distasteful, but sadly accurate phrase. Warehouses are places to store goods – lumber, pork bellies, and machine parts – for temporary safekeeping until they are needed in the future. But when children become goods – things to be shelved, isolated, and rendered inert – they are kept only from learning, cut off from proper intellectual development, and as a result they will never be ready in time for the future. In the circumstance, schooling becomes a vast bureaucratic maw into which countless children simply disappear without a trace, appearing only in record books as ciphers. Anonymity becomes a way of life. The individual student is too often forgotten, or as it was poignantly expressed by one young black, "Somebody is in charge of everything at the regular high schools – attendance, schedules, lunch. But nobody is in charge of caring" (K. Epstein, 1989, p. 36). In short, a vast underclass of children become damaged goods, increasingly held down against their will and increasingly disenfranchised.

For many disadvantaged students school is an endless daily cycling through crowded, decaying classrooms managed by overburdened teachers who serve up listless, make-work assignments with little or no hope that these youngsters will ever catch up and escape an adult life limited to dead-end, marginal jobs. These students are rarely exposed to what has been called "high-status knowledge" (Tobias, 1989), the kind of knowledge that might be useful in college, like reasoning and decision-making skills (Davis, 1986; Powell, Farrar, & Cohen, 1985; Trimble & Sinclair, 1986). Instead, according to Jeannie Oakes (1985), a researcher concerned with classroom inequality, low-track classrooms typically focus year after year on basic arithmetic facts and rarely, if ever, move beyond simple measurement skills such as converting English measures to metric. This kind of functional literacy is not functional at all. It provides students with neither relevance nor rigor (Levin, 1988). No one would deny the need for such arithmetic skills, not as ends in themselves, however, but rather as stepping stones. In the absence of at least some formal academic training worthy of the name, tracking formalizes a castelike system, engenders ethnic humiliation, and leads to doubts about what schools can do to improve the lives of their clients.

The seeds of doubt and failure sprout remarkably early, often triggered innocently, for example, by the mere fact that simple number concepts may remain a mystery for a second grader. This youngster is likely to be judged "backward," a bureaucratic label that will probably stick, as demonstrated earlier by the observational research of Ray Rist. In an earlier, gentler time such a poor showing would have signified the need for greater effort both on the part of the student and the teacher. Today, however, it is just as likely to mean that the child *cannot* learn. This message is profoundly unfair and wasteful of human talent, a predictable consequence of the widely held view among students that it is ability, not effort, that counts the most. And, as we know, ability status counts for more and more in the minds of children as they grow older, magnified by competition, by the demise of intrinsic task involvement, and by the fact that more and more course work is grouped by ability. As Oakes (1985) points out, by the ninth grade, 80% to 90% of all students are in separate classes determined by whether they are judged to be "fast," "average," or "slow."

So far I have described the problems faced by many minority children who continue to endure the noxious gauntlet of competitive sorting year after year. But what of those students who drop out along the way, before high school graduation – by some estimates, up to 60% of all inner-city youngsters? There are many reasons for this exodus. Some students drop out simply for having no good reason to continue or because they are intellectually marginal. Dropouts are not necessarily the poorest students, however. In fact, the Houston school district, the fourth largest in the United States, recently reported that 25% of all its dropouts scored above the 75th percentile on standardized reading and mathematics tests (Maugh, 1987).

Why do such promising individuals quit? Kathryn Epstein (1989) conducted extensive interviews with some 20 high school dropouts from inner-city neighborhoods in Oakland, California – youngsters who subsequently returned to alternative schools to complete their degrees and then, in many instances, began college. The reasons given for having dropped out originally are surprising. Such factors as economic hardship and family problems were rarely mentioned. Feeling unfairly treated in school and saddled with a sense of boredom were far more frequently cited. Raymond, a gifted black student, captures perfectly the essence of such complaints. Although he eventually completed several years of college, he refused to sit through his high school classes because, he said, "Nothing happens. It is totally pointless for me to be there" (Epstein, p. 39). Anger at being treated as a nameless cipher also figured prominently in the complaints of Epstein's youngsters. Another black informant put it this way:

I was invisible, man. I knew it. I sat in those schools for two years. I sat in the back of the room and I did nothing. I didn't speak to anyone and no one spoke to me. Nobody said, "Do your work" or nothing. Then one day I said it, "Man, I'm invisible here." I got up and walked out the door and I never went back. (Epstein, p. 1)

Nor did Epstein find any evidence that the parents of these students encouraged their youngsters to drop out. Actually, most parents expressed eagerness to help, but their efforts to get information about their children's progress, even their whereabouts during the school day, was typically frustrated by school bureaucracy. Every parent in Epstein's sample, without exception, reported that their children had cut classes for periods ranging from 20 to 60 days before they were notified by the school, far too late to prevent their youngsters from receiving F's, which according to school policy were issued automatically after only 6 days of unexcused absence. Why return to school for the rest of the year, these students wondered, reasonably, if they had already earned an F in every class? Such a seemingly dysfunctional school policy can be altered easily, but not the reasoning behind such rules that assumes that dropouts are educational deadweight and incapable of further instruction.

Although it is true that Epstein's interviewees were creating their own interpretation of events, and perhaps putting the best face on failure, still there is little here to support the traditional view of dropouts as incorrigible or marginal. It appears that dropping out for many students represents the failure of schools as institutions and not simply the failure of families to provide encouragement, or of economic dislocation, or of personal upheaval including pregnancy or illness. In one recent nationwide survey of some 50,000 high school students, the only major reason for dropping out that came close to reflecting personal circumstances was that of being offered a job (Jones, 1982).

Yet in fairness to schools the dynamics of self-fulfilling prophecy are subtle and difficult to combat once they are set in motion. Everything students do, or do *not* do – such as refusing to participate in class or ignoring homework assignments – simply reinforces the teacher's view that they are, indeed, unprepared, antagonistic, and marginal; and often teachers are right. But the conditions that create such underpreparation and anger are not right.

Conclusions

It has long been believed that the use of competition – *healthy competition,* that is, in modest amounts – guarantees the highest average performance for the group by maximizing the output of each individual member. Actually, as we now know, the facts do not support this contention. The notion of healthy competition is a contradiction in terms and cannot be justified educationally if it is meant to imply that competition in small, carefully administered doses will increase school performance. The evidence simply does not encourage such distinctions by degree. The introduction of competitive incentives, in any form or amount, produces a decrease not an increase in school achievement. And we have seen why. When students are busy avoiding failure, there is little to encourage true task involvement. So much for the argument that competition enhances academic productivity. In reality, it is the presence of competition, not its absence, that threatens school achievement at all ability levels.

Likewise, the claim that achieving under adversity (competition) builds character is flatly contradicted by the evidence. In the process of scrambling, children learn that the purpose of school is to avoid losing – or, worse, yet, to make others lose. Children quickly learn to cheat, lie, and become saboteurs. They band together, not for the purpose of learning, but in temporary alliances to keep others from winning or to avenge themselves for imaginary injustices. Where is the nobility of purpose here? Far from building character, it appears that competition in schools contributes to a breakdown of personal integrity and encourages a mentality that favors ganging and fractious rivalries.

Even among the winners, the psychological casualty rate is prohibitive whether it be reflected in the young, upward-striving entrepreneur who sacrifices the joy of discovery for the sake of conformity, or the gifted child who amasses an enviable academic record as a way to offset persistent self-doubts about her worth, doubts that linger nonetheless. Also, the rewards of competitive success are often tarnished by the realization that one's pride is based on the ignoble sentiment of being better or more deserving than others. In effect, winning tends to breed feelings of guilt for having denied others success.

We have implicated a scarcity of meaningful rewards as a major cause of the current educational crisis. But to indict only the most blatant mechanisms of competition such as grading on a curve or grouping by ability is to miss the larger point. Competition is more than a dubious way to arouse children to learn. Competition is also an *ethos,* a worldview that prescribes manners, establishes customs, espouses ideals, and, above all, determines the rules by which people relate to each other – in this case, rules that set person against person and discourage cooperation. Many beliefs and practices form this vanguard of competitive rivalry in schools, not the least being America's preoccupation with the sorting of children by ability and the uncritical acceptance of motives as drives – inner states to be manipulated and aroused at will by others – and our tolerance of testing procedures that shortchange children through the dynamics of self-fulfilling prophecy.

Thus it is not only a specific set of practices that must be changed, but also a broader philosophy as well. This is an extraordinary challenge, made even more difficult by the fact that not all of what has been criticized here is necessarily wrong. Consider, for example, the need to take account of ability. There can be no denying that ability is a major source of individual differences among learners, a reality that must never be forgotten by teachers. Indeed, as we know, the key to motivating students properly depends on providing instruction that is neither too easy nor too difficult for each individual. Such fine-tuning requires that teachers know as much about how their students differ as the ways in which they are alike. But ability grouping is not the preferred way to achieve this balance. Grouping by ability comes to grief, not because the goal of providing instruction according to student readiness is pedagogically unsound, but rather because when grouping is employed in a competitive atmosphere *differences* invariably become equated with *deficits.*

We must seek ways to celebrate and encourage the special qualities of each student while recognizing the fact that ability differences are, after all, part of that uniqueness.

Basically, this means encouraging beliefs about ability that empower students, not constrain them unduly. The suggestions made earlier (pp. 137–138) for ways to halt the drift toward unidimensional classrooms are a case in point. However, the purpose of permitting students some choice over *what* they learn, *how* and *when* they learn, and to participate in groups not always defined by ability, is not to halt the formation of ability estimates among children. Children will inevitably compare themselves no matter what teachers do. Rather, the true purpose is to broaden student beliefs about the multidimensional nature of ability – including reasoning, visual, and intuitive skills – and to increase an appreciation of the various ways that differing patterns of ability can be brought to bear on different problems. By recognizing that there are as many approaches to a task as there are problem solvers, it is hoped that a unidimensional view of ability and the social stratification that follows can be moderated. Whether these hopes are realistic is a question to be taken up in the remaining chapters.

Finally, it is useful once again to place our arguments in a larger societal context. Just as we must not focus on only one competitive practice, say, grading on a curve, as the exclusive cause of America's massive failure to educate, neither can we blame the broader competitive ethos alone. There are other demeaning forces at work as well both within and outside the school. Within schools there is the failure to create a sense of academic community and the general absence of mechanisms to involve parents in their children's learning, especially minority parents, to mention only two shortcomings (Carnegie Council on Adolescent Development, 1989). From this perspective the problem is not only the quality of the relationship between specific teachers and individual children, but also a broad set of institutional conditions that make real education difficult for many, if not virtually impossible (Levin, 1986, 1988).

Then there are the horrendous out-of-school problems that threaten to swamp even the best concerted efforts of teachers, parents, and community. These include malnutrition, the sexual exploitation of children, childhood pregnancy, drug abuse, and homelessness – problems over which schools have little or no control and about which teachers often have little knowledge. Still, schools must continue to struggle, not only to do traditional things better, like improving test scores, but also to do new things, too, because schools are the last best hope for countless youngsters. For example, most of the proposed solutions for virtually every catastrophic social problem facing America today involves an educational component. The public looks to schools to develop and administer antiviolence programs, deliver health care messages, and provide job counseling. Yet no solutions that depend importantly on schools will succeed fully until the reasons for attending school are set right.

We have now completed our analysis of the motivational roots of the classroom crisis in America, thanks largely to the theme of motives-as-drives. In the next chapter we begin considering recommendations for change that call for a different motivational metaphor. In preparing for this step, it is useful to recall the STARPOWER game, and ask if competition is not after all an unavoidable fact of life, or even basic to human nature. Certainly one might think so after watching players consistently misuse power in such arrogant ways in what is, after all, only a game. Is it in the nature of individuals to seek out inequality? Whatever the answer to this age-old question, one thing seems quite clear. Changing the way people behave will depend on more than simply exhorting them to exercise reason and act in good faith. Aggressive, authoritarian, and rebellious behavior is virtually assured in situations of inequality. Changing such behavior requires that we change the system in which the behavior occurs. R. Garry Shirts (1969), the developer of STARPOWER, believes that

> it would be possible to take a group of aggressive STARPOWER players and put them in a social system that rewards openness, honesty, warmth and tenderness and have them act entirely different; not because they are any better or worse as individuals but because they are operating in a different social system. (p. 19)

What kinds of games might these be, and if there are no losers would they still be worth playing?

7

Motivational equity and the will to learn

Be happy in your work.
COLONEL SITU IN PIERRE BOULLE, The Bridge over the River Kwai

It was inevitable that Colonel Situ's advice would fail to move the British prisoners under his control. After all, the work in question was building a railroad bridge that would advance Japan's cause in World War II, and to comply – happily or not – would mean collaborating with the enemy. As a result, Situ had few motivational cards to play. Yet he needed British help. At first he sought to persuade the prisoners by increasing their food ration. Later, when these *positive inducements* failed, Situ applied the principle of *negative reinforcement*. By resuming work the prisoners could escape brutal beatings. Still British cooperation was only half-hearted and punctuated by numerous acts of sabotage.

Situ's frustration compellingly illustrates what we already know about achievement dynamics: The quality of one's effort, whether it be enthusiastic engagement, timid reluctance, or active resistance, depends largely on the reasons for performing. Clearly, defiance and anger are a poor basis on which to build anything – not bridges and certainly not the future.

In the first six chapters we explored the consequences of using competition as a means to motivate students, and in the process were led to investigate the complex relationship between school achievement, on the one hand, and fear-of-failure dynamics and anxiety, on the other – all thanks to the perspective provided by drive theory. In essence, we learned that competition arouses short-sighted, divisive reasons to learn, namely, to win over others and when necessary to avoid losing. Competing in schools for limited rewards in a climate of scarcity, like Situ's cunning use of food as a bribe, arouses little in the way of true enthusiasm. Students no longer focus on learning, but only on the gold stars and grades that follow compliance. Likewise, avoiding failure and ridicule (or beatings, in the case of the British prisoners) like other forms of negative reinforcement cannot sustain task involvement. A competitive, ability-stratified environment provides few prospects for being happy in one's work.

In the remaining chapters we will consider the possibility for reducing the threat to school achievement posed by competitive incentives and by the wrongheaded policy of intensification that focuses on performance, not necessarily on learning. To do this we must now shift our attention away from the metaphor of motives as drives – forces that impel action – and consider instead motives as goals – reasons that draw or inspire individuals to action. As explained earlier, the reason for adopting a goal orientation is not because it is necessarily the better way to characterize human motivation but rather because goals are more readily changeable than drives, and when goals change so does behavior. It is precisely this malleability – viewing motives as a *state* of mind subject to change and not as an immutable *trait,* to borrow a distinction from test anxiety research – that recommends motives-as-goals as the best way to think about educational reform.

The kinds of goals we must foster are intrinsic in nature, that is, involving the desire to become more effective as a person or to perform actions for their own sake (Deci & Ryan, 1980, 1985; Lepper, 1988). Recall the properties of intrinsic goals. First, because intrinsic reasons are their own reward, the psychic payoffs for learning are not limited to a few individuals, but are open to all. Second, when the individual is intrinsically motivated learning becomes the means to an end, not an isolated event whose only purpose is to get the right answer or to please the teacher. Where education is concerned things go better when intrinsic motives predominate for several reasons. For one, intrinsic involvement is a necessary condition for creative thinking and innovative thought (Amabile, 1982; Moran, McCullers, & Fabes, 1984). For another, students who see schools as agents for promoting learning for its own sake get better grades, are more satisfied with school, and are less likely to drop out (Nicholls, 1984; Nicholls et al., 1985).

For these reasons, the remaining chapters belong to Colonel Nicholson, Situ's counterpart, the highest-ranking British officer in the jungle prison camp. What Situ was unable to accomplish by cunning and brutality, Nicholson achieved by appealing to a higher purpose. Nicholson gave the men under his command a reason for living: to create something worthwhile, even though he could offer them little in the way of tangible rewards. But I am getting slightly ahead of the story.

Before proceeding, we need to pause briefly and take stock. It is essential that we be clear about the likely causes of the current crises in education, at least those that can be deduced from a motivational perspective. The kinds of solutions I recommend will depend closely on my analysis of the problem, and particularly on those features of school life I believe should be altered in order to enhance feelings of competency, task-engagement, and satisfaction. Constructive change is always difficult to initiate even under the best of circumstances, so we can ill afford to address the wrong problem. Then, after targeting the problem, we will draw together the many lessons learned so far into a single set of guidelines for change.

The problem

Nothing is more despicable than respect based on fear.
ALBERT CAMUS

We will proceed to identify the problem by the process of elimination. What then are *not* the likely causes of the widespread failure to learn in our schools?

First, and fundamentally, the problem does not appear to reside in the process of learning itself. Nowhere in our review have we found any evidence to suggest that the act of learning is inherently abrasive. It is only when the egotistic goals of self-aggrandizement and status seeking predominate that the learning process becomes threatening. This suggests that the problem of student indifference lies as much in the kinds of goals that society chooses for its children as in the means by which these goals are achieved.

Second, the root cause of the educational crisis is not poor school performance; inadequate achievement is merely a symptom. The causes go deeper to underlying motivational concerns. Indeed, the logic of our position so far argues that an exclusive concern with improved test scores not only overlooks the real problem, but is also largely irrelevant to the solution. Better academic performance should not be the primary objective we seek. Actually, academic gains are the byproduct of attaining other more fundamental objectives. In fact, as we have seen, a preoccupation with performance – and its handmaiden, ability – tends to inhibit the very excellence we hope to promote. Increasing test scores alone will not ensure future excellence as long as the pupil's sense of worth is linked to succeeding competitively. The student may improve, but then so will others, and the competitive race will simply escalate. Ultimately, it is the value and meaning of what is learned – more particularly, the sense of satisfaction arising from enhanced understanding – rather than accumulating knowledge for the sake of power or prestige that will determine whether or not the will to learn is maintained. This is not to suggest that achievement is irrelevant. It is through one's accomplishments that self-confidence is nurtured. But it is equally true that confidence depends on the reasons students learn. In effect, competency and confidence must prosper together, in tandem, and for the right reasons, if either is to advance. Otherwise, the will to learn will suffer.

Third, we must also be wary of attributing the problem of educational failure simply to inadequate motivation. Again, such a conclusion points only to symptoms. Characterizing student indifference as unmotivated does not *explain* the problem; neither does it really *identify* the problem. Based on the research presented so far, it seems reasonable to conclude that the failure to achieve is as much the result of being *overmotivated,* but for the wrong reasons, as it is of not being motivated at all. By this logic, preferred solutions lie in the direction of altering motivational intent or goals rather than simply arousing motivation per se as is implied by intensification policy.

Fourth, and finally, the collective failure of will does not derive from the fact that the quality of school achievement depends heavily on academic ability or from the fact that children compare abilities, even though some observers have pointed to the "tyranny of intelligence" as a major culprit. These misguided reformers suggest that schools should treat all students more alike – in effect, encouraging a uniformity of achievement outcomes – thereby creating a kind of egalitarianism that is thought to produce a shared sense of dignity among all learners. However, these proponents do not understand what we have come to discover, namely, that dignity is achieved through striving for excellence, not equivalency. As Covington and Beery (1976) observe, "Bringing the achievement of all to the same level will only result in mediocrity and in the process destroy the spirit of individual initiative so crucial to high accomplishment" (p. 90).

With these comments in mind, what is the central cause of the widespread disruption of school learning from a motivational perspective? And in what directions might effective solutions lie? Fundamentally, the failure to learn arises whenever the individual's sense of worth becomes equated with the ability to achieve competitively. Individuals who anchor their sense of personal value in ability are placed at considerable risk because schools, like the rest of life, cannot guarantee an unbroken string of successes. If pride in success depends largely on self-perceptions of ability, then students' involvement in learning will continue only for as long as they continue to aggrandize ability. But once failure, with its legacy of shame and anger, threatens a self-image of competency, students will likely withdraw from learning and may even make it difficult for others to learn.

What parts do schools play in forging this potentially destructive ability–worth axis? Basically, as I have argued, this linkage is strengthened by school environments that magnify the importance of ability and, as a result, tend to limit the supply of meaningful rewards. When classrooms provide insufficient incentives for success, many, if not most, youngsters must shift their achievement goals (Botkin, 1990). They must now struggle to avoid failure and its accompanying sense of worthlessness. As we have seen, in a competitive climate the supply of meaningful rewards shrinks largely because students come to judge the value of their accomplishments relative to the achievements of others. For example, even though Gloria merits high praise for a job well done, she may still not feel successful because her efforts are less polished or less complete than those of others. Such harsh, self-imposed standards push the possibilities for genuine pride further and further out of reach.

An important proposition emerges from this self-worth analysis. It is the structure of classroom learning and the educational goals implied by a particular incentive system that control the amount, duration, and quality of student involvement in learning. If this argument is correct, then we should be able to change both the rate of failure and its meaning by restructuring the "rules of the learning game," to use Alschuler's (1969, 1973) phrase. This observation reminds us of our earlier contention that preferred solutions lie in the direction of altering the reasons (or goals) for learning rather than increasing motivation (drive) per se.

Solutions

Colonel Nicholson had the sort of faith which moves mountains, built pyramids, cathedrals, or even bridges, and makes dying men go to work with a smile on their lips. They succumbed to his appeal that they should pull their weight. They went down to the river without a murmur. With this fresh impetus, the bridge was soon finished.
PIERRE BOULLE, The Bridge over the River Kwai

It was a proper bridge, too, not a shoddy, makeshift affair, but an accomplishment worthy of civilized men working in squalid places. For the sake of pride, dignity, and the awe of creation, Colonel Nicholson's men toiled, suffered, and occasionally died. Yet, curiously, they remained indifferent to the blows and curses rained down on them by Colonel Situ. Free men and slaves differ in their reasons for working. Slaves perform to avoid punishment; at their best, free men aspire to higher goals.

Likewise, in schools the reasons for learning control not only the quality of understanding but, of equal importance, the meaning of one's accomplishments for the continued will to learn. As we have seen, some goals are unworthy and disrupt learning: avoiding failure, aggrandizing ability status for the sake of power, and gaining favor at the expense of others. By contrast, other goals encourage those behaviors associated with task-engagement and creativity. We must identify these latter goals and systematically reinforce them. One is the goal of mastery – becoming the best one can be. A second goal is to help others, or as defined more broadly by Nicholls (1984, 1989), a commitment to solving society's problems. A third goal is the satisfaction of curiosity.

Such goals promote *motivational equity* – equity in that the satisfaction that comes from the struggle to achieve these goals is within the reach of all students, irrespective of background or ability. This source of equity is denied students when excellence is defined competitively.

Instructional guidelines

How do we encourage the pursuit of these egalitarian goals? What guidelines emerge from the diverse array of research findings reviewed so far? Six broad generalizations suggest themselves.

1. INHERENTLY ENGAGING ASSIGNMENTS

Schools must provide the opportunity for intrinsic goals to emerge in the course of daily work. In effect, when possible schools should turn work into play, recalling Mark Twain's distinction between *work* – "whatever a body is obliged to do" – and *play* – "what a body is not obliged to do." What, then, are the task characteristics that promote a sense of playful involvement and personal commitment? Thomas Malone (1981a, 1981b) suggests three:

Manageable challenges. Tasks are engaging to the degree they challenge the individual's present capacity, yet permit some control over the level of challenge faced. So far Hoppe's ring-toss experiment has served as our prototype. But there are many everyday examples as well. The childhood game of tag readily comes to mind. Tag permits each participant to adjust the level of challenge to his or her own physical abilities by choosing whom to chase and by modifying the distance to stay away from whoever is It (Eifferman, 1974). Such subtle adjustments create drama and excitement, which is to say that the outcome of each round is left in doubt. As we shall see, this game has any number of serious academic counterparts.

Curiosity arousal. Assignments are also inherently appealing to the extent they arouse and then satisfy curiosity. The arousal of curiosity depends on providing sufficient complexity so that outcomes are not always certain. Complexity that stimulates rather than overwhelms can be introduced by providing for the possibility of multiple goals that emerge within the same task as work proceeds (Csikszentmihalyi, 1975). This process is described wonderfully by James Diggory (1966):

> [But] once this exploration ends . . . he tries to produce a result as good as the last one, but quicker. Next, he may disregard time altogether and try to improve the product. Later he may concentrate on the smoothness of the process and attempt to swing elegantly through a well-ordered and efficient routine. He may discover and invent new processes or adapt new materials or new methods of work. (pp. 125–126)

It is the natural progression of goals described here that maximizes playful involvement. Assignments that feature emerging multiple goals can be contrasted to those tasks that are dominated by one constant overweening purpose, that of winning over others, and to those tasks characterized by rigid, fixed conventions. In these latter instances there is little incentive to take the risks associated with discovering and meeting challenges; one is too busy worrying about who is ahead and who is behind.

Fantasy arousal. Assignments are inherently captivating to the extent they elicit fantasy. By fantasy I do not mean merely unbridled wish fulfillment or fairy tales, but rather the creation of imaginary circumstances that permit the free and unfettered use of one's growing abilities (Malone, 1981b). The child who uses books as a medium of passage into new worlds of his or her own creation is but one example of this phenomenon. Such fantasizing stimulates the child to read more and better, thus closing the circle between self-reverie and competency.

The larger point is that if educators are clever enough in their curriculum design, they should be able to arouse students to greater involvement, and for the best of reasons – for the satisfaction of curiosity, the stimulation of personally valued imagery, and for meeting manageable yet challenging goals.

2. PROVIDING SUFFICIENT REINFORCERS

Once teachers arrange assignments in ways that encourage intrinsic involvement, they must then systematically reward students for setting meaningful goals, for posing questions that lead to new ways of thinking, and for satisfying their curiosity. In essence, this means modifying the rules of the learning game. These rule changes must accomplish two basic objectives: First, they must correct the economics of scarcity and, second, rewards must be arranged so that the act of learning itself becomes a sought-after goal. Consider a simple example of how such an alteration might work as described by Covington & Beery (1976):

> For all the good-natured fun and excitement it generates, the "spelling bee" is in many ways the epitome of classroom competition. By necessity there is *the* winner (usually a girl). There are also several near-winners, and the rest are losers to one degree or another. Yet by introducing only modest changes, Richard de Charms (1972) transformed this game into an object lesson in the importance of recognizing and working within one's limits. Rather than assigning spelling words to students on a random basis as is typically the case, this experimenter gave each student

a choice of three kinds of words to spell: easy, moderately difficult, and difficult. Students were kept from automatically choosing an easy word because spelling it gave their team only one point, whereas spelling the moderately difficult word meant two points, and three points were given for the hard words. . . . The scale of difficulty was tailored to each individual. Easy words were those that the student had spelled correctly on a test several days before; moderately difficult words were those he had previously misspelled but had studied in the meantime; and hard words were taken from the next spelling assignment which no student had yet seen. By this arrangement students quickly learned that success depends on a careful evaluation of one's own skills – in this case, spelling skills – and that if they disregard these realities, no matter how bright they might be, they penalized themselves by failing. Moreover, they learned that a realistic goal is the most challenging kind, and incidentally the one that yields the greatest payoff. (pp. 94–95)

Economics of scarcity. These lessons are possible only because de Charms corrected the economics of scarcity. By changing the reasons for learning from being largely competitive – as is the nature of most spelling bees – to self-challenge and cooperative team effort, rewards became plentiful, yet individually meaningful. And of equal importance, it was the actions of students *themselves* that determined how plentiful were the rewards, not the actions of the teacher. Such rewards have a special characteristic. They are distributed on an absolute, not on a relative basis, that is, not depending on how well one student does compared to another, but depending on *what* tasks the student chooses, with the rewards going most often to the realistic goal setter. Such absolute reference points also provide built-in criteria for gauging one's progress, or lack of it, and for judging when one's work is finished or still incomplete.

Many, if not most, school tasks can be cast in absolute terms and have numerous counterparts in the outside world. Witness the Boy Scout who is working for a merit badge in photography, and the eager 16-year-old preparing to pass his driver's license test, or the insurance executive studying to pass an examination that will certify her as a life underwriter. In effect, any number of merit badges can be awarded or driving tests passed. The struggle now focuses on the obstacles imposed by the nature of the task itself and on the varying levels of excellence required, not on individuals competing against one another for diminishing rewards. Naturally, not everyone wants a merit badge in photography. And not everyone is capable of becoming a life underwriter, nor should everyone try; it doesn't make economic sense. But when it comes to schooling, it *does* make sense for *all* students to master as many of the basic lessons as possible. These observations bring us to the second important feature of restructuring.

Learning as a conditioned reinforcer. These plentiful, absolute rewards must be arranged so that the act of learning itself becomes a *conditioned reinforcer*, to use the terminology of behavioral modification. Money is a common conditioned reinforcer. Clearly, money itself is not good to eat or drink, nor does it provide entertainment (unless one is a Midas). But money will *buy* all these things and that is the source of its reinforcing value. Conditioned reinforcers commonly used in school include points, tokens, or credit that can be accumulated by students and then later cashed in for long-awaited privileges or prizes. Thus, for example, students can accumulate points for doing well (learning) on a series of weekly spelling quizzes with the ultimate payoff being free passes to the zoo or time out in class to listen to music (with earphones) or the chance to talk with friends. In the early stages of such a *token economy,* learning is likely to be viewed expediently as something one does to get a reward. But the prevailing evidence suggests that eventually the experience of learning itself will begin to acquire intrinsic properties. When this happen students often prefer different kinds of payoffs, especially those that increase the chances to learn even more. This transformation from extrinsic to intrinsic control of learning is demonstrated by the findings of Harold Cohen and James Filipczak (1971) who worked with delinquent boys. Tokens were dispensed as rewards for completing homework assignments and could be "spent" in various ways, including the purchase of items from a mail-order catalogue. In the beginning, the mail-order business was lively. But eventually, as their school performance increased, the boys became dissatisfied with material rewards. They began to purchase library time with their tokens and paid rent on study cubicles. In effect, the boys were willing to pay for the privilege to study.

The experience of Bernadine Allen (1975) is even more impressive, perhaps because of the long-term changes involved. Allen agreed to reward ten failing high school students from minority backgrounds if they would improve their grades. Most of these students chose monetary rewards and received $5 for every A or B grade they received in each course throughout the school year. The remaining students set up individually tailored incentives, which in one case was being a timekeeper for football games at a nearby college. By the end of the year all the students had raised their grades to at least a passing level, and several were earning A's and B's. The students attended classes regularly and completed their homework assignments on time, something they had rarely done before. Eight years later, all the students had graduated from high school and five had gone on to college. Of these latter students, two had completed three years of college, and the remaining three had graduated from a four-year college or university. This is a remarkable record of persistence, one that could never have been sustained by financial inducements alone, especially for such low wages.

These several studies demonstrate just how powerful intrinsic payoffs can be and how, despite their intangible qualities, they can be arranged for and deliberately promoted using positive reinforcers. (For an excellent account of the classroom management strategies involved, see Cangelosi, 1988). But how can this be?

Plentiful rewards. If there are sufficient rewards to go around, will not the value of these plentiful rewards be degraded? Will not students work less hard to attain rewards, especially if they are no longer evidence of one's ability status? Not necessarily.

It is largely when rewards (e.g., grades) are dispensed on a competitive basis that their value depends on scarcity. When rewards are distributed on an absolute basis, then pride in accomplishment comes to depend more on how hard one chooses to work. A study by Covington and Jacoby (1973) illustrates this point. College students enrolled in an introductory psychology course could work for any grade they desired, but the grade requirements were commensurate with the level of excellence sought: The standards were quite demanding for an A, somewhat less stringent for a B, and so on. Satisfaction with a given grade, say, an A, depended not so much on how many other top grades were awarded – in this case far more than under conventional grading systems – but on how hard the task was perceived to be and on whether or not students thought their work measured up favorably to the instructor's expectations. In short, goals that are seen as challenging and require much hard work are deemed valuable, no matter how many other students also succeed at or above that level of attainment.

Overjustification effect revisited. All this may be true, but what happens when teachers begin rewarding actions they hope students will undertake freely, such as browsing through library books on their own? According to the *overjustification* hypothesis (chapter 6), when students are offered tangible rewards for what they might otherwise do unprompted, learning simply becomes a way of obtaining rewards. In effect, students may end up merely internalizing teacher reinforcement schedules. In some respects such "internal motivation," as Christine Chandler and James Connell (1987) call it, does resemble intrinsic motivation. But they are not the same. Consider Chandler and Connell's example of the young boy who dutifully cleans his room without being reminded by his parents. It is true that this good conduct is internalized. It occurs without the threat of punishment or the promise of rewards. But it does lack the joyful, spontaneous qualities associated with true task involvement.

These same concerns can be expressed differently. Recall our example of the driver's license test. Few teenagers choose to master the complexities of driving a car out of any intrinsic curiosity about the principles of applied physics. Typically their goals are more social and economic if not competitive – the boy with the car gets the girl, or so it used to be. Likewise, the merit badge holder may seek the prestige of becoming an Eagle Scout out of vanity, not out of any high-minded ideals. These examples indicate that true task engagement requires that the reasons for mastery must be right.

Actually, tangible rewards need not interfere with intrinsic task involvement, and depending on several factors may even enhance it. First, as was just noted, rewards encourage learning, not just performance, if they are distributed on an absolute, noncompetitive basis (Boggiano & Ruble, 1979). Second, it is when extrinsic rewards are used as *motivators* to arouse greater effort that intrinsic involvement is most imperiled. However, when rewards are used as *information* about how well students are doing or as a signal that a different approach is needed, then feedback messages can themselves take on intrinsic properties. Moreover, such feedback need not always be positive to be effective. For example, Ruth Butler and Mordici Nisan (1986) provided a group of sixth-grade students with feedback describing one aspect of a task that they had performed well and another aspect performed less well (e.g., "You thought of many ideas, but not many *unusual* ones."). These students continued to express interest in the task and to improve their performance over several work sessions compared to another group that received feedback designed simply to arouse effort level, in the form of a numerical score indicating how well each student performed relative to others. The performance of this latter group deteriorated over time; the children later explained in poststudy interviews that they were worried about failure and were trying to avoid losing. Clearly, then, it is the context in which feedback is provided, as well as its purpose, that is important to continued striving. When rewards smack of surveillance, of being compared to others, or if they imply manipulation and control, even if it is for the students' own good, youngsters – like adults – are likely to respond with anger, resentment, and fear (Boggiano et al., 1988; Deci, 1975; Deci & Ryan, 1987).

Minimal sufficiency. Sometimes extrinsic rewards are necessary to sustain student involvement long enough to ensure mastery. For example, the importance of learning to diagram sentences as a gateway to more satisfying future activities – such as expressing one's ideas sufficiently well to win the argument or poetically enough to win the girl – may be lost on young students who see no majesty here, no larger purpose, but only tedium. In such cases artificial inducements may be needed to engage the student, especially in the early stages of learning. But extrinsic rewards should be used sparingly and withdrawn as soon as skills are adequately mastered.

This realization has prompted Mark Lepper (1981) to propose the principle of "minimal-sufficiency," that is, teachers should rely on extrinsic rewards only as absolutely necessary and no more: The less powerful the extrinsic controls employed by teachers, the more likely students will be to internalize what they learn and apply it spontaneously without being prompted to do so. This principle has been demonstrated not only for school learning but also for a range of other valued behaviors as well, including the willingness to act altruistically and to resist tempting but dangerous activities (Boggiano et al., 1987).

But how can rewards be administered in ways consistent with the principle of minimal-sufficiency? Several possibilities come to mind. For one thing, the effects of rewarding individuals for merely participating or for completing an assignment are different from using rewards as a way to control the quality of performance. The weight of research evidence suggests that giving rewards for participation alone is unlikely to inhibit task involvement (See Olsen, 1991).

For another thing, grading is most compatible with the goals of learning when it is to some extent under the control of students. For instance, students might choose the particular assignments on which they are to be judged or they might become involved directly in the grading process itself. Here the grade might be the average of the student's and teacher's appraisal. Self-grading is also a possibility. Interestingly, when teachers provide the criteria for a good performance, students tend to judge themselves according to these rules with the result that self-assigned grades usually correspond closely to those that the teacher would otherwise assign (Anderson, 1966).

Placed in the context of self-appraisal and personal decision making, the issue of grading properly becomes a question of how students can best learn to judge their own abilities and then to make the most of them. In this role grading is most compatible with the overall objectives of fostering competency, personal growth, and feelings of self-worth (Kirschenbaum, Simon, & Napier, 1971).

3. ENHANCING EFFORT–OUTCOME BELIEFS

Obviously, plentiful rewards by themselves are insufficient to sustain the will to learn. Students must also come to interpret their newly won successes as caused by their own skillful effort. Gaining a sense of personal control over events involves the strengthening of an effort–outcome attribution linkage. This is no easy proposition. As we know, expending effort represents a potential threat to those students caught up in a competitive mentality. However, by shifting the focus from competitive goals to equity goals, teachers can encourage plausible interpretations of failure other than low ability (Ames et al., 1977; Ames, 1978; Stephan et al., 1977). For example, if students choose tasks within their level of competency – as was the case in de Charm's spelling bee experiment – then effort and good judgment become the main perceived causes of success, and failure occurs because of unrealistically high aspirations, greed, or because of inappropriate or ill-timed study. These causes are within the power of students to correct, and for this reason learning need no longer be aversive, nor effort something to be feared.

Indeed, teachers should begin to see the emergence of effort patterns that comply more with rational expectations. No longer should effort expenditure serve a predominantly defensive function, as when – contrary to all logical considerations – students choose to work only on tasks that are so difficult that success becomes impossible or on assignments that are so easy that success is virtually assured. Rather, students ought to begin exerting effort as required by the nature of the problem: As task difficulty increases, so will effort, and in the case of exceedingly difficult problems, students may choose not to try at all, not necessarily to avoid the implications of failure but to husband their energy and resources for other tasks more within their capacities and experience (Sigall & Gould, 1977).

These observations take on special meaning in the light of David Mettee's (1971) answer to the question of how the cycle of despair might be broken for failure-prone students who deny success and on occasion even sabotage their own efforts. Mettee proposed that such individuals might eventually accept total responsibility for their successes if they first started by taking only partial credit – just enough to engender some pride but not enough to arouse fear. Hopefully, then as individuals become more comfortable with success and the sense of pride it engenders, they will assume more of the credit. My self-worth analysis suggests a different approach. Overcoming fear of success is not so much a matter of growing used to feelings of pride, but of restructuring the meaning of success. Failure-prone individuals are afraid that if they accept credit for their successes, they will be unable to repeat them later for lack of ability. But if these students exercise proper task analysis and set realistic goals, then success is repeatable. Presumably, then, these students will not only accept credit for their successes – and not just partial credit – but will also become increasingly confident about their future chances.

To secure these benefits students must be free to set their own learning goals. This point has been vividly demonstrated by Alschuler (1969) who transformed a previously uninspired fifth-grade mathematics class into a highly rewarding experience by introducing a simple goal-setting component. Alschuler merely asked students to indicate in advance what percentage of test problems they would strive to answer correctly on each weekly quiz. Students were paid for the accuracy of their judgments – the coin of the realm being Monopoly money. Realistic aspirations were critical because students would lose money if they either overestimated or underestimated their eventual performance. Thus, just as in the case of de Charms's spelling bee, success depended more on an accurate match between the student's aspirations and his or her current knowledge than on the absolute level of performance. And because the implied goal was to maximize one's earnings, students were expected to make their estimates near the upper reach of their present ability, thereby setting in motion an upward cycling of achievement – just as Hoppe's ring-toss subjects had done nearly half a century earlier. This is exactly what happened. On average, math achievements scores increased three grade levels for this group during the school year! Students who had done nothing in mathematics before now began completing homework assignments on time and taking their books home.

More rigorous laboratory research has since confirmed Aschuler's compelling anecdotal findings regarding the importance of student goal setting (Bandura & Schunk, 1981; Schunk, 1983, 1984; Thomas, 1980; Wang & Stiles, 1976; Zimmerman, 1989). As only one example, James Sofia (1978) found that when students analyzed learning tasks for sources of difficulty and indicated the levels of performance to which they aspired, they did better on achievement tests and were more likely to interpret their successes in terms of effort expended. These goal setters also felt most satisfied with the results of those tests for which they studied the hardest, irrespective of the score they received.

An important sidelight on these self-monitoring dynamics is provided by Giora Keinan and Moshe Zeidner (1987). These researchers demonstrated that merely providing students a choice of which practice problems they would work on, rather than being assigned the practice items by a teacher, reduced feelings of anxiety (tension) during study and also led to higher test scores. By gaining some measure of personal control over events, these students were better able to concentrate on the task at hand.

4. STRENGTHENING AN EFFORT–WORTH LINKAGE
Under competitive goals, emotions such as shame in failure and pride in success depend largely on self-perceptions of ability. As a result, as long as the individual continues to win all is well; feelings of pride will act as a powerful

source of self-reinforcement. But in this case it is pride in ability, not necessarily pride in accomplishment, that sustains student involvement. Eventually, however, if failure threatens students' self-images of competency, then they are likely to withdraw from learning, particularly those who already harbor doubts about their ability.

Conversely, by shifting to equity goals, self-praise will come to depend more on the quality and amount of effort expended and less on winning (Ames, 1978; Ames & Ames, 1981). Likewise, in the case of falling short, self-criticism will more likely be linked to inadequate or improper effort (Crockenberg, Bryant, & Wilce, 1976). For all the unpleasantness they create, effort-linked emotions such as guilt and remorse act as negative reinforcers – they can be avoided by working harder, and for that reason have a beneficial side. Not so, however, with ability-linked emotions. Shame and humiliation are unlikely to arouse positive reactions under any circumstance. Rather they promote only despair, anger, and feelings of helplessness.

5. PROMOTING POSITIVE BELIEFS ABOUT ABILITY

According to self-worth theory, a preoccupation with ability status is the central, oppressive reality of school life and must be dealt with constructively if we are ever to promote the will to learn. This cannot be done simply by dismissing the importance of ability or ignoring individual gifts. Far from minimizing the importance of ability, teachers must, in fact, actively promote implicit theories of ability, but theories that are conducive to sustained motivation. What ability beliefs have we considered so far, and which are likely candidates?

Ability as capacity. First, there is the view of ability as a capacity, something best thought of as a *noun,* a fixed amount or quantity. This belief is a powerful organizer of behavior. In fact, a growing number of researchers regard differences in perceived capacity as the essence of achievement motivation. Overall, the evidence is quite compelling. For one thing, self-perceptions of ability (as capacity) guide the individual's choice of tasks (Buckert, Meyer, & Schmalt, 1979). For another thing, ability perceptions determine how much effort the individual is likely to exert, and for how long once difficulties arise or failure occurs (Hallermann & Meyer, 1978; Hallermann, 1980; Licht, Kistner, Ozkarogoz, Shapiro, & Clausen, 1985). Finally, depressed self-perceptions of ability lead to avoidance behavior and to anxiety and, as we have seen, are the main trigger for learned helplessness (Covington, 1985a).

If perceived capacity controls so much of what we take to be motivated behavior, then perhaps schools should encourage greater perceived capacity among its students. There can be little doubt about the potential benefits of doing this, at least in a narrow, experimental context. For instance, Robert Miller, Philip Brickman, and Diana Bolen (1975) supplied second-grade students with ability-enhancing feedback as they worked on arithmetic assignments (e.g., "You have excellent ability"). This manipulation produced dramatic increases in math achievement scores. However, despite this and other similar demonstrations, there is reason to believe that in the long run such an emphasis may actually be counterproductive. For one thing, any attempt to manipulate ability perceptions directly is at best artificial and not always convincing. When students already doubt their ability, contrary information does little to enhance self-confidence (Marston, 1968). Worse yet, suspect feedback may cause students to doubt the honesty of teachers and jeopardize their credibility (Gergen, 1971). For another thing, a capacity-enhancing approach is likely to encourage further the view of ability as fixed and immutable (an *entity* belief), which carries with it the fear of being judged as inadequate and consequently being unworthy. For these reasons the prospects for enhancing sustained motivation via altering perceptions of capacity appear remote.

Ability as attributions. Recall from the evidence presented in chapter 3 (Figures 3.1 and 3.2) that ability attributions strongly influence expectations for future success as well as feelings of pride in success and humiliation in failure. As we know, these findings have led some researchers to alter achievement attributions experimentally in order to maximize the perceived importance of effort compared to ability. I have already expressed concern over the wisdom of using attribution retraining as an educational strategy, especially in competitive circumstances and among older students who might not share the teacher's enthusiasm about increasing their effort level when risking failure.

Ability as strategy. Ability can also be viewed as fulfilling an executive or strategic planning function (Covington, 1969, 1986b; Resnick, 1987). Here the notion of a *static* capacity gives way to a more animated, *plastic* view of ability as a repertoire of skills that can be improved and expanded through instruction and experience – the so-called *incremental* perspective. Here ability is a *verb*. Recall that those students who embrace an incremental view of ability are more likely to focus on the task at hand, display greater involvement, and are less preoccupied with learning as a test of their worth compared to students who hold an entity view (e.g., Dweck & Bempechat, 1983).

It is this incremental view of intelligence that must be fostered in schools, not to discourage peer comparisons, which are inevitable anyway, but rather to broaden student beliefs about the true multidimensional nature of human talent. There is, however, a subtle irony in this proposal. Developmentally speaking, an incremental view reflects the most primitive notion of ability – ironic because in order to sustain the creative side of adulthood, it would appear that we must help students retain a perception of the world that occurs naturally among only the very young. Pablo Picasso put the dilemma well when he remarked that "every child is an artist. The problem is how to remain an artist once he grows up."

6. IMPROVING TEACHER–STUDENT RELATIONS

We have pictured students and teachers as adversaries in the competitive learning game, a no-win situation in which both sides lose. The authority of teachers to control student attention is severely limited, their only power being the power to cajole, reprimand, and punish; as for students, they can only disrupt or avoid learning, not change the basic causes of their frustration and fear. Neither teachers nor students are to blame, but rather together they are caught up in a contest that neither can win, and teachers are helpless to change things so long as the dominant classroom incentive structure remains failure oriented.

According to this analysis, by promoting a condition of motivational equity, the rules of the game will change so that power is shared by both teachers and students. Naturally, many teachers are wary of sharing power. As Bill Cosby wryly observes, "You don't defend yourself by leaning into the punch!" And, by analogy, you do not compound an already difficult teaching situation by putting more power in potentially irresponsible hands. Indeed, one of the major fears of both beginning and veteran teachers is that they may lose control of their classroom. Today this is no idle worry. What teachers need, many will tell you, is more, not less, power.

Teachers can be reassured, however, by the results of several studies that have sensitized teachers to the ways in which they and their students antagonize one another. For example, Alschuler and his colleagues (1975) trained the staff and student body of a large urban junior high school to analyze the disruptive dynamics of the "discipline game," (as portrayed in chapter 6). This exercise eventually gave way to a mutual spirit of experimentation in which, class by class, individual teachers and their students set about establishing new rules so that teachers could teach more and students had more freedom to learn on their own. Most often such restructuring involved setting time aside – what Alschuler called "mutual agreed learning time" – during which teachers had their student's undivided attention. Similar restructuring, with equally positive results – this time among high school dropouts and migrant workers – has been reported by Arthur Pearl (see Silberman, 1970, p. 346).

As a group these six guidelines represent the essence of the paradigm shift in thinking about school learning and motivation of which we spoke earlier (chapter 1). But what might these changes look like in practice with all these guidelines joined and operating together in harness? Consider the following example.

Global Gambit

Speak to the earth, and it shall teach thee.
JOB 12:8

A hush falls over Mr. Rodriguez's ninth-grade social science class as the first international conference on global warming is convened at Jefferson High. This conference marks the concluding phase of a month-long instructional unit called Global Gambit. Six teams of students, each representing a different nation at risk are poised, eager to make the case for their particular needs in a world of limited resources and dubious prospects. This electric atmosphere has prevailed ever since Mr. Rodriguez first presented some of the possible consequences of global warming, the Greenhouse effect: whole cities, like London, drowned in rising oceans; drought severe enough to trigger riots in Los Angeles when it was learned that an old woman had been secretly watering an ivy plant in her home; and the prospects for a bumper cotton crop in Siberia, which has become the new agricultural land of plenty.

The object of the conference is to negotiate a plan to deal with these and other potential dislocations. Two broad strategies suggest themselves. First, each country (team) can prepare its own local defenses against the warming trend without regard for the actions of other countries. Second, all the countries can band together to seek broader, regional, or worldwide solutions that may forestall or even eliminate the need for local responses. Whatever plans are devised, they must take into account the varying needs of the six participating countries. Several of these countries, like Holland, are peculiarly vulnerable to any rise in ocean levels and tide surges. But Holland is highly industrialized and can better afford the costs of preparing to meet this threat than can other equally endangered but poorer countries. Consider Indonesia, for example, which possesses 15% of the world's coastlines with about 40% of its land vulnerable to a sea-level rise of as little as half a meter. Some experts project the rise to be as high as 3 meters by the end of the 21st century!

Mr. Rodriguez warned his students in advance that their negotiations will be complicated by several factors. First, as just noted, the threat of global warming and the resources available to withstand it vary from country to country. To reflect this reality, Mr. Rodriguez provides each team with different amounts of credit at the World Bank. The richest countries receive the most credit because of their proven ability to repay debt. Each team is free to create its own safeguards but within the limits of its resources, and different solutions have different price tags. For example, one likely consequence of warming is that the level of freshwater lakes will fall due to increased rates of evaporation. For the joint American-Canadian team the cost of dredging the Great Lakes shipping channels 5 feet deeper is 200 credits; dredging 10 feet deeper costs 300 credits.

If an underdeveloped country is not rich enough to create all the safeguards it believes necessary for survival, then it must negotiate to borrow credits from the wealthier teams. But the industrial nations are unlikely to be willing lenders. This is the second complication. Global Gambit has another cross-cutting objective – a game within a game. The industrial nations are placed in competition to determine who becomes the world's leading economic power. The winner of this minigame is the country that amasses the greatest wealth by the end of game play. Yet the wealthy nations cannot entirely ignore the plight of their poorer neighbors because these countries are most vulnerable to any rapid change in climate. Even small dislocations in weather patterns can lead to disproportionate increases in hunger, trigger mass migration, and encourage political unrest, factors that can easily threaten world stability and end game play prematurely.

A third complication is that even in scientific circles, nothing is entirely certain. There is always room for controversy and the margin of error in making predictions is often great. Mr. Rodriquez's students soon learn that although there is general agreement that increases in global temperature are closely associated with rises in global carbon dioxide (CO_2) levels, such correlations are not necessarily evidence for causation. Moreover, even if all the teams agree that CO_2 buildup *causes* warming, it can still be argued that a world with twice as much CO_2 is not always bad and may, in fact, compensate for some of its own negative effects, like the projected reductions in usable farmland. More specifically, some laboratory experiments suggest that CO_2 acts as a sort of fertilizer that accelerates the growth and size of plants. So perhaps less farmland will be needed for the same amount of production. However, these findings can be debated if Mr. Rodriguez's students are clever enough to draw certain conclusions from the graphs and charts he will provide them. Do only the leaves and stems of the plants get bigger, or the grain and fruit as well?

By presenting his students with a series of such debates, Mr. Rodriguez expects them to recognize the range of uncertainty that surrounds their choices, and hopes they will come up with what, according to many experts, is the key question regarding global warming (Schneider, 1989): How fast and how far will climate conditions change relative to the world's ability to cope? It is out of this array of unevenly distributed resources, uncertainty, and mixed motives – some favoring competition and others cooperation – that Mr. Rodriguez's students must hammer out a prudent plan for dealing with the potential crisis.

But there was much to do before the conference could begin. For starters each team had to familiarize itself with the country it represents – the particular geography involved, the economic base, and population density – in order to assess their country's potential vulnerability to global warming. Mr. Rodriguez provided each team with a list of primary sources where the necessary information could be found. He also drew up a test covering the assigned material. Each student had to pass the test at a minimally acceptable level before his or her team could proceed. This requirement posed no particular problem for any of the teams, not because the questions were easy, but because passing the test became a matter of cooperative teamwork. Team members paired up and monitored one another's study, and anyone falling below the minimum on his or her first test try was permitted a second chance after additional peer tutoring. Things were also made easier, especially for test-anxious students, by Mr. Rodriguez's decision to allow unlimited time to answer the questions. As a further inducement to excel, all students scoring above the minimum had their surplus points converted into additional credits at the World Bank for their team.

The real payoff for learning, however, was the opportunity to work on several additional assignments that represented the final gateway to the negotiating table. One task was designed to acquaint students with the various consequences of global warming, some of which are economic, others political, and some medical. In this latter case, the Moroccan team was dismayed to find that increased temperatures in central Africa might spread encephalitis-bearing flies out of their current living range to adjacent territories that are presently free of the disease. Because of the enormity of this global search for consequences, Mr. Rodriguez proposed that the teams assign each of their members to become expert on specific topics, with one student responsible for, say, surveying the possible effects of warming on agricultural production and another for exploring the potential psychological impact on the country's citizens. After all the "experts" had done their homework, each team reconvened and combined these various knowledge sources in much the same way that pieces of a jigsaw puzzle are put together.

Although most students enjoyed these assignments, this was not true of Ralph, the *failure-accepting* student whom we first met in chapter 2. Ralph was a constant source of disruption – handing in assignments late if at all, losing team notes, and always talking out of turn. Clearly, he was out to sabotage Global Gambit. Things were not helped by the fact that Ralph was the last person in class to be picked for a team – actually not picked as much as simply assigned by default as a booby prize to the group unlucky enough to have no choices left. Ralph's reputation as a troublemaker had preceded him from Mrs. Sorensen's room even before he was transferred in the hope that a male teacher might have more luck in providing a much needed source of authority and discipline in Ralph's life.

In order to minimize Ralph's disruptiveness yet also provide him with some sense of accomplishment, Mr. Rodriguez decided to negotiate a series of learning contracts. During their first conference, Mr. Rodriguez gave Ralph some pages from a science text and asked him to choose one of the several experiments that demonstrates how acid rain is created. "Ralph, if you set up the experiment and give a demonstration to the whole class next Wednesday, I will give your team 20 extra credits at the World Bank," offered Mr. Rodriguez, "and 5 additional points if you follow the steps in the text exactly. How much is being careful worth to you?" Ralph looked startled. It had been a long time since anyone had asked his opinion.

Postmortem

The conference has just ended. An overall global plan was ratified, but barely. As Mr. Rodriguez had expected, the negotiations were often acrimonious, sometimes confused, but always engaging. Predictably, the wealthier nations spent much of their time maneuvering among themselves, seeking competitive advantage while often ignoring the proposals and needs of the poorer countries. In the end, however, eight regional projects were funded to aid specific countries in addition to three larger projects involving worldwide cooperation, including an unprecedented reforestation project in which Madagascar would be turned into a giant forest preserve to capture carbon from the atmosphere. And no country went bankrupt! This success was achieved because the total plan was based on the assumption that the effects of global warming, even if they were to prove substantial, would occur only slowly – slowly enough that additional adjustments could be made at 5-year intervals.

"But was our solution OK?" demanded several students. They had a right to know, they pleaded, after all this work. They were being both serious and playful in their question. They were secretly pleased with themselves and intoxicated by the knowledge that Mr. Rodriguez was also delighted. At this point Mr. Rodriguez provided a final surprise. Unbeknownst to his students, Global Gambit had also been played by several atmospheric scientists. The scientists' solutions were accompanied by a detailed explanation of their reasoning at each step, a list of the facts each scientist weighed most heavily in making their decisions, various sources of controversy, and how these controversies were settled, if at all.

Mr. Rodriguez's students spent the next few days in a lively postmortem, huddled together in their respective teams, pouring over the scientists' reports – whispering, grumbling, and variously exclaiming, *"Our* team knew this graph was important, but Argentina refused to see it," and, "So that's why our idea about plankton won't work." The scientists, too, came in for some withering criticism, especially when their reasoning differed substantially from that of the students. "After all," as one student was overheard to remark haughtily, "experts are only people from out of town."

In the end, most students felt comfortable with the probabilistic nature of their decisions, but others were still not sure. "What *really* is the answer?" someone asked. Mr. Rodriguez was about to dismiss the question, but suddenly stopped. He had long wondered how best to pursue further the topic of certainty and knowledge, and to debate the proposition that even in science truth is often socially defined. Now he knew how to spend the last two weeks of the spring term.

Postscript

In what ways does the Global Gambit scenario satisfy our instructional guidelines? And, is it a reasonable example of what is meant by a paradigm shift in the way we need now to think about schooling? Before taking up the first question, the answer to the second question is "yes, more or less," with the usual caveat that no single example can fully capture the larger concept it is meant to illustrate.

Still, it seems natural to ask if this is all there is? Is there really anything new in this example? No, not fundamentally. Virtually everything about Global Gambit is standard teaching practice. The popular "jigsaw" method of cooperative learning is much in evidence as is, of course, the use of educational games and the emphasis on primary source material such as charts and maps. All these techniques are well known to teachers, even venerable. For instance, arguments favoring the use of primary source documents as the best way to stimulate children's thinking surfaced as long ago as the 1890s (Barnes, 1894).

Nor is there anything particularly novel with regard to educational philosophy. Clearly, this example embraces the philosophy of *reflective inquiry,* which was first promoted by John Dewey (1916), later articulated by Gordon Hullfish and Phillip Smith (1961), and most recently defended by Richard Pratte (1988). Reflective inquiry assumes that for a society to remain open there must be a free flow of information and an informed citizenry capable of evaluating it critically. Likewise, Global Gambit makes common cause with a *decision-making* approach to education (Engle & Ochoa, 1988) that assumes that informed choice stands at the heart of good citizenship and that education must ultimately be concerned with society and how individuals live in it and contribute to it. From this perspective, schools should draw their subject matter from such issues as hunger, pollution, poverty, and gender discrimination.

And, finally, just to add a spark of controversy – if more be needed – there is the hint (if not obvious here, it will be in later examples) of what has been called *critical pedagogy* (Giroux, 1983). Critical pedagogy assumes that scientific knowledge, especially in the social sciences, is the product of distorted ideologies that unjustly favor some groups and deprive others. The creation of knowledge, so the argument goes, has been male dominated, overly dependent on *logic* to the relative exclusion of *intuition,* and preoccupied with Western values; such imbalances can only be put right by using schools as an open forum in which any reasonable questions may be raised and all positions fully represented.

Controversial or not, the various educational priorities implied by this example are at least familiar and the criticisms of each are well known (for a review, see Cherryholmes, 1982). In short, there is nothing particularly new here either.

But no promises were made about desired changes being new, only that they should be workable and relatively easy to implement so long as they also satisfy the requirements of a motivational perspective. Thus in an important sense, the purpose of this book is to elevate the commonplace to a new order of significance – in short, to help teachers recognize the profound in the ordinary. If this can be done, then familiarity becomes a hopeful sign, not grounds for contempt or dismissal, and for several reasons. First, a sense of the familiar tells us that what is needed is not only plausible but possible. Second, it suggests that most teachers are already on the right track; that they have been warm all along, but may not have always realized it or always known why. This is why there is nothing as practical as a good theory! Good theories tell us how warm we are and how to get warmer still.

So just what is so profound about the Global Gambit scenario from a motivational perspective? Basically, the answer is the difference between being *task oriented* or being *ego involved*. Mr. Rodriguez's students were more concerned with answers than with who thought of them, more excited by the challenge of the problem than worried about the risks of failure, and caught up, at least briefly, in an intellectual drama that demanded more of them than they may have thought themselves capable. Under the circumstances, time was no longer the property of Hermes – something to be sold, bought, or saved. Rather, for these students time reflected the flow of which Mihaly Csikszentmihalyi (1975) speaks, when ideas come effortlessly, and when without warning or without previous intent "we discover only retrospectively that we have spent time improving ourselves and our work, completely oblivious of our surroundings or of the passage of time, trapped in the pathway to mastery" (Diggory, 1966, p. 126). It is this capacity for self-absorption that has been identified as the hallmark of creativity (Barron, 1965; MacKinnon, 1962).

These transformations occurred for several reasons, each related to the instructional guidelines.

INHERENTLY INTERESTING PROBLEMS

First, Mr. Rodriguez's overall assignment was highly engaging, not only because of its ghoulish appeal to adolescents – the imagined (fantasy) destruction of everything they are rebelling against anyway – but also because of its curiosity value, which depended largely on uncertainty and controversy. In fact, uncertainty was sustained until the very end. And even then, the scientists' feedback created as much controversy as closure. Also, the students had a wide latitude of choice regarding *how* and *when* to learn, and to some extent *what* to learn as they prepared for the final negotiations stage. Such control over events creates a sense of manageable challenge. Finally, by entrusting youngsters with a real problem that alarms us all, Mr. Rodriguez unlocked the supreme source of motivation for all human beings – being respected enough for our counsel that others seek out our advice on urgent matters.

MOTIVATIONAL EQUITY

By daring his students to solve a problem that combined novelty and curiosity value with manageable complexity, Mr. Rodriguez unleashed a host of intrinsic reasons for learning. And because these reasons are their own reward, the payoffs became plentiful and available to all, among them the rewards inherent in discovering connections, creating understanding, and in knowing that one has made a significant contribution to the larger group effort. Of equal importance, Mr. Rodriguez arranged the rules of the learning game so that the act of learning itself became a conditioned reinforcer. In effect, his students learned that knowledge, like money, buys things. For one thing, it buys power. The team that best understood the dynamics of global weather was placed at a decided advantage later when it came time to negotiate. For another thing, knowledge buys resources. Recall Mr. Rodriguez's built-in incentive for learning more than just the minimum number of facts – earning extra credits at the World Bank.

Mastery learning. Mr. Rodriguez also placed knowledge acquisition on an absolute basis. Remember that every team member had to demonstrate a common, minimal level of competency before his or her team could proceed with negotiations. This is an example of a *mastery* or *outcome-based* approach to learning (Block, 1977, 1984; Block & Burns, 1976; Burns, 1987; Mitchell & Spady, 1978; Spady, 1977, 1978, 1982). Here objectives are coached in clear, absolute terms and students are given sufficient opportunity to surpass these standards through extra practice, corrective feedback, and, when necessary, remedial assistance. In this particular case, remedial help was provided for slower learners by those team members who finished early, a feature of *team-assisted instruction* (Slavin, 1978, 1983). Another example of the mastery learning paradigm is *contingency contracting,* which Mr. Rodriguez used successfully with Ralph. Here a teacher negotiates with students work contracts that involve a statement of what is to be done, when the task is to be finished, and the kinds of rewards or payoffs that are contingent upon completion of the contract (Atwood, Williams, & Long, 1974; Homme, 1970; Sapp, 1971).

Contingency contracting well illustrates the potential motivational benefits of mastery learning as they apply to our guidelines. First, contract learning is essentially noncompetitive, with success or failure depending on the actions of the individual students, not on how well others do by comparison. Second, if properly established, contracts create a match between the student's current skill level and his or her aspirations, thus avoiding both the frustration of working beyond one's ability and the boredom of being unchallenged. A proper match also ensures that success is not only more likely but that it is perceived as depending on the quality and amount of effort expended. In this way the all-important effort–outcome linkage is strengthened, also ensuring that the emotions that follow success or failure will promote rather than inhibit intellectual growth (i.e., effort–worth linkage). Third, recall that giving rewards for participation alone is unlikely to inhibit intrinsic task involvement (chapter 6). Contingency contracting would seem to be an ideal vehicle for taking advantage of this fact. Here the offering or withholding of a reward depends totally on the individual's decision to participate or not, and it is largely up to the student to set his or her own standards of excellence once the process of contract negotiation begins. Fourth, unlike ability-grouped instruction, which carries with it the expectation that slow learners are unlikely to succeed (Weinstein & Middlestadt, 1979), learning contracts communicate the expectation that all students will complete their work successfully. Additionally, clear expectations make learning more task oriented (Helmke, 1986; Zatz & Chassin, 1983) and as a result less threatening to anxious, failure-avoiding students who would otherwise expect the worst in the absence of feedback and judge their performance as unacceptable (Butler & Nisan, 1986; Meunier & Rule, 1967). Fifth, mastery rewards tend to serve an *informational*, not an arousal, function. For instance, grades or points become meaningful because they herald a specific accomplishment – a study unit turned in on time or a term paper adequately completed, or in Ralph's case, the experiment conducted exactly according to instructions. Moreover, when grades signal a disappointing performance in the context of a mastery goal, they carry direct implications for how to improve. Furthermore, when rewards are assigned on the basis of absolute standards, they tend to foster a positive interpretation of failure. Failure to achieve under a well-defined standard motivates students to try harder, whereas those failures that occur without any reference to explicit standards tend to lower motivation (Kennedy & Willcutt, 1964). Finally, contingency contracting in particular and mastery learning in general have the potential for making the teacher an ally of the student because the emphasis is on accomplishment rather than on avoiding teacher disapproval (Knight, 1974).

A more detailed analysis of the costs and benefits of mastery learning will be found in Appendix A. The interested reader will also find out what happens next to John, our *failure-avoiding* student, whom we last left in a state of despair at the end of his first semester in college.

Cooperative learning. Mr. Rodriguez also encouraged another source of motivational equity – cooperation for the sake of the group (Slavin, 1983, 1984). Any number of players can win when learning is seen as a cooperative venture. When each student achieves his or her goal – in our example, passing

Mr. Rodriguez's mastery test – then all those with whom the individual is cooperating likewise achieve the common goal, that of moving on to the negotiation stage of Global Gambit. These same dynamics also operated in the jigsaw example (Aronson, Blaney, Stephan, Sikes, & Snapp, 1978; Blaney, Stephan, Rosenfield, Aronson, & Sikes, 1977) where each team member contributed to the group welfare by supplying specialized (expert) information about the consequences of global warming. Here, too, are possibilities for strengthening students' beliefs about the multidimensional nature of ability and their recognition that there are as many different approaches to a task as there are problem solvers.

When properly used, cooperative learning equalizes the opportunity for everyone to feel successful both as individuals and as members of a group so long as each person maximizes his or her effort and shares in the risks of failure (Ames, 1981; Harris & Covington, 1989). Ultimately, the individual's accomplishments take on meaning because they add to the welfare of the group and promote a sense of belonging (Cooper, Johnson, Johnson, & Wilderson, 1980). These benefits are above and beyond the intrinsic pleasure that comes from the process of learning itself. Appendix B explores more fully the potential of cooperative learning techniques as well as some of the risks.

ALTERING THE MEANING OF SUCCESS AND FAILURE

When rewards are scarce, failure takes on an exaggerated presence owing to its implication of low ability. But in Global Gambit, this distortion stands to be corrected. In fact, the very meaning of failure was transformed by the introduction of the scientists' feedback. No longer was a miss (failure) as good as a mile – hopeless and irretrievable (Clifford, 1978). Not only did both students and scientists share a common task, but most important, their reasoning revealed more similarities than differences. And because near misses are subject to correction, mistakes are likely to qualify for what John Holt (1964) has referred to as *nonsuccesses,* events that reflect the vast middle ground between outright perfection and abject failure. Here, too, we can appreciate the potential of game-play for changing the meaning of help seeking from implying incompetency to testimony that sometimes problems are so demanding that all of us, even experts, need all the help we can get.

Global Gambit also demonstrates how the otherwise divisive issues of winners versus losers can be used for constructive purposes. A competitive element was deliberately introduced into Global Gambit, not to arouse interest, however (the teams were already heavily engaged), but rather to instruct. Competition is an important reality and its dynamics must be understood, not denied – understood in light of other legitimate realities such as the possibilities of personal goals. According to Terry Orlick (1982), personal goals such as recovering from mistakes, improving self control, and mastering new skills, moves, and routines have little to do with winning over others; in fact, the presence of competitive dynamics can be used to promote positive values. "What better place is there to discuss the true meaning of values that are important to children and adults alike, such as winning, losing, success, failure, anxiety, rejection, fair play, acceptance . . .? What better place to help children become aware of their own feelings and the feelings of others'' (Orlick, 1982, p. 102)?

TEACHER AS ALLY

Up to this point teachers and students have been portrayed as opponents in the learning game. This negative relationship was transformed when Mr. Rodriguez became an ally of his students – a coach, mentor, and a resource – as they prepared themselves for the upcoming contest of nations. This change from adversary to ally can have important, positive ripple effects in classrooms. For one thing, Mr. Rodriguez was no longer the sole disciplinarian, nor was he the only person concerned with intellectual excellence. His use of cooperative learning automatically placed much of this responsibility on the students themselves, where it must ultimately reside anyway. Whenever the fate of the group is tied to the actions of each individual, then there are powerful incentives within the group to see that everyone learns and to discourage off-target behavior such as loafing, ''goofing off,'' or being tardy.

For another thing, when teachers become advocates for students, they, too, are allowed to make mistakes, even to admit to them, and apologize openly yet still be forgiven, even admired by students because they are allies. As Herbert Kohl (1967) points out, it is the teacher's struggle to be fair and honest, not always right or righteous, that moves and excites students. Kohl goes on to reflect that his ghetto pupils

> did not want to be defiant, insulting, idle; nor were they any less afraid of chaos than I was. They wanted more than anything to feel they were facing it with me and not against me. These discoveries were my greatest strength when I began to explore new things to teach the children. They were as impatient to learn something exciting as I was to find something that would excite them. (p. 31)

The key to teacher goodwill, as illustrated in Global Gambit and reinforced by Kohl's remark, is to arrange circumstances so that teachers and students face obstacles together and in the process learn together. Teachers, like everyone else, are most alive when they are learning.

These observations suggest the need for an important corrective. Until now we have largely characterized good teachers as *managers* whose primary task is to optimize the conditions for learning; in effect, to simplify and present complex topics like history, mathematics, and geography in ways that are accurate, honest, and open to development and discovery (Leinhardt & Greeno, 1986). But good teachers are more than stage directors. Fortunately so, because the motivational objectives we seek cannot be attained solely by arranging information and reinforcement schedules in optimal ways. Inspiring a lifelong commitment to learning also requires warmth, intensity, patience, encouragement, and above all, the presence of a mentor who exudes a genuine interest in young people. This observation is self-evident. But cliché or not, researchers are just now beginning to understand why it is true.

Consider the dimension of teacher expressiveness. Whenever students describe the ideal teacher, expressiveness is always mentioned (Feldman, 1976; Kulik & McKeachie, 1975). Expressiveness refers to a common core of behaviors: eye contact, voice modulation, and facial mobility. Raymond Perry and his colleagues (Perry, 1981; Perry & Magnusson, 1987; Perry & Dickens, 1984) have demonstrated that when teachers (actually actors posing as teachers) deliver information in an animated fashion – upbeat, open, and with enthusiasm – students are more likely to attribute their own successes to effort rather than ability or luck. Interestingly, these benefits also depend on students believing themselves to be the agents of their own success. When students think that success or failure is largely in the hands of the teacher, or is simply a matter of caprice, then there is little teachers can do to arouse student enthusiasm, no matter how animated they may be. Indeed, in this case teachers' jokes and antics are often misinterpreted as taunts or sarcastic put-downs. But when students are allowed to take charge of their own learning, then enthusiasm of the kind expressed by Mr. Rodriguez makes an already positive climate even better. In short, good teachers combine both *support* and *managerial* functions.

Global Gambit is a fictitious example, but a useful fiction nonetheless. Above all, it represents a vision of what might be, and to some extent what is already happening in some classrooms. But will real students respond in the same positive ways as Mr. Rodriguez's hypothetical pupils? In principle, they should. The restructuring portrayed here conforms closely to our instructional guidelines, which themselves are well grounded in theory and fully buttressed by existing laboratory research. Moreover, the behavior of Mr. Rodriguez's students faithfully reproduces the findings of various applied field studies conducted in actual classrooms where success and failure experiences are real, not artificially induced. In addition to those studies already cited, several others have been particularly important in creating the Global Gambit scenario. For example, its conceptualization owes much to the work of Carole Ames and her colleagues (Ames, 1990; Ames & Archer, 1987a; Ames & Maehr, 1989) who recently modified the rules of the learning game in 100 elementary school classrooms favoring noncompetitive successes and the sharing of authority among teachers and students. Early results indicate the restructuring has changed the learning climate for the better in ways portrayed in Global Gambit, especially among high-risk students.

Also influential is the research of Andres Helmke (1988) who studied classroom factors that perpetuate student anxiety. Helmke found that anxiety is particularly disruptive of school achievement whenever a premium is placed on performance per se; that is, on winning versus losing rather than on learning, and when teachers provide little in the way of help for poor students, including periodic feedback, study review, and clear standards. Helmke's work provides some of the best empirical justification for the use of mastery learning approaches in the quest for motivational equity.

So far our research examples for creating motivational change have been confined to the individual classroom. But as Martin Maehr and Carol Midgley (in press) point out,

The classroom is not an island. It is part of a broader social system and it is difficult to develop and sustain changes in the classroom without dealing with the wider school environment. Moreover, teachers cannot alone carry the burden of significant school change; one must also engage school leadership if the deepest structure of teaching and learning is to change. (p. 7)

To be sure there are occasional examples of efforts to restructure entire schools, some of which have already been mentioned (e.g., Alschuler, 1975), but for the most part they remain isolated efforts. Seldom do educational researchers speak directly to school leaders and to the school community at large. Fortunately, things are beginning to change in this arena as well, thanks to research of the kind being initiated by investigators affiliated with the National Center for School Leadership at the University of Illinois (Champaign-Urbana). For instance, Maehr and his colleagues (Maehr, 1989, 1991; Maehr & Braskamp, 1986) have convincingly demonstrated that school climate, defined by the collective instructional goals of the entire teaching staff and administration, impacts the quality of classroom motivation as surely as does individual classroom incentives, and that school climate can also be changed for the better (Baden & Maehr, 1986; Maehr, 1991).

Conclusions

There is more to Global Gambit than merely setting motives right, critical as that is. There are also broad hints about another critical objective of schooling: enriching our children's capacity to think, to reason free of rhetoric, and to create plans for desired futures rather than merely accept the future by default. This additional objective will come as no surprise to the reader given the rationale presented so far. Indeed, our analysis now comes full circle, back to the opening arguments in chapter 1 regarding problem solving and future survival. This round trip represents a natural progression. First, we considered the question of *why* achieve and concluded that for learning to endure and enrich, the reasons or motives for learning must be positive. Then we took up the question of *how* to achieve – how to arrange the conditions of learning to enhance the will to learn? Now we come to the question of *what* to achieve – what lessons are worth knowing as students struggle to create their own futures? Two kinds of knowledge stand out: first, knowing *how to learn* and, second, knowing *how to think*.

By this reckoning, *learning* and *thinking* are not the same thing, although it is often assumed that if people simply have enough information they will also think about it effectively. Obviously, this is not necessarily true. We cannot teach facts alone and expect understanding to occur automatically. As Emily Dickinson remarked, "He has the facts, but not the phosphorescence of thought." Learning and thinking are different because they involve different goals – in the first instance, to recall what is memorable, and in the second, to make meaningful what is remembered. These different goals also involve different mental operations. Learning places a premium on the skills of precise rehearsal and effective recall, whereas thinking demands flexibility, openness, and a spontaneous play of mind.

In the next chapter we will consider the possibility of teaching facts in ways that encourage understanding. We will also explore the prospects for teaching children strategies of thinking, and ask if such instruction also enhances the *willingness* to use one's mind in creative ways. Thinking strategies are necessary for solving what J. W. Getzels (1975) calls *discovered* problems as contrasted to *presented* problems.

Presented problems have a solution that is known to the presenter in advance (usually a teacher) and must be worked out by the learner. Typically, such problems are presented in a neatly packaged, highly structured form, with all the information provided for a solution – no more, no less. Most presented problems are in themselves quite trivial. Who really cares how old Ruthie is if her age is two-thirds that of Mary's age? The answer is useful only as evidence that students have learned the concept of fractions.

Rarely in schools is presented knowledge put to work for solving *discovered* or *created* problems for which the presenter (who may be the student) usually *does* care about answers and not just about the process – sometimes caring passionately, even desperately, and precisely because there is no known or preset solution, or at least no single answer on which everyone (not even their teachers) can agree. This is the domain of the truly creative act: seeking ways to help one's younger brother kick the cocaine habit, painting a picture that forces the viewer to see the world in novel ways, or creating a worldwide network of cooperation to deal with global warming. By their nature, discovered problems typically must be solved not once, but repeatedly, and sometimes by different players. For instance, the answer that satisfies a husband as to why the family budget was overrun may not satisfy his wife. Nor are the insights achieved by one generation always agreeable to the next. Today's assessment of the threat of global warming will change as decades pass. But just how these later appraisals will differ, no one can say except that they will likely prove the point made by R. H. Tawney that "the certainties of one age are the problems of the next." It is all part of the drama associated with what James Carse (1986) calls *infinite games*.

Infinite games are defined as those human endeavors in which the goal is to extend play (or inquiry) indefinitely. Science is an infinite game, as is civilization, and so is the playing out of the lives of young children who must repeatedly renegotiate relationships with others as they grow into adulthood.

What are the prospects for teaching young people the broad mental strategies for creating the proper moves and countermoves involved in such infinite game play?

8

Strategic thinking and the will to learn

> *Long-range planning does not deal with future decisions, but with the future of present decisions.*
> PETER DRUCKER

Drucker's remark captures the essence of the relationship between discovered problems and the future. The future depends on, indeed, eventually *becomes* a history of, the kinds of problems we choose either to ignore, postpone, or solve, and of the wisdom of those choices and solutions.

It is not that we are without some guidelines for making the best present decisions. Common sense provides one source, as do the lessons of history. Another oracle, largely neglected, is the accumulation of folk wisdom known as Murphy's laws or the "official rules" (Dickson, 1978). This neglect is all the more puzzling given the uncanny accuracy of these laws. In projecting future outcomes, who can easily dismiss the observation that for every human problem there is a neat, plain solution – and it is always wrong – or ignore the warning, If you think the problem is bad now, just wait until you've solved it.

Murphy's laws form a user's manual for dealing with an unpredictable world of perversity, surprises, and contrary events. Naturally, they cannot tell us precisely *what* will happen or exactly *when*. Still, Murphy and his intrepid band of lawgivers have put us on notice *in advance* for *why* things may turn out badly, or at least differently than expected.

By taking Murphy's laws seriously we are compelled to wonder, for example, if the simplest solution is so often wrong, then why are we not more suspicious of simplicity to begin with? And, what is it about our solutions that so often makes them worse than the original problem? If the future is just a lot of mistakes waiting to happen – the same ones made by past generations and similar to those *we* are now busily committing ourselves before the future overtakes *us* – then the message seems clear. Schools must work for the repeal of Murphy's laws! This means schools must teach children *how* to think, not merely *what* to think.

The topic of this chapter is the nature and facilitation of the kinds of thinking engaged in by Mr. Rodriguez's students as they struggled to reach a global accord in the last chapter. We will inquire about the kinds of intellectual skills and knowledge needed when, in the words of Max Wertheimer (1959), individuals "discover, envision, and go into deeper questions." We will also glimpse something of the frailty and limits of human problem solving, and ask if the capacity for reflective thought can be increased through instruction. And, finally, given our larger motivational concerns, we will inquire if learning *how* to think will increase one's *willingness* to think.

All these questions are predicated on knowing what *thinking* is.

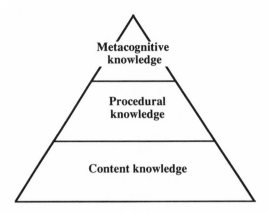

Figure 8.1. Knowledge hierarchy

What is thinking?

Currently, there is a great deal of interest in improving student's thinking abilities, but there is also a great deal of confusion about what thinking is.
BARBARA PRESSEISEN

One contemporary textbook on problem solving (Phye & Andre, 1986) defines thinking as the mental operations involved in dealing with problems. Today most cognitive psychologists think of these mental operations in terms of different kinds of knowledge arranged in a hierarchical, top-down structure of the type portrayed in Figure 8.1 (for a review see Frederiksen, 1984; Prendergast, 1986).

The significance of this model is best conveyed by example. Mr. Rodriguez assigned several tasks to acquaint his students with the basic mechanisms of global warming. One exercise required the creation of an "environmental danger hierarchy" in which students rank-ordered various practices such as deforestation and the use of artificial fertilizers from the least to the most damaging. Mr. Rodriguez explained that burning fossil fuels had always been thought to be the main cause of global warming. "But what is the latest evidence?" he wondered. "Are there greater dangers? And, are there any wild card players in this game, potential but as yet underappreciated or overlooked sources of danger?" This was no simple assignment. In order to succeed, Mr. Rodriguez's students had to draw on the collective sources of knowledge portrayed in Figure. 8.1.

Content knowledge

The first-order requirement for all thinking is access to information: dozens, perhaps hundreds of facts, figures, and other forms of data arranged in charts, graphs, or text that together represent what cognitive scientists (e.g., Flavell, 1979) call *content* or *declarative* knowledge – knowing *that,* for example, each year Brazil burns or cuts down forests whose land area is the size of

Pennsylvania or *that* methane comes from leaks in natural gas lines, from belching cows, and is also produced by forest fires. Facts are the basic ingredient of all thinking. They are not thinking, but thinking is not possible without them.

Procedural knowledge

Next comes a repertoire of mental *procedures* needed to make sense of the facts. Procedural knowledge represents the *how* of problem solving, knowing, for example, *how* things work – simple things like the rules of the Global Gambit game, or more complex things like *how* the credit banking system works. Typically, procedural knowledge relates closely to the content of the problem itself, so close in fact that sometimes procedural and content knowledge literally fuse. For example, in order to identify the most important causes of CO_2 buildup, Mr. Rodriguez's students must first understand *that* each potential source of warming – be it deforestation or methane gas leaks – is itself a larger natural system, and only one system among many complex systems, including the atmosphere, the biosphere, and the geosphere. Second, they must appreciate *how* changes in just one system, such as reduced CO_2 levels, can alter the growth rate of trees, which in turn can have many effects on the atmosphere, some of which may cause additional warming and others which may actually cause cooling.

Procedural knowledge can also transcend a given subject-matter strand and apply broadly across disciplines. This is the realm of knowing *how* to think of ideas, to evaluate hypotheses, and to look at problems in new ways. These procedures often have specific *skill* components.

IDEA GENERATION

One powerful procedure for generating lots of ideas is to conduct an orderly exploration of all possibilities by imagining an "idea tree": First, identify the general possibilities in a situation (main branches) and then spell out all the specific ideas that follow (specific branches). For instance, if the assignment is to generate various *natural* explanations for the Loch Ness monster, students might divide their attention between two main possibilities – that the monster is some kind of nonliving floating object or, alternatively, some kind of familiar living creature. Having once established these categories many specific ideas present themselves, including an overturned rowboat, floating weeds, a log, or even a group of seals cavorting through the water in single file. With the advent of a third category, *weather changes,* yet additional hypotheses spring to mind as youngsters exhaust a veritable forest of idea trees – a rainstorm boiling up the water, the wind causing dark rolling waves, or the sun casting moving shadows on the water.

RESTRUCTURING PROBLEMS

Another general procedural tool for thinking involves knowing *how* to restructure problems. The classic demonstration of restructuring was conducted some years ago by Wertheimer (1959). A group of elementary schoolchildren first mastered the formula for calculating the area of a rectangle and then were given the task of determining the area of a parallelogram. This new problem defied all the best efforts of these students until they were shown how to view a parallelogram as a kind of rectangle. A similar turn of mind led biochemist Ralph Sachs (Griver, 1979) to ask himself not what drug might kill leukemia cells that refuse to age – then the current method of treatment – but rather what kind of drug might make leukemia cells grow old and simply die. This fresh question opened a wide range of previously unforeseen possibilities.

Restructuring one's view of a problem requires abandoning conventional, popular thinking and overcoming rigid preconceptions. The skills of insightful mental reformulation are among the least studied and least understood of all the thought processes. Yet, as we will see, there is reason to believe that they, too, like other general thinking skills are susceptible to training.

IDEA EVALUATION

Knowing *how* to evaluate and rethink ideas in light of new information is also part of the procedural knowledge base of problem solving. For instance, *initially* Mr. Rodriguez's students might place methane gas leaks near the bottom of the danger hierarchy owing to the *fact* that only a small volume is released into the atmosphere each year, initially, that is, until they consider the implications of another fact: that each methane molecule contributes 15 to 30 times more to global warming than does one CO_2 molecule. Perhaps methane gas is a greater danger than they had originally thought! To extend this example, rethinking the danger status of methane gas should prompt further concerns about the relative threat of deforestation, which in light of these new data now appears to represent not just one danger – reduction of the global capacity to absorb CO_2 – but a second danger as well – the creation of methane gas through burning.

This example illustrates something of the circular quality of rethinking prior decisions, detecting relationships, and generating implications. In this connection, the appropriateness of an idea may depend more on the future consequences of putting it to work than on its immediate intended impact. For example, had planners accurately anticipated the negative effects of building the Aswan Dam in the upper Nile River in the late 1960s – erosion of the Nile basin and the collapse of the aquatic food chain in the eastern Mediterranean – they might have modified their plans for turning the Egyptian desert into farmlands. The capacity to envision the many future consequences of present decisions, to recall Drucker's remark, involves what cognitive scientists refer to as *divergent thinking* (Guilford, 1957). Divergent thinking involves much searching for ideas, speculating, and going off in different directions, sometimes playfully, even mischievously, while suspending assumptions about present realities and exploring unlikely but not illogical possibilities. These processes also exhibit skill-like qualities in that they, too, are subject to improvement through instruction.

Metacognitive knowledge

Finally, at the pinnacle of the knowledge hierarchy comes an overall executive function – the integration of all prior sources of knowledge. Successful thinkers view problems in their entirety, not just as an assortment of isolated subroutines, disconnected facts, or disembodied skills. Nowhere is the statement, The whole is greater than the sum of its parts, more apt than when applied to problem solving. This dictum asserts that good thinking is more than the simple total of all procedural and content knowledge. And there is the corollary that good thinking does not depend solely on the size of one's content and procedural knowledge base. It is what one does with one's knowledge that counts most – how information is selected, arranged, and prioritized. This is the realm of *metacognitions*. The essence of metacognitive knowledge is embodied in Albert Camus's celebrated quip, "An intellectual is someone whose mind watches itself." For our purposes metacognitive knowledge can be divided roughly into three functions (see Flavell, 1976, 1979; Forrest-Pressley, MacKinnon, & Waller, 1985; Weinert & Kluwe, 1987): self-monitoring, conditional knowledge, and plans of action.

SELF-MONITORING

A capacity for self-monitoring involves knowledge about one's own intellectual strengths, limitations, and preferred styles of thinking (McCombs, 1984, 1987). People possess such knowledge if they know that some things are harder for them to do than other things. For example, as a result of carrying out his contingency contract with Mr. Rodriguez, Ralph realized that he does best when the task is clearly defined. Self-knowledge also involves being able to judge accurately one's capacity for recall, or what has been called "metamemory" (Flavell, Friedrichs, & Hoyt, 1970), and estimating correctly the amount of time one needs to learn something (Neimark, Slotnick, & Ulrich, 1971). There is a wide range in the accuracy with which individuals make such judgments, and marked developmental trends as well (Flavell & Wellman, 1977; Yussen, 1985). We have already seen how poor some children are at estimating their ability to learn (Yussen & Levy, 1975). At the same time, there is disquieting evidence that adults, too, are far from perfect when it comes to realistic self-monitoring (Denhiere, 1974).

CONDITIONAL KNOWLEDGE

A second aspect of metacognition involves *conditional* knowledge (Paris, Lipson, & Wixson, 1983). Conditional knowledge means knowing *why* one should create idea trees or divide a difficult problem into more manageable subparts. A particularly important conditional message is that strategy application takes conscious effort and patience (Borkowski, Weything, & Turner, 1986). When students do not understand this message, they may possess the necessary procedural knowledge but not apply it unless directed specifically to do so. Such failures to act are referred to as *production deficiencies*. Motivational factors may also be involved in these deficits. Students who lack confidence in their knowledge are unlikely to use it. On this note, it is reassuring to find that conditional knowledge can be taught (Pressley, Borkowski, & O'Sullivan, 1984, 1985).

PLANS OF ACTION

The third aspect of metacognitive knowledge involves knowing how to create plans of action and monitor them. (For a recent review, see Friedman, Scholnick, & Cocking, 1986). The parallel between *planful* thinking and a military campaign is nearly perfect. Successful generals arrange their troops (cognitions) in a marching order that is best suited for some overall purpose, whether it be to defeat the enemy outright or to withdraw gracefully to fight another day. These moves and countermoves are controlled by broad plans of action that, in the case of potentially less violent pursuits such as plotting one's next move at the negotiating table or on the playing field, involve checking the results of that move, and then revising one's strategies accordingly.

Broad planning strategies have wide application by analogy. For example, like chess masters who must protect the center of the board, politicians must protect their flanks, and TV evangelists must control their revenue base among the elderly and gullible by at least appearing to be respectable and pious. And even the youngest of problem solvers have their survival strategies, a fact appreciated by all parents who have been victimized by the divide (mom and dad)-and-conquer ruse.

Sometimes these plans of action are best conceived of as a series of abstract steps or mental operations that must be properly sequenced. From this angle effective problem solving involves deciding at a given point in one's work, for instance, whether it is more fruitful to suspend judgment and give free rein to speculation in search of entirely new ideas or approaches, or whether, on balance, it would be best to begin anew by evaluating the ideas one already has. This balancing act implies appreciating when one is on the right track or, conversely, recognizing the danger of being overwhelmed by too much information, and once having realized the danger, knowing what to do about it.

At one point Mr. Rodriguez worried that his students might collapse beneath the combined weight of too many new unfamiliar concepts, introduced too quickly. The last straw was the notion that climate change depends on a complex interaction among several global ecosystems, including the oceans, the continental land masses, and the vast ice fields of Antarctica and Greenland, not to mention plant and animal life. Mr. Rodriguez saved the day by asking his students to think of analogies or metaphors (a procedural skill) that would convert this complex concept into a simpler, more recognizable form (Gick & Holyoak, 1983; Mayer, 1989; Spencer & Weisberg, 1986). One team decided to liken the dynamics of climate change to a mobile: both weather and mobiles are in constant motion, with any change in one element (e.g., the oceans) creating corresponding changes in the total configuration.

Fortunately, there is evidence that individuals can be taught to create and use analogies as a problem-solving tool. In one study, Ann Brown and her colleagues (Brown, Campione, Reeve, Ferrara, & Palincsar, 1991) report that following the administration of a special reading comprehension program (Brown & Palincsar, 1989), children easily deduced why farmers use lady-bugs to destroy aphids and then were able to apply this same reasoning several weeks later when they learned about using manatees to rid inland waterways of weeds.

By helping his students transform the strange into the familiar, Mr. Rod-riguez not only reduced cognitive overload but also promoted further inquiry. The ability to grasp the essential elements of a complex situation is the bench-mark of effective thinking. As Friedrich Nietzsche said, "He is a thinker. That means, he knows how to make things simpler than they are."

Summary and prospects

The educational significance of the hierarchical knowledge model is reflected in a growing awareness that thinking, far from being a passive activity, is an active, constructive attempt by the learner to create meaning (e.g., Shuell, 1986; Weinstein & Mayer, 1986). Above all, this process involves the capac-ity to think about thinking and the purposeful arrangement, assembly, and orchestration of different kinds of knowledge to achieve a larger goal.

By this accounting, thinking is a far more demanding and complex activity than typically envisioned by schools. This analysis is also breathtaking in its scope. It appeals to the broadest educational context and pertains to all subject-matter domains. As Richard Crutchfield (1969) explains it,

> Both simple and highly complex problems must be included; so must precisely-stated and well-structured problems as well as those which are loosely defined and weakly structured. The spectrum of problems must include the briefest, lasting but a few seconds, and also those which stretch out over prolonged periods of time with many sessions of work by the individual. And problems may not only be fixed and static in nature, but may also be such as to undergo constant changes in structure and con-ditions as they are worked on.
>
> Problems include those for which there are unique solutions as well as those for which there are multiple solutions, and partial solutions as well as complete solutions. Problems differ in the type of solution sought: some pertain to the achievement of understanding, as in the assimilation of new information . . . others pertain to explanation, as in the account-ing for a puzzling phenomenon in science; others pertain to the creation of an innovative way of accomplishing an end, such as in resolving a conflict in human relations. (pp. 6–7)

Given all the complexities involved, and the many forms that problems can take, it is a wonder that humans think at all. Of course, there are those cynics who wonder openly if this indeed is not the case. Paul Fix asserts that "the only reason some people get lost in thought is because it's unfamiliar territory." Somerset Maugham put it this way: "Their [people's] hearts are in the right place but their head is a thoroughly inefficient organ.'' The accumulated research tends to support these amusing if bleak appraisals. At every level of the knowledge hierarchy there is evidence of massive deficits (e.g., Oka & Paris, 1987; Reusser, 1987; Sowder, 1987). Recall those primary-grade youngsters who (at a metacognitive level) blithely calculated the captain's age in terms of the number of sheep and goats on his ship, and were none the wiser, and the teenager's unintentionally witty stab at identifying Chernobyl (content knowledge) as Cher's real name.

We can place much of the blame for such ''thoughtlessness'' on the fact that in school youngsters are rarely led to see the larger utility of what they are learning or doing. Surprisingly, many students do not realize that in order to write checks and balance a checkbook – in effect, to take charge of one's economic life – one must first know how to add and subtract; and in order to vote one must first be able to read the ballot. Moreover, even on those relatively few occasions when such functional relationships are discussed in school, it is rarer still that students are allowed to practice voting or setting up their own household budgets – all in simulated form, of course – in order to appreciate firsthand what it means to be cut adrift without benefit of basic survival skills. As a result, students are typically unable to recognize that what they are studying in one subject-matter domain relates to other areas (Bailin, 1987), nor do they readily appreciate the relationship between their current understanding and what they might or must accomplish in the future (Stake & Easley, 1978).

We have also implicated the fear of failure as a cause of ''thoughtless'' learning. When students are driven to outperform others, they retreat to low-level thinking strategies that favor rote memorization (Nolen, 1987, 1988). Anxiety degrades intellectual functioning to the point that many students operate at an almost witless level of existence.

We can now add a third reason for thoughtless learning. The goal of teaching thinking in schools is honored more in the breach than in the observance. In actuality very little time is devoted to thinking. All too often students believe that the reason for studying mathematics is to get the right answers, not to improve their quantitative thinking skills; likewise, they believe the purpose of studying history is to memorize names, dates, and places; and the reason for writing compositions is because they must! But the goals of content mastery and learning need not proceed in a mindless fashion. From a metacognitive perspective, content acquisition is best conceived of as a process of assimilating new information to be fitted meaningfully into the child's conceptual world, and in turn to stimulate the expansion of that world. As William James remarked, ''The art of remembering is the art of thinking. . . . Our conscious effort should not be so much to *impress* or *retain* (knowledge) as to connect it with something already there.''

This goal requires that children learn to think about thinking in the profound hierarchial sense already described (Figure 8.1), an observation that brings us to the central question of this chapter: Can the capacity to think about thinking and the ability to assemble and use different kinds of knowledge be taught to schoolchildren?

The evidence

A child's mind is like a field for which an expert farmer has advised a change in the method of cultivation, with the result that in place of desert land, we now have a harvest.
ALFRED BINET

The literature on teaching children to think is truly monumental (see Adams, 1989; Glaser, 1984; McKeachie, Pintrich, & Lin, 1985; Nickerson, Perkins, & Smith, 1985; Perkins, 1982; Segal, Chipman, & Glaser, 1984). Yet only a tiny fraction of this literature is appropriate to our concerns. The relevant research is restricted drastically by the fact that most published sources provide little more than anecdotal, hearsay information regarding the value of instruction. Additionally, of the few actual research-based studies available, many are either inadequately evaluated or subject to various methodological criticisms (for a critique, see Mansfield, Busse, & Krepelka, 1978). For our purposes, the best evidence comes from a handful of studies conducted in schools using instructional programs of sufficient scope to qualify as general skill training, and with enough data gathered under sufficiently rigorous conditions to permit reliable conclusions.

The following review focuses mainly on the *Productive Thinking Program* because of its emphasis on the training of cognitive assembly and planning mechanisms, and because of the relatively large body of research that has accumulated around this program over the past two decades. Several other instructional programs will also be reviewed as they become relevant to our inquiries.

The productive thinking program

The Productive Thinking Program (PTP) is a course in learning to think designed for upper elementary schoolchildren (Covington, Crutchfield, Davies, & Olton, 1974). The main teaching component of the PTP consists of a series of 16 self-instructional lessons, each centering on a complex detective-type mystery problem. As the problem unfolds page-by-page, students are required to perform various problem-solving operations: writing down ideas, formulating the mystery in their own words, and suggesting what additional information is needed. On successive pages, students receive immediate feedback on their efforts in the form of a range of possible suggestions or ideas that are appropriate at that particular point in the problem. Through such guided practice students are lead to understand what constitutes relevant and original ideas, how best to proceed in the face of uncertainty, and what strategies to employ whenever they encounter difficulties. This practice–feedback sequence is built around a set of 16 *thinking guides* (see Table 8.1).

The managerial schema taught by the PTP is primitive but serviceable. Whenever students get stuck on a problem they are directed to consult the thinking guides. In this way students are encouraged to review problems periodically, consider whether or not the task has changed, judge what has been accomplished up to that point, and then decide what additional facts or next steps are needed to achieve a solution.

Table 8.1. *The thinking guides from the Productive Thinking Program*

1. Take time to reflect on a problem before you begin work. Decide exactly what the problem is that you are trying to solve.
2. Get all the facts of the problem clearly in mind.
3. Work on the problem in a planful way.
4. Keep an open mind. Don't jump to conclusions about the answer to a problem.
5. Think of many ideas for solving a problem. Don't stop with just a few.
6. Try to think of unusual ideas.
7. As a way of getting ideas, pick out all the important objects and persons in the problem and think carefully about each one.
8. Think of several general possibilities for a solution and then figure out many particular ideas for each possibility.
9. As you search for ideas, let your mind freely explore things around you. Almost anything can suggest ideas for a solution.
10. Always check each idea with the facts to decide how likely the idea is.
11. If you get stuck on a problem, keep thinking. Don't be discouraged or give up.
12. When you run out of ideas, try looking at the problem in a new and different way.
13. Go back and review all the facts of the problem to make sure you have not missed something important.
14. Start with an unlikely idea. Just suppose that it is possible, and then figure out how it could be.
15. Be on the lookout for odd or puzzling facts in a problem. Explaining them can lead you to new ideas for a solution.
16. When there are several different puzzling things in a problem, try to explain them with a single idea that will connect them all together.

Source: From M. V. Covington, R. S. Crutchfield, L. B. Davies, & R. M. Olton. (1974). *The Productive Thinking Program: A course in learning to think.*

Cognitive skill instruction is reinforced through the use of indentification models. A story line is developed around two school-age children – Jim and Lila, brother and sister. Students work on a problem in concert with Jim and Lila: First, students produce their own ideas, then Jim and Lila respond with theirs (feedback). The models are not meant to be perfect; they are depicted as making mistakes but also learning from those mistakes, and as a result they gradually improve. Moreover, students can deal with misunderstandings about the nature of thinking and learn about the benefits of skillful persistence. A sample sequence (see Figure 8.2) illustrates how such positive attitudes are systematically strengthened using a variation on attribution retraining. This particular example involves enhancing beliefs about ability as a modifiable set of strategies.

The results of some 20 different experimental studies are summarized here (for reviews, see Covington, 1986b; Mansfield et al., 1978; Polson & Jeffries, 1985). Although these studies vary somewhat in specifics, in all cases they involve a comparison between an instructed group and a matched, but un-trained control group. All participants are administered a battery of thinking

Figure 8.2. Sampler from The Productive Thinking Program

tests both *before* the instructional period, in order to establish an initial base-line of thinking proficiency, and then again *after* instruction.

The test battery consists of a number of problems drawn from different subject-matter fields, including the medical sciences, biology, history, and anthropology. Many of these problems are *convergent* in nature. Convergent problems (as distinct from divergent problems) yield to only one or two best answers. Convergent solutions depend on the individual's capacity to gener-ate, test, and then eliminate a number of less elegant ideas in a progressive manner so that the search eventually converges on a few good ideas that best fit the constraints of the problem. One convergent task is a simplified version of Karl Duncker's venerable X-ray problem (1945). Here the individual thinks of ways to kill a malignant tumor deep inside the human body using X-rays, but without harming the surrounding healthy tissue. In another convergent task (the ancient city problem) students give their best explanation as to why an apparently thriving civilization came to an abrupt end, given a variety of seemingly unrelated pieces of physical evidence.

Enhancing procedural knowledge

CONVERGENT THINKING

The accumulated evidence suggests that systematic instruction improves the procedural skills associated with convergent thinking. Typically, PTP students generated more ideas and ideas of higher quality than did matched control students (Covington & Crutchfield, 1965; Moreno & Hogan, 1976; Ripple & Darcey, 1967; Shively, Feldhusen & Treffinger, 1972; Treffinger, 1971; Treffinger & Ripple, 1970). Instructed students were also quicker to recognize how they might restructure problems in ways that afford new perspectives (Olton & Crutchfield, 1969). They also demonstrated an improved ability to ask questions, especially when it came to strategic inquiries that help identify the nature of the problem (Blank & Covington, 1965; Greer & Blank, 1977).

The number of convergent solutions also increased after instruction. In one study (Covington & Crutchfield, 1965) instructed students discovered classic solutions to the X-ray problem (which included the idea of focusing a number of weakened X-ray beams on the tumor from different directions) twice as often as did control students. In another convergent problem students were provided with information describing the flight pattern of a flock of migrating birds. Embedded in the text were three puzzling pieces of information, one of which indicated a precipitous decline in the size of the flock at a certain point in the flight. Robert Olton & Richard Crutchfield (1969) reported that control children identified and explained satisfactorily one of the three facts on average, whereas the instructed students explained an average of two of the facts. Moreover, 38% of the instructed students explained all three facts with their best solution, whereas only 12% of the control children were able to do so. The fact that this particular problem was administered 4 months after training attests to the longevity of the instructional effects. Finally, of considerable significance is the fact that these thinking gains occurred on problems that were quite different in content from those used for practice.

Similar findings have been reported by researchers using the teacher-led *Philosophy For Children Program* (Lipman, 1976, 1985). This program emphasizes training on the more logical aspects of thinking such as drawing syllogistic inferences. Some half-dozen studies conducted by Matthew Lipman and his colleagues provide strong evidence that systematic instruction leads to substantial increases in the capacity of children to provide reasons for puzzling events, to identify fallacies in reasoning, and to discover alternative interpretations of data (Lipman, 1985; Lipman, Sharp, & Oscanyan, 1977). These positive outcomes also were accompanied by improved teacher ratings of student academic readiness as well as corresponding gains in math and reading skills.

Likewise, Marilyn Adams and her colleagues (Adams, 1989, 1986; Hernstein, Nickerson, de Sanchez, & Swets, 1986) have reported positively on a course designed to teach Venezuelan schoolchildren various observational and classification skills as well as reasoning and decision-making strategies. This program is unique because it was developed under the auspices of the Venezuelan Ministry of Education as part of a countrywide effort to improve the intellectual functioning of all its citizens (Cordes, 1985).

DIVERGENT THINKING

The results of other studies also suggest that originality (defined as divergent thinking) can be fostered through general strategy training. Most germane is research using the *Purdue Creative Thinking Program* (Feldhusen, Speedie, & Treffinger, 1971). This program consists of several dozen audio tapes that provide practice on various divergent thinking techniques. The evidence of five studies employing the *Purdue Program* with middle and upper-elementary schoolchildren indicates that the quality of divergent search strategies improves with instruction. For instance, in one study (Feldhusen, Treffinger, & Bahlke, 1970) 54 elementary-level classrooms were administered the program at the rate of two lessons a week for 14 weeks. The experimental design involved the presentation of various components of the program with some children receiving all of the lessons and other children only a few lessons. The instructed groups generally outperformed a control group that received no training.

Enhancing executive knowledge

Having considered the evidence for enhancing the specific procedural components of problem solving, what are the prospects for fostering its metacognitive, managerial aspects? In one study employing the *Productive Thinking Program* (Olton et al., 1967) students were given an unfamiliar problem and asked to select the best planning steps from a list of alternative actions as the problem unfolded. Each set of decision-making options differed in quality and appropriateness depending on previous events, but they always included a "best" decision, a "second best" decision (reasonable, but not as good as the first), a "contrary fact" decision (one that ignored an already established fact), an "appealing but irrelevant" decision, and, finally, a decision that would bring the problem to a premature closure. Instructed students were better able than control students to track the most effective course of action throughout the entire problem-solving episode, and in the process were less attracted to appealing but irrelevant actions and less likely to be seduced by contrary actions.

Instructed students have also proven better able than controls to create their own plans of action. In another PTP study (Cox, Swain, & Hartsough, 1982)

1000 middle grade youngsters were asked to plan a hypothetical school report. Instructed students posed more strategic questions about the sequence and timing of various subtasks within the larger project than did the control children. Instructed students were also more likely to judge the success of their plans in terms of intrinsic criteria such as how much might be learned from writing the report apart from any grade they might receive. These findings are particularly welcome in light of our earlier comments concerning the importance of self-defined success.

The fact that students can be taught to plan better takes on considerable importance in light of speculation that links intelligence to the quality of cognitive assembly (Butterfield & Belmont, 1971, 1977; R. J. Sternberg, 1985; R. M. Sternberg, 1987). It has been proposed that intelligence, in actuality, represents the ability to think strategically, that is, the capacity to plan for and make the most of one's personal resources as situations change (Berg, 1986; Covington, 1984b, 1984c; Derry & Murphy, 1986). But if *behaving* intelligently as distinguished from *intelligence* per se depends on the capacity to plan and act in a strategic manner, then in what ways does this capacity emerge through instruction?

To answer this question additional analyses were undertaken using PTP data (Covington & Fedan, 1978). It was found that among children who had not yet received cognitive instruction, the quality of their ideas depended heavily on tested intelligence (IQ) – brighter students produced the better ideas. In fact, IQ was the most important factor in this process, far more important than the possession of procedural knowledge, say, knowing how best to generate ideas. Things changed after instruction, however: Trainable skills now became as important as ability in the process of generating good ideas. This means that many of the less bright instructed students who were previously unable to do well owing to low ability were now able to perform as well as innately brighter untrained children who already knew intuitively how to think; moreover, these same instructed students easily outperformed other less bright control students who possessed neither the trainable skills nor the capacity to generate them spontaneously.

These findings suggest that strategy instruction stimulates a higher-order, harmonious integration of cognitive processes that tend to operate in compensatory ways. This is likely what Alfred Binet had in mind almost a century ago when he observed:

> It is in this particular sense, the one which is significant that we can say the intelligence of children may be increased. One increases that which constitutes the intelligence of the school child, namely the capacity to learn and improve with instruction. (1909, p. 54–55).

Binet would almost certainly have embraced the concept of *working intelligence* (Scribner, 1984), In school, working intelligence means being able to recognize when one does not understand a concept, knowing how to make a difficult assignment easier, and knowing what to do when previously successful learning strategies are no longer effective. All these actions are governable by rules and strategies that can be taught, and it is in this sense that Binet says ability can be modified and improved. A more contemporary but quite compatible interpretation of Binet's position was recently offered by Terry McNabb (1987) when she proposed that ability also implies strategy, in that those students who possess larger arsenals of strategies are better able to achieve success. Strategies, then, suggest a more fluid type of ability – more a resource than a capacity.

Motivational consequences

McNabb's comments lead to the question of the motivational benefits of cognitive skill training. Does strategy instruction increase the *willingness* of students to think deeply about problems now that they are more capable of doing so? The prospects are encouraging for the fact that the notion of strategic planning bridges both cognitive and motivational domains in several ways. First, strategy knowledge increases beliefs that ability is an incremental process. As one child put it, "Thinking is like a flower. It unfolds as you work" (Covington, 1967). We know that such incremental beliefs are associated with an increased willingness to tackle more difficult problems, for longer periods, and with greater resolve and confidence (Dweck & Bempechat, 1983; Dweck & Goetz, 1978). Second, a strategic view of thinking is also likely to alter the meaning of failure. If students can analyze problems, identify sources of difficulty, and create plans of action to overcome these obstacles, then should a particular problem still prove too difficult, alternative explanations for failure other than low ability are possible (see Figure 8.2). For instance, one might try hard and still fail simply because one's original aspirations were unrealistic. Such a strategy interpretation is task oriented and as a consequence does not necessarily lead to the kinds of self-doubt and paralysis caused by ego-involved failure.

A study by McNabb (1987) confirms this point. A series of mathematics problems was administered to two groups of upper elementary students. One group received strategy-related messages ("To successfully solve problems like these, you have to use good methods"). The other group was given effort-related messages ("To successfully solve problems like these, you will have to try harder"). Recall that simply exhorting students to greater effort may do little to improve performance. Although both groups received the same procedural training – how, for example, to diagram math problems – only the strategy group consistently employed these procedures and, as a result, performed better on a final achievement test. Moreover, when computational errors occurred, the strategy-method group was more likely to ascribe these lapses to modifiable causes such as inattention. Furthermore, strategy messages significantly increased task involvement as defined by the degree of enjoyment expressed by these students, by their willingness to work on the math problems, and by an increased expectation that they would succeed on similar problems in the future. Finally, those students who originally exhibited the lowest levels of perceived competency in mathematics benefited the most from strategy-message training.

McNabb interpreted this latter finding as being consistent with self-worth formulations in that strategy-linked messages provide insecure students with plausible nonability explanations for their performances, thereby freeing them to work harder. Interestingly, these feelings of liberation do not necessarily occur by reducing anxiety. In fact, in one PTP study (Covington, 1984a) self-reported anxiety levels remained the same after strategy instruction as before. But after instruction, anxiety mobilized students to use their newly acquired thinking skills so that now they produced a few ideas of high quality compared to before when anxiety aroused an unbridled production of many ideas of indifferent quality.

Strategy training also appears to increase intellectual self-confidence. One index of self-confidence is the degree of independence exhibited by individuals in judging the merits of their own ideas. Following PTP instruction, Vernon Allen and J. Levine (1967) gave students false feedback allegedly representing the opinion of their peers regarding the correctness of various answers to a problem. Instructed students were less likely than control students to give up their own ideas simply because they differed from peer group opinion. Moreover, these instructed students were selective in their judgments. Sometimes they changed their minds in favor of the group position when the group was clearly correct, and at other times defended their own ideas when they believed they and not the group were right. The fact that independence of judgment can be encouraged through strategy training is highly significant given the importance of self-regulated learning. And, perhaps even greater importance can be attached to these findings in light of Binet's celebrated definition of intelligence: "Comprehension, planfulness, invention and *judgment* [italics added] – in these four words lies the essence of intelligence" (1909, p. 54).

Another mark of intellectual self-confidence is the individual's readiness to think. As part of PTP evaluation students are often asked to write an essay on the topic of poverty. The task is entirely open ended. Students are free to respond in any way they wish. Both instructed and control children tend to produce the same number of *descriptions* of poverty (e.g., "These people don't have any money"). But whereas most control youngsters stop short at this declarative (content) level, instructed students do not. In one study (Olton & Crutchfield, 1969), by a margin of 3 to 1, instructed students went on to mention various *causes* of poverty (e.g., "They were replaced by machines"). And all of the few students who went further still to suggest *solutions* were from the instructed group. These findings indicate that strategy instruction strengthens the readiness of students to use their minds in productive ways – "discovering, envisioning, and going into deeper questions," to recall Wertheimer's phrase (1959). Such a positive set should be a prime goal of education.

Strategic problems

Wisdom is merely knowing what to do next.
ANONYMOUS

So far we have focused on problems that involve the creation and use of knowledge – whether it be understanding a puzzling event (the bird migration problem) or designing a more powerful technology (the X-ray problem). This kind of thinking reflects the scientific method with its emphasis on hypothesis generation, experimentation, and hypothesis testing. Such problems depend on creating plans of action for their solution; in effect, plans are in the service of a solution. Now we turn to an analysis of two other kinds of problems: first, strategic problems for which the plan *is* the solution and, second, those situations in which there is no plan because as yet there is no problem!

For what problems is the plan the solution? The answer is those situations in which the goal or desired state of affairs is known in advance and the task is to figure out how to transform these hopes into reality. Such strategic problems are commonplace. They are illustrated by the football coach who vows to have a winning season next year and now must figure out how to achieve it, and by the hostess who hopes to have a successful dinner party in which each course will be delivered on time, in the right order, and at the proper temperature. Troubleshooting of the kind practiced by car mechanics to detect an electrical fault also involves strategic thinking, as do the efforts of a systems analyst to trace the source of breakdown in a railroad network. Strategic planning also involves the pursuit of occupational and career goals whenever young people start out to work their way to the top of a chosen profession.

Whatever form it takes, strategic planning calls for what Herbert Simon (1972, 1973, 1980) describes as a means–ends analysis. The successful problem solver must be able to represent a problem both in its present state and as a desired end state, and be sensitive to the broad problem-solving steps and moves needed to reduce and eventually eliminate these differences. For instance, in the case of debugging an electrical fault this means that, first of all, the auto mechanic must define the elements of the problem space – the battery, carburetor, fuel pump, and starter – and then, second, begin testing all the elements of the system, singly and in combination, to locate the defect. Means–ends processing also involves the ability to recognize and deal with the strategic implications of new, unexpected events – potential windfalls or unexpected obstacles – that can change the character of a problem in unanticipated ways, because a plan of action that is effective at one point can quickly become inappropriate or even counterproductive as circumstances change. And not only are plans subject to change, but so are the goals. For instance, labor negotiators invariably settle for less than originally desired, but on balance the contract they sign must approximate the initial hopes and demands of those workers they represent. Likewise, budget as well as time limits may force the hostess to serve a more modest meal to her guests, but the original purpose of creating a convivial evening can still be achieved.

Most school tasks involve elements of strategic planning. For example, writing essays consists largely of iterative cycles of planning, drafting, and revising, and, when necessary, redrafting the entire composition as the student strives to create a more satisfying product. Likewise, reading for comprehension usually involves successive cycling as well – looking ahead to anticipate, looking back to check and test one's recall, summarizing what is important so far, and filtering new information through the lens of prior understanding (Brown & Campione, 1990; Haller, Child, & Walberg, 1988; Paris & Oka, 1986). At its most effective, academic study is also an exercise in strategic planning.

Academic study

Researchers have just begun to appreciate the complexities of good study (see Biggs, 1984). John Thomas and William Rohwer (Rohwer, 1984; Thomas, 1988; Thomas & Rohwer, 1986) point out that academic study is, by its nature, self-initiating. In the last analysis, it is the student who must acknowledge that study is needed – yet study is sometimes painful, laborious, and often unrewarded. Moreover, study typically proceeds in isolation, often without corrective feedback until it is too late. For another thing, studying demands considerable effort, and a willingness – often at the risk of failure – to persist or to seek out and organize seemingly unrelated sources of information into manageable and meaningful forms. Finally, above all, Thomas and Rohwer conclude that academic study is ill-defined. It is not always clear what the teacher expects students to learn or what performance standards will prevail from time to time. For instance, it has been shown that although experts might agree about the performance criteria that define an adequate or inadequate product within their own particular expertise, this consensus dissolves when these same experts in the role of teachers are asked to specify criteria for the performance of novices (Thomas & Rohwer, 1986). In the face of such disagreement, it is hardly surprising that students often suffer a lack of clarity of purpose in their studies. Yet to be effective in school youngsters must persist with intensity and verve despite all these vagaries.

J. W. Getzels (1975) captures the essence of all these complications when he describes the most demanding kind of problem: "problem unknown, with the solution thereby free to vary and the means or methods to attain a solution unclear." Academic study is not quite as uncertain as this, yet, realistically, this description is not a bad approximation. Ann Brown and Joseph Campione (1990) discovered a profound lack of understanding among high school students about how to proceed with their studies:

> For example, one student claimed that when called upon to study, "I stare real hard at the page, blink my eyes and then open them – and cross my fingers that it will be right here" (pointing at his head). A somewhat better informed peer replied, "It's easy; if she (the teacher) says study, I read it twice. If she says read, it's just once through." A third answer: "I just read the first line in each paragraph – it's usually all there." (p. 111)

In a masterpiece of understatement Brown and Campione observe that "these are not expert readers."

Better students do, of course, possess a large repertoire of study methods, knowledge-acquisition strategies, and mnemonic devices (Davis & Annis, 1982). But as to problem formulation, most students can, at best, only dimly anticipate potential test questions; and, at worst, problem formulation goes little beyond a beleaguered, negative expression of hope: The problem is not to fail.

The struggle for students is to bring the study task into focus and under manageable control. When the information load is heavy, individuals tend to focus on the text in selected ways (Frase, 1968, 1970), and it is precisely during this process of spontaneous reorganization that deficiencies appear among poor learners (Cromer & Wiener, 1966; Steiner, Wiener, & Cromer, 1971). Knowledgeable students seek out information about the test to determine the kinds of demands it will place on them, by inquiring, variously: "What must I remember?" "Must I remember it again later?" "What kind of test?" "What aspects of the assignment will be most emphasized" (Bransford, Nitsch, & Franks, 1977)? Effective recall occurs when learners anticipate correctly the form in which the information will later be tested, and study accordingly. Researchers refer to this process as encoding specificity (Postman, 1975; Tulving & Thomson, 1973). For example, if the test is an exercise in rote recall, then rehearsing (encoding) the material originally as isolated, unconnected facts may be sufficient for later recall. But if the test requires the application of these facts in new situations, then rote overlearning will be inadequate (Covington, 1985b).

DEFICITS

The available evidence makes clear just how inadequately prepared students are to meet these strategic challenges. Alan Schnur (1981) asked junior-high students to predict how well hypothetical classmates would do on an upcoming test (that was either easy or difficult) if they were either (1) high or low in ability and (2) had studied a lot or little. Students readily identified those situations that either augured well for success (high ability × much study × easy test) or, conversely, presaged imminent failure (low ability × little study × hard test). Other than this, however, students were quite insensitive. Many did not realize that a combination of high effort and easy task presents a greater likelihood of success than does either high effort or task ease alone, nor did they always appreciate that individuals can study less if the test is easier than if it is hard and still do just as well. These surprising findings have been corroborated by other investigators (e.g., Nicholls, 1978).

Schnur also asked his informants to suggest how these hypothetical classmates might improve their future performance, and what they might do if forced to change their study plans (e.g., the date of the test is moved up). Most students simply advised studying harder – responses that reveal a complete lack of appreciation for *how* best to work harder, such as taking more complete notes or asking questions.

At a time (junior high school) when youngsters stand on the threshold of truly independent learning in the form of take-home examinations and long-term projects like Global Gambit, they appear hopelessly naive about even the simplest elements of achievement management. To make things worse, these planning deficiencies likely involve motivational deficits as well. Schnur also told his subjects that their hypothetical classmates had either passed or failed a previous test. This information proved more important to students in making predictions about future outcomes than knowing about the specific circumstances of the upcoming test. If someone had succeeded before, they were judged likely to succeed again, and likewise, they were judged less likely to succeed if they had failed previously, irrespective of whether the upcoming test was easy or hard, or whether their study had been described as adequate or inadequate. Many students see themselves and their peers trapped in the past, for good or bad; if their past is a failure, then there is little reason to imagine things changing.

Joy Cullen (1985) not only confirmed the existence of these same cognitive deficiencies among younger primary-grade students but also found that for some of her subjects inadequate problem-solving responses were associated with anger, aggressiveness, and frustration in contemplation of failure. Other students identified by Cullen as anxiety oriented were dominated by feelings of embarrassment and guilt about impending failure.

Finally, just to complete this glum picture, there is no reason to suppose that these deficits will spontaneously correct themselves as students grow older. Higher-order thinking skills do not automatically emerge out of simpler skills; nor is the situation necessarily corrected through maturation or by accumulating content knowledge. If this were true, then we would expect adults to exhibit few if any of the deficits found in children. Unfortunately, this is not the case. Compelling evidence comes from the work of Barbara Hayes-Roth (1980) who studied how adults create and carry out plans of action for such everyday tasks as completing the greatest number of shopping errands in the briefest time. Adult subjects consistently overestimated what they believed they could accomplish in the time available. Moreover, as the importance of achieving their goals increased, these subjects became increasingly unrealistic about how much they could do. Finally, when they were required to modify their overblown expectations these adults focused on the least important goals! Sound familiar?

REMEDIES

Still, for all these strategic deficits, there is reason to believe they can be remedied. Even the simplest school learning task such as memorizing a list of Spanish-English equivalents or recalling the 12 cranial nerves can be construed as exercises in strategic rehearsal (Dansereau, 1987). At its most significant, active rehearsal implies the ability to recognize which rehearsal method is best for a given task and to appreciate that the method of choice may change as work on the assignment proceeds.

Such metacognitive knowledge can be enhanced by using what Michael Pressley and his colleagues (Pressley et al., 1985; Borkowski, Johnston, & Reid, 1987) call *meta-memory acquisition*. For example, in one study (Lodico, Ghatala, Levin, Pressley, & Bell, 1983) young adolescents learned two different rehearsal strategies, one that was more effective for free-recall tasks (e.g., recalling the cranial nerves in any order) and the other better suited for learning paired associates (e.g., Spanish-English equivalents). In addition to this basic rehearsal training, half of the subjects learned about the importance of choosing between these two strategies depending on the nature of the task.

The remaining subjects received no such instruction. Then these two groups were given both paired-associate and free-recall tasks. Those students who had been provided with conditional knowledge more often used the most effective rehearsal strategy of the two, depending on the task, and were better able to justify their choice.

The larger significance of this and other similar strategy training studies, which include instruction in paragraph summation (Winograd, 1984), reading comprehension (Duffy et al., 1986; Paris, Cross, & Lipson, 1984), and writing (Englert & Raphael, 1988; Graham & Harris, 1987), is that school learning need not proceed in a mindless fashion. From a metacognitive perspective, knowledge acquisition is best thought of as an active, highly deliberate process in which the learner brings to bear various mental resources and techniques depending on task demands (Loper & Murphy, 1985). These findings underscore the profound difference between simply trying (sheer effort) and trying in a planful, strategic fashion, or as Craig Anderson and Dennis Jennings (1980) express it, "Motivation requires a *directing* component as well as the more typical *energizing* component labelled effort. This directing component can be viewed as 'strategy' – a particular approach, tactic, or method one uses in attempting to achieve a goal or to solve a problem" (p. 394).

Cooperation for its own sake

Nowhere are the demands on strategic planning greater or success more imperative than in those cases that require the cooperation of individuals within the family, among communities, and across nations. Today cooperation usually means sharing. As human and natural resources dwindle compared to rising global needs, greater sharing – of time, space, talent, even of one's own possessions – will be the key to collective survival.

Ultimately, then, what makes teaching cooperation so important is not its potential for promoting individual excellence, important as that is, but rather learning how to cooperate for its own sake. Sometimes in the course of solving discovered problems we seek the best (single) solution, not just an improved performance by all team members. Best ideas often depend on pooling the collective wisdom of many individuals. This point is strikingly illustrated by the *Lost on the Moon Game* (Hall, 1971). The task is to rank-order the survival value of 10 pieces of equipment for astronauts who become separated from their mother ship on the moon, including matches, a supply of water, and a flare gun. Almost always a single group consensus is a closer approximation to the "official" rankings (as provided by actual NASA astronauts) than is the average of all individuals working separately. But not always. Occasionally the group solution suffers when cooperation falters. Rancorous conflicts of opinion or attempts to control the group by an unruly minority can obscure facts that are critical to the best decisions (e.g., matches are virtually worthless on the moon since there is no oxygen to sustain a flame).

Fortunately, there is clear evidence that young students can be taught to cooperate. Recall the study by Nelson and Kagan (chapter 6) who demonstrated that under competitive rules, where rewards were insufficient for the number of players, children preferred to sabotage the game and lose any chance of winning themselves rather than let others win. These same investigators and their colleagues also showed than when children practiced cooperation first, they were more willing to work cooperatively under competitive conditions later on (Kagan & Madsen, 1971). Often these enlightened students simply divided the few prizes among the players at the end of the game. Also, in some cases they decided jointly to alternate which of the players would receive the reward on a particular round as the game progressed. Interestingly, again it was urban whites who proved least able to adopt such strategies (Kagan & Madsen, 1971). By contrast, children from rural, agrarian cultures respond more readily to the lessons of cooperation (Madsen, 1967; Madsen & Shapira, 1970; Shapira & Madsen, 1969).

Several techniques appear helpful in reducing competitive rivalry, and as far as present research can determine, all are about equally effective (Sagotsky, Wood-Schneider, & Konop, 1981). One strategy involves having children observe adults on videotape working out simple strategies for cooperation. Another approach calls on teachers simply to describe the advantages of cooperation – stating, for example, that each player will receive more rewards if everyone cooperates than if they do not.

Heeding such advice is extremely difficult, however. One's good intentions to share can easily fall prey to greed, panic, and mistrust. This sad fact is the basis for one of the most disheartening problems of our time, the "tragedy of the commons" (Edney, 1980; Hardin, 1968). The *commons* is any communal resource; it referred originally to a grazing pasture shared by farmers from several nearby villages. If the carrying capacity of the pasture is 10 cows, for example, then as long as 10 farmers graze only 1 cow each, the commons is not in danger of being overgrazed. The trouble begins when one farmer, more ambitious than the rest, concludes that by adding another cow he can double his milk production. The typical result is a stampede of farmers acting like cattle – all desperately seeking their "fair" share before it is too late. It is only later, usually after the commons lies depleted, that someone remembers the advice simple enough for children to follow: Each player will receive more if everyone cooperates. The commons can be any shared but limited resource, including both renewable and nonrenewable items – air, water, or even the inadequate supply of rewards provided by Nelson and Kagan in their experiments on competition.

The obstacles to cooperation are ancient and many, part of a legacy of fear and suspicion that is not entirely irrational. Human history is a roll call of broken pledges and abused trust. But more stands in the way of cooperation than the tragedy of the commons. There are also certain human peculiarities that make the sowing of doubt and mutual suspicion virtually inevitable. One is the *fundamental attributional error*. As humans we tend to explain the negative behavior of others in traitlike terms ("He cheated because he is dishonest."), while attributing the same behavior in ourselves to the situation ("I cheated because everyone else did."). The reader will recognize this "error" as part of the more pervasive self-serving tendency to maintain feelings of respectability and as likely the reason why in the study conducted by Covington and Omelich (chapter 4) students estimated the ability of others as less than their own under identical conditions of failure. Also, because we know more about our own situation personally, we are more likely to ascribe situational explanations to our own behavior. Although understandable, and only too human, such biases bode ill for the kinds of delicate negotiations and planning required in emotionally charged situations where the stakes are high and the intentions of other participants already suspect.

Consider the problem of nuclear proliferation. According to these attributional dynamics, during the heyday of the cold war both the Soviet Union and the United States probably overestimated the hostility of the other (Lindskold, 1978). Each interpreted any nuclear buildup by the other side as driven by an inherent (traitlike) aggressive tendency, yet justified increases in their own arsenal of weapons out of necessity as only a natural (situational) response to those hostile intentions, and all without recognizing that this countermove would be seen as equally menacing by the other side. This "spiral" effect was compounded whenever a proposal made by one side to reduce nuclear arms – presumably for the sake of conciliation – was discounted by the other side as only a ploy to gain political advantage. Naturally, of course, sometimes adversaries are treacherous and ill-disposed, and to perceive them as such may be critical to one's survival. Nonetheless, it is equally important to remain sensitive to these signs of potential change when confronting an increasingly agreeable competitor.

These same kinds of distortions and stresses are at work in any situation where emotions run high and resources are limited or contested, including courtroom battles between divorcing parents, costly commercial litigation, and acrimonious labor disputes. Given the growing necessity for cooperation, it seems clear that systematic instruction and practice in conflict management, planning, and the joint resolution of issues must form an indispensable part of the curriculum. Among other things, children must learn about attributional errors and other forms of mental and perceptual bias – how they can cloud one's judgment, when they are most likely to operate, and how to discount them. Moreover, students should experience for themselves and then master the stresses, uncertainty, and occasional failure of nerve that are an inevitable part of solving discovered problems – all, of course, in manageable amounts and limited to the instructional context. If properly orchestrated, hands-on experience with conflict management can promote the kinds of mature, stabilizing perspective that was so characteristic of Secretary of State George C. Marshall, who when asked why he could remain so calm in the face of the Berlin airlift crisis replied, "I have seen worse".

Problem discovery

To raise new questions, new possibilities, to regard old questions from a new angle, requires creative imagination and marks real advances in science.
ALBERT EINSTEIN

By Einstein's reckoning, problem discovery is the highest expression of humankind's remarkable intellect. The dynamics of problem discovery can be described as no problem at all, at least not in the beginning and, as a consequence, not even the glimmer of a solution, and, of course, no known steps to be taken. This null condition describes many circumstances: the incisive question yet to be asked, the human need unrecognized and hence unmet, and the potentially dangerous condition gone undetected. In its essential form problem discovery reflects the challenge described by Getzels (1975), "Pose an important problem and solve it!" The fundamental ingredients of this process are the continual readiness of individuals to find problems everywhere, to be puzzled by the obvious, and to see the extraordinary in the ordinary, and the willingness to turn the familiar, prosaic event into a profound revelation (Arlin, 1975; Ghiselin, 1955; Wakefield, 1988).

Thanks to the media, we are made aware constantly of both newly emerging problems and the reoccurrence of old problems that were once thought to have been solved. Examples of this endless cycle of intrigue and tragedy include reliving the specter of famine that periodically sweeps third world countries, the discovery of new forms of toxic waste pollutants, and the ever-expanding, previously unforeseen economic and political consequences of the AIDS epidemic. These examples suggest that at its most passive, problem finding involves little more than turning on the nightly television news.

The process of discovering problems on one's own, however, not just finding out what others already know or fear, depends largely on the ability to detect inconsistencies and incongruities in nature or to discover something strange that violates what would otherwise be expected (Dillon, 1982; Getzels, 1975). This description typifies the process of scientific discovery. The history of science is replete with examples of breakthrough discoveries that depended on being sensitive to the unexpected. Occasionally, these discoveries have provided new insights into old problems. This process involves *serendipity*, the art of finding something of value when you are looking for something else (Shapiro, 1986). The classic example of serendipity is Alexander Fleming's discovery of penicillin. Instead of simply throwing out the bacteria killed by a strange green mold that spoiled his research and starting over again, Fleming paused to consider the meaning of this accident. Obviously, serendipity involves more than luck; it is not simply accidental. In Fleming's case, several other researchers had already seen bacteria destroyed in a similar fashion, but they did not recognize the full importance of what they saw; in effect, for them the familiar held no surprises. Fleming possessed the capacity to see the profound in the ordinary. Likewise, Wilhelm Roentgen saw the same fogged photographic plate as had other scientists before him, but whereas they considered it a nuisance, Roentgen asked why the plate was fogged, a question that led to the discovery of X rays and eventually to atomic research.

The process of problem finding and the possibility of serendipitous discovery are largely omitted from the kinds of problem solving found in schools. Yet these dynamics, too, are the stuff of which the future is made. It is the advent of new problems and new ways to deal with old problems that propels the observation that 90% of the jobs that will occupy America's labor force in the year 2020 do not yet exist. It is not typically the case, as some have argued, that humans solve their problems by outliving them, but rather in the process of solving them we create new needs and difficulties, and reshuffle our priorities. Most school tasks are presented as exercises in rote reproductive thinking, yet the potential for problem finding in the curriculum is ever present. Problem finding comes into play whenever students are confronted with the task of deciding for themselves what counts as an important enterprise. This occurs in college as well as at the professional and postgraduate level whenever students are expected to define and carry out original, independent research. It also occurs in high school whenever students search for a worthwhile science project, and in junior high when children must generate worthy term paper topics.

The transfer of knowledge

We don't know what problems the future will have. . . . So the best way of preparation for the future is to learn to solve complex problems today.
CARL ROGERS

As D. N. Perkins and Gavriel Salomon (1987) explain it, *transfer* refers to a fringe benefit: By learning task A an individual finds it easier to master task B. George learns to play tennis and discovers a talent for playing squash. Likewise, after learning to read musical notation for the piano, Bette finds that reading for the trumpet follows easily. Transfer of knowledge is the name of the game when it comes to preparing for the future. Since no one can possibly anticipate all future contingencies, it is vital that students be exposed to knowledge that has broad application. So far I have argued that the best preparation is to teach for general problem-solving strategies and for their metacognitive assembly. The merits of this generalist position seem self-evident. Although not always guaranteeing a solution, general strategies for mental management should at least help in solving problems, no matter what the future circumstance (Holland, Holyoak, Nisbett, & Thagard, 1986; Perkins & Salomon, 1989; Sternberg & Kastoor, 1986).

There is much evidence to support this view, including that generated from research on the *Productive Thinking Program*. General knowledge about how to think appears to promote performance on tasks quite different from those previously experienced by students (see pp. 194–196). As a further example, Douglas Clements and Dominic Gullo (1984) report that teaching programming languages to primary-grade youngsters increases their reflectivity, divergent thinking, and comprehension monitoring when working on problems unrelated to computer programming. Even retarded youngsters can be trained in self-management procedures that transfer to other contexts. In one case retardates studied a memory strategy for learning lists of words and continued to exhibit improved performance one year later when they learned a complex prose passage (Belmont, Butterfield, & Ferretti, 1982).

However, not all attempts to demonstrate the transfer value of general thinking strategies have been positive. For instance, researchers have been largely unsuccessful in demonstrating the benefits of teaching broad heuristics for mathematics problem solving. Students may understand these rules in the abstract, but they do not always understand mathematics well enough to make use of them (Schoenfeld, 1985). Such failure of transfer led Allen Newell and Herbert Simon (1972) to conclude that focusing on broad mental principles is best characterized as a general-weak approach – *general* in that broad strategies are clearly applicable to all problems, but *weak* because their usefulness for solving a *specific* problem may be negligible.

Actually, much of the present evidence on the dynamics of transfer suggests a very different strategy than the one we have proposed for promoting good problem solving: simply acquiring lots of specific knowledge about the detailed ins and outs of a particular field. No problem can be solved unless the individual appreciates the permissible limits under which problem solving can proceed (e.g., McPeck, 1981). For instance, the successful ballerina must abide by the principles of the classical ballet, just as the poet who composes a sonnet is constrained to a form with 14 lines and a specific meter and rhyme scheme. Likewise, the habit of proper spelling and procedural knowledge, such as knowing how to fractionate chemicals, and even those manual dexterity skills associated with the piano keyboard are the foundations for more complex achievement.

In a classic study, William Chase and Herbert Simon (1973) used chess players to demonstrate the importance of rich content knowledge in problem solving. These investigators found that master chess players were no better than beginners at memorizing the layout of pieces on a chess board if the patterns were purely random. But recalling the past moves that emerged in the course of actual game play was another matter. Here the grand masters excelled. In fact, their memories were prodigious. They could remember all the various moves of both players in the right order for hundreds of previous games. This suggests that grand masters know something very powerful but very specific to chess play, otherwise they would have done better at recalling the random layouts. Grand masters appear to think in terms of patterns or sequences of specific moves with a repertoire of some 50,000 chess configurations, according to the conservative estimates of Chase and Simon. Knowledge of general strategies such as controlling the center of the board appear to play little part in winning at chess once sufficient experience is accumulated. Additional research in other fields, including physics (Larkin, 1982; Larkin, McDermott, Simon, & Simon, 1980) and computer programming (Erlich & Soloway, 1984), confirm the importance to problem solving of a large knowledge base of specific moves, procedures, and patterns (also see Chi, Glaser, & Rees, 1982).

At the same time, unfortunately, for all of its undeniable importance the accumulation of specific content seems decidedly limited when it comes to transfer. Once learned, subject-matter knowledge in one domain appears to have little positive impact on performance in other domains (see Ennis, 1989). Surprisingly, for example, learning to play chess does not ensure that students will be better able to solve logic problems. Given these findings, Newell and Simon (1972) characterized the accumulation of specific content knowledge as a strong-specific approach when it comes to transfer – *strong* in the sense that subject-matter knowledge is a powerful component of effective thought within a given discipline such as biochemistry or astrophysics, but decidedly limited when it comes to solving a wider array of problems outside the discipline.

Here are the makings of a profound dilemma. If the evidence for the transfer of broad thinking strategies is spotty, and specific knowledge is also of limited generality, can we *really* prepare students for a future of unknown possibilities where the specific content as well as the very nature of the problems themselves will likely be quite different if unrecognizable today?

A dilemma resolved

Actually the picture is far less dismal than this, if only we are clever enough to look at the problem differently. The research of John Clement (1982) provides the proper perspective. Instead of asking expert chess players to solve chess problems, Clement gave grand masters unfamiliar, novel tasks for which their current experience was insufficient. Under these circumstances, grand masters as well as experts in other fields revert to broad thinking strategies in an attempt to discover the underlying structure of the problem. They create analogies and metaphors to convert the unfamiliar to the familiar, just as Mr. Rodriguez's students were taught to do. Experts also construct simple versions of the problem in an effort to detect the workings of the more complicated case. And, almost invariably they try to identify the specific problem as belonging to a larger class of problems (Adelson, 1981). Additionally, experts establish a context for solving unfamiliar problems. For instance, before studying the specifics of a legal case, attorneys locate the particular decision in the larger context of who judged the case, the type of court that tried the case, and the kinds of parties involved (Adelson, 1981).

It is in the face of unknown contingencies that general thinking strategies come into their own. And it is just this problem-framing quality and the fact that future problems are by definition likely to be novel that justify the emphasis on training for broad problem-solving skills. Brown and Campione (1990) refer to youngsters who possess these general strategies as *intelligent novices*. Intelligent novices may not have all the background knowledge needed for exploring a new field, but they know how to get it.

Recent research on the dynamics of transfer has led to a much more sophisticated understanding of the relationship between general thinking strategies and specific context knowledge. General and local knowledge are not rivals. Rather they both fill important functions in the overall process of problem solving. When tasks are unfamiliar, overly complicated, or fraught with emotional overtones, then general strategies are most valuable; indeed, they are indispensable (Anderson, 1987). Yet, conversely, the ability of individuals to solve these same problems with increasing sophistication, faster, and with greater assurance depends on the creation of a rich knowledge base of experience that is specific to the particular task. It is at this juncture that general thinking strategies recede in importance; eventually, with enough experience even highly complex tasks like chess play may take on the superficial appearance of lower-level, rote functioning.

This interplay between general and specific knowledge is extraordinarily complex. For instance, in order to benefit most from instruction in general knowledge, students must already possess a good deal of content knowledge on the topic to which the broad strategies will apply (Hasselhorn & Körkel, 1986; Gay, 1986). Furthermore, as learners acquire more content knowledge, they seem more adept at creating abstract representations of a particular problem on their own (Alexander & Judy, 1988).

Teaching for transfer

On the whole, the evidence reviewed in this chapter reinforces a vague impression that children are capable of thinking in terms of general strategies, that they will do so on occasion, but usually not unless directed to do so. This uneven record reflects the fact that transfer is potential, not automatic. Whether or not transfer occurs depends on making explicit the future utility of present knowledge. For instance, teachers can aid transfer by showing students how problems resemble one another (Shoenfeld, 1987), discussing how students have solved similar problems in the past, and talking about what they might do in the future (Charles & Lester, 1984). Basically, this means teaching for *conditional* knowledge – pointing out *when* and particularly *why* students should use strategy knowledge. Such lessons are largely neglected in school.

In teaching for transfer, educators will find the analogy of a tool kit useful. Carpenters use a hammer differently depending on whether the task is to set a nail or to remove it. By the same token, effective thinkers apply the dictum of "getting all the facts clearly in mind" differently depending on whether they are classifying botanical specimens or wrestling with an algebraic word problem. Moreover, fields differ in what counts as a proper approach. For instance, in the social sciences statistical significance is a central consideration, but in some branches of physics it is largely ignored; and in the arts subjectivity is the norm, whereas in the sciences subjectivity is usually discouraged. Yet for all this diversity, there are many cognitive similarities from field to field as well as a common core of basic thinking principles that apply, although not every principle applies to all fields (Resnick, 1987; Toulmin, Reike, & Janik, 1979). These observations conjure up the advice of Alfred North Whitehead (1929) when he insists that we must "let the main ideas which are introduced into a child's education be . . . thrown into every combination possible" (p. 14).

Having pressed the importance of transfer, it must now be acknowledged that cognitive scientists still understand relatively little about the mechanisms by which transfer occurs and even less about which broad thinking strategies should or can be promoted at any given age. If it is true that to be effective, general cognitive skill training must proceed developmentally over a period of years, not just for a few weeks or months, then the staging of such instruction becomes crucial. Yet we are basically uninformed about what thinking skills are the true precursors of adult thought (see Carey, 1985). For instance, it is by no means certain that those strategies often associated with childhood creativity such as divergent thinking or ideational fluency (e.g., Torrance,

1965, 1972) are synonymous with or even similar to the cognitive functions responsible for creativity in adulthood (Covington, 1969; Nicholls, 1972). Hopefully, we have demonstrated the urgent need to search for answers to these questions and to incorporate them into the process of educational reform.

Analysis and conclusions

The most important implication of this chapter stems from the fact that researchers have not always fully appreciated that both *knowing* (as in knowing the facts) and *knowing how to know* (as in thinking) are essential to academic success (see Alexander & Judy, 1988; Katz, 1976). But now having understood this, how can we best combine the teaching of local domain-specific knowledge and broad metacognitive knowledge in ways that maximize task involvement as well as the chances for future transfer?

We have already provided an answer by example in the case of the Global Gambit scenario (chapter 7) where high school students are portrayed as mastering the finer points of economic theory, meteorology, and conflict management (at a deep level of processing), all for the purpose of responding to the greenhouse effect. In short, school learning should be arranged around the discovery and investigation of inherently interesting problems – not just the solving of disembodied, mindless work sheet problems, 10 to a page, a practice that trades effectiveness for efficiency.

Such a problem orientation heralds several important changes in the way we must think about school curricula. One involves the role of content knowledge. In our example, content knowledge becomes subordinated to the higher purposes of inquiry. Facts should be introduced sparingly, only as needed, and associated with a particular problem or series of problems. This can be accomplished in several different ways. First, as illustrated by Global Gambit, students can acquire factual detail in *anticipation* of problem solving. Here the demands of content acquisition readily conform to the mastery learning paradigm in which students are held responsible for various levels of understanding before they are allowed to proceed. Second, facts can also be introduced *during* problem solving, even at the crucial moment of decision making, when, for example, students acting as emergency room physicians consult the patient's vital signs or past history (facts) in a last-ditch effort to discover a life-saving clue. What better way to convince students of the value of having the right information at the right moment? Third, content acquisition can also proceed *after* the fact by way of a postmortem review, as also occurred in the Global Gambit scenario. Students can search for, identify, and then learn those facts and principles that, had they been available earlier, might have saved the patient, secured peace, or explained the mystery. Ultimately, the value of learning facts in these ways, as part of a meaningful endeavor, is that they transcend their traditional purpose as only things to think *about;* facts now can also become things to think *with.*

How then should procedural knowledge be taught in a problem-focused curriculum, especially those subject-matter strands whose acquisition is largely a cumulative affair? Consider the logical scaffolding of mathematical knowledge that presumes the progressive step-by-step mastery of propositions, theorems, postulates, and proofs. Obviously, Mr. Rodriguez's students cannot properly interpret graphs on population growth or fully appreciate the meaning of the phrase "parts per million of oxygen" until they understand, respectively, the notion of rate of change among variables and the concept of percentage. Such understanding depends on starting at the beginning, years earlier, with basic number facts no matter what discovered problems these students may encounter along the way, and to begin anywhere else would invite disaster.

But being a novice does not mean having to learn in a "thoughtless" way. The research of Gordon Cavana and William Leonard (1985) demonstrates that acquiring procedural knowledge merges comfortably with the goal of self-regulated learning. These researchers distinguish between the *proscriptive* aspects of scientific investigation – knowing, for example, how to use a microscope or a titration buret – and its *discretionary* aspects – deciding which of several specific methods to use in demonstrating a process, for example, mitosis. Most commercial science experiments are predominantly proscriptive training activities (what we have called *presented problems*) that are divided into a number of sequential steps that students must complete in a virtual lockstep. As only one example, the Biological Sciences Curriculum Study (1968) unit on water loss from plants consists of 12 interlocking tasks, each taking an average of 5 minutes to complete.

Cavana and Leonard have altered these curricula by combining several steps into one, thereby transforming largely proscriptive exercises into partially discretionary tasks over which the student can exercise more personal control, independent of both the teacher and textbook. In one experiment that involved changing the curriculum of entire biology departments in three urban high schools, students demonstrated an increasing ability to exercise discretion and for longer and longer periods of time (Leonard, 1980; Leonard, Cavana, & Lowrey, 1981). Many students who initially could not work without direct guidance for more than 15 minutes at a time extended their discretionary capacity to periods of 2 to 3 hours by the end of the school year. Moreover, these same students demonstrated a significantly greater understanding of laboratory concepts and produced higher quality written reports than did students using the unaltered commercial versions of the same exercises.

Research of this kind suggests that effective educational reform lies not in tampering with the inherent organizational structure of subject-matter knowledge, but in arranging content in thought-evoking ways and also in making certain that children realize that what they are learning now about mathematics, science, or grammar has both immediate and future utility. This means that discovered problems must be coordinated closely with the growth and development of the child's procedural knowledge base so that the act of problem solving itself fulfills the promise of content relevance and also spurs further learning in the belief that this new knowledge, too, will eventually prove useful for some as yet undisclosed purpose or problem.

Granted, encouraging students to persist in the face of delayed, even quite remote, payoffs is a difficult proposition, but certainly not impossible. Consider providing the proper perspective by means of a spiral lesson plan, spiral in that the same discovered problem is reintroduced from time to time, say, once every year or two, so that children can gauge for themselves how much better and more sophisticated their reasoning is now than before, with the implication that the next time they meet this same problem their present thinking will also appear naive by comparison. Just as children are fascinated by the physical changes they see in themselves as they leaf through the family photo album, so, too, by returning repeatedly to the same problem, can they develop an appreciation for their own mental growth and recognize that although day-to-day intellectual gains are rarely obvious, they do accumulate and lead eventually to entirely new forms of thought and perspective.

Dangers of dilettantism

For all its potential benefits, problem-oriented schooling raises several legitimate concerns. First, is it possible that by arranging learning around problem-solving episodes rather than around chapters in a textbook that subject-matter coverage of, say, chemistry or biology will become spotty and uneven? Certainly this is a potential danger. We must be careful not to create the kind of dilettantism reflected in the world's first (and greatest) consulting detective. Sherlock Holmes simply followed his interests from one mystery (discovered problem) to another, capriciously and often on a whim. As a consequence his ignorance was as remarkable as his knowledge. Holmes was scathing in his rebuke of any content knowledge that was neither appropriate nor relevant to his immediate concerns: ''What the deuce is it to me? . . . You [Watson] say that we go around the sun. If we went around the moon it would not make a penny's worth of difference to me or my work'' (Doyle, 1967, p. 154). Holmes could afford this self-absorbed perspective because his peculiar talents suited his chosen profession so well. But today such a cavalier attitude bodes ill for future survival, at least among lesser mortals. Obviously, teachers must sample discovered problems carefully to ensure a wider subject-matter exposure than if students were totally free to choose only those tasks that hold immediate appeal as Sherlock Holmes was lucky enough to do.

However, having once acknowledged the need for caution, does a problem-oriented focus hold any greater dangers than those associated with the current hodge-podge approach to content coverage? As things stand today student understanding of most topics is confused, plagued by an overemphasis on the trivial to the neglect of the profound, and characterized by wide-ranging misconceptions and misinformation. According to Andrew Porter (1989) this occurs in part because of the widespread practice of ''teaching for exposure.'' He reports that at the elementary level most key mathematics concepts receive only the briefest coverage. For example, Porter found that during the entire school year fourth-grade teachers in one sample devoted less than 30 minutes *each* to 70% of the mathematics topics scheduled for introduction, including multidigit multiplication, number facts, and subtraction with borrowing! Although the reasons for this ''once over lightly'' approach to content coverage may seem plausible enough – briefly introducing work to be treated in later grades or reintroducing work from the previous years for review – the results are potentially disastrous. Quite apart from guaranteeing superficial, disjointed preparation, which is bad enough, students may also conclude what is even worse, that knowing very little about a lot of things is better than a deep understanding of a few central concepts.

Also at fault is the fact that school instruction is not well designed to help students make sense out of complex events. One might suppose that history, a topic that presupposes a rich variegated network of cause-and-effect relationships, would be organized around narrative themes involving people's reactions to events and the consequences of their reactions. Not so, according to the research of Isabel Beck and Margaret McKeown (1988) who analyzed the treatment of the topic of prerevolutionary America in several elementary school history books. Apart from the usual ambiguous statements, confusing references, and simple errors of fact, all deplorable enough, the larger problem was that these texts failed to provide information that would allow students to see connections between events or to understand why events overtake people. For instance, in no case was there a discussion of why previously loyal British colonists would become revolutionaries within one generation. In effect, little was offered that would help students begin to build a sophisticated understanding of American history, so that, when the factual details are long forgotten – it seems the colonists were especially fond of porridge – students will still be able to draw cogent relationships and attach the proper meaning to historic events. These same kinds of deficiencies have also been reported in grade school science texts (Mergendoller, Marchman, Mitman, & Packer, 1988) where passage follows passage with no coherent theme. As Brown and Campione (1990) discovered to their dismay, "A passage about volcanos might follow one on dinosaurs, that follows a description of aquanauts, two poems and a fairytale" (p. 113).

The cult of efficiency

A second concern about problem-focused schooling involves assigning the highest priority to teaching students how to think. By realigning priorities we challenge the cult of efficiency. Americans are known for their ability to get the job done, quickly and on time. And when productivity suffers we become uneasy. It is not surprising, then, that a mentality of efficiency pervades our schools, aided in part by a factory model of education that, although sufficient for promoting the interchangeable assembly-line skills needed during rapid industrial growth in the 19th and early 20th centuries, has proven hopelessly outdated today. Nonetheless, the vision of schools as factories or as a workplace still lingers (for a critique, see Marshall, 1988).

Compared to acquiring content knowledge, thinking is an enormously inefficient proposition. Solving problems takes time, lots of it – time to reflect, define, speculate, and then true to the convoluted nature of thinking, additional time to *redefine* the problem, to discard false leads, and sometimes to start over. Group problem-solving is the most cumbersome and time-consuming of all – time out to negotiate with others for their cooperation; time taken to overcome stalemates by searching for the next-most-acceptable alternative for all parties; and even extra time to create controversy deliberately in order to challenge overly simplistic solutions. The importance of this latter function cannot be overstated. For instance, testimony to the presidential commission on the explosion shortly after the launch of the American space shuttle *Challenger* indicated that no one on the launch team wished to voice his concerns about its safety for fear of appearing troublesome or not being a "team player."

Patience is a virtue when it comes to interpersonal negotiation, problem solving, and crisis management. On the face of it, then, teaching thinking confronts schools with a cruel tradeoff between promoting breadth of content coverage or depth of processing. Actually, in the final analysis, this dilemma may be more apparent than real. As we have seen, by improving the ability of students to think strategically, they also increase their capacity to learn and to retain more of what they learn. What could be more efficient?

9

An immodest proposal

Had I been present at the act of creation I would have had some helpful suggestions.
ANONYMOUS

We can now turn to recommendations. No simple remedies are involved, nor just a few, but hopefully workable ones nonetheless. There is no easy way out of the problems caused by the massive default of education that faces America today, but there are at least some constructive avenues to pursue. We have anticipated these recommendations to a greater or lesser extent. It is time to draw them together into a single, unified proposal.

To recap, we argued from the outset in favor of John Dewey's observation (1938/1963) that "the most important attitude that can be formed [in schools] is that of the desire to go on learning" (p. 48). Our analysis of achievement motivation led to a set of instructional guidelines intended to foster the will to learn, which depends largely on viewing motives as goals. Indeed, one of the greatest challenges for schools today is to rearrange the prevailing incentive systems to promote intrinsic goals such as playful curiosity and to establish meaningful payoffs in the struggle for self-improvement (Maehr, 1976, 1989).

Then, to complete our analysis, we added a distinctively cognitive element to these motivational concerns, something also anticipated by Dewey (1938/1963) when he remarked that "all which the school can or need do for pupils, so far as their minds are concerned, is to develop their capacity to think" (p. 152). In contemporary terms, this means strengthening the ability of students to reflect on their thinking, to create their own mental strategies, and to encourage a view of learning as an ongoing, open-ended process in which meaning is created by the learner, not simply dispensed by authority.

The point of contact between these two educational objectives – one cognitive, the other motivational – is the concept of strategic thinking. A strategy orientation mobilizes the will to learn because it encourages a belief that capacity expands through the wise management of one's resources. Also, by focusing on mental strategies, not on ability per se, students become task oriented, and as a result more positive, empowering explanations for failure become possible.

Finally, we have steadfastly maintained a future-oriented perspective. In chapter 1 we proposed three essential ingredients for future building. The first concerned the need for students to develop a set of marketable skills, be they reflected occupationally as a carpenter, a social worker, or an architect, and in any event to do the job well. The second was a sense of commitment, a willingness to become engaged. The third element involved preparing for change and accepting with grace the inevitability of change. How, then, can we restructure prevailing educational experiences to accommodate this entire future-oriented legacy and the diverse demands it places on schools? That is the fundamental question addressed in this chapter.

Serious games

Play used to be regarded as a harmless release of surplus energy, but it has come to be regarded as useful to the process of learning. Under the guise of play, new forms of behavior can be invented with impunity and thus it becomes an inspiration to innovation.
JEREMY CAMPBELL

My proposal can be summarized in a nutshell: Schools should teach students how to play games – serious games, to use Clark Abt's (1987) colorful oxymoron – under instructional conditions that (1) favor motivational equality, (2) promote strategic thinking, and (3) reinforce the positive lessons to be learned from failure. Serious games are essentially synonymous with what we have called discovered problems – the domain of truly creative products – whose outcomes and consequences cannot always be known in advance. Most discovered problems can be viewed as games. Any political, economic, or social issue, whether it involves a nation, a neighborhood, or an individual is a contest of sorts typically played by adversaries with specific objectives in mind and with various resources available, including knowledge, skill, and power. Even luck and chance play a part. And, perhaps most notably, adversaries are not always other players. In the case of many, if not most, discovered problems players must cooperate to achieve common cause against obstacles not of their own making. Sometimes these long odds are due to a lack of information, sometimes to simply not having enough time to act in full deliberation. At other times the adversary may be nature itself, which yields up its secrets only reluctantly.

The word *game* has a rich surplus meaning that goes far beyond the barest dictionary definition that suggests mere amusement, frivolous diversion, or recreation. On the more serious side, games can also mean any test of skill, courage, or an ideal endurance, as in the *game of life*. Games also refer to objects of pursuit, especially business and vocational pursuits, as in the *sales game*. Also, we play for high stakes, risk danger, and sometimes gamble recklessly, all for the sake of winning the *big game*.

It is this combination of the joyous and creative coexisting with the serious side of play – the analytic, the empirical, and the deliberate – that most recommends gaming and role playing as ideal vehicles for encouraging both the will to learn and the capacity to think (McLoyd, 1985). Abt (1987) puts it well when he suggests that "in dreams begin responsibilities . . . and in games begin realities" (p. 5). These realities benefit particularly from the fact that serious games provide a union between thought and action. They offer an unparalleled opportunity for an active yet risk-controlled exploration of significant intellectual, personal, and social problems – the *thought* side of the equation – and for the accumulation of experience by *doing* – on the action side – all through the process of role playing that prepares youngsters for the real roles they will play in later life.

> It is not difficult to imagine a school of the future as a "laboratory school" – a school making massive use of educational simulation games, laboratory exercises, and creative projects – a school in which almost everything to be learned is to be manipulated, physically or mentally. (Abt, 1987, pp. 120–21).

Before I spell out some of the further benefits of such a vision and address its limitations, consider several additional examples of serious educational games besides Global Gambit.

Nuclear Countdown: A mixed-motive paradigm

The U.S. military command in Europe has just received reports of a large Russian fleet moving through the Dardanelles. There is also evidence of Soviet jet fighters over Turkey, and a further report that a British bomber has been shot down over Syria. Given this scenario the NATO operations plan calls for an all-out nuclear attack on the Soviet Union. Improbable as these events may seem, they actually occurred in 1956 – or, more accurately, were *thought* to have occurred (as reported in "Avoiding Nuclear War," 1989). In actuality, the "jets" turned out to be a flock of swans incorrectly identified on radar. The Soviet fleet was engaging in a long-scheduled, well-publicized naval exercise, and the British bomber had mechanical trouble.

A group of high school students representing the NATO countries has just been given an order to stand down from their nuclear alert, just another one of the scores of "near accidents" in the 40 years since the United States and the Soviet Union became nuclear rivals. But now that the Soviet Union has dissolved, there is real hope that the world can move beyond crisis prevention to a basic improvement in the climate for peace. The task of this NATO team and that of a second group of students representing the Soviet Union and the nations of the (now defunct) Warsaw Pact is to launch a peace offensive whose ultimate goal is the bilateral elimination of both nuclear stockpiles and conventional weaponry, and the revitalization of domestic economies drained by years of inflationary defense spending.

For a period of 3 weeks the two teams have been preparing a variety of topics specific to U.S.–Soviet relations. These include a review of the history of international diplomacy since 1945, an analysis of the root causes of World War II, and a study of the geopolitical implications of the Soviet land mass.

The rules of negotiation are simple, but nonetheless reflect the essential realities that have confronted and plagued both the Americans and the Soviets for nearly half a century. Following a given round of negotiations, each team can either decrease, increase, or maintain their weapons arsenals at the status quo. The seeds of mistrust and suspicion are sown by the fact that these moves and countermoves are carried out largely in secret so that public agreements can be violated without the other side being the wiser. The temptation to cheat is enormous because the payoffs in this game, as in all real international diplomacy, favor competition as much as cooperation, hence the term *mixed-motive paradigm* (Axelrod, 1976; Jervis, 1976). Yet neither side is entirely in the dark. Some partial information about the moves of each side is made available to the other team. If construed properly, these data provide clues to the private intentions of each team, although nothing is completely certain.

It is only when both sides disarm simultaneously that real progress is made. And there are considerable benefits to cooperation. In this scenario both sides can divert defense funds to badly needed domestic programs. If the negotiating teams do not succeed in making this transfer from military to domestic spending, they run the risk of being replaced or overthrown by an impatient electorate (a third group of students).

Simulation games of this kind have been used widely by arms control specialists in both the Pentagon and the State Department in order to discover unanticipated dangers and flaws in their reasoning that, if allowed to go unchecked, could trigger nuclear war. Students can profit, too, by learning firsthand about the art of making decisions under pressure and in the face of incomplete, often conflicting information. Of equal importance is the possibility of a fresh understanding of the workings of the human mind and how human beings are biased toward making the simplest, most meaningful interpretation of events driven not by logic necessarily, but by immediate needs. In this particular case, students must struggle to remain sensitive to signals for potential change in the attitude of their adversaries yet, at the same time, remain prudent.

These dynamics apply generally to any mixed-motive paradigm, including conflict resolution at a personal level between parents and children, husbands and wives, and at the societal level as well among ethnic groups, between the sexes, and in business and industry. Such negotiations are also reminiscent of other classic dilemmas that are only likely to intensify in the future, including the tragedy of the commons that, as we know, arises whenever the collective consumption of a scarce but shared resource exceeds the supply.

Exponential Growth: A mathematics game

Not everyone was satisfied with Sally's approach. She tried again, raising her voice for emphasis: "Assume the original pair is labeled (0); and that the first offsprings of these parents are labelled (0) (1)." Sally and her classmates are struggling with a precollege mathematics problem dealing with growth functions. Their task is to figure out ways to verify that a single pair of rats (male and female) and their progeny would multiple into a colony of 1,808 rats by the end of 1 year given various parameters, including an average gestation period of 21 days and an average litter size of six, half of which are female (de Lange Jzn, 1987, p. 46).

Here mathematics is being taught basically as an empirical discipline, one consisting of data and discovery much like biology, physics, and chemistry. What is being discovered are the rules of the mathematics game rather than the rote application of presented rules. In this context learning becomes a community enterprise in which truth, according to Alan Schoenfeld (1989), becomes "that for which the majority of the community believes it has compelling arguments. In mathematics truth is socially negotiated, as it is in science" (p. 9). Sally's team is engaged in this truth-seeking process whenever any one member argues for his or her own notation system. And the teacher's task is not necessarily to certify which is correct, but rather to draw students into more sophisticated ways of stating problems in mathematical terms, which in the rat colony example means bringing students to the threshold of matrix algebra. Indeed, herein lies the most formidable challenge facing teachers whenever they arrange learning as a discovery process: recognizing when the child's intuitive appreciation of a situation outstrips his or her formal knowledge, and then knowing how to help consolidate these informal insights into more advanced systems of thought so that the stage is set for the next intuitive leap forward. Immanuel Kant said it all when he observed: "Thus all human cognition begins with intuitions, proceeds from hence to conceptions and ends with ideas."

This progression as applied to mathematics teaching is in vogue today. The Netherlands has built a nationwide high school mathematics curriculum around such a problem-focused approach (the rat colony problem is but one example from this curriculum). And because of its success, the program is currently being extended downward to the elementary levels (de Lange Jzn, 1987). Likewise, over a decade ago in the United States the National Council of Teachers of Mathematics (1980) identified problem solving as the recommended focus for school mathematics. Since then it has become widely understood that mathematics instruction should explicitly emphasize the role of evidence and argument, and that instructors need to emphasize problem finding and problem defining. Of special relevance to our arguments is the growing recognition that problems should be drawn from real-life situations with a playful engaging twist if possible, what John Bransford and his colleagues (Bransford, Hasselbring, Barron, Kulewicz, Littlefield, & Goin, in press) refer to as mathematical thinking in a "micro-context." Bransford describes an experimental math program for the upper elementary level in which youngsters learn to "mathematize" many of the problems faced by Indiana Jones in the first 10 minutes of the film *Raiders of the Lost Ark*. When Indy comes to a large pit, the film is stopped and students are asked how they might estimate its width. One ingenious idea is to measure the length of the bullwhip Indiana uses to swing over the pit and then estimate the arc of the swing, a suggestion that brought the fifth graders in at least one classroom perilously close to the basic principles of geometry as well as to the gateway to classic Newtonian physics.

Although ultimately by our definition such exercises are presented problems, they also share an important element of discovery because it is the process, not the answer correctly calculated, that remains the focus. The means by which Leibnitz created the calculus shares more in common with the struggle of the schoolchild to discover and understand it than was once suspected. In effect, the capacity for productive thinking can be found in every individual and among all ethnic groups, not merely among a chosen few.

The Health Futures Game

A group of junior high students is huddled around a game board, absorbed in the task of negotiating for freindships (Covington, 1981). In the early rounds (representing the teenage years) the goal is to gain "popularity" points. One of the simplest ways to be in demand is to provide one's peers with a ready supply of cigarettes and to smoke whenever others light up. Actually, the real purpose of this game goes deeper than teaching youngsters about the best, and worst, ways to negotiate friendships. It is also designed to illustrate that the means to immediate and future goals may not always be compatible, and that a tactic that may be effective now can become ineffective or, in this case, even destructive later on as situations change. Having chosen to smoke in the earlier rounds of the game puts players at a decided handicap in future rounds where the objective, now in the adult years, is to establish financial independence and provide for one's family. This task is made more uncertain by increasing health risks, ineligibility for life insurance, and unexpected medical expenses due to having been a smoker in earlier years.

It is now widely accepted that before physical health messages can be truly effective in altering risky behavior, the perceived linkage between one's actions (e.g., smoking) and their consequences (e.g., decreased lung capacity) must be strengthened. Also the relationship between one's intentions and actual outcomes must be clarified. In our society accountabilty for one's actions depends as much on intentions as on the gravity of the actions themselves. For instance, if one person harms another, but without intending to do so, then his or her culpability is diminished. Applying this same logic to health risks, many adolescents truly believe that if they do not *intend* to smoke (but do so because of social pressure), then they will suffer fewer negative health consequences compared to those instances in which they choose freely to smoke (Covington & Omelich, 1988b). Such primitive thinking represents a major obstacle to health promotion. Demonstrating the fallacies of magical reasoning is best pursued by providing youngsters with a life-cycle perspective that relates short-term decisions to long-term consequences. In this particular simulation, cause-and-effect dynamics can be discovered and the implications more readily appreciated by the young adolescent without adult preaching, and in a situation that is inherently interesting and that encourages the development of an extended future time frame.

Forbidding Planet: The Space Colony Game

A group of high school students is given the task of designing a space colony that will occupy a drone planet in a nearby galaxy for the purpose of harvesting minerals for commercial use. As a first step, team members must discover those laws of physics, chemistry, and biology that prevail in this distant world – laws that may not conform to more familiar earthly patterns. What, for example, would conditions be like if life was based on methane, not carbon, building blocks? What would be the consequences and risks to humans? Or what if these explorers were confronted with a world of only two dimensions, a situation that faced the inhabitants of Edwin Abbot's classic science fiction fantasy, *Flatland* (1983). Certainly the numerical base for mathematics would be different, likely requiring a binary base, which incidentally provides a convenient introduction to the fundamentals of computer language.

In this simulation, our explorer-students have available a limited set of experiments as the means to discover these prevailing laws and conditions. Team members may take on the roles of individual subject-matter experts – chemists, engineers, and even biostatisticians – each of whom learns to conduct a single experiment, record the results, and then interpret them. Naturally, certain levels of technological sophistication must be attained before these experiments can be run because so much rides on their accuracy. Under the circumstances it is the students, not the teacher, who will likely monitor the quality of individual contributions. Once all the experiments are completed, team members meet to share their individual findings and search for a larger pattern of meaning, reminiscent of the rules of the cooperative jigsaw paradigm.

If mistakes are made and false conclusions drawn about the nature of the planet, then the wrong kinds of equipment will be chosen for the voyage. The success of the mission is measured by whether or not the colony survives and for how long, and also by the quality of the life that evolves for the colonists. Criteria for judging life quality both in physical and psychological terms are established by the team itself before setting out on the voyage.

Viral Invasion: The Bioalert Game

Several fifth-grade students stand by watching anxiously as one of their friends struggles to save himself from a massive viral invasion, all thanks to a computer simulation. With the cunning of video-game junkies, students organize and arrange their antibodies to mow down wave after wave of invaders. Although good motor coordination is a decided advantage, ultimately the patient will be saved only by understanding the intricate relationships found among the body's various immune systems, and in particular by specialized knowledge about the use of antibiotics. Prior to game play students master the necessary information and concepts. For example, they learn that antibiotics, for all their benefits, are still potentially dangerous and may actually increase the risk to the patient if they are administered in improper combinations, under the wrong circumstances, or in inappropriate dosages. For these young students, the rewards of play include surviving the viral attack and the opportunity to learn more about the human body so that they can challenge an even more virulent breed of invaders in the next round of the BioAlert Game.

Psychic Income: The Career Placement Game

Mrs. Rollins's students remained skeptical. Could it really be that most adults find their jobs more satisfying than leisure activities such as watching television or going to movies (Juster, 1985)? But if true, conceded the students, then something very strange indeed must happen between junior high school and the future because everyone knows TV is more fun than work! Then there was the other bombshell: Those same loopy adults report that happiness on the job depends on more than how much money they make.

This young, disbelieving audience is about to be transported into the adult world of work where things would become clearer, thanks to the Psychic Income Game (after Abt, 1987). In this simulation students become employees and employers in a small electronics manufacturing firm. The firm is structured hierarchically with most job openings at the production level (hourly wages), fewer jobs in middle management (annual salary), and fewer still at the top management level (annual salary plus bonus). The task for the players is to assign themselves to available job openings while maximizing satisfaction for all. One approach is to make every job equally attractive despite the differential pay rates.

Players begin by listing various sources of on-the-job satisfaction besides money, what economists call *psychic income* (Strober, 1987) – security, independence, power, status, and opportunity for leisure. *Power* is measured by the number of people one supervises; *independence,* conversely, by the number of supervisors above one's level; and *leisure* by the number of free, nonworking hours per week. Players establish their own personal priorities and then begin negotiating among themselves for their own ideal mix of pay, leisure time, and status. One player may value monetary rewards so much that she is willing to give up all the leisure credits allotted her if she can but find someone willing to trade time for money. Another player finds the idea of rotating among different lower-paying production jobs (lateral movement) attractive because the resulting diversity of experience will make him more marketable in the event of a layoff (besides, having to endure four years of college just to enter management is not an agreeable prospect).

Today many youngsters make career and vocational choices inadvertently without an accurate understanding of how these decisions will affect their lives. Some children drift from one part-time job to another in essentially a random fashion, often accepting the first offer of permanent employment even though they may have applied for many jobs of widely varying characteristics (Osterman, 1989). Other young people aspire for something better but lack the preparation to implement their dreams. For instance, black females often express career aspirations that are comparable to or even higher than those of white females (Gibbs, 1985; Moerk, 1974; Smith, 1982), but they may lack sufficient information to make realistic plans to achieve these goals (Wallace, 1974).

An important part of career education involves providing youngsters with systematic opportunities to gauge their own strengths and weaknesses, to discover preferred working styles, and to consider life goals. When students must determine their own "winning" formula in the Psychic Income Game, they are considering just what they want from a job. For many, this may be the first time they have consciously thought about their life aims. Hopefully, such self-reflection will encourage the beginning of a rational choice of occupation, especially coming to terms with the fact that the most prestigious, well-paying jobs in our society are in relatively short supply compared with the number of young people who aspire to them (see chapter 10).

Playing school

Education will also become creative – a game under the control of the person being educated. Everyone will have a chance to discover exactly what he or she enjoys.
LEE KRAVITZ

There is little that is novel in the proposal to organize schools around discovery projects, lifelike simulations, and role playing. Actually, what John Stevenson (1921) called the ''project method'' of teaching was already well established in American educational circles long before the turn of the present century. In those early years the emphasis was on teaching the principles of science through their application to farm management and home economics. Today, although there have been dramatic changes in content and emphasis, survival and the pursuit of a better life are still the objectives. Educational gaming has since gained widespread acceptance in schools, especially with the advent of microcomputers beginning in the early 1980s (for a recent annotated review, see Cruickshank, Telfer, Ezell, & Manford, 1987). Today hundreds of simulation games are commercially available. For example, there exist some 400 computer war games, and hundreds of millions of dollars are spent yearly by the public on additional simulations covering virtually every content topic, including both board games and computer-based games. Of course, not all of these, perhaps only a relatively few, are what we would consider *serious* games whose purposes go beyond the merely recreational. But true educational games are in sufficient supply to illustrate their potential as the vanguard of change.

If there is anything new in my proposal, it is the suggestion that discovered problems should form the core of the entire school experience, not merely provide another source of novelty, distraction, or enrichment. Simply to suggest the occasional use of serious games would at best improve things only marginally. Rather the intention is to transform educational policy. Ideally, the challenge of arranging schools around the solving of discovered problems will force educators to deal with new and (hopefully) more appropriate concerns as well as to view old problems from new perspectives. No small part of this renewal involves focusing attention squarely on our motivational objectives and on the future. Indeed, whether or not this proposal can be justified depends largely on how well it satisfies the motivational, metacognitive, and future-oriented issues raised in earlier chapters.

In chapter 7 we marshaled various motivational arguments in favor of serious games. The additional examples just presented strengthen these arguments.

First, these examples further illustrate how task involvement can be aroused by combining novelty with the opportunity for youngsters to exert some control over the challenges they face. The BioAlert Game creates drama and excitement by leaving the chances of success uncertain but not hopelessly out of reach. There is that delicious moment when players realize that this time they may have given the virus too much of a head start. But if they try their hardest and learn just enough, they still might snatch victory from the jaws of defeat. Here there is room for the playful exploration of what it means to take risks, and how it feels to fail after having given it one's best shot – hopefully not shattered, as would almost certainly be the case if failure were defined competitively around ability status, but rather self-accepting, secure in the knowledge that personal satisfaction comes not only from achieving excellence but from striving for excellence as well.

Second, these examples also reinforce the potential of serious games for arousing intrinsic reasons for learning. And because these reasons are their own reward, the payoffs become plentiful as long as the quality of one's thinking brings a satisfactory conclusion to a particular assignment, whether it involves creating a viable theory about the workings of alternative worlds (Space Colony Game) or resolving a frightening standoff between rival powers (Nuclear Countdown).

Third, these examples illustrate anew the potential for altering the student –teacher relationship. The adversary is no longer adult authority, but rather the challenge of achieving a valued goal. The role of the teacher in the Nuclear Countdown Game is largely that of a research coordinator and coach, an ally of the students in preparation for their upcoming contest rather than a disciplinarian or lecturer.

Fourth, it is also clear just how easily rewards can be incorporated as an integral part of the learning activity itself rather than being imposed extraneously. In the BioAlert Game the reward for defeating one virus is the opportunity to learn more in order to play better next time.

If Tom Sawyer could make whitewashing a fence so attractive that his friends begged for the chance to help, then educators should also be able to turn work into play. And, by *play* it is now clear that we do not mean frivolous or undisciplined activity. Rather, we mean perceiving that an activity is interesting or worthwhile enough in its own right to commit all of one's resources, unreservedly, even joyously. Other more colloquial meanings of the word *play* also broaden its meaning for true learning: to use one's resources in the most effective manner, as in *"playing* one's cards right"; mobilizing one's skills to best advantage, as in "making a *play* for"; or enjoying the "subtle *play* of the mind." By the same token, not everything about *work* is contrastingly bad. Not when we recall that work implies purposeful activity as in the "collected *works* of Walt Whitman," or the importance of "good *works,*" or the quality of *"workmanship."* Unfortunately, it is these uplifting interpretations of work that too easily become the casualties of schooling as presently structured.

In addition to these motivational benefits, serious games also encourage a future orientation and have the potential to remedy various metacognitive deficits. First, consider the prospects for a future orientation.

A future orientation

Serious games typically involve strategic thinking for the purpose of future building. The goal of strategic thinking, or plan-generating behavior, is to achieve a desired state of affairs at a future time, whether it be a brighter world devoid of nuclear weapons (Nuclear Countdown) or having survived attractive but potentially lethal health risks associated with adolescent experimentation (The Health Futures Game).

Perhaps the ultimate demand for future-oriented thinking is reflected in the literature of science fiction. Science fiction asks that we temporarily suspend our assumptions about present realities and explore the implications of different worlds and different times – all through the passport of imagination. The essence of future-oriented thought involves the capacity to imagine the improbable as potentially possible, the unknown as eventually knowable, and the impossible as perhaps only contrary to today's facts (Covington, 1986a). These qualities of thought led Christopher Cockerell to invent the hovercraft when he toyed with the unlikely, farfetched possibility of moving ships *over* the water, not through it. They are the same characteristics of mind that permitted researchers to unravel the mysteries of Legionnaires Disease, an illness that for a time defied all known laws of contagion.

Such mental gifts would seem best promoted by confronting students with fictional worlds – worlds that operate on the basis of strange, remote, or wholly unlikely rules, but lawful rules nonetheless, rules whose regularities can be discovered by applying the skills of both inductive and deductive reasoning. Laboratory research indicates that discovering lawful relationships of the kinds suggested by the Space Colony Game depends on the ability of individuals to detect discrepancies in data patterns, to formulate and test hypotheses, and to keep systematic records of the results of their experiments (Kahn, 1979). Happily, as was demonstrated in chapter 8, research also indicates that these capabilities can be improved with practice, beginning as early as the elementary school years.

Serious games also provide an ideal vehicle for dealing with those issues that most experts believe will increasingly characterize the future. First, the future is problematic, and becoming more so, because the greatest dangers are not necessarily the most obvious ones. Second, more and more future problems will be without precedent in human history. And, finally, it is increasingly clear that these problems cannot be solved in isolation, one from another.

LOW-PROFILE RISKS

Robert Ornstein and Paul Ehrlich (1989) remind us that humans are notoriously prone to react quickly and often ineffectually to the dramatic but infrequent threat – being held hostage by terrorists, falling victim to a mass murderer, or being struck by lightning – and slow to respond, if at all, to the more insidious, low-profile threats that adversely affect everyone – the rising tide of human population, the accelerating extinction of animal and plant life, and the slow-but-sure poisoning of our environment.

An example from the field of public health illustrates the difficulties of teaching for such awareness. The consequences of some health risks, such as using heroin and skateboarding, are immediate, potentially fatal, and capable of graphic portrayal. But other risks, such as poor diet and chronic cigarette smoking, are more subtle. They involve low probabilities of occurrence over extended periods of time. For instance, relatively few smokers will die of cancer. Moreover, the harmful effects of smoking are often long delayed. Thinking seriously about such low probability, time-delayed risks depends on the emergence (during adolescence if we are lucky) of a capacity for formal logic as well as a tolerance for ambiguity and a growing understanding of the probabilistic nature of future events. It also requires that youngsters put aside childhood demands for certainty and the need for unwavering assurances from adult authority.

Specific examples of such future-oriented reasoning include being able to entertain the idea that the benefits of taking preventive actions now, for example, going on a low-sodium diet, may be delayed in their appearance sometimes for years, and then may only become manifest, if at all, through an *absence* of symptoms like heart disease. Then there is the possibility that taking risks now may never have an adverse impact on one's health unless other seemingly unrelated risks are also taken at a later time. For instance, the lung damage done by heavy smoking in adolescence may not manifest itself as emphysema until years later when the individual (by now, a longtime ex-smoker) moves to a polluted metropolitan area.

Such understanding is exceedingly difficult to convey, if not nearly impossible, because of a compressed view of future time and the concrete, absolute nature of the thinking of young people. However, by incorporating these lessons in realistic scenarios, like the Health Futures Game, and starting in the earliest grades, hopefully we can promote a true appreciation of the low-profile risk.

PROBLEMS WITHOUT PRECEDENT

Future problem solving will be increasingly characterized by either too little or too much information. The former case includes situations so novel to human experience that there are few precedents for decision making and for which the future consequences of our present actions can only be dimly foreseen today: decisions about the commercial exploitation of outer space or the ethical consequences of humankind's capacity to change its very nature through biochemical technology. Fortunately, however, as will be recalled, these are the very kinds of problems that are most responsive to broad problem-framing strategies, skills that can be readily practiced in the naturally occurring context of serious games.

Another precedent-shattering development is the phenomenon of information overload. Today the information glut is so severe that even experts working in highly arcane, narrowly defined specialties cannot keep up with all that is potentially important. The statistics are staggering. Worldwide, 7,000 books are published each day (Wurman, 1989). There is also the daily blizzard of memos, abstracts, and reports, most of it generated and stored by computer, and much of it only marginally relevant to any particular problem. This means that tomorrow's adults must be prepared to handle large masses of information, certainly not to remember it all, but at least to be able to make decisions about what is relevant and what to ignore. Such preparation takes practice.

For example, it would seem reasonable that students spend as much time learning whether or not problems can be solved in the form stated and, if necessary, how to reformulate them as is now devoted to practicing specific procedural rules for adding double columns or subtracting with borrowing. Subject-matter experts in all fields differ from novices in the amount of time they spend in the problem-formulation stage (Johnson, 1990). Novices tend to look immediately for a solution, whereas experts begin by analyzing the available information. Only after the dimensions of the problem are well understood do experts begin the search for answers. If children were taught these lessons early on, far fewer of them would try to calculate the ship captain's age in terms of the size and content of his cargo (chapter 1).

INTERCONNECTED ISSUES

The future of present decisions will depend increasingly on how well we handle deeply interconnected issues. For example, pesticides control plant-eating pests, but only up to a point. Overspraying, by even a small margin, can have a more devastating effect on insect enemies of plant eaters than on the plant eaters themselves. Thus a hoped-for solution to the problem of the global food shortage can in the end be counterproductive by creating an unexpected dislocation in a larger chain of related events. Human nature also illustrates the theme of interconnectednees. As powerful a technique as punishment is for controlling the actions of humans, punished behavior is rarely extinguished; it is only suppressed. The child punished for lying to his parents may continue to lie outside the home, an action that in turn may create greater problems than if the parents had treated the original problem differently.

These examples illustrate the need for a *systems* approach to problem solving. Michael Polanyi reminds us that "we cannot comprehend the whole without seeing its parts, but we cannot see the parts without comprehending the whole" (quoted in Reich, 1989, p. 17). Serious games are admirable vehicles for promoting an appreciation of this whole–part relationship that involves the capacity to view any given problem as part of a larger system, whether it be a psychological, a biological, or an economic system; or, what is more likely, some combination of all three.

Global Gambit illustrates the kinds of thinking and cooperation demanded by this perspective. It demonstrates that neither the players nor society at large can succeed solely by doubling up on their brain power, that is, by simply creating more specialists. Such a narrow frontal assault on problems exposes too many knowledge gaps. Rather, we must prepare our students to array their expert knowledge in an overlapping fashion more akin to the pattern of fish scales so that common, continuous fields of knowledge are created (Campbell, 1986). These lessons are taught in Global Gambit by requiring students to arrange their individual knowledge in a collective jigsaw fashion (Aronson et al. 1978). Teaching these jigsaw dynamics is also illustrated by the Space Colony Game in which students must assign overall meaning to a series of scientific experiments conducted by individual team members.

Interdisciplinary cooperation is exceedingly difficult to achieve. Experts not only speak different technical languages, but they think differently about issues. Like the proverbial ships that pass in the night, all too often experts talk past one another; and, in fact, sometimes do just about everything but bring different perspectives to bear on the same problem. Some systems researchers suggest that interdisciplinary teams must spend months if not years in preliminary discussion before formal work on a problem can profitably proceed (Chubin, Porter, Rossini, & Connolly, 1986). But even this is no guarantee. Spending time together is just as likely to increase barriers to understanding, with team members breaking up into isolated or competing factions. Recall the advice about cooperation that is easier to give than to follow: Each player will receive more rewards if everyone cooperates than if they do not. To be heeded, this advice must be practiced systematically in schools from the earliest years in situations that simulate all aspects of human nature, including greed, ambition, and altruism. Students must shift their view of themselves as separate entities, each seeking to satisfy only his or her particular goals, to a broader, collective conception of group well-being and to appreciate anew the deep interconnectedness of events and issues. Serious gaming seems an ideal vehicle for this purpose.

Enhancing metacognitions

We have surveyed the quality of planning that typifies both children and adults and found it depressing. On the brighter side, we now know that these deficiencies can be offset by systematic instruction. Also, encouraging the proper reasons for learning will help. No one can think effectively when fear is the instigator. Now a third source of help presents itself: serious games.

Serious games automatically reinforce a strategic, metacognitive perspective for several reasons. First, rhetorical questions about what one should know, how well, for how long, and for what purpose are all answerable in terms of the demands of the larger problem. In effect, the problem itself becomes the advanced organizer of the kinds of working knowledge needed for a solution. And solutions in turn become feedback, confirmation that enough information was acquired and the proper meaning extracted to get the job done. Second, serious game play transforms the purpose and function of knowledge. No longer does learning imply the rote recall of isolated facts for no particular purpose other than getting the right answer. For instance, many geography textbooks routinely dispatch the topic of Siberia (if it is covered at all) in a few sentences concerning its remoteness and frigid climate. However, for those students about to negotiate a nuclear disarmament treaty, Siberia takes on enormous geopolitical importance, and given the stakes involved, the desire to learn more increases and in ways that promote game play.

In effect, facts should be acquired to serve a larger purpose. If in the process they are retained longer, so much the better. But factual retention is not the real purpose of serious games, nor should discovered problems be contrived simply as a way to make rote learning like memorizing the multiplication tables more palatable or fun. Rather, it is quite the reverse. Serious games can show how applying the logic of multiplication will aid a greater understanding or reveal errors in reasoning that might otherwise support catastrophic conclusions. Ornstein and Ehrlich (1989) provide a timely example. It is widely held that economic growth can continue indefinitely. But if students simply compute economic growth at the rate of 1% per year, they will find that in 2,500 years the average Englishman would have 200 times as much buying power as *all* Americans have today. Does the earth have the carrying capacity to sustain a real growth rate of even this low magnitude? Here the use of multiplication facts sets the stage for debate and potential insights. In the context of discovered problems, facts become tools, not merely an end in themselves. As one further example, if students wonder why the American colonists increased their protests even after the British lowered the price of tea, then learning that England used price fixing as a way to manipulate trade is more than just a fact. It also becomes an explanation. In this case, to recall a point made earlier, facts become things to think *with*, not just things to think *about*. Little wonder that the colonists were so furious, no matter what the price of tea.

The elevation of local subject knowledge to the realm of metacognitive substance is best accomplished by allowing students to practice thinking in the same ways as do real-life practitioners in the context of what Jean Lave (1988) refers to as *authentic activities*. Authentic activities like serious games have their counterparts throughout the real world, especially in the crafts and trades – cooking, woodworking, gardening, and weaving.When individuals learn to perform authentic tasks they become apprentices and enter into the life and community of the practitioner. Even highly formal occupations, including medicine and the law, are taught largely through a process of apprenticeship. As John Sealey Brown and his colleagues point out (Brown, Collins, & Duguid, 1989), graduate students in the sciences and the humanities refine their research skills by apprenticing to senior researchers who themselves are working on authentic (discovered) problems that require the resolution of ill-defined issues and the clarification of controversy, as contrasted to those kinds of well-defined workbook (presented) exercises that make up so much of school life. In effect, at this stage of their development these advanced students no longer act like students, but rather have become authentic practitioners who hone the skills of their craft through group collaboration and social interaction. And, we know, groups are more than an effective means for transmitting knowledge to their individual members. Groups also give rise to ideas and solutions otherwise impossible without community input. Moreover, groups are essential to the detection of misconceptions and false leads that otherwise might be perpetuated if a single problem-solver keeps his or her own council. Also, groups are a source of collective wisdom that arises out of the conspiratorial sharing of shortcuts and little-known "tricks of the trade." It is in this realm that *intuitive* knowledge is born and thrives. Intuition is perhaps the highest expression of metacognitive sophistication, and what ultimately sets the expert apart from the beginner.

In school students are most often treated as novices, or worse yet as supplicants – in the most passive, infantilized sense of that term – whereas by contrast the expert is a practitioner. But beginners need not wait to become practitioners despite their fledgling conceptual knowledge. They need only enter into a community of apprentices, much as did Mr. Rodriguez's students in the Global Gambit scenario. By modeling the feedback provided them by the atmospheric scientists, these young students were well on their way to gaining membership in the trade of scientific inquiry and discourse.

Passing a history or mathematics test is not the same as entering into the world of the historian or the mathematician. To do this students must practice the conceptual tools and ways of thinking specific to various domains in authentic ways – perhaps by engaging in diplomacy and negotiation (Nuclear Countdown Game) or by teasing out the biological parameters that spell success or failure for the players in the BioAlert Game. At times the process of acquiring authentic knowledge may appear informal, unpredictable, and even chaotic. But this process can lead to robust, versatile (transferable) knowledge in deeply informative ways; it can decontextualize textbook examples and encourage connections between facts and concepts that would otherwise remain isolated and inert.

The benefits of failure

We have concluded that it is the meaning individuals attach to failure, and not necessarily its occurrence, that controls the quality of achievement motivation. Serious games are especially well suited for conveying the invaluable lessons of failure. As Max Beerbohm remarked, "There is much to be said for failure. It is more interesting than success." Failure is interesting partly for the fact that successful thinkers actually make more mistakes than those who give up easily and therefore preserve their unblemished record of mediocrity, and also for the fact that mistakes can usually be set right by trying again.

Many cases illustrate the value of persistence, including Edison's trial-and-error attempts to find a suitable filament for the first electric light. Legend has it that Edison made over 1,000 mistakes before succeeding, an impressive but unenviable record that caused him to observe that "invention is 99% perspiration and 1% inspiration." According to Richard Wurman (1989, p. 194), Jonas Salk, discoverer of the polio vaccine, spent 98% of his time documenting the things that did not work until he found the thing that did. Likewise, Charlie Chaplin often insisted on several hundred retakes of a single movie scene before he was satisfied with the results.

Edison may have relied too much on blind variation, and perhaps Chaplin persisted to a fault. Nonetheless, the value of not giving up easily is plain to see. Indeed, there are others besides Beerbohm who extol the virtues of failure as long as it is done with wit, grace, and style. In the words of Tom Robbins, author of *Even Cowgirls Get the Blues,* "A mediocre failure is as insufferable as a mediocre success. Embrace failure. Seek it out. Learn to love it. That may be the only way any of us will be free." Although Robbins may be overselling failure, it is also true that rarely in school is the case made for the importance of risking mistakes.

It should also prove instructive for students to replay famous failures in history. The title of James Welles's (1988) fascinating book suggests that we are in no danger of running out of teaching examples anytime soon: *The Story of Stupidity: A History of Western Idiocy from the Days of Greece to the Moment You Saw This Book.* By being properly forearmed, perhaps a new generation can do better than its predecessors at avoiding some of the great planning disasters of history (Hall, 1980). For instance, after students witness the conditions of leadership that led to the disastrous Bay of Pigs invasion of Cuba, they could replay events again, this time hopefully avoiding the divisive consequences of *groupthink,* a condition in which groups value harmony above dissent (Janis, 1982). In the same vein, one might challenge students to discover the flaws in reasoning that led authorities to build a nearly disastrous rapid transit system in the San Francisco Bay area. In hindsight the mistakes seem obvious (Hall, 1980). But students will need to combine their expertise at strategic thinking with a working knowledge of political systems, tax structure, and various principles of social psychology in order to improve on the record of these transportation planners.

Given our concern for the future, it would also seem wise for students to make a study of the failure of humans to anticipate the future. The record of prediction is basically dismal; it is not even a history of near misses. In fact, even when the projected target dates are only one or two decades hence, most expert guesses still prove wide of the mark, often ludicrously so. One of the most stunning examples of technological predictions gone wrong is TRW's "Probe." This 1960 study claimed to anticipate the products of the 1980s. Virtually all the predictions were either flatly wrong or the predicted time frame for their occurrence wildly optimistic. For example, it was estimated that the first manned lunar base would be established by 1977 and that by 1980 commercial passenger rockets would transport people to the moon and back around the clock. These wrong guesses were largely the result of psychological errors, including the tendency to be overly impressed by the wonders of technology, or what has been called the "gee whiz effect." Other mistakes in forecasting are driven by wishful thinking. Consider the often predicted cure for cancer. And then there is egocentrism, the presumption that consumers will see the same value in a new product as does the inventor. Obviously, these kinds of errors have implications for individual decision making and should be well understood by students lest they, too, make the same kinds of mistakes in arranging their personal and collective lives that have lead to enormous miscalculations in political and social policy in this century.

Serious games and minorities

Educational reform must also address the special problems associated with disenfranchised youth, immigrants, and children of color. For many of these youngsters, school is essentially a foreign country, foreign in that the goals traditionally associated with schooling are narrowly defined around unfamiliar middle-class values, including achievement for the sake of competitive excellence or merely for attaining a high test score. Moreover, the *means* to these predominately middle-class goals are foreign to many minority students who prefer the cooperation that comes from tight-knit neighborhood and family traditions. If black ghetto youngsters and their families survive by a kind of collective sharing, as documented by Carol Stack (1974), then it is only natural that these same children would feel most comfortable learning by cooperative means (Au & Jorda, 1981; Richmond & Weiner, 1973; Shade, 1987; Slavin & Oickle, 1981; Spencer, 1985). Yet if minorities want to play school, they must play by essentially competitive rules. Finally, schools rarely demonstrate how traditional textbook knowledge will benefit youngsters now or in the future (Marchant, 1990). As a result, many minority students "see studying as a sucker's game and school as a waste of time" (Steele, 1989).

We concluded earlier (chapter 2) that these sources of estrangement can be overcome in part by encouraging more varied achievement goals than those associated with high test scores and by honoring alternate ways of achieving largely through noncompetitive approaches. Serious games can promote these changes in several ways.

First, serious games are well suited for demonstrating the functional value of knowledge. Schools need no longer be seen as purveyors of irrelevant or useless information, cut off from the realities of daily living. These benefits would seem particularly important in the case of helping students make decisions about jobs and about their place in the world of work (see The Career Placement Game, this chapter).

Second, serious games provide a naturally occurring vehicle for a cooperative approach to learning. They do so without abandoning individual accountability or sacrificing the virtues of independent thought and judgment.

Third, we have already noted how playing serious games can transform the teacher–student relationship for the better. Such changes would seem especially welcome for disenfranchised youngsters who often see adult authority as an intrusion into their lives. For example, as will be recalled, the early withdrawal of emotional support from children in some black families leads to anger and resentment (see chapter 2), emotions that will likely generalize to other adult authority figures, including teachers (Ladner, 1978; Silverstein & Krate, 1975). But when the rules decree that the goal of school is to solve problems, not to usurp power or defend against powerful others, then the role of the teacher as a potential adversary can give way to the teacher as helper, explainer, and possibly even a player. Evidence reported by Abt (1987, p. 70) suggests that even the most rebellious student, fearing exclusion by peers, is more likely to accept and play by those rules mutually agreed upon by the group than by the rules of discipline imposed by a teacher.

Fourth, because game play is a familiar concrete activity it makes an ideal vehicle for the introduction and mental manipulation of complex concepts like history, justice, and civilization in ways that might not otherwise be possible if these topics were presented solely as abstractions. Indeed, some researchers suggest that black and Hispanic children favor learning environments that focus on whole concepts and real situations rather than on fragmented skills (Cohen & DeAvila, 1983; Gilbert & Gay, 1985; Ramirez & Castaneda, 1974).

Additionally, children of widely differing intellectual capacities and social backgrounds can participate in the same game with equal enthusiasm, yet learn quite different lessons. John Blaxall, one of the developers of a simulation designed to demonstrate the economic forces at work in the industrial revolution of the 1880s, observed that quite apart from the original intentions of the designers, slow learners came to understand for the first time about the idea of charging interest on money, and more advanced students learned about the effects that fluctuating demand has on prices (see Abt, 1987, p. 75).

Fifth, and finally, serious games, especially those that encourage cooperation, can be a significant force for overcoming ethnic bias, prejudice, and stereotyping. It is well known that increased contacts between ethnic groups can reduce prejudice so long as the contacts are not forced, and particularly when individuals band together to solve a common problem. Also knowing that another person has tried his or her best to help the group is enough to induce linking and to encourage the feeling that others care (Tjosvold, Johnson, & Johnson, 1984).

The problem of minority education is not that disadvantaged youth lack the ability to learn or that they are disinterested in learning. Rather, what is being taught is too often perceived as irrelevant to their lives. When it really counts, however, minority children, like all youngsters, are capable of extraordinary achievements. The research of Geoffrey Saxe (1988) illustrates just how extraordinary. Saxe studied poor children in the urban barrios of Brazil who survive by selling candy. These young entrepreneurs (many of whom never attended school and some as young as five years old) created a serviceable, intuitively based system of arithmetic rules and notations that allowed them to carry out the complex calculations involved in buying candy wholesale and then to set the daily retail price that must take into account the Brazilian inflation rate, which often exceeds 250% per year! Improvisation is the name of the game. For example, the youngest children, who are as yet unable to identify the numerical value of currency – not knowing the difference between a 1,000 cruzeiro and a 10,000 cruzeiro bill – make due nonetheless by substituting the color of the bill as the way to distinguish value! In these circumstances learning also became a social event. Older children (sometimes brothers and sisters or older candy sellers) teach the younger children how to count and calculate, and sometimes wholesale store clerks help sellers with their purchases by reading the prices of the candy boxes. Saxe's research is but one example of the newly emerging field of ethnomathematics (D'Amborsio, 1985, 1987; Millroy, 1991), which investigates different modes of mathematical knowledge that arise outside formal schooling and across different cultures.

One can envision a classroom counterpart of Saxe's real-life situation in which students – not just minorities, but all children – acquire and manipulate the basic number facts through exchange, bartering, and trade, all in a larger social and economic context in which learning serves an immediate tangible purpose and children are encouraged to help one another. Perhaps, too, older children and even parents can be drawn into this process of game play.

I do not propose that teaching mathematics, or any topic, remain solely an intuitive exercise driven by expediency. Intuitive knowledge as Kant rightly points out (p. 220) is a starting point, but intuition alone is not enough. Although Saxe's candy sellers who did not attend school made do for a time, in the long run they were unable to build on their intuitive understanding of mathematics in the same ways that school attenders were able to do. I do suggest, however, that teachers can help students make explicit their tacit, working knowledge on any topic by using the youngsters' intuitive understanding as a gateway and stimulant to abstract knowledge and by modeling formal concepts and strategies, all for the purpose of encouraging students to continue learning on their own.

The approach taken by Magdalene Lampert (1986) for teaching mathematics to fourth graders illustrates this progression. Lampert begins by using coin problems as a way to exploit the students' implicit knowledge and interest in money (e.g., "using only nickels and pennies, make 82 cents"). Next, students are encouraged to create stories for manipulation problems. For example, they are shown pictures of 12 glass jars, each of which contains 4 butterflies, and asked to think of different ways to group the jars that would make it easier to count the total number of butterflies. And, of course, different groupings still lead to the same answer, because as one child recognized triumphantly, "We have the same number of jars and they still have 4 butterflies in each." Through these kinds of mental manipulations students come to decontextualize the multiplicative properties of numbers. They learn that there is no "right" grouping, just more or less useful combinations depending on the purposes of the problem solver. Finally, the students are introduced to the standard multiplication algorithm now that the larger concept has acquired meaning and utility – multiplication makes unnecessary the otherwise laborious process of counting all the butterflies in each set of jars. It is no accident that Lambert's approach also incorporates a community of inquiry and an apprenticeship function in which there is an emerging classroom heritage of shared ideas and examples.

By these illustrations I do not suggest that minority students can learn only by concrete example. Actually, the evidence indicates that *all* children are likely to profit from authentic, hands-on experience as the first step toward abstract knowledge (Oakes, 1987). Such a playful approach permits students to take personal ownership of what they are learning and to see directly how knowledge is useful.

Saxe rightly observes that the gap between formal school mathematics and the mathematics used in everyday life is not unique to his Brazilian candy sellers. American youth likely suffer this same dislocation, not only in mathematics but probably with respect to most content domains. For instance, the way students create their own personal chronology and think about the concept of time differs radically from traditional, didactic approaches to the teaching of history (Downey & Levstik, 1988).

Schools must offer learning experiences that meet children on their own terms, not only developmentally but culturally as well, tasks that do more than hold their attention only briefly, tasks that also can command their loyalty and passions. Kevin Huston, a youth director in New Haven makes this point most urgently: "Get black youths interested in anything that won't get them killed or arrested" (reported in Finnegan, 1990). Insofar as possible the serious but *meaningful* games that children might play in school must become critical competitors to the serious but *deadly* games many of them play in the streets. Ganging is a game of sorts played by adversaries who abide by rules that involve real rewards and punishments, the rewards including a sense of belonging and a source of protection. Likewise candy-selling mathematics on the streets must not become a gateway to drug dealing, which also has its own rules and deadly risks. The positive lesson to be learned from drug dealing – if we dare think of drugs in that light – is the enormous entrepreneurial spirit it creates. In school many minority children are at a loss, but outside in the neighborhood and on the streets, they learn what is necessary to negotiate their daily survival and they improvise creatively even though some of their solutions are hazardous to themselves and others.

No matter what approach is taken toward minority education, we must be careful that the school experience does not imply or require that children of color must assimilate into the white middle-class culture. In the words of John Ogbu (1985):

> Some inner-city black children need to know, for example, that one person can be a good mathematician and be black; another person could be a good mathematician and Chinese. Yet both may have become good mathematicians because they learned similar rules of behavior and skills that make people anywhere good mathematicians, without requiring them to give up their cultural, ethnic or racial identities.'' (p. 66)

Obviously, in the last analysis, the massive problems associated with minority education – the horrendous dropout rate to mention just one example – will not be solved easily or quickly, and certainly not simply by restructuring schools around the lessons learned from solving meaningful problems. Other changes must also be initiated simultaneously, many of which lie outside the influence of schools. These changes include reducing the barriers to minority employment and relieving the crushing burden of poverty that stalks America's urban ghettos and barrios. It is one thing to arrange learning so that disadvantaged youth will come to appreciate that how much and how well they learn now will influence their lifetime income on the job (Bishop, 1989). However, if in the end there is no tangible payoff for trying hard in the form of enough jobs that offer a living wage and provide a reasonable source of dignity, then only disillusionment and resentment will result.

Schools and jobs

The end of the rainbow, you know, is not training and a diploma. The end of the rainbow is placement in a job and work.
RUSSELL TERSHY

Schools should provide opportunities for students to produce something of merit in the real world. The concepts of vocational and career education come as close as any to describing this linkage between schools, intellectual productivity, and the outside world of ideas and work. Today vocational education in America represents an enormous investment of time and resources. It is estimated that in California alone public secondary school students spend one million hours per day on some form of vocational education preparing for jobs and careers (Stern, Hoachlander, Choy, & Benson, 1986). Yet for all its prominence, the vocational education movement is beset by a host of problems. For one thing, despite its heavy focus on preparing disenfranchised youth for productive lives, vocational programs appear just as likely to track minorities and working-class students out of traditional academic curricula, thereby contributing inadvertently to the warehousing phenomenon. For another thing, in a fundamental sense schools are basically ill suited to the task of preparing students for employment; presumably, youngsters are being trained for work, but in an institution that keeps them from working! Despite some similarities in appearance, like equating the earning of grades with making money, working in the classroom and working on the job are quite different. As Donald Hansen and Vicki Johnson (1989) explain it, "Schools ostensibly are dedicated to the development of the individual; the workplace, to the delivery of [a] product or service" (p. 77).

The unsatisfactory nature of this arrangement is reflected in the growing perception of young people throughout Western Europe and America, as well as in Japan, that school is irrelevant to the work they will do after graduation (Coleman & Husen, 1985) and by the increasing numbers of students who get part-time jobs whenever they can (Greenberger & Steinberg, 1986). Surveys have found that from 80% to 90% of American students have held at least one paid job at some time during their high school years (Lewin-Epstein, 1981; Lewis, Gardner, & Seitz, 1983). Economic necessity appears to play little part in increasing teenage employment because parental income has been on the rise since the early 1960s. Rather, the evidence suggests that work provides a sense of meaning and pride not available in schools (Grubb, 1989).

> As one young man put it, At school you are treated like kids. . . . This year I'm expected to be more responsible to work. I felt really babied last year. Sometimes I feel like telling my teachers where to put it. They were talking to me like I was five years old. (Gaskell & Lazerson, 1980)

Of course, work experiences are not always positive. Many jobs involve repetitive, menial, unskilled activities that make it unlikely that students will actually acquire a sense of initiative and responsibility. Rather, youngsters are likely to become alienated from a work ethic, cynical about the intrinsic value of work, and even dishonest. For example, a near majority of one sample of young workers admitted to stealing on the job or lying to employers by calling in sick when they were not (Greenberger & Steinberg, 1981). Moreover, working long hours in out-of-school jobs can contribute to depressed grades in school (Steinberg, Greenberger, Garduque, & McAuliff, 1982).

This troubling situation is scarcely improved by the lack of evidence that vocational education helps students find regular employment after high school graduation. For instance, those California high school students who concentrated on vocational subjects during the 1981 school year had a 26% unemployment rate in the spring of 1982, a figure slightly greater than the unemployment rate for all 16- to 19-year-olds in the state (Stern et al., 1986).

Moreover, in that same spring a sample of California dropouts from the high-school class of 1982 had an unemployment rate of 27%.

Evidently, vocational training does not give high school students any particular edge in finding jobs after they graduate (Rumberger & Daymont, 1984). There are several reasons for this. First, David Stern and his colleagues (Stern et al., 1986) point out that the traditional goal of vocational education, that of preparing students for a first job, is unworkable because it emphasizes a result over which educators have little control. Vocational training may produce skills sufficient for entry-level employment, but skills alone cannot guarantee a job, especially when job markets are tight. Second, youth employment programs typically emphasize the training of relatively narrow job-related skills, such as filing and record keeping, skills that are less important than the lessons to be learned on the job (Johnson, 1990). In effect, specific job skills are no longer a sufficient condition for employment.

Actually, many prospective employers do not see vocational training or even the quality of academic preparation itself as the main issue. Various business surveys indicate that the greatest deficiencies among recent high school graduates are their unwillingness to show up for work, to take directions, to work together, and to take responsibility for their jobs (McGuire & Lund, 1984). The findings of the National Academy of Sciences Panel on Secondary School Education for the Changing Workplace (1984) echo these same concerns. Employers were asked to describe the kinds of employees they will need in the years ahead. Overwhelmingly, the answer was individuals who are able to take responsibility and are willing to learn throughout a lifetime. The panel went on to describe the necessary skills that characterize such individuals: "Able to identify problems, . . . adjust to unanticipated situations, . . . work out new ways of handling reoccurring problems, . . . determine what is needed to accomplish work assignments" (pp. 20–21).

Clearly, what is being called for is preparation for a working life of constant learning, problem solving, teamwork, and effective communication rather than a continuation of the outmoded practice of preparing most students for what Robert Reich (1983, 1989) calls "cog" jobs – being trained to follow directions for relatively simple, routine tasks that can be repeated over and over – while sending only a small minority of students on an advanced track to become decision makers at the top of the heap. Reich argues that productivity in America can no longer be viewed as a matter of producing a greater volume of goods, like cars or refrigerators, at a low cost per unit. Today there are simply too many other countries able to mass produce things better and cheaper. According to Reich, America must now rely on producing fewer goods, but of higher quality and tailored to the needs of specific customers in a timely fashion. By this reasoning, the manufacturing of TV sets must be replaced by the production of TV shows for specialized audiences worldwide. Likewise, mass producing refrigerators must give way to the job of filling these refrigerators with specialized kinds of food.

In order to maintain a competitive edge, American industry must continually improve its ability to respond quickly to changing tastes. This vision implies not only a rapid turnover in jobs, but also requires flexibility in shifting work roles within a company so that, for instance, a worker may become a production engineer on one project and part of the sales force on another. One recent trend involving decentralizing authority and dismantling bureaucratic layers also illustrates the new demands being placed on the work force. Branch managers of banks are increasingly encouraged to make decisions about loans without waiting for instructions or permission from superiors. Likewise, production workers are increasingly expected to maintain and make repairs on equipment themselves, thereby reducing the need for expensive specialized mechanics (Bailey, 1990). These expanding responsibilities require that the work force be capable of upgrading skills continuously and of acquiring new skills as well as the ability to think about information, not simply to remember it.

W. Norton Grubb (1989) sees schools in a quandary about how to respond to these new challenges and old failings. At one extreme, schools can simply get out of the business of vocational education and replace the demands of the labor market with curricula for the development of thoughtful individuals who are well versed in broad competencies. This is the vision of a true liberal education. At the other extreme, schools can intensify their present vocational mission and reemphasize utilitarian concerns. In practice, according to Grubb, we have an awkward combination of the two approaches, "with students pulled toward vocational purposes while reformers and educators try to remind us of the moral, intellectual, and political purposes of school" (p. 41).

There is, however, a third option: neither more nor less vocational education, but vocational education of a different kind, consistent with Stern's notion of "enterprise training" (Stern, 1990; Stern et al., 1986), that is, helping students become job ready through systematic instruction in individual and group problem-solving techniques and by learning to communicate effectively. Stern's recommendations are entirely compatible, uncannily so, with *our* evolving arguments that have approached the problem of student unpreparedness largely from a motivational perspective. The point of clearest overlap is an agreement that all students should practice creating potentially useful and personally meaningful ideas and products. By this reckoning, the world of work becomes another subject-matter topic equal in status to, say, physics or chemistry – in fact, a premier opportunity for the practical application of physical and biological principles.

The world of work and career development should be recognized as another rich source of discovered problems that can be posed in the form of serious games, and whose solutions depend on the exercise of productive thinking and strategic planning. Discovered problems associated with careers and work are legion, as are the spinoffs to traditional content domains, including such obvious candidates as economics. According to Myra Strober (1987) these topics should extend to everyday economic transactions such as buying a car and establishing a credit rating. Discovered problems should also include the nonmarket sector such as considering the choices people make for spending their leisure time and the economics of family households. These issues are of special interest to young adolescents who are in the process of questioning their place in their parent's home and are beginning to anticipate family life and work roles for themselves.

These lessons can start surprisingly early as Strober found to her amusement when she began to cut in half a dollar bill borrowed from a fourth grader whose room she was visiting (Strober, 1990).

> The children began wailing "Oh no!" So I asked them, "Why is this piece of paper special? How is it different from any other piece of green paper?" [Strober repeated the same maneuver on a credit card,] and again they cried out as only fourth-graders can, "Oh no!" From there we discussed what money means – and what kind of trust one needs in a society to have money as a medium of exchange. We discussed why these kids would be willing to take money for chores and not insist on having food or a sweater, or whatever else they were going to buy with the money. And we looked at the dollar bill – and we looked at the pyramid on it and the god's eye, and talked about what these symbols mean. (p. 5)

Predictably, Strober's demonstration opened a floodgate of questions driven by a healthy curiosity about real events. So, too, did the actions of one third-grade teacher who decided to share the details of her paycheck in class as a way to explore the concept of benefits and deductions and demonstrate why her take-home pay was so little!

This spirit of inquiry can be rekindled later when these same youngsters begin to wonder what their parents do when they go to work, and again later still when they begin to contemplate those mysterious factories and offices that they themselves will soon be entering. Serious games serve not only to keep these curiosities alive, but they also help provide a fundamental grasp of business law and accounting, as well as the principles of industrial psychology and labor relations. Consider, for instance, the Production-line Game through which youngsters can experience first-hand the dynamics of mass production and division of labor in the workplace (as described in Jamieson, Miller, & Watts, 1988). Students are organized into teams whose task it is to assemble a finished product out of component parts – perhaps building toy cars or fabricating paper notebooks out of raw materials. Students quickly realized that they can increase their efficiency (and the payoff) by assigning themselves to subtasks within the larger process. Eventually this division of labor may become complicated enough that the group will choose supervisors from within their ranks to coordinate the production process. In more sophisticated versions of this game students can experience key facets of the real work environment, including the wearing of industrial clothes, clocking in, and taking work breaks. During such breaks students might receive printouts describing the financial condition of the company, its cash flow, earnings, and daily production schedules. When the financial well-being of the company – and, in effect, the opportunity for continued gameplay – depends on the proper interpretation of such data, we can count on students to be motivated to learn.

In the hands of older players, such games can become the vehicle for experiencing a variety of work roles, including that of supervisor, shop steward, quality-control expert, and assembly-line worker. Students can also negotiate for pay rates and better working conditions, and in the process learn why some jobs are valued more than others, at least in terms of differential pay. Production simulations also provide an ideal setting for dealing with sex and ethnic stereotyping. In some experiments girls, women, and minorities have been assigned deliberately to nontraditional roles in the higher echelons of management. Although as yet there is little formal evidence on the value of such practices for reducing prejudice, anecdotal case study reports are favorable (see Featherston High School Study, in Jamieson et al., 1988).

Obviously, business decisions also can be practiced in lifelike situations, a prospect well illustrated by the Teddytronics Game in which young entrepreneurs manufacture teddy bears (as reported in Jamieson et al., 1988). In the process of studying the topic of yearly quotas, players learn to distinguish between fixed and variable costs. The seasonable (variable) nature of the teddy bear market introduces unexpected complications that may make these lessons quite graphic, even painful unto bankruptcy. For instance, students must figure out how to negotiate favorable interest rates with a banker (teacher) and minimize rent increases in periods of low demand in order to stay in business.

The use of business and career games can also help repair many of the problems besetting education in general and vocational education in particular.

First, as to the broader implications of serious games, it has already been remarked that many students rarely see any relationship between what they are learning now and what they must or might accomplish in the future. Serious vocational games can make vivid the future utility of what is being learned now. Moreover, such games help create a fusion of thought and action. For instance, consider the Production-line Game, which is not overly academic and therefore satisfies the need for relevance in the minds of players. Yet, at the same time, this game is not so narrowly defined as simply to mimic the demands of the marketplace. In this case effective business play depends on a larger set of academic concepts that make up the formal curriculum, thereby satisfying the need for pure or abstract knowledge.

In effect, vocational education need not trade academic rigor for watered-down relevance. Serious games provide an ideal context in which imminently practical issues and even the most humdrum procedural knowledge, like computing interest rates, can be taken up and mastered in a context that allows for the practice of what we have called higher-status knowledge – the kind of strategic skills useful in college, such as reasoning and decision making, and, according to employers, of particular value in the future world of work. Warehousing should be a game played to illustrate how goods are distributed and flow throughout the marketplace, not the consequence of a limited educational vision.

Second, by casting vocational education in the form of serious games, the quality of learning can be controlled directly by schools. Students need not be thrown willy-nilly into the marketplace of jobs in order to gain experience, which often turns out to be a brutalizing and demeaning experience. Ian Jamieson, Alan Miller, and A. G. Watts (1988) describe a number of school-linked work experiences including refurbishing old houses, tutoring young children, running recycling centers, and setting up food-growing coopera-tives. Stern (1984) calls these experiences "good work" because the evidence he presents suggests that they better prepare youngsters for future careers than does their random placement in odd jobs and part-time employment.

Third, and finally, we have concluded that although competition is a poor reason for learning, it is an undeniable force in society that cannot be ignored. Serious games provide an ideal springboard for creating a broader context within which to consider competitive dynamics: for clarifying the differences between cooperation and competition, for demonstrating how they blend as mixed motives in the marketplace, and for identifying what kinds of activities are best reserved for cooperation (Deutsch & Krauss, 1960). In the Teddy-tronics Game competition favors the consumer when teams compete among themselves in order to offer the most attractive product at the lowest cost. But when players within a team compete among themselves for competitive ad-vantage, everyone is the loser. Here game play largely follows gambling prin-ciples and features random trial-and-error moves driven by the need for a team to recoup its losses quickly before players are fired or demoted. These deci-sions depend little on the reality of cash flow, production demands, or on market variations. The usual result is a rapid expansion of teddy bear output followed by a drastic reduction in the labor force when hundreds of teddy bears remain unsold during periods of low demand (Jamieson et al., 1988).

There is broad agreement that schools should prepare students for the world of work as it now exists. This is part of John Dewey's legacy. So, too, is the conviction that schools should encourage a vision of what work might become at its best – part of Stern's (1984) notion of "good work." Good work means an environment free of physical danger, fair wages, and the chance for indi-viduals to do those things they do best. The quality of life in the workplace, like that in schools, also depends on the rules by which people relate. And these rules, too, can be changed for the better, a possibility to be explored beginning in the earliest years of school by the very individuals who will eventually inherit the workplaces of the future.

Grubb (1989) suggests three present realities that urgently require the at-tention of our youth. First, children should learn that work is largely done for money, not necessarily for intrinsic satisfaction. Having once understood this, students should then address the question of why this is so, and how work might be restructured to promote maximum psychic income. Second, students should learn about discrimination in the workplace – understanding, for ex-ample, that on average women are paid less than men and minorities are paid less than whites for the same work – and then consider how to remedy the situation. Third, students should learn about chronic unemployment – how it saps morale and erodes human dignity – and what might be done to minimize it. Many additional concerns can be added to this list, perhaps chief among them the need to teach students that our nation's economic well-being de-pends ultimately on issues of ecology and on the preservation of nature.

Obviously, these are not neglected topics. Much of the welfare and protective legislation in this century is a response to the cynicism, exploitation, and inequities of opportunity found in the workplace. But these problems and their solutions are never static. New ideas are constantly needed in response to a rapidly changing world of work and to evolving notions of fairness and human rights – issues that will shape the destiny of our young people. All the more reason why youngsters should have a hand in thinking about the process of change.

This perspective suggests that dealing with issues of work, employment, and economics are in the final analysis as much a moral enterprise as a scientific or sociological activity. As Strober (1987) puts it, "I want students who study economics to come away not simply with an ability to analyze but with an ability to care, to feel deeply the excitement and pathos of trying to meet human wants with scarce resources" (p. 136). Achieving this objective requires that students gain a unifying perspective of how each of us and the problems we confront fit into the physical, social, and biological worlds. Note then that our earlier Global Gambit example is as much an economics game whose purpose is, in Strober's words, "to meet human wants with scarce resources," as it is an exercise in ecology. Such a perspective does not render learning about morals obsolete, but rather creates a world in which the nature of moral choice is unprecedented.

This vision of serious gaming requires that schools shift from being places characterized by deep divisions between vocational and academic subject matter to places that integrate disciplines and draw together college-bound and employment-bound students to the mutual benefit of all. Equally pronounced today are differences in teaching style and pedagogical method, namely, the didactic, teacher-focused approach favored by academic instructors versus student-initiated, project-oriented approaches associated with vocational classes. Here, too, the possibilities for creative borrowing are unlimited, especially when teachers begin collaborating to establish interdisciplinary programs.

A number of models for integrating academic and vocational education have been identified (Grubb, 1990). One possibility is to replace conventional vocational and academic programs at the school site with departments arranged around occupational groupings such as technology, health, and business or communications. This arrangement would provide academic instructors with a vocational theme that they can incorporate into their own teaching. As Grubb points out, the more ambitious of these proposals go far beyond attempts simply to integrate academic and vocational strands and can be regarded as efforts to overcome some of the more serious failings of schools, including the isolation of teachers both from their students and from one another.

Prospects and conclusions

To reiterate, my proposal can be stated quite simply: Educational reform should proceed by teaching students (and teachers) to play serious games using rules that promote positive, ennobling reasons for learning – reasons accessible to all students – and that will sustain game play into the future. In many respects this proposal is quite modest compared to the enormity of the problems facing American education today. It has become axiomatic that big problems require big solutions. Yet, as promised, these recommendations require no major dislocation in educating our youth. Educators and teachers remain in control and ultimately would still be subject to the wishes of the community. Neither is a massive infusion of additional monies necessarily called for because limits on spending is not the most serious roadblock to change (Hanushek, 1989), although at a minimum clearly something must be done to repair the physical blight and decay of schools, upgrade antiquated equipment, replace books, and bring teachers' salaries more in line with the indispensable services they provide. Moreover, as already noted, none of the key ingredients of this proposal is new. Cooperative learning has been around for decades, as have been the techniques of mastery learning. And since their introduction in the 1960s, educational games have played an increasingly important, albeit still quite modest, part in the lives of schoolchildren. All this suggests that my proposal is capable of relatively rapid implementation. The ingredients of change are all around us.

Yet despite the appearances of modesty, I have described this proposal as immodest. There are several reasons for this. First, the proposal is clearly controversial, if for no other reason than the fact that the emphasis on thinking threatens the status quo. As Dewey correctly observes, ''Let us admit the case of the conservative: If we once start thinking, no one can guarantee where we shall come out; except that many ends, objects and institutions are doomed.'' We can already hear the complaints of some parents as anticipated by Ornstein and Ehrlich (1989):

> Children can learn about how their minds work in college. . . . My child doesn't need to waste his time learning about farming; I want him to become a lawyer. . . . Concentrate on the basics. . . . Youngsters need to learn *our* values not those of other people. . . . [Our] kids don't even know what the Bill of Rights is or who was president during the Civil War.
>
> Teachers will chime in too: I can teach Roman History, but I don't know Lucy from Neanderthal. . . . Probability? I have enough trouble explaining Geometry! . . . Anthropology should wait until college. (p. 201)

Second, the proposal is immodest because it challenges deeply held beliefs about the nature of teaching and learning. Chief among these beliefs is the proposition that teachers can control the quality of student effort through an appeal to tangible rewards and to the threat of punishment, and its corollary: The more valued (scarce) the reward, the more eagerly students will compete. We have shown these beliefs to be largely illusory, but still they are intuitively appealing and difficult to give up. The Protestant work ethic and the entrepreneurial system of extrinsic rewards that sustains it are deeply ingrained in the American experience.

Third, and finally, it is worth noting that this proposal requires more than merely shifting instructional priorities. It also means flying directly in the face of current trends that stress teacher accountability, which these days is increasingly defined by how well students do on standardized achievement tests. Teachers themselves are perceived as competent to the extent that their students excel, with excellence defined in an ever-narrowing arc. Whenever teachers believe that their role is to ensure high test scores rather than to help students learn, they pressure themselves, and in the process use controlling, autocratic teaching techniques (Boggiano & Barret, in press). In this case, control means emphasizing extrinsic rewards (particularly when they are dispensed competitively), allowing students little choice for how they go about learning, and threatening to withdraw emotional support as a means of punishment (Maehr & Stallings, 1972).

Such a regimen perpetuated in the name of efficiency forces teachers to de-emphasize topics not covered on standardized tests (Darling-Hammond & Wise, 1985; Shepard, 1989) with the result that although scores in basic reading and computing skills may have increased slightly in recent times, scores in science, writing, and more advanced analytic reading skills have actually declined (National Assessment of Educational Progress, 1979, 1981; National Research Council, 1979). Moreover, not only is the *content* of instruction altered by such narrow preoccupations but, more importantly, the *depth* of instruction is affected negatively as well. With increased standardization and greater accountability comes superficial coverage, and the possibility that we may be simply teaching children a series of "tricks" that enable them to perform well on standardized tests yet leave them deficient in basic understanding (Cunningham, 1990). What the advocates of intensification have forgotten is that *standardization* and *standards* are not the same thing.

All these concerns are reflected in what John Fredericksen and Allan Collins (1989) call the *systemic validity* of tests. A test is systemically valid to the extent it induces changes in instruction that promote the very skills the test is designed to measure. A particularly compelling – and from our vantage point, chilling – example of this process gone awry is how a high score on the statewide Regents Examination has become the main goal of instruction in many New York schools. The major part of the geometry section of the Regents Examination requires students to produce proofs. But as Allan Schoenfeld (1991) discovered to his dismay, instead of teaching students how to generate proofs on their own, many teachers require students simply to memorize the steps for each of the 12 proofs typically found on the examination. If the goal of teaching geometry is to reproduce formal proofs flawlessly, then the Regents Exam is systemically valid. However, if mathematical reasoning involves more than the slavish memorization and mindless recall of formulae, then the test is doing students a disservice.

The cult of efficiency has long been a driving force in American education and at present is growing stronger. A particularly insidious example was the recent proposal to screen nursery school toddlers for competency in prereading skills before admitting them to public kindergarten (Georgia Department of Education, 1988). If such a proposal had been enacted, we would face the very real, frightening prospect that some children might fail to reach even the first rung of the educational ladder. Fortunately, this particular plan has since been abandoned amidst great public opposition. But the mentality that breeds such schemes remains. Today it is only the brave, dedicated teacher who de-emphasizes immediate performance goals for the sake of teaching more lasting objectives, which include encouraging the will to learn and the productive use of the mind, especially when these goals are not always easily measured.

Fortunately, it is now possible to assess these illusive objectives thanks to the advent of new measurement techniques referred to collectively as *authentic* or *performance-based* assessment (Brown et al., 1989; Covington, 1968; Wiggins, 1989). Fredericksen and Collins (1989) explain these techniques using the example of *verbal aptitude,* which might be defined as the ability to formulate and express arguments in verbal form. Traditionally this construct is assessed using tests of vocabulary knowledge or verbal analogies. By contrast, in the case of authentic tests the cognitive skills associated with verbal aptitude are evaluated as they are expressed in the performance of some extended, meaningful problem such as requiring students to develop arguments favoring their side of the law in a small claims court action.

A number of authentic assessment tasks are currently undergoing development and large-scale tryouts under the auspices of the Common Core of Learning Assessment project (COMPACT Dialogue, 1989) sponsored jointly by the state of Connecticut and the National Science Foundation. For instance, high school students are required to use principles of physics and mathematics to determine whether or not speeding contributed to the death of a pedestrian in A Case of Manslaughter. In another problem students are given evidence that the earth is flat and are then asked to figure out ways to prove their belief that the earth is really round. In the area of social science students are given a number of artifacts from various civilizations in different time periods and required to make inferences about these long-extinct cultures.

Authentic measurement is not limited to direct performance tests alone. This type of measurement also includes long-term projects, playbills, logs, and students journals, as well as writing samples and even testimonials (Costa, 1989; Wolf, 1989). Of special interest is the use of student portfolios modeled after the kinds of resumes collected by artists and writers (Levin, 1990). Portfolios can reflect a whole range of student experiences and accomplishments, and they can be arranged chronologically or by subject-matter areas. For instance, science portfolios might contain a journal used to record observations collected during science experiments, student-generated graphs and tables, as well as field drawings from nature.

Performance-based tests are designed to reveal the primary characteristics that define excellence, which in our example of the small claims action might include such dimensions as clarity and persuasiveness of communication. To be sure, the evaluation of authentic products and their underlying processes is formidable. Not only is it time-consuming and labor-intensive, but just to complicate things authentic assessment provides information that is not easily converted into a single score for the sake of convenience. On the other hand, however, the information is potentially far more diagnostic of student progress, and the teacher can avoid the dangers inherent in attaching too much meaning to a single score made up of many isolated (multiple-choice) answers gathered under potentially artificial circumstances (Gitomer, 1989, cited in Frederickson & Collins, 1989). Moreover, when the criteria for judging quality are made clear, scoring can be done with a high degree of agreement among raters (Mullis, 1980).

Ultimately, the extra work is justified by the fact that authentic testing involves more than merely identifying the best students for promotion to college – the major preoccupation of most traditional standardized tests. At its most profound, authentic testing becomes an integral part of the instructional process itself (de Lange Jzn, 1987). Above all, authentic testing stands as a means of diagnosis and feedback. For example, authentic testing has the potential for providing students with various absolute landmarks of success and near success in the form of sample answers that might be labeled "beginner," "intermediate," and "expert." Students should have unrestricted access to sample answers of varying quality so that it becomes clear just how a particular performance is being judged and how students can improve. Hopefully, authentic testing will encourage students to become their own critics and autobiographers and to begin to notice what is distinctive about their own work, what has changed for them over time, and what is still missing and needs to be accomplished (Levin, 1990). This is precisely the reason that Mr. Rodriguez provided his students with expert feedback at the conclusion of the Global Gambit scenario.

The idea of performance-based assessment also helps place the issue of transfer of learning in its proper perspective. If complex behaviors, for example, developing authoritative arguments and presenting them persuasively, are judged important enough to target in schools, then the skills that support effective communication should be both trained and assessed directly and transparently. In effect, teaching to the test – recalling the notion of systemic validity – is no vice if the test itself reflects highly valued human qualities that have broad application. If students can learn to express themselves clearly and forcefully, perhaps as judged by their performance in a simulated legal action, then it is likely that they can also act as effective advocates for themselves in other related, real-life situations as well. Conversely, however, simply passing a word-recognition vocabulary test is no guarantee that these words can or will be used properly or to good advantage in *any* situation.

This is not to suggest that vocabulary is unimportant. Nor do I mean to downplay the importance of mastering the steps involved in creating geometric proofs. The subject-matter mechanics of every field is essential to good thinking. What concerns me, however, is that those kinds of learning that are most *easily* measured, like vocabulary acquisition, are not necessarily the most *important*. We laugh at the bizarre logic of the drunk who upon losing his car keys one night decides to search for them on another street where the light is better. Yet when it comes to educational matters, the public often insists on asking students questions whose answers are the easiest to assess and interpret; but these are not necessarily the right questions. Where education is concerned, easy is rarely best. By focusing attention on the memorization of proofs, students can doubtless be coached into passing standardized tests with flying colors, but they will not necessarily learn how to reason mathematically. The point is put bluntly by Elfrieda Hiebert and Robert Calfee (1989):

> Citizens in the 21st century will not be judged by their ability to bubble in answers on test forms: Their success both personally and professionally will depend on their capacity to analyze, predict, and adapt—in short, to think for a living. (p. 54)

10

Obstacles to change: The myths of competition

Competition prepares one for life. But what kind of life?
MARIE HART

Today when parents are asked to rank various educational goals, they typically give high ratings to promoting self-esteem and the will to learn, right along with competency in reading, writing, and mathematics (Reasoner, 1986). This is surprising for the fact that only a few decades ago proficiency in reading and mathematics dominated these polls, with esteem and motivational goals trailing badly. Perhaps even more remarkable is the fact that these shifts in priority hold across a broad socioeconomic spectrum. Both working-class parents and those in the professions endorse self-worth values. It seems that the lay public has come to intuit what we have demonstrated empirically, that self-worth considerations stand at the center of the achievement process, and that competency and feelings of worthiness are inseparable.

These ratings are also remarkable for what they do not reveal about public perceptions of the instructional process. Other expectations are also at work behind the scenes – factors that threaten the delicate balance between competency and confidence. First, as we know, there is the widely shared belief that schooling should be efficient. Second, many believe that arranging incentives around competition is the best way to ensure efficiency as well as creativity (Collins, 1975; Elleson, 1983; Grenis, 1975). This latter belief is so pervasive that, as will be recalled, George Leonard (1968) charged that competition is taught in schools as an end in itself. If Leonard is correct, then a major, if misguided, value perpetuated by our schools never appears on any public relations statement of the educational mission: competitiveness for its own sake!

What may not be so obvious to the lay public is that the values associated with efficiency and competitiveness are essentially incompatible with the promotion of self-esteem. I have argued from the outset that it is through improved performance that self-confidence grows, and increased self-assurance in turn triggers further achievement (e.g., Skaalvik & Hagtvet, 1990). However, it is not always the case that confidence and competency act in mutually reinforcing ways. I have shown repeatedly that despite records of great distinction, some students never feel personally secure. Recall the *overstriver* who accomplishes much, not out of curiosity or caring, but out of a compulsive need to demonstrate perfection. Indeed, much of our attention has been devoted to understanding why esteem and competency do not always grow apace.

How, then, are all these potentially contentious values to be reconciled so that the goals of self-acceptance and competency will prosper despite the presence of competition in schools and a growing clamor for efficiency? Regarding the cult of efficiency, our answer (chapter 8) was that the goal of efficient learning need not be rejected as much as subordinated to the larger concerns of effective thinking. *Efficient* learning and *effective* thought are not the same; but neither are they incompatible. By increasing their capacity to think, students learn faster and retain more of what is important.

Dealing with competition is more complex because the issue is not simply one of degree of compatibility. Competition in any amount – even in moderation, whatever that means – creates noticeable declines in academic performance (Boggiano et al., 1985; Rubin, 1980). This suggests that competition should be minimized whenever possible, not just moderated. Yet can we risk jeopardizing the very factor that some observers (e.g., Ford, 1974; Levin, 1983) argue has brought America to preeminence in the world? This question requires that we reevaluate the wisdom of abandoning the competitive mode of learning in schools. At first blush, this suggestion appears deeply contrary to the entire weight of our earlier arguments. Is there *any* legitimate reason to teach children to treat others as impediments to their own success? One would think not. Nonetheless, there still remain powerful reasons thought by many to justify competition as a central enabling force in our schools. These claims must be dealt with, and if possible dismissed, before we can take seriously the possibilities for educational change along the lines proposed in previous chapters.

The myths of competition

We say that if you win, you're dedicated, hardworking, altruistic. If you lose, you're none of the above.
THOMAS TUTKO

A major obstacle to true reform involves the uniquely American commitment to competition, and its corollary that competition is the best way to ensure at least a minimum level of competency among all our students. This beguiling but mistaken belief is enormously powerful because of its intuitive appeal to reason. After all, if a competitive edge has sustained America's unprecedented economic prosperity through most of the 20th century, will not the same formula work in our schools? The answer, as we now know, is probably not. But the reasons why are not always immediately obvious. Moreover, even after demonstrating the falseness of the argument that competitive adversity builds character (as was done in chapter 6) and pointing out the flaws in the belief that competition motivates students to do their best (also, see chapter 6), there still remain two other powerful arguments favoring competition as a way of life, arguments that have little to do with the process of learning itself. These reasons relate to the undeniable fact that there must be some orderly way to distribute individuals proportionately across the available jobs in our society, some of which are more attractive than others. Competitive grading in schools has long been the primary mechanism for assigning talent according to job demands and availability (Campbell, 1974). In effect, the better a student's grades, the more likely he or she is to be picked out for further schooling, and it is higher education that forms the gateway to the most prestigious occupations. If competition is de-emphasized in schools, by what mechanisms will individuals be apportioned to jobs? A related question concerns the second, remaining argument favoring competition: By minimizing competition in schools, do we not do an injustice to students who will grow up ill prepared to survive in the world of adulthood? What about these arguments? Are they fatal to suggestions for reform that depend on de-emphasizing the role of competition in learning? Let us consider each in turn.

Competition and survival

Will not the future of our children be jeopardized if the competitive nature of the learning game is changed? This question implies that teaching competition prepares children for survival later on in an impersonal job market and, conversely, that to elevate cooperation or individual excellence as the higher good is to prepare them for a world that does not exist. Faced with this argument, many teachers may feel coerced into accepting the status quo, despite noble sentiments to the contrary. After all, resistance to competition is viewed in many quarters as faintly unAmerican anyhow (Hart, 1973), and the arguments that competition is an unavoidable fact of life or even basic to human nature are numerous and beguiling (Klein, 1982; Nouwen, 1975; M. Rosenbaum, 1980). (For an excellent critique of the "human nature" myth, see Kohn, 1986.)

If we accept the argument that schools serve a transitional function that moves children progressively from the support-centered family group in their early years to an uncaring world of adulthood, then it might seem that requiring children to compete is basically a beneficial exercise. Getting used to losing is considered to be no small part of this benefit. Aside from the perfectly valid point that schools should teach students how to deal with failure, this argument falls short on several counts. First, far from preparing children for the rigors of the future, competition actually undercuts their ability to succeed in *any* kind of world, competitive or otherwise. Second, the world of work as it presently exists is far less competitive than is often assumed.

EARLY ADVERSITY

If competition is as devastating to student productivity and self-esteem as it appears, then the real issue is not one of preparing students for a cutthroat world, but rather facing the prospect of delivering them into adulthood without the skills to cope effectively on any terms. Despairing of one's ability to face an unknown, quixotic future is not the kind of preparation we would choose for our children; nor is growing up with high ambitions driven out of compulsive attempts to resolve doubts about one's worth. Yet these are the eventual legacies of competitive incentives. And as to the argument that children ought to compete in order to get used to losing, this notion is based on the largely discredited assumption that depriving children is the best way to prepare them for the rude shocks of life (Kohn, 1986). Even philosopher

Richard Eggerman (1982), who argues in favor of competition as a "mixed good," concedes that "children may be peculiarly liable to dangers of comparisons of relative worth in a way that adults are not, just as it is reasonable to suppose that children should not be exposed to pornography, violence, and so forth" (p. 48). Although some experience with failure is important for maturity, the context within which it occurs and its meaning are pivotal. When failure is judged by competitive norms, it signals falling short as a person. This exceedingly noxious message carries with it feelings of self-loathing and humiliation. On the other hand, when students fall short of their *own* expectations, failure encourages the very virtues often mentioned as the fruits of competition: self-discipline, tenacity, and resiliency (Kennedy & Wilcutt, 1964).

The point is that even if survival in adulthood depends on being competitive to the degree that some claim, then teaching these lessons in childhood destroys the will to compete long before most youngsters enter the battle for economic survival. Herein lies the essential paradox facing advocates of competition in schools: Preparing for a competitive world destroys the capacity to compete in that world. And, what is more, we are unwilling to concede the basic assumption on which this wrongheaded argument rests – that competition is the fundamental reality of adulthood.

OUTPERFORMING OTHERS

The tenacity of the myth of early adversity derives largely from a false reading of the true nature of the world of work, and of the personal qualities best suited for survival. This brings us to the second flaw in the argument that links competition and survival. Basically, proponents of competition have overstated the extent to which the economic well-being of individuals depends on outperforming others. What, in fact, is the role of competition in keeping a job and of getting ahead?

Keeping a job. It is an undeniable fact that the American economic system is grounded in competition. However, what is less often appreciated, but of equal significance, is the fact that the mechanisms of supply, demand, and productivity that operate on a broad economic macroscale depend, in the final analysis, on the collective efforts of millions of individuals who are themselves unlikely to be in direct competition with one another. Competition in the sense of a pure zero-sum game operates largely between corporations, within business sectors, and between countries, but far less frequently among the individuals who make up these larger aggregates.

Interestingly, one of the most effective cooperative learning paradigms mimics this reality precisely. When individuals cooperate among themselves in smaller groups in order to compete against other groups, the achievement of each group member is maximized (Deutsch, 1949).

Arthur Combs (1957) makes the case for cooperation as the ultimate enabling force in American society:

> We are impressed by the competitive features of our society and like to think of ourselves as essentially a competitive people. Yet we are thoroughly and completely dependent upon the goodwill and cooperation of millions of our fellow men. From the engineer who keeps the electric tur-

bines running through the night to the garbage men who keep our cities livable, each of us must rely on others to carry out the tasks we cannot perform ourselves. . . . Although it is true that we occasionally compete with others, competition is not the rule of life but the exception. Competition makes the news, while cooperation supplies the progress. (p. 265)

Of course, it is true that when a business fails or is substantially restructured in order to remain competitive, individual workers will be affected. But it is difficult to see how learning to be competitive from an early age will prepare employees for the trauma associated with unemployment and dislocation. Advocates for competition can only hold out the forlorn hope that by learning to outwit one's peers, it will be *someone else,* and not *oneself* who is the victim of future economic upheaval. Obviously, schools cannot give such guarantees. Nor should they. The mission of schools is not to provide a training ground for future rivalries. Nor can schools ensure against future job loss. Even if they were to try, enhancing competitiveness is the wrong way to proceed, because in most cases holding a job does not depend on outperforming others. It has been estimated that the vast majority of American workers, some 80% of them, are compensated on the basis of group effort or simply by being competent enough (Deutsch, 1979). Less than 20% of the work force is paid according to individual productivity, that is, paid strictly on a merit basis – the more one produces the more one earns. This arrangement includes, for example, piece-rate workers in garment factories and salespeople on commission. But most important is the fact that only a small fraction of these relatively few merit workers – probably less than 1% of the total work force overall – owes its livelihood to being able to outperform potential competitors. These data suggest that for the overwhelming majority of jobs merely being competent is enough; most workers need not be either overqualified or demonstrably better at what they do than anyone else, but only capable of performing satisfactorily.

Certainly there are exceptions to this general observation, but these exceptions are exceedingly few. It is only because of their exceptionality that they capture the public imagination, and in doing so are often thought to be representative of the larger world of work. The corporate executive whose year-end bonus depends on being more ruthless than his rivals is an image that readily comes to mind. Another is the professional athlete whose starting position on the team depends not simply on being good enough, but on being better than any upcoming rookie, year after year. And then there is the professional musician whose position as first-chair violinist in the orchestra is perpetually in jeopardy from the challenges of any other member of the violin section. These examples conjure up arguments about the inevitability of competition on the grounds that it is all simply a matter of economic necessity. The social reform literature of the early 1900s is replete with images of unscrupulous business tycoons and other cutthroat predators who acted on the principle of survival of the fittest. Although these portrayals were doubtless true then, and are still partly true today, they misrepresent the vast majority of jobs and occupations.

Direct economic competition among individuals is likely to occur only when the total number of goods or services offered for sale or hire exceeds the demand. The unemployed music teacher who moves to a new community only to find that a cadre of well-established teachers have already cornered the market on young, aspiring pianists is but one example of this supply–demand imbalance. So too is the cyclical overabundance of unemployed aerospace engineers caused by reduced federal spending on defense. But the economic hardships caused by these imbalances will not be corrected by teaching young children to be ruthless. This would simply encourage further a mentality of winning and losing. Rather, schools must help youngsters gauge the wisdom of their career choices in advance against projected needs for their services in the future, and help them develop alternative skills should their best guesses go awry or if their chosen life-style no longer appeals.

Finally, it is important to realize that very few individuals lose their jobs merely because someone else is marginally better qualified. In part this is because it is simply not economical for most businesses to pursue a policy of pure competition in which jobs remain continuously open to challenge by other workers much in the same way that the starting quarterback's job is always up for grabs. The cost of pursuing such a policy in the workplace would quickly become prohibitive in terms of falling productivity caused by plummeting morale. There would also be costs associated with upgrading or relocating displaced workers, not to mention the possible illegality of such practices. "Revolving door" competition is largely unworkable in the business world, yet we tolerate it in our schools whenever children are required to compete for a shrinking supply of rewards that depend on doing better than others. Of all the groups in our society, it is children who are the most subject to continuous, unremitting public scrutiny and evaluation, and all too often in a competitive atmosphere. This combination of factors is rarely experienced in adulthood; and when it does occur, as in the case of professional athletes, at least the financial rewards are proportional to the stress involved.

These observations place the arguments for early adversity in the proper perspective. Presently many children are not only being prepared for the rigors of adult life, but because its competitive nature is exaggerated, they are being *overprepared!* Rarely will the economic well-being of young adults depend on outwitting and outmaneuvering others in the caustic fashion we have come to associate with the zero-sum game in schools. In the final analysis, apart from sheer incompetency or simply not caring, the major causes of job loss are impersonal, cyclical economic forces over which individuals have little direct control. The best way for individuals to prepare for the vicissitudes of automation, foreign competition, overspecialization, and seasonal fluctuation in jobs is to increase their range of marketable skills (Hull, Friedman, & Rodgers, 1982; Jaffe & Froomkin, 1968).

Getting ahead. So far we have spoken only of keeping jobs. But what about being promoted once the individual enters the job market? Leaving aside seniority – which is the major reason for promotion in most jobs (Berg, 1970) – upward mobility otherwise depends on becoming increasingly valuable as an employee. Doing so typically involves further schooling and the development of additional skills or technical expertise. As long as one's competencies keep pace with potential opportunities, promotions will likely depend on those personal qualities associated with noncompetitive striving such as cooperativeness. By contrast, neither intellectual ability nor educational level have much to do with longevity on the job. It appears that brighter, better-educated people get ahead by moving from one firm to another, and that their less-educated peers stay behind and move into the higher-paying, if not always higher-skilled, jobs vacated by employee turnover (Berg, 1970). Meanwhile, higher-skilled jobs are filled by the better-educated workers who have quit other employers. Incidentally, we see here one of the hidden costs of competition reflected in high employee turnover. The upwardly mobile better-educated workers often do not stay long enough on one job to master it fully (Kanter, 1977).

I do not mean to imply that ranking employees for relative competency plays no part in the promotion process. Promotions that depend on being more competent than others occur frequently in hierarchically structured occupations where there are fewer and fewer job openings as one moves up the career ladder. Consider the military. Officers on the promotion list at any step in rank typically outnumber the openings available at the next higher rank. As a result, many qualified officers are denied promotion on a given round, and must await advancement at a later time. In this way, all officers will rise through the ranks until eventually each is promoted no further, even though he or she may be perfectly capable of discharging the duties associated with a higher rank. Much the same can be said about management positions in many business organizations.

Hierarchical job structures are an economic fact of life. They cannot be ignored; but neither should they serve as a model for how students are taught. Parents can certainly expect schools to aid in the development of their children's talents but in the clear knowledge that even an outstanding record of school achievement is no guarantee of limitless promotions or of unrestricted financial rewards later on. No matter how well prepared students may become, barriers to further progress will eventually be encountered whether they be limits of talent, unfavorable economic realities, poor timing, or just plain bad luck.

But, surely, won't those individuals who are more aggressive and ambitious (in the spirit of Hermes) enjoy greater occupational success? Not necessarily, according to the findings of Janet Spence and Robert Helmreich (1983). These researchers studied the relationship between the successes of adults in several career fields and personal dispositions such as competitiveness, a willingness to work hard, and a mastery orientation (e.g., "If I am not good at something I would rather keep struggling to master it than move on to something I may already be good at."). In one sample involving scientists, success was defined as the number of times each participant's research was cited by colleagues; for a sample of businessmen, success was calculated in terms of yearly income; and for a sample of college students, GPA was the measure of success. The results for these disparate groups were remarkably similar and striking. In all three cases, the more individuals preferred hard work and the mastering of new skills, the more successful they were. For task-oriented individuals personal competitiveness was an unnecessary ingredient for achieving at the highest levels. In fact, being competitive actually interfered with the productivity of these high-achieving individuals. The image of the successful businessperson as highly competitive, and the presumption that competition is necessary for a successful career are called into question by these data. What really counts in the march toward career prominence is being task engaged, being interested in one's work, and always striving to become more skillful.

To summarize so far, I have argued against using schools to indoctrinate students into a competitive life-style on the grounds that the world of work is simply not as competitive as some believe. In fact, competitiveness as a life-style may actually get in the way. Once students become competent, it is those personal qualities engendered by cooperation, sharing, and achieving by independence that best predict their future productivity. Certainly these are the qualities that most attract the attention of potential employers (chapter 9).

Competition as head start

Although competitiveness may play a negligible, even contrary role in succeeding on the job, what about landing the job to begin with? It is a truism that individuals aspire to more rather than less prestigious jobs, and it is the high-paying, challenging jobs that are in shortest supply. Schools have become the central selection agent by which individuals are allocated proportionally to the available jobs. This is done largely by assigning relative rankings to students in the form of grades. Morton Deutsch (1979) puts it this way: "In the contest for individual success, grades are to the student what occupational status and income are to the adult" (p. 394). Not only is this relationship correct metaphorically, but it is true in fact. Adult occupational status depends closely on the kinds of grades received by individuals in school. This linkage between grades and continued access to education holds schools hostage in the battle for future economic security and prestige, a contest that absorbs millions of American parents and turns their teenagers into compulsive, test-anxious, grade-grubbers.

Thus although a spirit of competitiveness may benefit individuals little once they are established on the job, competition is a vital part of the race to acquire sufficient educational credentials for access to the most desired career paths. Obviously, too, the process of competitive selection occurs not just once at the juncture between high school and college, but numerous other times as well. This is why some parents are so desperate to enroll their toddlers in just the right nursery school as a kind of head-start insurance. Moreover, the impact of this competitive gauntlet is felt not only by those who stand to gain the most by such maneuvering – the children of upwardly mobile, affluent parents – but also by those who have relatively less access to the top – largely minorities and youngsters from low-income families. These children, too, are ensnared in the same grade-grabbing game, perhaps not as active participants, but they become savaged nonetheless. If disadvantaged youngsters should choose to stop playing the competitive game or simply drop out, as many do, they will likely feel themselves as failures rather than recognizing the game as a failure. Ultimately everyone pays for a contest that is actively engaged in for profit by only a relative few.

Given the potential cost in human terms, powerful forces indeed must be perpetuating this selection function of schools. The main benefactors are business, government, and industry. Business relies heavily on schools to sort individuals into various occupational tracks based on ability and intellectual potential so that eventually only a relatively few persons remain to compete for the most prestigious jobs in the professional ranks, while lesser-endowed or less well-prepared individuals compete for less demanding jobs. Thus much of the task of job sorting is done in advance of the time individuals actually apply for work. It is this selection function that has most enraged educational critics who charge that the domination of school learning by competition is driven primarily by economic factors rather than pedagogical concerns. For instance, David Campbell (1974) observes that the whole frantic, irrational scramble to beat others is essential for the kind of institutions that our schools are, namely, "bargain-basement personnel screening agencies for business and government" (pp. 145–146).

There is no denying that competitive sorting serves an important economic function: the allocation of individuals to jobs. Indeed, it can be argued that the system works with considerable efficiency because (1) once outstanding talent is identified (through competition), then (2) competitive rewards arouse and sustain the enormous effort needed for these gifted individuals to acquire advanced degrees. Consider these two claims briefly.

Competition and effort. First, take the latter proposition that competitiveness drives the kind of dedicated effort needed to prepare for entry into prestigious occupations. If a link can be established between personal competitiveness, on the one hand, and persistence in school, on the other, then the case would be strengthened for encouraging competition on the grounds that only the strongest and best prepared candidates will eventually prevail. We have already reviewed the available evidence on this point (chapters 1 and 6) and found quite the opposite. When youngsters perceive school solely as a way to further their economic interests or to enhance their prestige at the expense of others, they are *less* rather than *more* likely to continue their education. It is reasonable to suppose that those youngsters who are dominated by considerations of status suffer the most from the competitive climate of schools, and as a result drop out sooner, perhaps driven to escape the noxious implications of failure, given the rules by which they have chosen to play. By contrast, for others the excitement of discovery and learning likely buffer the harsh competitive lessons of school.

Identifying talent. As to the other interlocking argument, there can be little doubt that competition is a highly efficient way to segregate individuals by talent. This is true for both athletic and academic gifts. But we can still inquire if competitive sorting by ability is the *best* way to assign students to jobs. As it turns out, competing for this purpose is costly and for many if not most individuals unnecessary. As to cost, we have already documented the decline in academic productivity caused by ability ranking and its devastating influence on the will to learn (chapter 6). As for being largely unnecessary, consider the fact that currently the vast majority of jobs in America demand no great intellectual talent, but only basic competencies within the grasp of most people. In fact, many entry-level jobs – some estimates range as high as 90% of them – can be performed successfully with only a high school diploma, irrespective of the student's GPA, and less than 6 months on-the-job training or technical instruction (Deutsch, 1975, 1979).

It appears that many policymakers may have overestimated the level of skills necessary for successful performance at entry level for most jobs. It may be a sad commentary on the times, but thanks to the dubious blessings of automation and the advent of work-related computer systems, the need for computational and organizational skills in many parts of the workplace may actually be declining (see Braverman, 1974; Gottfredson, 1986; Gottfredson & Sharf, 1988; Spenner, 1985). Of course this is no reason to de-emphasize the teaching of the basics. Being able to read, write, and compute is important for more than job survival. These are the gateway skills to creativity and innovation, which is all the more reason why the basics should be acquired in ways that are not subject to the corrosive effects of competition. The virtues of sensitivity, understanding, and creativity transcend any temporary benefits of competition as a goad to learning. No one wants to apply conditions of scarcity to these human qualities.

The important point is that the teaching and certification of broad competencies, at relatively modest levels, is all that schools should or need do to prepare the vast majority of students for successful entry into the work force. This preparation is best achieved through noncompetitive means.

Granting this, however, isn't competitive sorting still necessary for assigning people to jobs that require extraordinary talent? Obviously, no one wants to trust the design of skyscrapers to architects of limited gifts, or undergo surgery at the hands of a physician of doubtful qualifications. Architecture, law, and medicine, as well as teaching and public service, deserve the best and the brightest. Actually, even in these special cases knowledge about ability adds less to the validity of the selection process than is often thought when future occupational success is the criterion. For instance, it is estimated that 40% of the general adult population in America possesses the intellectual capacity to become physicians (Collins, 1979). Less than one half of 1% of the population ever become physicians, however, so selection factors other than ability must also be at work, such as availability of financial support, interest, and willingness to persist. But what makes for outstanding, not just competent, physicians? If the research of Spence and Helmreich is any indication, extraordinary success (by any definition) will depend on more than a combative spirit (and perhaps even on its relative absence). In any event, it cannot be assumed that those gifted youngsters who survive the high-stakes scramble for grades are always the best suited for professional and public service. Students who jostle their way to the top by reason of a near perfect academic record are often driven by motives that may work against career success once they finish their formal schooling and enter the job market. Our self-worth analysis of the *overstriver* provides a glimpse of this possibility.

Little wonder, then, that neither high school nor college GPA predicts the quality of performance on the job or one's satisfaction as a worker (see Berg, 1970; Spenner, 1985). It is not the grades themselves so much as the underlying reasons for achieving them that count most in sustained occupational success. Obviously, we cannot tolerate incompetency in high places; but neither can we afford to promote the fear and self-doubt that, once having driven individuals to positions of power, then compromises their ability to use that power wisely. Cheating is but one form of such abuse, whether it be industrial espionage, deceptive advertising practices, or a failure to disclose potential defects in commercial products. Such deception would seem inevitable if it is true, as Combs (1957) argues, that competition triggers not necessarily a search for better products, but a scramble to sell competing products at any cost.

Given all these observations, one wonders once again why schools do not de-emphasize the competitive nature of classroom learning. Such a move is long overdue and would appear highly beneficial. As things stand, the preemptive use of competitive incentives undercuts academic productivity, jeopardizes self-confidence – and no less troublesome – encourages timidity and opportunism; moreover, competition dislocates talent and teaches students to strive for selfish goals.

Yet, for all these arguments, there is still one overarching reality that works against change. Parents fear that if their children do not enter the star-spangled scramble for grades, others will, and as a result their youngsters may lose forever the chance at prestigious occupations and economic security. Basically, competition in schools is perpetuated by the fear of being left out. And these fears are real enough. They are confirmed by the undeniable fact that the occupational status of individuals as well as their eventual income level depend heavily on the number of years spent in school (Bishop, 1989; Mincer, 1989).

As long as these anxieties persist, change is unlikely. What, then, are the possibilities for more open access to higher education and jobs through noncompetitive avenues? Can things be altered so that young people (and their parents) have less reason to feel left behind? There is no shortage of reform proposals, all of which address the basic question posed originally by Morton Deutsch (1979): "Suppose . . . everyone was equally qualified to do the more interesting, challenging and rewarding jobs available in the community. And also suppose that only a small fraction of the jobs were desirable. How would one allocate these scarce, good jobs" (p. 394)?

Would people bid for the better jobs? Would they be assigned them by seniority? Some reformers argue that educational credentials should be banned entirely as the basis for job selection and that all workers be allowed to share both attractive and not so attractive jobs. According to one theorist (Collins, 1979), "the great majority of all jobs can be learned through practice by almost any literate person. . . . How hard people work and with what dexterity and cleverness, depends on how much other people can require of them to do'' (p. 54). As a practical example of this reasoning, workers might rotate through jobs, or job ladders might be created so that over time individuals could move up from less rewarding to more rewarding tasks. For instance, a person might work up to the full status of a physician through a series of steps, beginning with hospital orderly.

Although these various proposals reflect considerable ingenuity, they are not particularly appropriate for our purposes because they are unlikely to be taken seriously, at least any time soon. We seek a more modest example of change, one that is both reasonable in scope and practically feasible; one that depends on altering educational policy, not society itself; and, finally, one that is broadly compatible with the arguments of the self-worth position, namely, that positive reasons for learning are jeopardized when the individual's sense of worth becomes equated with the ability to achieve competitively.

Perhaps the one proposal that comes closest to fulfilling these conditions was suggested some 20 years ago by Robert Wolff (1969) in a thought-provoking essay concerning a blueprint for the ideal university. Wolff identified the root cause of competition in schools as a shortage of openings in the first-ranked colleges of America. To relieve this constriction, Wolff proposed that more modest academic standards be established for admission to the top colleges. These standards should be rigorous enough to exclude the truly disinterested, he argued, but generous enough to permit eligibility for far more students than currently apply. Once high school graduates established their eligibility for admission to these elite schools, they would then be assigned to available openings in the freshman class by lottery! Similar adjustments would be made by all colleges whenever applications outran available openings, with schools of lesser rank and reputation establishing somewhat lesser entrance requirements. Wolff reasoned that once the external pressures arising from the college admissions scramble were relieved, most students would likely accumulate academic credits above the minimum cutoffs anyway, but for far different reasons than those that drove them before. Students could now turn to the task of learning rather than competing for the rewards of scarcity.

Consider Wolff's plan on its merits. First, it is only fair to say that Wolff's plan, like any reform proposal, cannot be expected to banish competition. For example, we know that test anxiety is greatest for those students who find themselves on the borderline between a passing and a failing grade (Becker, 1982, 1983). Extrapolating these findings, we would expect considerable residual anxiety among those high school students whose academic records are only marginal for admission to a preferred college. Moreover, there is nothing inherent in Wolff's proposal that precludes students from still maneuvering for that competitive edge. Once admitted to college, students could take additional courses or pursue special extracurricular activities not out of any particular intrinsic interest but in order to present the most attractive profile to potential employers. All that Wolff can offer, and all anyone can reasonably expect, is a way to discourage such practices in excess, and hopefully before they compromise the will to learn.

A somewhat different objection to Wolff's plan concerns what appears to be a violation of our American sense of fair play and the deep conviction that hard work and success should be rewarded. Where, we might ask, is the justice in excluding highly gifted, deserving high school students from the best educational opportunities solely through the luck of the draw? Although fair enough, such a question assumes that the present system is more likely than Wolff's scheme to sort students on the basis of merit. This is a dubious assumption. In reality, luck likely plays no less a role in the current college sweepstakes than it would under Wolff's minimal competency plan. Given the current oversupply of highly qualified college applicants for a few top schools, today admissions officers stand ankle deep in file folders containing applications from the nation's high school elite. Admissions staff must increasingly shoulder the onerous task of turning away more and more candidates who are just as likely to succeed as those who are accepted. Consider the University of California at Berkeley. In recent years applicants to the freshman class (which is limited to approximately 4,500 students per year) have exceeded 22,000. At least half of these applicants have a high school GPA that exceeds 3.80 (with 4.0 being a straight A average). Moreover, in 1989, approximately one-fourth of these applicants were valedictorians, senior class presidents, or student body presidents. No admission procedure has yet been devised that reliably predicts academic success in college among such exceptional applicants; in effect, the admission of some and not others is basically random if the intent is to encourage talent and future promise. This situation is not limited to Berkeley alone, but is found among all other top public and private colleges and universities in America.

Wolff's proposal merely *appears* more capricious because randomness is the admitted cornerstone of *his* system and the key to its potential effectiveness. But what would be the fate of those highly gifted youngsters denied admission to an elite school under Wolff's schema? The answer is the same as what happens to unsuccessful candidates presently. To continue our example at Berkeley, the majority of rejected candidates are admitted to one or more of several other top schools to which they also typically apply, with no small thanks to luck. Wolff does not argue that reform will entirely eradicate losers in the college admissions game. No system can do that as long as there are more qualified applicants than openings. Rather, the essence of Wolff's point is that under his plan those students who eventually attend college will do so for different and presumably more positive reasons than is presently the case.

Should Wolff's plan be adopted on at least a limited, trial basis? Perhaps so, but it almost certainly will not be. But why not? After all, Wolff's basic assertion appears reasonable and the hoped-for outcomes are more than merely plausible if we extrapolate from the psychological arguments marshaled throughout this book. Moreover, the plan can be implemented relatively quickly by the educational community, and without a catastrophic dislocation of educational resources. For another thing, Wolff's basic rationale is straightforward, simple, and remarkably free of rhetoric. Finally, it is entirely democratic. No student has a right to be admitted to a particular college, but only the right that the system of allocation be equitable in its treatment of all students.

The problem is not that Wolff's plan is utopian in the sense of being unworkable. Rather, the difficulty is that once launched the plan may work *too* well and lead to alternative educational futures that are so different from current experience that few of its consequences can be envisioned, let alone prepared for.

If not competition, then what?

It is a trifle unsettling, I grant, to contemplate the idea of going to college merely for an education, rather than for a degree. But after one lives with the notion for a while, its strangeness somewhat recedes.
ROBERT WOLFF

If modest proposals like Wolff's cannot be taken seriously, then where does that leave the prospects for genuine reform? Perhaps this question is best answered by posing another: Can schools themselves do anything to moderate the competitive scramble by changing their objectives? And, are there any words of reassurance that can be offered students (and their parents) here and now if they do not get top grades? First, consider the matter of reassurances.

Reassurances

Although it is true that the single best predictor of lifetime income is the number of years completed in school, it is also the case that this relationship does not necessarily depend on where one's schooling was obtained (Berg, Bibb, Finegan, & Swafford, 1981). Having gone to Yale or Harvard may be more impressive than having started one's college career at a local community college. But the prestige of the postsecondary institution attended is essentially unrelated to one's eventual standard of living. Nor is institutional prestige a good predictor of later on-the-job satisfaction; neither does it predict well one's effectiveness on the job as rated by supervisors. In effect, Ivy League graduates on average are not richer (holding their parents's wealth constant, of course), more famous, or feel they are any more successful in their work than do graduates from schools of lesser reputation. These statistics may dismay some parents, but they can also give powerful reassurances. If a student is denied access to the most prestigious colleges, it is not the end of the world.

From this perspective it is important that America continue to ensure open access to postsecondary education with the main gatekeepers being only the desire to learn and evidence that one is willing to work hard. Today the community college system provides one such source of upward mobility in a society heavily stratified by wealth and power. Typically, anyone can attend community colleges (and at bargain basement fees) as long as they hold a high school diploma or continuation certificate. There are even provisions for completing a high school degree on many campuses. Here the standards for admission are just high enough to command some commitment to learning yet are not so prohibitive as to discourage further schooling – just what Wolff had in mind (minus the lottery of course).

Recently community colleges have been criticized for de-emphasizing the preparation of students for transfer to regular four-year colleges in favor of short-term vocational and career education. But despite these charges and the controversy sparked by counterclaims that they are unwarranted (for the debate, see Brint & Karabel, 1989; Deegan, Tillery, & Associates, 1985), it is still the case that the majority of community college entrants plan to get a bachelors degree or higher (Astin, Hemond, & Richardson, 1982). In 1980, 56% of all postsecondary minority students nationwide were enrolled in community colleges (Grant & Eiden, 1982), a figure that included one-half of all black college students and two-thirds of all Hispanics (Astin, 1982). Moreover, the vast majority of minority students who eventually receive a bachelor's degree – up to 50% of them by one estimate (Reagan, 1990) – began their postsecondary schooling at a community college. Such developments tend to loosen the choke hold of high school GPA on access to further schooling that has often precluded all but the most able or the most fortunate from better jobs, because a poor start in school or detours along the way need no longer represent unsurmountable barriers.

A second kind of reassurance, a reminder actually, is that a successful career depends not only on the amount of one's education but also on the reasons for learning. Recall that students who perceive schools as an opportunity to better themselves are likely to persist longer, whereas those who see schools as a way to bolster a sense of worth by outscoring others are likely to quit sooner (e.g., Nicholls et al., 1985). Given the importance of motivational factors in the decision to continue in school or not, parents often fear the wrong thing. Far from being worried if their children do not enter the frenzied rat race for grades, they should start worrying when their children do. All too often the result is not excellence but self-doubt, anger, and a decline in true task involvement. Competition focuses attention on the wrong issues. What matters ultimately is not performance but learning; not short-term gains, but the reasons for achieving. If the reasons are right, achievement will likely flourish without the goad of competition. Otherwise children may do just enough to win the prize and little more.

A modest proposal

What can schools do to moderate the competitive scramble for grades? This scramble is activated largely by the fact that too many individuals are chasing too few positions at the top of the occupational ladder: 80% of our young people aspire to 20% of the available jobs (Paterson, 1956). This mismatch is driven in part by positive factors – by youthful exuberance and the natural desire of individuals to excel. It is also propelled by wishful thinking, ignorance, and parental pressure despite the fact that their children's interests and talents may lie elsewhere. Schools should encourage realistic dreaming, dispel ignorance, and at the same time promote a healthy perspective for dealing with the massive disappointment reflected in the statistic just cited.

In chapter 9, I argued for the creation of a work force that could respond flexibly to the changing needs of the workplace, which today stresses independence of judgment and a willingness to cooperate. Now I argue also for providing students with sufficient information and self-knowledge to make informed judgments about which kinds of jobs would be most meaningful to them personally. Among other things, this involves helping students assess the risks, challenges, and satisfactions associated with different careers and encouraging an understanding that occupational satisfaction depends largely on matching job demands with one's interests, personal styles of thinking, and tolerance for risks (Spenner, 1985). Consider competitiveness as a personal style. Some individuals clearly seek more risks and are more combative than others. The same can be said for jobs: Some are riskier and less secure, especially those we have characterized as being hierarchically organized. As part of career education one can envision students living and working for a time in competitively structured climates – where individuals compete for fewer and fewer placements at each rung of the promotion ladder – all vicariously, of course, through realistic simulations and role-playing exercises. They would also sample other alternative occupational structures where, for instance, rewards may be best pursued by moving laterally rather than vertically within an organization. Students can also benefit from games like Psychic Income (chapter 9), in which the players seek out their own preferred mix of status, pay, and leisure time as different compensatory sources of reward.

Hopefully, such instruction would also help redress a potential irony inherent in the policy of open access to higher education (Thurow, 1975). If students can drop out of school and subsequently reenter the educational mainstream without prejudice and continue learning despite false starts and detours, then won't the job scramble simply intensify, given more rather than fewer qualified candidates? Not necessarily if increased competency also implies greater self-realism and an improved capacity for making informed occupational choices. I do not suggest that children be encouraged to accept second best for themselves. Nor is it likely that schools can completely cure the overmatch between aspirations and opportunity already cited; people will always aspire to something better, as they should. What I do suggest, however, is that students can learn that there are often many unforeseen employment opportunities, potential windfalls waiting to be discovered, and always the prospect for substituting one career goal for another. For instance, a student may choose to become a paramedic rather than a physician, or a paralegal, not an attorney – consoled in the knowledge that the attractiveness of a given occupation is not simply a matter of more or less money or only a matter of status, but rather depends on a mixture of compensatory factors. Physicians may have a higher annual income, but paramedics have better hours and are less subject to malpractice suits.

Approaching occupational choice as informed self-selection, not as a matter of job sorting, makes students active participants in the process of their own future building. If one particular move proves unsatisfactory, they can always design a new route without feeling they have fallen short as a person. This dynamic has all the characteristics of partially contingent paths (chapter 2), a concept used to describe Atkinson's success-oriented individuals.

Elevating the goals of competency and good judgment over competition is no easy proposition, and there are risks involved. Actually, the perils are considerable. Perhaps the greatest risks are those inherent in defining competency. On the one hand, we must encourage students to do more than the minimum. This much is obvious, but the dangers are more subtle than one might imagine. For instance, David Ainsworth (1977) points out that the psychological implications of the language of achievement itself may well discourage excellence, that is, "If a student is competent, then surely that is enough" (p. 329). Obviously, it is not enough if by competency we mean simply tolerating the lowest common denominator of performance. Competency in school must never be equated with mediocrity. On the other hand, demanding too much of students in the absence of the skills needed to pursue excellence can be equally devastating. Fortunately, as we know, there is a middle ground between *too much* and *too little,* where one's aspirations hover at or near the upper bounds of present competencies. It is in this zone of challenge, so to speak, that excellence is promoted. For all the difficulties involved in maintaining this balance on a day-to-day basis, at least we know it can be done. Competitiveness offers no such prospects. There is no middle ground here, no such thing as "just enough" competition.

In the struggle to change priorities educators can be reassured on several counts. First, those who desire change are not limited to a handful of academic troublemakers or professional curmudgeons. Many parents, too, are convinced of the need to foster competency, not competition, if we can judge from the research of Carole Ames and Jennifer Archer (1987b). These investigators found at least as many mothers of elementary schoolchildren who preferred that schools promote *mastery* goals – striving for the sake of self-improvement through effort – as mothers who believed in *performance* goals, that is, striving to do better than someone else by reason of ability.

Second, and of equal significance, Ames and Archer (1987a) also discovered that promoting mastery goals does not require the complete elimination of competition. They observed various kinds of classrooms: those in which students perceived a mastery orientation to predominate, those perceived to be largely performance-oriented, and combinations of both performance and mastery orientations. As long as mastery goals were in evidence, the presence of competition did not diminish those behaviors we have come to associate with intrinsic task engagement. Students focused on effort explanations, used sophisticated planning strategies, and preferred problems where "you can learn a lot of new things but will also have some difficulty and make many mistakes." And, most important of all, student enthusiasm for such challenges did not depend on their self-perceived ability level.

These findings are critical because if the pursuit of excellence required the virtual absence of competition, then the chances for reform would be bleak, indeed. In reality, competitiveness can never be entirely banished from schools. Witness the many students as well as some parents who have an uncanny knack for turning everything, even joyous games, into competitive contests. The question of how much or how little an emphasis on mastery is needed to offset the inevitable press of competition was not part of the original Ames and Archer research, but obviously it is an important next point of inquiry. Yet whatever the eventual answer, there is cause for optimism. Perhaps far fewer and less radical changes are needed to tip the classroom balance in favor of spontaneity, involvement, and creativity than was ever thought.

Conclusion

Now that our blueprint for change is in place, we come to a potential new beginning. The proposal can be stated quite simply: Educational reform should proceed by teaching students (and teachers) how to play serious games as a way to promote strategic thinking and a sense of real-world and personal relevance, using incentive systems that encourage positive reasons for learning – reasons accessible to all students and that will sustain game play and learning into the indefinite future. This proposal enjoys the benefits of being closely guided by theory and well-grounded empirically. Moreover, it appears workable. The practical elements are already in place, existing if not thriving in individual classrooms across America despite the presence of powerful contrary forces. Many teachers already encourage the proper motives for learning by holding fast when possible to absolute standards of excellence, by encouraging students rather than praising them, and by dispensing incentives in ways that permit unlimited rewards, open to all, which despite their frequency, remain undiminished in their motivational value. These recommendations come not as strangers but rather as overlooked, often underappreciated ways of thinking about schooling.

Indeed, there is nothing new here when we consider each component singly. Rather, the novelty (and value) of the approach and the force of its sustaining arguments turn on the fact that familiar, even commonplace ideas, once rearranged or combined in new ways, can excite new perspectives. In effect, we have sought to establish the "throbbing vital center" of which Ernest Becker spoke earlier (chapter 1) by drawing together a kaleidoscope of isolated possibilities, tantalizing but often untried theories, and commonsense answers that, to quote Becker's words once again, "were strewn all over the place."

But what of the potential benefits of these remedies? Are they worth all the effort? Can the value of such change be measured in terms of increased school achievement scores, reduced dropout rates, revenue savings to the states, or perhaps reflected as improvements in America's economic standing worldwide? Obviously, such tangible benefits are difficult to estimate, and it may be downright dangerous to try. Many reform movements have ended in disaster following exaggerated claims for success.

Ultimately, the benefits of this proposal cannot be calculated in dollars and cents, but rather in terms of a broad, hoped-for vision, one that is perhaps best reflected through the reactions of those young Cuban children described in the closing paragraph of chapter 1. Recall that when these young revolutionaries of the 1960s were asked to describe the study of history, they hotly proclaimed themselves to be history in the making. Without realizing it they had become players in an *infinite game*. James Carse (1986) defines infinite games as those in which the goal is to extend play indefinitely and where there is no victory or defeat in the usual sense, but only the changing of rules to suit the evolving needs of players. By comparison, Carse characterizes *finite games* as inherently self-limiting. The goal of finite games is to end play as soon as possible in order to determine winners and losers. By now this win–lose mentality is quite familiar and recalls to mind the competitive features of the learning game. In competitive games, as we know, the past (history) has little standing. It is only the outcome of the current contest that counts. By contrast, those who play infinite games look forward to ongoing play in which the past requires repeated examination. The rise and development of cultures is an infinite game on a vast scale; so, too, is history itself. More modest but highly personal examples include marriage, parenthood, and the development of a career – any sequence of meaningful events that place players in transition and passage.

Strategic thinking clearly fits the category of infinite games for which the end is merely arbitrary, and to continue play means to be constantly discovering and growing, with the possibility of occasional surprises that may lead to a radical transformation of the game itself. Indeed, we have argued that cultivating a capacity for surprise (serendipity) is one of the best preparations for personal future building. Although it is true that the Nuclear Countdown Game (chapter 9) can be concluded successfully (or disastrously) at a given point in time, it is equally true that the peace-keeping process is never ending and subject to constant destabilization. When one side (e.g., Russia) initiates economic and political reforms (e.g., *glasnost* and *perestroika*), the rules of the game are dramatically altered with a prospect for new relationships and renewed play.

History as an infinite game is also reflected in the BioAlert exercise. When stripped of all its packaging, this game stands as an allegory for adaptation and change on an infinite scale. All biological systems, including the broader concept of nature, are open and dynamic, a point that can be vividly conveyed to students when they encounter dangerous viruses that play by different, unfamiliar rules – rules that fortunately can be deciphered, controlled, and then eventually altered by human ingenuity. And so it is with the game of human relations. Here, too, there is change and infinite variability with no end (and sometimes no relief) in sight. The rules that define the relationship between parent and child change as both grow older; so do the rules that govern the relationships between newlyweds and elderly couples. These examples convey best the meaning of change and its inevitability, and underscore the need to accept change, even welcome it as part of nature's order.

Infinite games are important to our story for other reasons as well. First, according to Carse, the concept of *power* that is associated with winning in finite game play is transformed in infinite play to mean *strength* – strength of will, strength of persuasion, and endurance. Anyone can be strong, a quality open to all and another source of equity. But only a few can be powerful, and only one the *most* powerful. Second, as Carse explains it, finite games are defined by boundaries, whereas infinite games are limited only by horizons, and there is nothing in the horizon itself that limits vision. To move toward one horizon is simply to create another.

Movement, growth, and passage – these are the qualities that define the future, a place of infinite moves. Infinite players, like our young Cuban students, cannot say how much of their studies they have completed, but only that much remains to be learned. Nor do they wish to determine when their education is over, but only what will become of what they know. Infinite players see themselves and their culture in transition, a most healthy educational perspective; and it is economically sound as well. Only by being open to future possibilities can we create new jobs and revitalize old market sectors sufficient to the needs of a free society. From this viewpoint, then, the most important obligation of American education as we enter the 21st century is to provide the means by which our children can continue to create that which they can never finish.

Appendix A

Mastery learning

John: The failure avoider revisited

John stands on the threshold of his next ordeal: the introductory psychology course. Recall that repeated academic failure has eroded John's faith in himself and in his ability to succeed in college. Fortunately for John, however, the rules of the learning game are about to change for the better, thanks to mastery learning. What, more precisely, is mastery learning?

Mastery learning comes in many forms. We have already described Mr. Rodriguez's use of contingency contracting as well as his elaboration on the simplest, most frequently employed type of mastery learning: the so-called Kellar Plan, named after Fred Kellar, a pioneer advocate of mastery learning. In this instance, Mr. Rodriguez established objectives for all Global Gambit teams that involved learning various facts about their respective countries. Then he developed a brief test for each team with questions that closely fit the preannounced objectives, meaning that the test was "criterion referenced." Mr. Rodriguez also set a passing score that represented a minimally acceptable performance. Those students who failed to pass the test initially could study more and then be retested.

The mastery philosophy assumes that most students can eventually assimilate the basic lessons taught in school if (1) these learning objectives are couched in clear, absolute terms, and (2) students are given sufficient opportunity to do so through repeated study, timely feedback, and adequate guidance. Unfortunately, some early advocates oversold the benefits of mastery instruction by contending that, for example, "it strives to make students more alike – by making them all excellent" (Born & Zlutnick, 1972, p. 30). The case for mastery learning is poorly served by such overzealous hype. Clearly, not everyone can become excellent if by that we mean creating uniform superiority. Still, the evidence is quite favorable. When given sufficient instruction in the context of absolute standards and clear goals, most students can achieve more than might otherwise be possible. To be sure, ability level still predicts how much students will profit from practice, how much they can eventually assimilate, and how quickly. But even low ability is no barrier to some improvement.

Consider the matter of *retention,* that is, how much students remember of what they learn. Virtually all the research indicates that the retention of course material is greater under mastery than under conventional course structures

(Born, Gledhill, & Davis, 1972; Kulik, Kulik, & Cohen, 1979). Undoubtedly, the most important factor in such superiority is the extra study afforded some students under the mastery paradigm (Corey & McMichael, 1974; Moore, Hauck, Gagne, 1973). Naturally, we would expect students who have additional study opportunities to retain more simply because they learned more to begin with compared to conventional instruction where students typically proceed to new material whether or not they have mastered earlier assignments.

Other factors also contribute to the superiority of mastery learning techniques. For one thing, students are often provided with examples of the kinds of knowledge they are expected to master and upon which their evaluation will be based. For another thing, mastery means providing students with systematic feedback as to the quality of their work as they proceed. Frequent corrective feedback reduces ambiguities about one's standing and about the quality of one's progress, or lack of it (Locke & Latham, 1984). As already noted, uncertainty is one of the major threats to learning. This is particularly true for anxious, failure-avoiding students who expect the worse in the absence of feedback, and tend to judge their performances as unacceptable (Meunier & Rule, 1967).

Additionally, mastery learning coordinates what is tested with what is learned, something that, surprisingly enough, is not always done in school. For instance, investigators (e.g., Armbruster, Stevens, & Rosenshine, 1977) have found that there is at best only a moderate overlap between the apparent objectives of many commercially available textbooks (e.g., improving reading comprehension skills such as drawing inferences) and the focus of the achievement tests that accompany these textbooks (e.g., locating factual information embedded in a written passage). Obviously, if students are evaluated on skills other than those for which they are trained, the resulting failure can be devastating, especially for those students who already doubt their ability. For these students, failure for any reason will likely be blamed on personal shortcomings, whether real or imagined, whereas the actual culprit may be the failure to arrange the conditions of learning in optimal ways.

In John's case, a relatively novel form of mastery learning was employed, namely, a grade-choice arrangement. John could work for any grade he chose, the only catch being that he must perform better and accomplish more, the higher the grade to which he aspires. But at least John is not in competition with other students; any number of students can achieve a given grade so long as each surpasses the necessary standards. Moreover, John can take each midterm exam a second time after additional study (and without penalty) if he wishes to improve his score.

In actuality, John was participating (along with some 500 real-life students) in a large-scale experimental field study designated to investigate the motivational benefits of mastery learning (Covington, 1984d; Covington & Jacoby, 1973; Covington & Omelich, 1984c). Half of the students in an introductory psychology class were randomly assigned to the mastery condition just described (John included), and the remaining half worked under a competitive arrangement. These latter students were graded on a curve with the best performers receiving the highest grades. Additionally, no one in this group was permitted to take a midterm more than once.

Both groups were tracked over the course of an entire semester, assignment by assignment, and test by test. A large amount of data was collected along the way, including indications of self-perceived ability, trait–state anxiety levels, how successful (or unsuccessful) the students believed their performances to be, and their attributions to each success or failure. These data were then subjected to path analysis, a statistical technique described in chapter 5. One final technical point. Unbeknownst to both groups, the two incentive systems were yoked so that the average final course grade was the same. Thus although the actual performance levels could vary between the groups, all students shared the same grading distribution. This was a necessary precaution because student course evaluations are known to depend on the grades they receive.

The single most important finding of this study was that the mastery students as a group outperformed the competitive students on each midterm and by a wide margin. This superiority was due entirely to the extra study–test opportunity. Mastery students simply spent more time studying, approximately twice as many hours as did those in the competitive group. John's experience was typical. As the first midterm approached, he set his sights on a conservative grade goal (a B-), one he felt was within his grasp since he knew he could always be reexamined. John still fell short on his first try. But fortunately, the shortfall was not great – just two points down – and now he knew the kinds of questions for which to study. John's performance improved markedly on retesting. He reacted with considerable pride and no small measure of relief.

As John approached the second midterm, he revised his sights upwards to a B+, and fortunately with the increased academic demands came a new confidence that he could succeed. In effect, John found himself caught in an upward, mutually reinforcing spiral of improving test performances, increasing self-confidence, and rising expectations – all triggered initially by the safety net of the study–retest opportunity. Succeeding after an initial disappointment serves several aspects of our instructional guidelines. Improving one's performance after more study strengthens an effort–outcome linkage. Also, recalling the effort–pride linkage, belated success is more satisfying than success achieved at first opportunity (Covington & Omelich, 1981). And the harder one tries, the greater the sense of pride in final attainment (Brickman & Hendricks, 1975; Weaver & Brickman, 1974).

The presence of absolute standards also made an important contribution to these positive dynamics, especially regarding the motivational components of confidence and rising aspirations. Absolute standards created a sense of fair play in John's mind and also reduced ambiguities regarding grading policy. Moreover, knowing that he could achieve a personally satisfying grade, although others might also do very well, revitalized John's faith in hard work, thereby further strengthening an effort–outcome linkage.

In sum, John was no longer playing an ability game. Granted, at first, John was worried that he was not able enough, but as the course progressed, his earlier self-doubts diminished as a significant predictor of performance. Simply put, John was doing much better than he (or we) would expect from his initially poor self-appraisal. Not so, however, for the competitive students whose self-perceptions of ability continued to be an important, even decisive, factor in their performance. Here only the brightest students achieved the top grades. This was because self-doubting, competitive students had no compensatory mechanisms available to offset their low ability attributions. For them it was business as usual: take a test, and no matter what the outcome, they had to move on. As a result, competitive students became increasingly threatened and sought ways to minimize the possibility that they might be revealed as incompetent. Some of these students stopped studying altogether; others indulged in magical thinking, hoping somehow the test would simply go away; while still others distanced themselves from failure by devaluating the importance of the course or blaming the teacher for their troubles (Covington & Omelich, 1982).

One additional finding, actually a potential paradox of sorts, deserves comment. Mastery students rated themselves as more able to succeed than did competitive students despite the fact that as a group the mastery students failed (fell short of their grade goals) more often, simply because they had more opportunities to fail! But how could this be, especially for failure-threatened students like John who typically interpret failure as the product of low ability? The answer became clear after additional data analysis (Covington & Omelich, 1982). As long as mastery students continued to learn and improve – improvement being the key – then isolated failure experiences along the way, although temporarily upsetting, had little lasting influence on their will to learn. These students attributed their successes to their own effort, and because the task was seen as challenging, they believed themselves able in the bargain. By contrast, students working under the competitive condition may have had available more self-serving explanations for failure such as unfair tests, ambiguous grading, or just plain bad luck. And, these excuses even remained credible for a time. But mastery structures provide a more substantial, lasting source of self-worth: the opportunity for self-improvement.

The advent of mastery learning raises a number of important issues and questions that not only challenge traditional educational practices, but also hopefully will permit a deeper understanding of the larger educational mission. Three issues are briefly considered here.

Content mastery versus content coverage

The mastery approach is effective largely because it requires that students not give up until they have learned a concept thoroughly (Arlin & Webster, 1983; Arlin, 1984). Yet as important as complete mastery is, especially from a motivational perspective, there is a price to pay. Because there is only so much instructional time available, time taken to master one topic thoroughly is time taken from other often equally deserving topics. Herein lies a dilemma that can be best described as a trade-off between content mastery and content coverage. Robert Slavin (1987b) put the issue this way: "Mastery learning proponents point out that material covered is not necessarily material learned. This is certainly true, but it is just as certainly true that material *not* covered is material *not* learned" (pp. 180–181).

Some critics, including Slavin, imply that this dilemma reveals an inherent weakness in the mastery learning philosophy (Mueller, 1976). Not necessarily so. Actually, mastery learning as a technique stands neutral on the issue of depth and breadth of coverage. Mastery learning is an instructional delivery system that controls the distribution of rewards and ensures effective conditions for learning (e.g., timely feedback, clear objectives), and as such can serve either broad or narrow content objectives. Equity structures are important because they promote positive reasons for learning, not because they tell us what should be mastered, or to what degree. These latter questions involve curricular decisions, not instructional decisions.

As to the question of coverage, we cannot teach everything worth knowing, and never could; there simply is not enough time. Hard decisions about what is worth teaching are long overdue. Presumably it is better to learn a few lessons well than many lessons imperfectly. But this is true only if we are careful about our choice of the few lessons. In chapter 8, we consider what these few good lessons might be.

The meaning of mastery

The concept of *mastery* is subject to a variety of meanings and interpretations, some of which – if we are not careful – can lead to a perversion of the larger educational mission. Because of the original emphasis by a few advocates on equating performance for *all* learners, mastery has become synonymous in the minds of some with *minimal* competency, that is, standards of performance that are within grasp of virtually every individual. Certainly there is a great deal to be said for the notion of minimal competency and competency testing as a means to certify that students have acquired the rudimentary skills in a specific knowledge domain (Resnick & Resnick, 1985). Yet we need not equate mastery with mediocrity as some critics have feared might happen (Mueller, 1976).

What is required is to think in terms of a hierarchy of standards – different kinds of excellence, perhaps – that involve the exercise of various levels and kinds of skills, ranging from minimal to extraordinarily complex. Sometimes minimal levels of processing will do just fine, as when one need only momentarily grasp the essential elements of an argument. And, even minimums can be highly demanding. Take the fact that every state in America has licensing procedures to ensure minimal competency among many professionals, including psychologists, attorneys, and pharmacists. In California, as in other states, any number of individuals can be licensed as a pharmacist in a given year as long as each person meets or surpasses exceedingly stringent standards of specialized knowledge, general intellectual functioning, and highly informed decision making. The success of such licensing procedures as gatekeepers for the protection of the public attests to the fact that even complex behaviors can be objectified and reliably measured using publicly agreed upon standards that are absolute, not relative, in nature.

The point is that students should be encouraged to develop a range of standards by which to judge or gauge the adequacy of their performances, standards that change as circumstances change. When students possess the capacity for such flexible self-regulation, free from the necessity of holding themselves to inappropriate, competitively driven, or perfectionistic standards, they will rarely ever be content with mediocrity. On this point we have the assurance of Hoppe's experimental observations about the value of self-regulated learning.

Having said this, it is also true that not everything worth encouraging can be stated in mastery terms. In the end, some behaviors *do* defy precise, behavioral definition. A list of competencies that is said to represent the total mastery of any but the most routine jobs or occupations can never be entirely complete. In what way, for instance, can we objectively specify all the critical dimensions of such elusive characteristics as charisma or leadership? Still, these dimensions are also markers of excellence. Actually, for most purposes of schooling, the *certification* of such qualities as leadership or creativity and good citizenship is probably not necessary. Naturally, we want to arrange school experiences to encourage those characteristics that ultimately define our humanness, but to describe them in terms of narrow, formal, behavioral objectives in hopes that they can be trained directly is likely to destroy the very qualities we hope to enhance. Happily, creativity and other valued qualities like the will to learn are likely to emerge spontaneously whenever the reasons for learning are uplifting and positive.

Mastery versus meaning

There is little doubt that mastery procedures can be highly effective for acquiring factual knowledge. But critics wonder if the exercise of conceptual skills is equally well served by mastery principles. There is good reason for their concern. For instance, Covington (1985b) provided a group of slow learners with several study sessions to master textbook material that required both conceptual learning (the understanding of principles) and rote learning (memorizing facts). As expected, these slow learners needed additional time to master the conceptual material, but eventually they performed as well as did brighter students who learned the same material far sooner. An unannounced retention test administered several months later revealed that the slow learners recalled just as many of the facts as did the fast learners. But they were decidedly poorer at recalling the conceptual material, despite the fact that both groups had originally mastered it equally. Does this mean that mastery learning is suitable only for the promotion of lower-level, rote objectives? No, not necessarily. But it does suggest that if we are to encourage meaningfulness, something more is needed than simply arranging the conditions of learning in optimal ways.

In this particular study, it was found that the slow learners simply did what they do best – memorizing information without necessarily understanding it. By overlearning the correct conceptual responses initially, they appeared to have reached mastery. But when information is rehearsed originally as a collection of isolated events, later recall is less resistant to forgetting than when information is organized around basic principles and concepts. Thus providing equalizing opportunities to master material does not guarantee equal understanding.

In the last analysis, mastery structures, like competitive ones, are systems for instructional delivery. They set the rules for what is to be learned, how well it is to be learned, and what is to become of learning; but the rules do not necessarily determine *how* students learn. The slow learners just described need more than the right reasons for learning. They also need practice in the thinking strategies that promote understanding, a point considered in chapter 8.

Appendix B

Cooperative learning

Educators have long been fascinated by the possibility of using groups to transform and revitalize classroom learning. For us, the promise of cooperative learning derives mainly from its equity orientation, namely the potential for encouraging constructive reasons for learning that are within the reach of *all* students.

There is little doubt that working toward a larger, common purpose can motivate students individually to their best efforts. A commonplace example is team sports, like volleyball, where the team's success depends on the joint and individual contributions of all its members. If the team wins, all savor victory – another source of equality, that is, a shared payoff – and if the team loses, then all suffer defeat collectively. Maximum effort is thereby assured because being rewarded individually depends on each team member trying his or her hardest (Deutsch, 1949). Many variants of cooperative learning have evolved over the years, but two types predominate.

Group-contribution mode

First, consider the *group-contribution* mode (Slavin, 1983, 1984). Here team members work or study together to produce a single product – perhaps a mural, a worksheet, or a report (e.g., Sharan & Sharan, 1989–1990). If the product measures up to the prevailing standards, then all members are rewarded, no matter how many other teams may also be working on the same task. Under this arrangement, the role of an individual team member may not be clear, and not everyone's contributions will necessarily be equally important.

Individual-contribution mode

In the second type of cooperative learning, the *individual-contribution* mode, the role of each team member is far more obvious and equal. The group works on a common task, say, learning the multiplication tables or solving worksheet problems provided by the teacher. Following this cooperative period, each individual is tested to determine how much he or she has learned. The test scores of all team members are then summed to form a total that serves as the basis for judging the entire group. Other methods of calculating rewards include limiting payoffs to the lowest individual score in the group – the lower the score the less the group reward – or even selecting an individual from the group at random to take the test (Dishon & O'Leary, 1984).

Clearly, two different patterns of work and cooperation are likely to emerge under these two forms of cooperative learning. Under the *group-contribution* mode, it is possible, even desirable, for one team member – typically the brightest, or the most energetic pupil – to do most of the work. In such cases, the contributions of the less able team players may be considered useless, or worse yet, an actual impediment to progress. By contrast, when group rewards are based on the quality of all individual performances, a truly cooperative learning environment is more likely. For instance, better-informed students may tutor their less able teammates. Also, teammates are more likely to reinforce one another for academic effort and apply social sanctions against those who do not try, or attempt to sabotage the work of the group by not coming prepared, or by leaving the group without permission. Interestingly, such peer norms likely play a more important role in school achievement than do either parent or teacher values, especially among students of lower socioeconomic status.

The powerful reward contingencies of cooperation cannot be doubted, especially when one's own success depends on how well one's partners do. Moreover, these effects can be very specific with respect to the behavior of individual team members. For example, a study by Hamblin, Hathaway, and Wodarski (1971) suggests that those students who learn the most from cooperative experiences are those on whom the team success depends most heavily. When teams were rewarded based on the average of the three highest scores in the group, high achievers learned more than the average or low achievers. Conversely, when rewards were based on the average of the three lowest scores, low achievers gained the most knowledge.

Learning benefits

Given the variety of cooperative techniques, it is refreshing to discover that certain basic consistencies emerge regarding their effectiveness. Robert Slavin (1983) located some 46 evaluation studies that met several important research criteria including the requirement that, no matter what cooperative mode was used, achievement measures be administered individually to all team members after the group reward was given. This precaution was taken because we know that groups are often better at solving problems than are individuals simply because if any one team member gets the answer, he or she will likely share this information as part of the cooperative arrangement (Johnson, Johnson, & Scott, 1978). However, the issue is not whether the sharing of answers is superior to individual discovery – which it most often is – but whether or not individual learning is enhanced more through cooperative procedures than when one simply learns on one's own.

Slavin found that generally it was only when rewards were based on the performance of individuals summed together – *the individual mode* – that achievement outcomes favored cooperative learning. When one's own fate is tied to the performance of others, there is a powerful incentive to help everyone learn. This dynamic likely accounts for the superior performance of youngsters taught under the *team-assisted* mode (chapter 7) when compared both to traditional group-based instruction (Slavin, Leavey, & Madden, 1984; Slavin, Madden, & Leavey, 1984) as well as to competitive procedures (e.g., Lewis & Cooney, 1986).

The evidence also suggests that cooperative incentives encourage the development of effective strategies for learning, presumably by providing slow learners with an opportunity to imitate the problem-solving behavior of their more able teammates (Johnson, Skon, & Johnson, 1980; Skon, Johnson, & Johnson, 1981). Less able students are deprived of this important source of intellectual stimulation under competitive conditions as well as under some individual mastery approaches. Perhaps it is this positive modeling that explains the occasionally reported superiority of cooperative learning over mastery learning (Slavin & Tanner, 1979; Sherman & Thomas, 1986) and the finding of no achievement differences between competitive and mastery learning structures when both are compared to cooperative systems (e.g., Johnson et al., 1980; Johnson, Johnson, & Stanne, 1985, 1986).

Whatever the causes of cooperative superiority, positive benefits have also been documented in the case of higher-order thinking skills, including identifying the main ideas in written passages and solving science experiments (for a review see Rolheiser-Bennett, 1986). This is not to suggest that cooperative arrangements always favor such objectives. In fact, in several cases cooperative gains in thinking proved no greater than those found under mastery approaches (Bargh & Schul, 1980; Okebukola & Ogunniyi, 1984; Rogan, 1988). The important point is that higher-order skills are trainable and cooperative techniques are compatible with these objectives.

In summary, individuals appear willing to work harder and learn more for the sake of the team, but typically only when group rewards depend on the quality of individual effort. Ironically, it is this source of performance superiority – the interlocking fate of team members – that also represents the greatest potential danger inherent in cooperative learning. Weaker students may fear reprisals from more able players, despite having done their best; and, stronger players may be driven to help their less well prepared brethren more out of self-interest than for the sake of community. It is against this backdrop of mixed motives that we must consider the motivational implications of cooperative learning.

Motivational benefits

Does cooperative learning enhance the will of individual students to continue learning when they are no longer aggregated in groups? Do students feel surer of themselves and of their ideas when they are part of a group effort? Evidence on such questions is far from complete. In theory, cooperative learning *should* advance our instructional guidelines (see chapter 7). Certainly, rewards can be made plentiful – everyone can succeed, but only when individual effort is maximal. Thus, a premium is placed on effort, and as a result, pride in success should be more contingent on diligence and less on ability. Moreover, allowances can be made for individual specialization within groups, as in the jigsaw method, which should encourage a more differentiated view of ability. Also, cooperative learning should help shift the teacher's role from that of antagonist to facilitator. However, no amount of theorizing can create a fact. Only research can do that. Fortunately, what little is presently known suggests that cooperative learning encourages task involvement, at least when groups succeed.

Success outcomes

Once again, the research of Carole Ames provides us with critical insights. One of her competitive versus mastery studies described earlier in chapter 6 (Ames, 1981) was augmented with a cooperative condition ("If you [pair of students] can solve a total of six puzzles, you will each get to a select a prize."). Under this cooperative arrangement, students in a given pair either solved enough puzzles collectively to earn a prize (team success) or fell short of the number of solutions required (team failure). As will be recalled, it was found that when students succeed competitively, they judge their own ability as greater than that of their partner, thereby arousing a misplaced sense of superiority (Ames, Ames, & Felker, 1977). By contrast, under conditions of cooperative success, the high-performing members of each pair evaluated both their own ability and that of their less productive partner as essentially the same and, most important, believed both to be equally deserving of the reward. Abi Harris and Martin Covington (1989) confirmed these positive findings using a similar methodology. In this study, the low-performing members of successful teams rated their ability to solve puzzles as greater than did students who succeeded by winning over others. Moreover, these same cooperative students believed themselves more worthy of a reward.

Obviously, everyone likes to succeed. Success reflects well on one's ability and provides the ultimate payoff for having worked hard. But *cooperative* success has certain additional advantages as well. It results in stronger beliefs that one is liked personally, is accepted by others, and that other team members care about how much one learns (Cooper, Johnson, Johnson, & Wilderson, 1980; Gunderson & Johnson, 1980). Also, perceptions that another person is exerting effort to help the group is enough to induce liking (Tjosvold et al., 1984). These dynamics are undoubtedly part of the reason that, compared to competition, cooperation promotes greater interpersonal attraction between ethnic minorities and middle-class white students (Cooper et al., 1980; Johnson, Johnson, Tiffany, & Zaidman, 1983) and between handicapped and nonhandicapped students (Armstrong, Balow, & Johnson, 1981; Nevin, Johnson, & Johnson, 1982). At a time when caring and commitment are in short supply, cooperation in schools will likely take on increased importance – a lifeline to many who might otherwise fall victim to isolation and despair.

Failure outcomes

A special peculiarity of the literature on cooperative learning is that relatively little attention has been paid to failure. In fact, proponents of cooperative learning tend to ignore the possibilities of failure, assuming either that failure is not indigenous to cooperation or that failure changes its character so radically as to be unrecognizable as such. Obviously, however, teams can fail as well as succeed, and like individual failure, team failure can take a variety of forms. It can refer to a team loss in intramural sports, the failure to finish a group project on time, or the inability to solve a collective problem. Low team productivity, a low grade, or a minimal team reward also implies an unsuccessful effort (Michaels, 1977; Miller & Hamblin, 1963).

Actually, from a self-worth perspective, there is reason to believe that members of a failing team may be placed in *double* jeopardy. Team failure may imply not only that the low performer is incompetent, thereby arousing shame, but irresponsible as well, thereby eliciting feelings of guilt. Fortunately, however, although such dangers are real enough, the available evidence suggests that they do not necessarily materialize. For instance in the study just described, Ames (1981) found that failing low performers in cooperative groups felt themselves no less able nor any less satisfied with their work than low performers in competition, and no less deserving of any rewards that might come their way. In the Harris and Covington study (1989), although low performers in groups were found to experience greater remorse at not having tried harder compared to individuals failing competitively, there were no differences between the two groups in their perceptions of ability.

There appears to be much to recommend cooperation as a way to cushion the impact of failure and to strengthen one's resolve for future accomplishment. One need only envision the locker room of the losing team and note the mutual aid and comfort provided one another by the players to know this is true. There are few, if any, comparable sources of consolation in individual competitive failure. On the other hand, however, failing groups are also notoriously prone to interpersonal conflict, scapegoating, and to other forms of divisive rivalry. Ultimately, which of these reactions to failure is the more likely – either solace or feelings of betrayal and anger – will depend on the original goal of the group. If the goal is to win over others, with cooperation seen only as a temporary mean to this end, as in some team sports (Sadler, 1976), then losing may well call out bitterness and recrimination. But if the reasons for banding together originally are ennobling, then failure – disagreeable as it may be – will more likely be interpreted as falling short of the goal, not necessarily falling short as a group or as individuals.

References

A look ahead: Education and the new decade. *Education Week* (1990, January 10), pp. 29–32.

Abbott, E. (1983). *Flatland: A romance of many dimensions.* Totowa, NJ: Barnes & Noble.

Abdul-Jabbar, K., & Knobles, P. (1983). *Giant steps: The autobiography of Kareem Abdul-Jabbar.* New York: Bantam.

Abramson, L. Y., & Sackeim, H. A. (1977). A paradox in depression: Uncontrollability and self-blame. *Psychological Bulletin, 84,* 838–851.

Abramson, L. Y., Seligman, M. E. P., & Teasdale, J. D. (1978). Learned helplessness in humans: Critique and reformulation. *Journal of Abnormal Psychology, 87,* 49–74.

Abt, C. C. (1987). *Serious games.* New York: Lanham.

Adams, M. J. (Ed.). (1986). *Odyssey: A curriculum for thinking* (Vols. 1–6). Watertown, MA: Charlesbridge.

Adams, M. J. (1989). Thinking skills curricula: Their promise and progress. *Educational Psychologist, 24,* 25–77.

Adelson, B. (1981). Problem solving and the development of abstract categories in programming languages. *Memory and Cognition, 9,* 422–423.

Adkins, D. C., Payne, F. D., & Ballif, B. L. (1972). Motivation factor scores and response set scores for ten ethnic-cultural groups of preschool children. *American Educational Research Journal, 9,* 557–572.

Ainsworth, D. (1977). Examining the basis for competency-based education. *Journal of Higher Education, 43,* 321–332.

Alexander, K. A., & McDill, E. L. (1976). Selection and allocation within schools: Some causes and consequences of curriculum placement. *American Sociological Review, 41,* 969–980.

Alexander, P. A., & Judy, J. E. (1988). The interaction of domain-specific and strategic knowledge in academic performance. *Review of Educational Research, 58,* 375–404.

Allen, B. V. (1975). Paying students to learn. *Personnel & Guidance Journal, 53*(10), 774–778.

Allen, G. J. (1971). Effectiveness of study counseling and desensitization in alleviating test anxiety in college students. *Journal of Abnormal Psychology, 77,* 282–289.

Allen, G. (1972). The behavioral treatment of test anxiety: Recent research and future trends. *Behavior Therapy, 3,* 253–262.

Allen, G. J., Elias, M. J., & Zlotow, S. F. (1980). Behavioral interventions for alleviating text anxiety: A methodological overview of current therapeutic practices. In I. G. Sarason (Ed.), *Test anxiety* (pp. 150–186). Hillsdale, NJ: Erlbaum.

Allen, V. L., & Levine, J. M. (1967). *Creativity and conformity* (Tech. Rep. No.

33). Madison, WI: University of Wisconsin Research and Development Center for Cognitive Learning.

Allington, R. (1980). Teacher interruption behaviors during primary grade oral reading. *Journal of Educational Psychology, 72,* 371–377.

Alpert, R., & Haber, R. N. (1960). Anxiety in academic achievement situations. *Journal of Abnormal and Social Psychology, 61,* 207–215.

Alschuler, A. S. (1969). The effects of classroom structure on achievement motivation and academic performance. *Educational Technology, 9,* 19–24.

Alschuler, A. S. (1973). *Developing achievement motivation in adolescents.* Englewood Cliffs, NJ: Educational Technology Publications.

Alschuler, A. S. (1975, March). *Radical psychological education.* Keynote address at the Convention of the Virginia Personnel and Guidance Association, Williamsburg, VA.

Alschuler, A. S., & Shea, I. V. (1974, Aug.–Sept.). The discipline game: Players without losers. *Learning Magazine.*

Amabile, T. M. (1979). Effects of external evaluations on artistic creativity. *Journal of Personality and Social Psychology, 37,* 221–233.

Amabile, T. M. (1982). Children's artistic creativity: Detrimental effects of competition in a field setting. *Personality and Social Psychology Bulletin, 8,* 573–587.

Amabile, T. M., & Hennessey, B. A. (in press). The motivation for creativity in children. In A. K. Boggiano & T. S. Pittman (Eds.), *Achievement and motivation: A social-developmental perspective.* New York: Cambridge University Press.

Ames, C. (1978). Children's achievement attributions and self-reinforcement: Effects of self-concept and competitive reward structure. *Journal of Educational Psychology, 70,* 345–355.

Ames, C. (1981). Competitive versus cooperative reward structures: The influence of individual and group performance factors on achievement attributions and affect. *American Educational Research Journal, 18,* 273–388.

Ames, C. (1984). Achievement attributions and self-instructions under competitive and individualistic goal structures. *Journal of Educational Psychology, 76,* 478–487.

Ames, C. (1990). *Achievement goals and classroom structure: Developing a learning orientation.* Paper presented at the Annual Meeting of the American Educational Research Association, Boston.

Ames, C., & Ames, R. (1981). Competitive versus individualistic goal structure: The salience of past performance information for causal attributions and affect. *Journal of Educational Psychology, 73,* 411–418.

Ames, C., & Ames, R. (1984). Systems of student and teacher motivation: Toward a qualitative definition. *Journal of Educational Psychology, 76,* 535–556.

Ames, C., Ames, R., & Felker, D. (1977). Effects of self-concept on children's causal attributions and self-reinforcement. *Journal of Educational Psychology, 71,* 613–619.

Ames, C., & Archer, J. (1987a, April). *Achievement goals in the classroom: Student learning strategies and motivation processes.* Paper presented at the annual meeting of the American Educational Research Association, Washington, DC.

Ames, C., & Archer, J. (1987b). Mothers' beliefs about the role of ability and effort in school learning. *Journal of Educational Psychology, 79,* 409–414.

Ames, C., & Felker, D. W. (1979). Effects of self-concept on children's causal attributions and self-reinforcement. *Journal of Educational Psychology, 71,* 613–619.

Ames, C., & Maehr, M. (1989). *Home and school cooperation in social and motiva-*

tional development (Contract No. DE-H023T80023). Research funded by the Office of Special Education and Rehabilitative Services.

Anderson, C. A., & Jennings, D. L. (1980). When experiences of failure promote expectations of success: The impact of attributing failure to ineffective strategies. *Journal of Personality, 48,* 393–405.

Anderson, D. G. (1966, Fall). Self-assigned grades. *Counselor Education and Supervision, 6,* 75–76.

Anderson, J. G., & Evans, F. B. (1974). Causal models in educational research: Recursive models. *American Education Research Journal, 11,* 29–39.

Anderson, J. R. (1987). Skill acquisition: Compilation of weak-method problem solutions. *Psychological Review, 94,* 192–210.

Anderson, L. (1981). Short-term student responses to classroom instruction. *Elementary School Journal, 82,* 97–108.

Andrews, G. R., & Debus, R. L. (1978). Persistence and the causal perception of failure: Modifying cognitive attributions. *Journal of Educational Psychology, 70,* 154–166.

Arkin, R. M., Detchon, C. S., & Maruyama, G. M. (1982). Roles of attribution, affect, and cognitive interference in test anxiety. *Journal of Personality and Social Psychology, 43,* 1111–1124.

Arlin, M. (1984). Time, equality, and mastery learning. *Review of Educational Research, 54,* 65–86.

Arlin, M., & Webster, J. (1983). Time costs of mastery learning. *Journal of Educational Psychology, 75,* 187–195.

Arlin, P. K. (1975). Cognitive development in adulthood: A fifth stage? *Developmental Psychology, 11,* 602–606.

Armbruster, B. B., Stevens, R. J., & Rosenshine, B. (1977). *Analyzing content coverage and emphasis: A study of three curricula and two tests* (Tech. Rep. No. 26). Urbana: Center for the Study of Reading, University of Illinois.

Armstrong, B., Balow, B., & Johnson, D. (1981). Cooperative goal structures as a means of integrating learning disabled with normal progress elementary school pupils. *Contemporary Educational Psychology, 6,* 102–109.

Aronfreed, J. (1964). The origin of self-criticism. *Psychological Review, 71,* 193–218.

Aronoff, J., & Litwin, G. H. (1966). *Achievement motivation training and executive advancement.* Unpublished manuscript, Harvard University.

Aronson, E., Blaney, N., Stephan, C., Sikes, J., & Snapp, M. (1978). *The jigsaw classroom.* Beverly Hills, CA: Sage.

Aronson, E., & Carlsmith, J. M. (1962). Performance expectancy as a determinant of actual performance. *Journal of Abnormal and Social Psychology, 65,* 178–182.

Aronson, E., & Mettee, D. R. (1968). Dishonest behavior as a function of differential levels of induced self-esteem. *Journal of Personality and Social Psychology, 9,* 121–127.

Astin, A. W. (1982). *Minorities in American higher education: Recent trends, current prospects, and recommendations.* San Francisco: Jossey-Bass.

Astin, A. W., Hemond, M. K., & Richardson, G. T. (1982). *The American freshman: National norms for fall 1982.* Los Angeles: University of California.

Atkinson, J. W. (1957). Motivational determinants of risk-taking behavior. *Psychological Review, 64,* 359–372.

Atkinson, J. W. (1958). *Motives in fantasy, action, and society.* Princeton, NJ: Van Nostrand.

Atkinson, J. W. (1964). *An introduction to motivation*. Princeton, NJ: Van Nostrand.

Atkinson, J. W. (1981). Studying personality in the context of an advanced motivational psychology. *American Psychologist, 36,* 117–128.

Atkinson, J. W. (1987). Michigan studies of fear failure. In F. Halisch & J. Kuhl (Eds.), *Motivation, intention and volition* (pp. 47–60). Berlin: Springer.

Atkinson, J. W., & Feather, N. T. (Eds.). (1966). *A theory of achievement motivation*. New York: Wiley.

Atkinson, J. W., & Litwin, G. H. (1960). Achievement motive and test anxiety conceived as motive to approach success and motive to avoid failure. *Journal of Abnormal and Social Psychology, 60,* 52–63.

Atkinson, J. W., & O'Connor, P. A. (1966). Neglected factors in studies of achievement-oriented performance: Social approval as an incentive and performance decrement. In J. W. Atkinson & N. T. Feather (Eds.), *A theory of achievement motivation* (pp. 299–325). New York: Wiley.

Atkinson, J. W., & Raynor, J. O. (1974). *Motivation and achievement*. New York: Wiley.

Atkinson, J. W., & Reitman, W. R. (1958). Performance as a function of motive strength and expectancy of goal attainment. *Journal of Abnormal and Social Psychology, 53,* 361–366. Also in J. W. Atkinson (Ed.), (1958), *Motives in fantasy, action, and society*. Princeton, NJ: Van Nostrand.

Atwood, B., Williams, R. L., & Long, J. D. (1974). The effects of behavior contracts and behavior proclamations on social conduct and academic achievement in a ninth grade English class. *Adolescence, 9,* 425–436.

Au, K. H., & Jordan, C. (1981). Teaching reading to Hawaiian children: Finding a culturally appropriate solution. In H. Trueba & K. H. Au (Eds.), *Culture and the bilingual classroom: Studies in classroom ethnography*. Rowley, MA: Newbury House.

Avoiding nuclear war: Lessons for the future of U.S.–Soviet relations. (1989, Summer/Fall), *Carnegie Quarterly, 34*(3,4)

Axelrod, R. (Ed.). (1976). *Structure of decision: The cognitive maps of political elites*. Princeton: Princeton University Press.

Backman, C., & Secord, P. E. (1968). The self and role selection. In C. Gordon & K. Gergen (Eds.), *The self in social interaction*. New York: Wiley.

Baden, B., & Maehr, M. L. (1986). Confronting culture with culture: A perspective for designing schools for children of diverse sociocultural backgrounds. In R. Feldman (Ed.), *Social psychology applied to education*. New York: Cambridge University Press.

Bailey, T. (1990). The changing world of work. *Educator,* The Graduate School of Education, University of California, Berkeley, *4*(3), 10–11.

Bailin, S. (1987). Creativity and skill. In D. Perkins, J. Lockhead, & J. Bishop (Eds.), *Thinking: The second international conference*. Hillsdale, NJ: Erlbaum.

Ball, S. J. (1981). *Beachside comprehensive: A case-study of secondary schooling*. Cambridge, UK: Cambridge University Press.

Bandura, A. (1971). *Social learning theory*. Morristown, NJ: General Learning Press.

Bandura, A., Grusec, J. E., & Menlove, F. L. (1967). Some determinants of self-monitoring reinforcement systems. *Journal of Personality and Social Psychology, 5,* 449–455.

Bandura, A., & Kupers, C. J. (1964). Transmission of patterns of self-reinforcement through modeling. *Journal of Abnormal and Social Psychology, 69,* 1–9.

Bandura, A., & Schunk, D. H. (1981). Cultivating competence, self-efficacy, and intrinsic interest through proximal self-motivation. *Journal of Personality and Social Psychology, 41*, 486–598.

Bangert-Drowns, R., Kulik, R., Jr., & Kulik, C. (1983). Effects of coaching programs on achievement test performance. *Review of Educational Research, 53*, 571–585.

Bargh, J., & Schul, Y. (1980). On the cognitive benefits of teaching. *Journal of Educational Psychology, 72*, 593–604.

Barker, R. G. (1942). Success and failure in the classroom. *Progressive Education, 19*, 221–224.

Barnard, J. W., Zimbardo, P. G., & Sarason, S. B. (1968). Teachers' ratings of student personality traits as they relate to IQ and social desirability. *Journal of Educational Psychology, 59*, 128–132.

Barnes, M. S. (1894). *Studies in general history: Teacher's manual*. Boston: D. C. Heath.

Barron, F. (1965). The psychology of creativity. In F. Barron, W. C. Dement, W. Edwards, H. Lindman, L. D. Phillips, J. Olds, & M. Olds (Eds.), *New directions in psychology* (Vol. 1). New York: Holt, Rinehart & Winston.

Bar-Tal, D., & Darom, E. (1979). Pupils' attributions of success and failure. *Child Development, 50*, 264–267.

Battle, E. S. (1965). Motivational determinants of academic task persistence. *Journal of Personality and Social Psychology, 2*, 209–218.

Battle, E. S. (1966). Motivational determinants of academic competence. *Journal of Personality and Social Psychology, 4*, 634–642.

Battle, E., & Rotter, J. (1963). Children's feelings of personal control as related to social class and ethnic group. *Journal of Personality, 31*, 428–490.

Baumeister, R. F., & Jones, E. E. (1978). When self-representation is constrained by the target's knowledge: Consistency and compensation. *Journal of Personality and Social Psychology, 36*, 608–618.

Beck, A. T. (1967). *Depression: Clinical, experimental, and theoretical aspects*. New York: Harper & Row.

Beck, A. T., & Clark, D. A. (1988). Anxiety and depression: An information processing perspective. *Anxiety Research, 1*, 23–36.

Beck, A. T., & Emery, G. (1985). *Anxiety disorders and phobias: A cognitive perspective*. New York: Basic Books.

Beck, I. L., & McKeown, M. G. (1988). Toward meaningful accounts in history texts for young learners. *Educational Researcher, 17*(6), 31–39.

Becker, E. (1981). *The denial of death*. New York: The Free Press.

Becker, P. (1982). Towards a process analysis of test anxiety: Some theoretical and methodological observations. In R. Schwarzer, H. M. van der Ploeg, & C. D. Spielberger (Eds.), *Advances in test anxiety research* (Vol. 1, pp. 11–17). Hillsdale, NJ: Erlbaum.

Becker, P. (1983). Test anxiety, examination stress, and achievement: Methodological remarks and some results of a longitudinal study. In H. M. van der Ploeg, R. Schwarzer, & C. D. Spielberger (Eds.), *Advances in test anxiety research* (Vol. 2, pp. 129–146). Hillsdale, NJ: Erlbaum.

Beery, R. G. (1975). Fear of failure in the student experience. *Personnel and Guidance Journal, 54*, 190–203.

Begley, S. (1982, February 8). Why scientists cheat. *Newsweek*, p. 90.

Belmont, J. M., Butterfield, E. C., & Ferretti, R. P. (1982). Transfer of training instruction in self-management skills. In D. K. Detterman & R. J. Sternberg (Eds.),

How and how much can intelligence be increased? (pp. 147–154). Norwood, NJ: Ablex.

Benjamin, M., McKeachie, W. J., Lin, Y.-G., & Holinger, D. P. (1981). Test anxiety: Deficits in information processing. *Journal of Educational Psychology, 73,* 816–824.

Benson, J., Urman, H., & Hocevar, D. (1986). Effects of testwiseness training and ethnicity on achievement of third- and fifth-grade students. *Measurement and Evaluation in Counseling and Development, 18,* 154–162.

Benware, C. A., & Deci, E. L. (1984). Quality of learning with an active versus passive motivational set. *American Educational Research Journal, 21,* 755–765.

Berg, C. A. (1986). The role of social competence in contextual theories of adult intellectual development. *Educational Gerontology, 12,* 313–325.

Berg, I. (1970). *Education and jobs: The great training robbery.* New York: Praeger.

Berg, I., Bibb, R., Finegan, T. A., & Swafford, M. (1981). Toward model specification in the structural unemployment thesis: Issues and prospects. In I. Berg (Ed.), *Sociological perspectives on labor markets* (pp. 347–367). New York: Academic Press.

Berglas, S., & Jones, E. (1978). Drug choice as a self-handicapping strategy in response to noncontingent success. *Journal of Personality and Social Psychology, 36,* 405–417.

Bernstein, W. M., Stephan, W. G., & Davis, M. H. (1979). Explaining attributions for achievement: A path analytic approach. *Journal of Personality and Social Psychology, 37,* 1810–1821.

Biaggio, A. M. B. (1978). Achievement motivation of Brazilian students. *International Journal of Intercultural Relations, 2,* 186–195.

Biggs, J. B. (1984). Learning strategies, student motivation patterns, and subjectively perceived success. In J. R. Kirby (Ed.), *Cognitive strategies and educational performance* (pp. 111–134). New York: Academic Press.

Binet, A. (1909). *Les idées modernes sur les enfants* [Modern ideas about children]. Paris: Flamarion.

Biological Sciences Curriculum Study (1968). *Biological science: An ecological approach.* Chicago: Rand McNally.

Birney, R. C., Burdick, H., & Teevan, R. C. (1969). *Fear of failure.* New York: Van Nostrand.

Bishop, John H. (1989, Jan.–Feb.). Why the apathy in American schools? *Perspective, 6*–10, 42.

Blaney, N. T., Stephan, C., Rosenfield, D., Aronson, E., & Sikes, J. (1977). Interdependence in the classroom: A field study. *Journal of Educational Psychology, 2,* 121–128.

Blank, S. S., & Covington, M. V. (1965). Inducing children to ask questions in solving problems. *Journal of Educational Research, 59,* 21–27.

Block, J., & Lanning, K. (1984). Attribution therapy requestioned: A secondary analysis of the Wilson-Linville study. *Journal of Personality and Social Psychology, 46,* 705–708.

Block, J. H. (1977). Motivation, evaluation, and mastery learning. *UCLA Educator, 12,* 31–37.

Block, J. H. (1984). Making school learning activities more playlike: Flow and mastery learning. *The Elementary School Journal, 85,* 65–75.

Block, J. H., & Burns, R. B. (1976). Mastery learning. In L. S. Schulman (Ed.), *Review of research in education.* Itasca, IL: Peacock.

Bloom, B. S., Davis, A., & Hess, R. (1965). *Compensatory education for cultural deprivation.* New York: Holt, Rinehart & Winston.

Blumenfeld, P., Pintrich, P., & Hamilton, V. (1986). Children's concepts of ability, effort, and conduct. *American Educational Research Journal, 23,* 95–104.

Blumenfeld, P. C., Pintrich, P. R., Meece, J., & Wessels, K. (1981, April). *The influence of instructional practices on children's criteria for judging ability, effort and conduct.* Paper presented at the meeting of the American Educational Research Association, Los Angeles.

Boggiano, A. K., Barrett, M., Weiher, A. W., McClelland, G. H., & Lusk, C. M. (1987). Use of the maximal-operant principle to motivate children's intrinsic interest. *Journal of Personality and Social Psychology, 53,* 866–879.

Boggiano, A. K., Harackiewicz, J. M., Bessette, J. M., & Main, D. S. (1985). Increasing children's interest through performance-contingent reward. *Social Cognition, 3,* 400–411.

Boggiano, A. K., Main, D. S., & Katz, P. A. (1988). Children's preference for challenge: The role of perceived competence and control. *Journal of Personality and Social Psychology, 54,* 134–141.

Boggiano, A. K., & Pittman, T. S. (Eds.). (in press). *Achievement and motivation: A social-developmental perspective.* New York: Cambridge University Press.

Boggiano, A. K., & Ruble, D. N. (1979). Competence and the overjustification effect: A developmental study. *Journal of Personality and Social Psychology, 37,* 1462–1468.

Borkovec, T. D., Robinson, E., Pruzinsky, T., & DePree, J. A. (1983). Preliminary exploration of worry: Some characteristics and processes. *Behaviour Research and Therapy, 21,* 9–16.

Borkowski, J. G., Johnston, M. B., & Reid, M. K. (1987). Metacognition, motivation, and controlled performance. In S. Ceci (Ed.), *Handbook of cognitive, social, and neurological aspects of learning disabilities* (Vol. 2, pp. 147–174). Hillsdale, NJ: Erlbaum.

Borkowski, J. G., Weyhing, R. S., & Turner, L. A. (1986). Attributional retraining and the teaching of strategies. *Exceptional Children, 2,* 130–137.

Bolles, R. C. (1967). *Theory of motivation.* New York: Harper & Row.

Born, D. G., Gledhill, S. N., & Davis, M. L. (1972). Examination performance in lecture-discussion and personalized instruction courses. *Journal of Applied Behavior Analysis, 5,* 33–43.

Born, D. G., & Zlutnick, S. (1972). Personalized instruction. *Educational Technology, 12,* 30–34.

Bossert, S. T. (1979). *Tasks and social relationships in classrooms.* Cambridge, UK: Cambridge University Press.

Botkin, M. J. (1990). *Differential teacher treatment and ego functioning: The relationship between perceived competence and defense.* Unpublished doctoral dissertation, University of California, Berkeley.

Botkin, M. J., & Weinstein, R. S. (1987). *Perceived social competence of friendship choice as a function of differential teacher treatment.* Manuscript in preparation, University of California, Berkeley.

Bower, G. H. (1981). Mood and memory. *American Psychologist, 36,* 129–148.

Bradshaw, G. D., & Gaudry, E. (1968). The effect of a single experience of success or failure on text anxiety. *Australian Journal of Psychology, 20,* 219–223.

Bransford, J., Hasselbring, T., Barron, B., Kulewicz, S., Littlefield, J., & Goin, L. (in press). In R. Charles & E. Silver (Eds.), *Teaching and evaluating mathematical problem solving.* Reston, VA: National Council of Teachers of Mathematics.

Bransford, J. D., Nitsch, K. E., & Franks, J. J. (1977). The facilitation of knowing. In R. C. Anderson, R. J. Spiro, & W. E. Montague (Eds.), *Schooling and the acquisition of knowledge*. Hillsdale, NJ: Erlbaum.

Brattesani, K. A., Weinstein, R. S., & Marshall, H. H. (1984). Student perceptions of differential teacher treatment as moderators of teacher expectation effects. *Journal of Educational Psychology, 76*, 236–247.

Braverman, H. (1974). *Labor and monopoly capital: The degradation of work in the twentieth century*. New York: Monthly Review Press.

Bricklin, B., & Bricklin, P. M. (1967). *Bright child – poor grades*. New York: Dell.

Brickman, P., & Hendricks, M. (1975). Expectancy for gradual or sudden improvement and reaction to success and failure. *Journal of Personality and Social Psychology, 32*, 893–900.

Bringing children out of the shadows. (1988, Spring). *Carnegie Quarterly, 33*(2).

Brint, S., & Karabel, J. (1989). *The diverted dream: Community colleges and the promise of educational opportunity in America, 1900–1985*. New York: Oxford University Press.

Brockner, J. (1979). Self-esteem, self-consciousness, and task performance: Replications, extensions, and possible explanations. *Journal of Personality and Social Psychology, 37*, 447–461.

Brockner, J., & Hulton, A. J. B. (1978). How to reverse the vicious cycle of low self-esteem: The importance of attentional focus. *Journal of Experimental Social Psychology, 14*, 564–578.

Brophy, J. E. (1983). Research on the self-fulfilling prophecy and teacher expectations. *Journal of Educational Psychology, 75*, 631–661.

Brophy, J. E. (1985). Teacher-student interaction. In J. B. Dusek, V. C. Hall, & W. J. Meyer (Eds.), *Teacher expectancies* (pp. 303–327). Hillsdale, NJ: Erlbaum.

Brophy, J., & Good, T. (1970). Teacher's communication of differential expectations for children's classroom performance: Some behavioral data. *Journal of Educational Psychology, 61*, 365–374.

Brophy, J., & Good, T. (1974). *Teacher–student relationships*. New York: Holt, Rinehart & Winston.

Brown, A. L., & Campione, J. C. (1990). Communities of learning and thinking, or a context by any other name. In D. Kuhn (Ed.), Contributions to Human Development [Special issue]. *Contributions to Human Development, 21*, 108–126.

Brown, A. L., Campione, J. C., Reeve, R. A., Ferrara, R. A., & Palincsar, A. S. (1991). Interactive learning, individual understanding: The case of reading and mathematics. In L. T. Landsmann (Ed.), *Culture, schooling and psychological development*. Hillsdale, NJ: Erlbaum.

Brown, A. L., & Palincsar, A. S. (1989). Guided cooperative learning and individual knowledge acquisition. In L. B. Resnick (Ed.), *Knowing, learning, and instruction: Essays in honor of Robert Glaser* (pp. 393–451). Hillsdale, NJ: Erlbaum.

Brown, J., & Weiner, B. (1984). Affective consequences of ability versus effort ascriptions: Controversies, resolutions, and quandaries. *Journal of Educational Psychology, 76*, 146–158.

Brown, J. S., Collins, A., & Duguid, P. (1989). Situated cognition and the culture of learning. *Educational Researcher, 18*(1), 32–42.

Bruch, M. A. (1978). Type of cognitive modeling, imitation of modeled tactics, and modification of test anxiety. *Cognitive Therapy and Research, 2*, 147–164.

Buckert, U., Meyer, W. U., & Schmalt, H. D. (1979). Effects of difficulty and diagnosticity on choice among tasks in relation to achievement motivation and perceived ability. *Journal of Personality and Social Psychology, 37*, 1172–1178.

Burns, R. (1987). *Models of instructional organization: A casebook on mastery learning and outcome-based education*. San Francisco: Far West Laboratory for Educational Research and Development.

Burton, D., & Martens, R. (1986). Pinned by their own goals: An exploratory investigation into why kids drop out of wrestling. *Journal of Sport Psychology, 8*, 1983–1997.

Butler, R. (1988). Enhancing and undermining intrinsic motivation: The effects of task-involving and ego-involving evaluation on interest and performance. *British Journal of Educational Psychology, 58*, 1–14.

Butler, R., & Nisan, M. (1986). Effects of no feedback, task-related comments, and grade on intrinsic instruction and performance. *Journal of Educational Psychology, 78*, 210–216.

Butterfield, E. C., & Belmont, J. M. (1971). Relations of storage and retrieval strategies as short-term memory processes. *Journal of Experimental Psychology, 89*, 319–328.

Butterfield, E. C., & Belmont, J. M. (1977). Assessing and improving the executive cognitive functions of mentally retarded people. In I. Bialer & M. Sternlicht (Eds.), *Psychological issues in mental retardation*. New York: Psychological Dimensions.

Calder, B. J., & Staw, B. M. (1975). Self-perception of intrinsic and extrinsic motivation. *Journal of Personality and Social Psychology, 31*, 599–605.

Calfee, R. C., & Brown, R. (1979). Grouping students for instruction. In D. L. Duke (Ed.), *Class management* (pp. 144–181). Chicago: University of Chicago Press.

Campbell, D. N. (1974, October). On being number one: Competition in education. *Phi Delta Kappan*, 143–146.

Campbell, D. T. (1986). Ethnocentrism of disciplines and the fish-scale model of omniscience. In D. E. Chubin, A. L. Porter, F. A. Rossini, & T. Connolly (Eds.), *Interdisciplinary analysis and research: Theory and practice of problem-focused research and development: Selected readings* (pp. 29–46). Mt. Airy, MD: Lomond.

Campeau, P. L. (1968). Test anxiety and feedback in programmed instruction. *Journal of Experimental Psychology, 59*, 159–163.

Cangelosi, J. S. (1988). *Classroom management strategies: Gaining and maintaining students' cooperation*. New York: Longman.

Carey, S. (1985). Are children fundamentally different kinds of thinkers and learners than adults? In S. F. Chipman, J. W. Segal, & R. Glaser (Eds.), *Thinking and learning skills* (Vol. 2, pp. 485–517). Hillsdale, NJ: Erlbaum.

Carnegie Council on Adolescent Development. (1989). *Turning points: Preparing American youth for the 21st century*. New York: Carnegie Corporation of New York.

Carse, J. P. (1986). *Finite and infinite games*. New York: Ballantine.

Carver, C. S., & Gaines, J. G. (1987). Optimism, pessimism, and postpartum depression. *Cognitive Theory and Research, 11*, 449–462.

Carver, C. S., & Scheier, M. F. (1986). Functional and dysfunctional responses to anxiety: The interaction between expectancies and self-focused attention. In R. Schwarzer (Ed.), *Self-related cognitions in anxiety and motivation* (pp. 111–141). Hillsdale, NJ: Erlbaum.

Carver, C. S., & Scheier, M. F. (1988). A control-process perspective on anxiety. *Anxiety Research, 1*, 17–22.

Casady, M. (1974). The tricky business of giving rewards. *Psychology Today, 8*, 52.

Castenell, L. A. (1983). Achievement motivation: An investigation of adolescents' achievement patterns. *American Educational Research Journal, 20*, 503–510.

Castenell, L. (1984). A cross-cultural look at achievement motivation research. *Journal of Negro Education, 53*, 435–443.

Cavana, G. R., & Leonard, W. H. (1985). Extending discretion in high school science curricula. *Science Education, 69*, 593–603.

Cervantes, R. A., & Bernal, H. H. (1976). *Psychosocial growth and academic achievement in Mexican-American students.* San Antonio: San Antonio Associates.

Chandler, C. L., & Connell, J. P. (1987). Children's intrinsic, extrinsic, and internalized motivation: A developmental study of children's reasons for liked and disliked behaviours. *British Journal of Developmental Psychology, 5*, 357–365.

Chandler, T. A., & Spies, C. J. (1983). *Semantic differential placement of attributions and dimensions in four different groups.* Unpublished manuscript, Kent State University.

Chapin, M., & Dyck, D. G. (1976). Persistence in children's reading behavior as a function of N length and attribution retraining. *Journal of Abnormal Psychology, 85*, 511–515.

Chapin, S. L., & Vito, R. (1988, April). *Patterns of family interaction style, self-system processes and engagement with schoolwork: An investigation of adolescents rated as at-risk, or not-at-risk for academic failure.* Paper presented at the American Educational Research Association Annual Meeting, New Orleans, LA.

Charles, R. I., & Lester, F. K., Jr. (1984). An evaluation of a process-oriented instructional program in mathematical problem solving in grades 5 and 7. *Journal for Research in Mathematics Education, 15*, 15–34.

Chase, W. C., & Simon, H. A. (1973). Perception in chess. *Cognitive Psychology, 4*, 55–81.

Cherryholmes, C. H. (1982). Discourse and criticism in the social studies classroom. *Theory and Research in Social Education, 9*(4), 57–73.

Chi, M. T. H., Glaser, R., & Rees, E. (1982). Expertise in problem solving. In R. Sternberg (Ed.), *Advances in the psychology of human intelligence* (Vol. 1, pp. 7–75). Hillsdale, NJ: Erlbaum.

Childress, M. (1990, August 19). Our life as a slave. *Image Magazine, San Francisco Examiner*, p. 25.

Chubin, D. E., Porter, A. L., Rossini, F. A., & Connolly, T. (Eds.) (1986). *Interdisciplinary analysis and research: Theory and practice of problem-focused research and development: Selected readings.* Mt. Airy, MD: Lomand.

Churchill, W. S. (1940, June 18). *Hansard Parliamentary Debates* (Commons), Vol. 362, col. 51–61.

Churchill, W. S. (1923). *The world crisis* (Vol. 1, Part 1). New York: Scribner's Sons.

Clark, K. (1969). *Civilisation.* New York: Harper & Row.

Clark, M. S., & Fiske, S. T. (Eds.). (1982). *Affect and cognition: The seventeenth annual Carnegie Symposium on cognition.* Hillsdale, NJ: Erlbaum.

Clark, R. M. (1983). *Family life and school achievement: Why poor black children succeed and fail.* Chicago: University of Chicago Press.

Clement, J. (1982). Analogical reasoning patterns in expert problem solving. *Proceedings of the Fourth Annual Conference of the Cognitive Science Society.* Ann Arbor: University of Michigan.

Clements, D. H., & Gullo, D. F. (1984). Effects of computer programming on young children's cognition. *Journal of Educational Psychology, 76*, 1051–1058.

Clifford, M. M. (1978). The effects of quantitative feedback on children's expectations of success. *British Journal of Educational Psychology, 48*, 220–226.

Clifford, M. M. (1984). Thoughts on a theory of constructive failure. *Educational Psychologist, 2,* 108–120.

Cohen, E. J., & DeAvila, E. (1983). *Learning to think in math and science: Improving local education for minority children* (Final report to The Walter S. Johnson Foundation). Stanford: School of Education, Stanford University.

Cohen, H., & Filipczak, J. (1971). *A new learning environment.* San Francisco: Jossey-Bass.

Coleman, J. S., & Husen, T. (1985). *Becoming adult in a changing society.* Paris: Centre for Educational Research and Innovation.

Collins, M. D. (1975). *Survival kit for teachers (and parents).* Pacific Palisades, CA: Goodyear.

Collins, R. (1979). *The credential society: An historical sociology of education and stratification.* New York: Academic Press.

Combs, A. W. (1957). The myth of competition. *Childhood Education.* Washington, DC: Association for Childhood Education International.

Commanday, R. (1992). *Sources of self-esteem: Investigating factors underlying achievement motives of high ability Afro-American students from a low income community.* Unpublished doctoral dissertation, University of California at Berkeley.

COMPACT Dialogue: Connecticut Multi-state Performance Assessment Collaborative Team in Math and Science. (1989), *1*(3). (A project sponsored by the National Science Foundation)

Condry, J. (1977). Enemies of exploration: Self-initiated versus other-initiated learning. *Journal of Personality and Social Psychology, 35,* 459–477.

Condry, J. D., & Chambers, J. (1978). Intrinsic motivation and the process of learning. In M. R. Lepper & D. Greene (Eds.), *The hidden costs of reward: New perspectives on the psychology of human motivation.* Hillsdale, NJ: Erlbaum.

Cooper, H. M., & Burger, J. M. (1980). How teachers explain students' academic performance: A categorization of free response academic attributions. *American Educational Research Journal, 17,* 95–109.

Cooper, H. M., & Good, T. L. (1983). *Pygmalion grows up: Studies in the expectation communication process.* New York: Longman.

Cooper, H., & Tom, D. (1984). Socioeconomic status and ethnic group differences in achievement motivation. In R. Ames & C. Ames (Eds.), *Research on motivation in education* (Vol. 1., pp. 209–242). New York: Academic Press.

Cooper, L., Johnson, D. W., Johnson, R., & Wilderson, R. (1980). The effects of cooperative, competitive and individualistic experiences on interpersonal attraction among heterogeneous peers. *The Journal of Social Psychology, 111,* 243–253.

Coopersmith, S. (1967). *The antecedents of self-esteem.* San Francisco: Freeman.

Corcoran, M. D., MacDougall, M. A., & Scarbrough, W. H. (1985). The interplay of worry and emotionality with anxiety and cognitive interference in predicting test performance. In H. M. van der Ploeg, R. Schwarzer, & C. D. Spielberger (Eds.), *Advances in test anxiety research* (Vol. 4, pp. 103–109). Lisse, Netherlands: Swets & Zeitlinger.

Cordes, C. (1985, March). Venezuela tests 6-year emphasis on thinking skills. *APA Monitor,* pp. 26–28.

Corey, J. R., & McMichael, J. S. (1974). The retention of material learned in a personalized introductory psychology course. In J. G. Sherman (Ed.), *PSI:41 Germinal papers.* Menlo Park, CA: W. A. Benjamin.

Costa, A. L. (1989). Re-assessing assessment. *Educational Leadership, 46*(7), 2.

Covington, M. V. (1967). *The effects of anxiety on various types of ideational output measures in complex problem solving.* Paper presented at the meeting of the Western Psychological Association, San Francisco.

Covington, M. V. (1968, February). *The affective components of productive thinking: Strategies of research and assessment.* Paper presented at the Definitions of Problem-solving Goals for the Elementary School Symposium, meeting of the American Educational Research Association, Chicago.

Covington, M. V. (1969). A cognitive curriculum: A process-oriented approach to education. In J. Hellmuth (Ed.), *Cognitive studies* (Vol. 1, pp. 491–502). Seattle: Special Child Publications.

Covington, M. V. (1981). Strategies for smoking prevention and resistance among young adolescents. *Journal of Early Adolescence, 1,* 349–356.

Covington, M. V. (1982, August). *Musical chairs: Who drops out of music instruction and why?* Proceedings of the National Symposium on the Applications of Psychology to the Teaching and Learning of Music: The Ann Arbor Symposium. Session III: Motivation and Creativity. Ann Arbor: University of Michigan.

Covington, M. V. (1983). Anxiety, task difficulty and childhood problem solving: A self-worth interpretation. In H. M. van der Ploeg, R. Schwarzer, & C. D. Spielberger (Eds.), *Advances in test anxiety research* (Vol. 2, pp. 101–109). Hillsdale, NJ: Erlbaum.

Covington, M. V. (1984a). Anxiety management via problem-solving instruction. In H. M. van der Ploeg, R. Schwarzer, & C. D. Spielberger (Eds.), *Advances in test anxiety research* (Vol. 3, pp. 39–52). Hillsdale, NJ: Erlbaum.

Covington, M. V. (1984b). Motivated cognitions. In S. G. Paris, G. M. Olson, & H. W. Stevenson (Eds.), *Learning and motivation in the classroom* (pp. 139–164). Hillsdale, NJ: Erlbaum.

Covington, M. V. (1984c). Strategic thinking and the fear of failure. In J. Segal, S. Chipman, & R. Glaser (Eds.), *Thinking and learning skills: Relating instruction to basic research* (pp. 389–416). Hillsdale, NJ: Erlbaum.

Covington, M. V. (1984d). The motive for self-worth. In R. Ames & C. Ames (Eds.), *Research on motivation in education* (Vol. 1, pp. 77–113). New York: Academic Press.

Covington, M. V. (1984e). The self-worth theory of achievement motivation: Findings and implications. *The Elementary School Journal, 85,* 5–20.

Covington, M. V. (1985a). Anatomy of failure-induced anxiety: The role of cognitive mediators. In R. Schwarzer (Ed.), *Self-related cognitions in anxiety and motivation* (pp. 247–263). Hillsdale, NJ: Erlbaum.

Covington, M. V. (1985b). The effects of multiple-testing opportunities on rote and conceptual learning and retention. *Human Learning, 4,* 57–72.

Covington, M. V. (1985c). The role of self-processes in applied social psychology. *Journal of the Theory of Social Behavior, 15,* 355–389.

Covington, M. V. (1985d). Text anxiety: Causes and effects over time. In H. M. van der Ploeg, R. Schwarzer, & C. D. Spielberger (Eds.), *Advances in test anxiety research* (Vol. 4, pp. 55–68). Hillsdale, NJ: Erlbaum.

Covington, M. V. (1986a, April). *Health and development: The adolescent as implicit politician and rationalist.* Keynote address presented at the National Invitational Conference on Health Futures of Adolescents, Daytona Beach, FL.

Covington, M. V. (1986b). Instruction in problem solving and planning. In S. L. Friedman, E. K. Scholnick, & R. R. Cocking (Eds.), *Blueprints for thinking: The role of planning in cognitive development* (pp. 469–511). New York: Cambridge University Press.

Covington, M. V. (1987). Achievement motivation, self-attributions and exceptionality. In J. D. Day & J. G. Borkowski (Eds.), *Intelligence and exceptionality* (pp. 173–213). Norwood, NJ: Ablex.

Covington, M. V. (1989). Self-esteem and failure in school: Analysis and policy implications. In A. M. Mecca, N. J. Semlser, & J. Vasconcellos (Eds.), *The social importance of self-esteem* (pp. 72–124). Berkeley: University of California Press.

Covington, M. V., & Beery, R. G. (1976). *Self-worth and school learning.* New York: Holt, Rinehart & Winston.

Covington, M. V., Crutchfield, R. S. (1965). Experiments in the use of programmed instruction for the facilitation of creative problem solving. *Programmed Instruction, 4,* 3–5, 10.

Covington, M. V., Crutchfield, R. S., Davis, L. B., & Olton, R. M. (1974). *The Productive Thinking Program: A course in learning to think.* (Address inquiries to Professor Martin Covington, Psychology Department, 3210 Tolman Hall, University of California, Berkeley, CA 94720).

Covington, M. V., & Fedan, N. (1978). *Metastrategies in productive thinking.* Unpublished manuscript, Department of Psychology, University of California, Berkeley.

Covington, M. V., & Jacoby, K. E. (1973). *Productive thinking and course satisfaction as a function of an independence-conformity dimension.* Paper presented at the annual meeting of the American Psychological Association, Montreal.

Covington, M. V., & Omelich, C. L. (1978). *Sex differences in self-aggrandizing tendencies.* Unpublished manuscript, Department of Psychology, University of California, Berkeley.

Covington, M. V., & Omelich, C. L. (1979a). Are causal attributions causal? A path analysis of the cognitive model of achievement motivation. *Journal of Personality and Social Psychology, 37,* 1487–1504.

Covington, M. V., & Omelich, C. L. (1979b). Effort: The double-edged sword in school achievement. *Journal of Educational Psychology, 71,* 169–182.

Covington, M. V., & Omelich, C. L. (1979c). It's best to be able and virtuous too: Student and teacher evaluative responses to successful effort. *Journal of Educational Psychology, 71,* 688–700.

Covington, M. V., & Omelich, C. L. (1981). As failures mount: Affective and cognitive consequences of ability demotion in the classroom. *Journal of Educational Psychology, 73,* 799–808.

Covington, M. V., & Omelich, C. L. (1982). Achievement anxiety, performance, and behavioral instruction: A cost/benefits analysis. In R. Schwarzer, H. M. van der Ploeg, & C. D. Spielberger (Eds.), *Advances in text anxiety research* (Vol. 1, pp. 139–154). Hillsdale, NJ: Erlbaum.

Covington, M. V., & Omelich, C. L. (1984a). An empirical examination of Weiner's critique of attribution research. *Journal of Educational Psychology, 76,* 1214–1225.

Covington, M. V., & Omelich, C. L. (1984b). Controversies or consistencies? A reply to Brown and Weiner. *Journal of Educational Psychology, 76,* 159–168.

Covington, M. V., & Omelich, C. L. (1984c). Task-oriented versus competitive learning structures: Motivational and performance consequences. *Journal of Educational Psychology, 76,* 1038–1050.

Covington, M. V., & Omelich, C. L. (1984d). The trouble with pitfalls: A reply to Weiner's critique of attribution research. *Journal of Educational Psychology, 76,* 1199–1213.

Covington, M. V., & Omelich, C. L. (1985). Ability and effort valuation among failure-avoiding and failure-accepting students. *Journal of Educational Psychology, 77,* 446–459.

Covington, M. V., & Omelich, C. L. (1987a). "I knew it cold before the exam": A test of the anxiety-blockage hypothesis. *Journal of Educational Psychology, 79,* 393–400.

Covington, M. V., & Omelich, C. L. (1987b). Item difficulty and test performance among high-anxious and low-anxious students. In R. Schwarzer, H. M. van der Ploeg, & C. D. Spielberger (Eds.), *Advances in test anxiety research* (Vol. 5, pp. 127–135). Hillsdale, NJ: Erlbaum.

Covington, M. V., & Omelich, C. L. (1988a). Achievement dynamics: The interaction of motives, cognitions and emotions over time. *Anxiety Journal, 1,* 165–183.

Covington, M. V., & Omelich, C. L. (1988b). I can resist anything but temptation: Adolescent expectations for smoking cigarettes. *Journal of Applied Social Psychology, 18,* 203–227.

Covington, M. V., & Omelich, C. L. (1990). *The second time around: Coping with repeated failures.* Unpublished manuscript, Department of Psychology, University of California, Berkeley.

Covington, M. V., & Omelich, C. L. (1991). Need achievement revisited: Verification of Atkinson's original 2 × 2 model. In C. D. Spielberger, I. G. Sarason, Z. Kulcsár, & G. L. Van Heck (Eds.), *Stress and emotion: Anxiety, anger, and curiosity* (Vol. 14, pp. 85–105). Washington, DC: Hemisphere.

Covington, M. V., Omelich, C. L., & Schwarzer, R. (1986). Anxiety, aspirations, and self-concept in the achievement process. A longitudinal model with latent variables. *Motivation and Emotion, 10,* 71–88.

Covington, M. V., Spratt, M. F., & Omelich, C. L. (1990). Is effort enough, or does diligence count too? Student and teacher reactions to effort stability in failure. *Journal of Educational Psychology, 72,* 717–729.

Coyne, J. C., & Lazarus, R. S. (1980). Cognitive style, stress perception, and coping. In I. L. Kutash & L. B. Schlesinger (Eds.), *Handbook on stress and anxiety.* San Francisco: Jossey-Bass.

Cox, H., Swain, C., & Hartsough, C. S. (1982). *Student success at school* (Final report: Elementary and Secondary Educational Act IV–C). Sonoma, CA: Sonoma County Office of Education.

Craik, F. I. M., & Lockhart, R. S. (1972). Levels of processing: A framework for memory research. *Journal of Verbal Learning and Verbal Behavior, 11,* 671–684.

Crandall, V. C., Katkovsky, W., & Crandall, V. J. (1965). Children's beliefs in their own control of reinforcements in intellectual-academic achievement situations. *Child Development, 36,* 91–109.

Crandall, V. J., Preston, A., & Rabson, A. (1960). Maternal reactions and the development of independence and achievement behavior in young children. *Child Development, 31,* 243–251.

Crockenberg, S., Bryant, B., & Wilce, L. (1976). The effects of cooperatively and competitively structured learning environments on inter- and intrapersonal behavior. *Child Development, 47,* 386–396.

Crocker, J., & Major, B. (1988). *Social stigma and self-esteem: The self-protective properties of stigma.* Unpublished manuscript.

Cromer, W., & Wiener, M. (1966). Idiosyncratic response patterns among good and poor readers. *Journal of Consulting Psychology, 30,* 1–10.

Croxton, J. S., & Klonsky, B. G. (1982). Sex differences in causal attributions for success and failure in real and hypothetical sport settings. *Sex Roles, 8,* 399–409.

Cruickshank, D. R., Telfer, R. A., Ezell, E., & Manford, R. (1987). *Simulations and games: An ERIC bibliography.* Washington, DC: U.S. Dept. of Education.

Crutchfield, R. S. (1969). Nurturing the cognitive skills of productive thinking. In L. J. Rubin (Ed.). *Yearbook of the Association for Supervision and Curriculum Development* (pp. 53–71). Washington, DC: National Educational Association.

Csikszentmihalyi, M. (1975). *Beyond boredom and anxiety.* San Francisco: Jossey-Bass.

Cullen, Joy L. (1985). Children's ability to cope with failure: Implications of a meta-cognitive approach for the classroom. In D. L. Forrest-Pressley, G. E. Mackinnon, & T. G. Waller (Eds.), *Metacognition, cognition, and human performance* (Vol. 2, pp. 267–300). New York: Academic Press.

Culler, R. E., & Holahan, C. J. (1980). Test anxiety and academic performance: The effects of study-related behaviors. *Journal of Educational Psychology, 72,* 16–20.

Cunningham, A. E. (1990). Explicit versus implicit instruction in phonemic awareness. *Journal of Experimental Child Psychology, 52,* 121–126.

D'Ambrosio, U. (1985). Ethnomathematics and its place in the history and pedagogy of mathematics. *For the Learning of Mathematics, 5*(1), 44–48.

D'Ambrosio, U. (1987). Ethnomathematics, what it might be. *International Study Group of Ethnomathematics Newsletter, 3*(1).

Dansereau, D. F. (1984). Learning strategy research. In J. Segal, S. Chipman, & R. Glaser (Eds.), *Thinking and learning skills: Relating instruction to basic research* (pp. 209–239). Hillsdale, NJ: Erlbaum.

Darling-Hammond, L., & Wise, A. E. (1985). Beyond standardization: State standards and school improvement. *Elementary School Journal, 85,* 315–336.

Davids, A., & Hainsworth, P. K. (1967). Maternal attitudes about family life and child rearing as avowed by mothers and perceived by their underachieving and high-achieving sons. *Journal of Consulting Psychology, 31,* 29–37.

Davis, D. G. (1986, April). *A pilot study to assess equity in selected curricular offerings across three diverse schools in a large urban school district: A search for methodology.* Paper presented at the annual meeting of the American Educational Research Association, San Francisco.

Davis, J. K., & Annis, L. (1982). Study techniques and the role of individual differences. *Communication & Cognition, 15,* 79–82.

Day, V. H. (1982). Validity of an attributional model for a specific life event. *Psychological Reports, 50,* 434.

DeCharms, R. (1957). Affiliation motivation and productivity in small groups. *Journal of Abnormal and Social Psychology, 55,* 222–226.

De Charms, R. (1968). *Personal causation: The internal affective determinants of behavior.* New York: Academic Press.

De Charms, R. (1972). Personal causation training in the schools. *Journal of Applied Social Psychology, 2,* 95–113.

Deci, E. L. (1975). *Intrinsic motivation.* New York: Plenum.

Deci, E. L., & Ryan, R. M. (1980). The empirical exploration of intrinsic motivational processes. In L. Berkowitz (Ed.), *Advances in experimental social psychology* (Vol. 13, pp. 39–80). New York: Academic Press.

Deci, E. L., & Ryan, R. M. (1985). *Intrinsic motivation and self-determination in human behavior.* New York: Plenum.

Dede, C. (1988). *The probable evolution of artificial intelligence based educational devices. Technological forecasting and social change.* Unpublished manuscript, University of Houston.

Deegan, W. L., Tillery, D., & Associates (1985). *Renewing the American community* college: Priorities and strategies for effective leadership. San Francisco: Jossey-Bass.

Deffenbacher, J. L. (1977). Relationship of worry and emotionality to performance on the Miller Analogies Test. *Journal of Educational Psychology, 69,* 191–195.

Deffenbacher, J. L. (1978). Worry, emotionality, and task-generated interference in test anxiety: An empirical test of attentional theory. *Journal of Educational Psychology, 70,* 248–254.

Deffenbacher, J. L. (1980). Worry and emotionality in test anxiety. In I. G. Sarason (Ed.), *Test anxiety: Theory, research and applications* (pp. 111–128). Hillsdale, NJ: Erlbaum.

Deffenbacher, J. L. (1986). Cognitive and physiological components of test anxiety in real-life exams. *Cognitive Therapy and Research, 10,* 635–644.

Deffenbacher, J. L., & Hazaleus, S. L. (1985). Cognitive, emotional, and physiological components of test anxiety. *Cognitive Therapy and Research, 9,* 169–180.

de Lange Jzn, J. (1987). *Mathematics, insight and meaning.* Vakgroep Onderzoek Wiskundeonderwijs en Onderwijscomputercentrum, Rijksuniversiteit Utrecht.

Denhiere, G. (1974, September–December). Apprentissages intentionnels à allure libre: Etude comparative d'enfants normaux et debiles mentaux [Learning in natural contexts: Comparative study of normal and mentally disabled children]. *Enfance,* 149–174.

Depreeuw, E. (1982). From test anxiety research to treatment: Some critical considerations and propositions. In R. Schwarzer, H. M. van der Ploeg, & C. D. Spielberger (Eds.), *Advances in test anxiety research* (Vol. 1, pp. 155–163). Hillsdale, NJ: Erlbaum.

Depreeuw, E. (1990a). *Explorative treatment outcome study on the role of time management training in passive test anxious students.* Belgium: University of Leuven.

Depreeuw, E. (1990b). *Fear of failure: A complex clinical phenomenon.* Belgium: University of Leuven.

Derry, S. H., & Murphy, D. A. (1986). Designing systems that train learning ability: From theory to practice. *Review of Educational Research, 56,* 1–39.

Desiderato, O., & Koskinen, P. (1969). Anxiety, study habits, and academic achievement. *Journal of Consulting Psychology, 16,* 162–165.

Deutsch, M. (1949). An experimental study of the effects of cooperation and competition upon group process. *Human Relations, 2,* 199–232.

Deutsch, M. (1975). Equity, equality, and need. *Journal of Social Issues, 31,* 137–149.

Deutsch, M. (1979). Education and distributive justice. *American Psychologist, 34,* 391–401.

Deutsch, M., & Krauss, R. M. (1960). The effect of threat upon interpersonal bargaining. *Journal of Abnormal and Social Psychology, 61,* 181–189.

Deutsch, M., & Solomon, L. (1959). Reactions to evaluations by others as influenced by self-evaluation. *Sociometry, 22,* 93–113.

De Volder, M., & Lens, W. (1982). Academic achievement and future time perspective as a cognitive-motivational concept. *Journal of Personality and Social Psychology, 42,* 566–571.

Dewey, J. (1916). *Democracy and education.* New York: Macmillan.

Dewey, J. (1963). *Experience and education.* New York: Collier. (Original work published 1938)

Dickson, P. (1978). *The official rules: The definitive, annotated collection of laws, principles, and instructions for dealing with the real world.* New York: Delacorte.

Diener, C. T., & Dweck, C. S. (1978). An analysis of learned helplessness: Continuous changes in performance, strategy and achievement cognitions following failure. *Journal of Personality and Social Psychology, 36*, 451–462.

Diener, C. T., & Dweck, C. S. (1980). An analysis of learned helplessness: II. The processing of success. *Journal of Personality and Social Psychology, 39*, 940–952.

Diggory, J. C. (1966). *Self-evaluation: Concepts and studies.* New York: Wiley.

Diggory, J. C., Riley, E. J., & Blumenfeld, R. (1960). Estimated probability of success for a fixed goal. *American Journal of Psychology, 73*, 41–55.

Dillon, D., & Searle, D. (1981). The role of language in one first grade classroom. *Research in the Teaching of English, 15*, 311–328.

Dillon, J. T. (1982). Problem finding and solving. *Journal of Creative Behavior, 16*, 97–111.

Dishon, D., & O'Leary, P. W. (1984). *A guidebook for cooperative learning: A technique for creating more effective schools.* Holmes Beach, FL: Learning Publications.

Doctor, R. M., & Altman, F. (1969). Worry and emotionality as components of test anxiety: Replication and further data. *Psychological Reports, 24*, 563–568.

Doctor, R. M., Aponte, J., Burry, A., & Welch, R. (1970). Group counseling versus behavior therapy in treatment of college underachievement. *Behavior Research and Therapy, 8*, 87–89.

Douglas, W. O. (1970). *Points of rebellion.* New York: Random House.

Downey, M. T., & Levstik, L. S. (1988, September). Teaching and learning history: The research base. *Social Education, 52*, 336–342.

Doyle, A. C. (1967). *The annotated Sherlock Holmes* (Vol. 1). New York: Clarkson N. Potter.

Doyle, W. (1983). Academic work. *Review of Educational Research, 53*, 159–199.

Dreeben, R. (1968). *On what is learned in school.* Reading, MA: Addison-Welsey.

Dryfoos, J. G. (1990). *Adolescents at risk: Prevalence and prevention.* New York: Oxford University Press.

Duffy, G. G., Roehler, L. R., Sivan, E., Rackliffe, G., Book, C., Meloth, M., Vavrus, L., Wesselman, R., Putnam, J., & Bassiri, D. (1986). *The effects of explaining the mental processing associated with using reading strategies on the awareness and achievement of low group third graders.* East Lansing: Michigan State University.

Duncker, K. (1945). On problem solving. *Psychological Monographs, 58* (No. 270).

Dunn, J. A. (1964). Factor structure of the Test Anxiety Scale for Children. *Journal of Consulting Psychology, 28*, 92.

Dunn, J. A. (1965). Stability of the factor structure of the Test Anxiety Scale for Children across age and sex groups. *Journal of Consulting Psychology, 29*, 1897.

Dweck, C. S. (1975). The role of expectations and attributions in the alleviation of learned helplessness. *Journal of Personality and Social Psychology, 31*, 674–685.

Dweck, C. S. (1986). Motivational processes affecting learning. *American Psychologist, 41*, 1040–1048.

Dweck, C. S., & Bempechat, J. (1983). Children's theories of intelligence: Consequences for learning. In S. G. Paris, G. M. Olson, & H. M. Stevenson (Eds.), *Learning and motivation in the classroom* (pp. 239–256). Hillsdale, NJ: Erlbaum.

Dweck, C. S., & Bush, E. S. (1976). Sex differences in learned helplessness. I: Differential debilitation with peer and adult evaluators. *Developmental Psychology, 12*, 147–156.

Dweck, C. S., Davidson, W., Nelson, S., & Enna, B. (1978). Sex differences in learned helplessness: II. The contingencies of evaluative feedback in the classroom and III. An experimental analysis. *Developmental Psychology, 14,* 268–276.

Dweck, C. S., & Goetz, T. E. (1978). Attributions and learned helplessness. In J. H. Harvey, W. Ickes, & R. F. Kidd (Eds.), *New directions in attribution research* (Vol. 2, pp. 157–179). Hillsdale, NJ: Erlbaum.

Dweck, C. S., & Reppucci, N. D. (1973). Learned helplessness and reinforcement responsibility in children. *Journal of Personality and Social Psychology, 25,* 109–116.

Dweck, C. S., & Wortman, C. B. (1982). Learned helplessness, anxiety, and achievement motivation: Neglected parallels in cognitive, affective, and coping responses. In H. W. Krohne & L. Laux (Eds.), *Achievement, stress, and anxiety* (pp. 93–126). Washington, DC: Hemisphere.

Eccles, J. (1983). Expectancies, values and academic behaviors. In J. T. Spence (Ed.), *Achievement and achievement motives* (pp. 75–146). San Francisco: Freeman.

Edney, J. J. (1980). The commons problem: Alternative perspectives. *American Psychologist, 2,* 131–150.

Edwards, W. (1953). Probability-preferences in gambling. *American Journal of Psychology, 66,* 349–364.

Eggerman, R. W. (1982, July–Aug.). Competition as a mixed good. *The Humanist,* 48–51.

Eifferman, R. R. (1974). It's child's play. In L. M. Shears & E. M. Bower (Eds.), *Games in education and development.* Springfield, IL: Charles C Thomas.

Elleson, V. J. (1983, Dec.). Competition: A cultural imperative. *The Personnel and Guidance Journal, 62,* 195–198.

Elliott, E. S., & Dweck, C. S. (1988). Goals: An approach to motivation and achievement. *Journal of Personality and Social Psychology, 54,* 5–12.

Ellis, A. (1962). *Reason and emotion in psychotherapy.* Secaucus, NJ: Citadel.

Ellis, A. (1971). The basic clinical theory of rational-emotive therapy. In A. Ellis & R. Grieger (Eds.), *Handbook of rational-emotive therapy.* New York: Springer.

Ellis, A., & Kraus, W. J. (1977). *Overcoming procrastination.* New York: Institute for Rational Living.

Engle, S. H., & Ocho, A. S. (1988). *Education for democratic citizenship: Decision making in the social studies.* New York: Teachers College Press.

Ennis, R. H. (1989). Critical thinking and subject specificity: Clarification and needed research. *Educational Researcher, 3,* 4–10.

Entwistle, D. R., & Hayduk, L. A. (1978). *Too great expectations.* Baltimore: Johns Hopkins University Press.

Epstein, K. K. (1989). *Early school leaving: What the leavers say.* Unpublished doctoral dissertation, University of California at Berkeley.

Erickson, F., & Mohatt, J. (1982). Cultural organization of participant structure in two classrooms of Indian students. In G. D. Spindler (Ed.), *Doing the ethnography of schooling: Educational anthropology in action* (pp. 132–175). New York: Holt.

Erlich, K., & Soloway, E. (1984). An empirical investigation of the tacit plan knowledge in programming. In J. Thomas & M. L. Schneider (Eds.), *Human factors in computer systems.* Norwood, NJ: Ablex.

Esposito, D. (1973). Homogeneous and heterogeneous ability grouping: Principal findings and implications for evaluating and designing more effective educational environments. *Review of Educational Research, 43,* 163–179.

Eswara, H. S. (1972). Administration of reward and punishment in relation to ability, effort, and performance. *Journal of Social Psychology, 87,* 139–140.

Etaugh, C., & Brown, B. (1975). Perceiving the causes of success and failure of male and female performers. *Developmental Psychology, 11*, 103.

Everson, H., & Millsap, R. (1987, June). *Test anxiety and competency testing: A cognitive capacity view*. Paper presented at the annual meeting of the International Society for Test Anxiety Research, Bergen, Norway.

Everson, H., Millsap, R. E., & Browne, J. (1989). Cognitive interference or skills deficit: An empirical test of two competing theories of test anxiety. *Anxiety Research, 2*, 313–325.

Eysenck, M. W. (1988). Anxiety and attention. *Anxiety Research, 1*, 9–15.

Eysenck, M. W. (1989). Anxiety and cognition: Theory and research. In T. Archer & L.-G. Nilsson (Eds.), *Aversion, avoidance and anxiety: Perspectives on aversively motivated behavior*. Hillsdale, NJ: Erlbaum.

Falbo, T., & Beck, R. C. (1979). Naive psychology and the attributional model of achievement. *Journal of Personality, 47*, 185–195.

Farber, I. E., & Spence, K. W. (1953). Complex learning and conditioning as a function of anxiety. *Journal of Experimental Psychology, 45*, 120–125.

Farber, J. (1969). *Student as nigger*. No. Hollywood, CA: Contax.

Feather, N. T. (1961). The relationship of persistence at a task to expectation of success and achievement-related motives. *Journal of Abnormal and Social Psychology, 63*, 552–561.

Feather, N. T. (1963). Persistence at a difficult task with an alternative task of intermediate difficulty. *Journal of Abnormal and Social Psychology, 66*, 604–609.

Feather, N. T. (1965). The relationship of expectation of success to achievement and test anxiety. *Journal of Personality and Social Psychology, 1*, 118–126.

Feather, N. T. (1969). Attribution of responsibility and valence of success and failure in relation to initial confidence and task performance. *Journal of Personality and Social Psychology, 13*, 129–144.

Feather, N. T., & Simon, J. G. (1971). Causal attributions for success and failure in relation to expectations of success based upon selective or manipulative control. *Journal of Personality, 39*, 528–541.

Feigenbaum, E. A. (1970). Information processing and memory. In D. A. Norman (Ed.), *Models of human memory*. New York: Academic Press.

Feld, S. C., & Lewis, J. (1969). The assessment of achievement anxieties in children. In C. P. Smith (Ed.), *Achievement-related motives in children* (pp. 150–199). New York: Russell Sage Foundation.

Feldhusen, J. F., Treffinger, D. J., & Bahlke, S. J. (1970). Developing creative thinking: The Purdue creativity program. *Journal of Creative Behavior, 4*, 85–90.

Feldhusen, J. F., Speedie, S. M., & Treffinger, D. J. (1971). The Purdue Creative Thinking Program: Research and evaluation. *NSPI Journal 10*(3), 5–9.

Feldman, K. A. (1976). The superior college teacher from the students' view. *Research in Higher Education, 5*, 243–288.

Felsenthal, H. M. (1970). Sex differences in teacher–pupil interactions and their relationship with teacher attitudes and pupil reading achievement. *Dissertation Abstracts, 30*, 3781A–3782A.

Festinger, L. (1957). *A theory of cognitive dissonance*. Stanford: Stanford University Press.

Fetterman, D. (1990, June). Wasted genius. *Stanford Magazine, 18*(2), 31–32.

Fincham, F. D., & Cain, K. M. (1986). Learned helplessness in humans: A developmental analysis. *Developmental Review, 6*, 301–333.

Findley, M. J., & Cooper, H. M. (1983). Locus of control and academic achievement: A literature review. *Journal of Personality and Social Psychology, 44*, 419–427.

Findley, W. G., & Bryan, M. (1971). *Ability grouping: 1970 status, impact, and alternatives*. Athens: Center for Educational Improvement, University of Georgia. (ERIC Document Reproduction Service No. ED 060-595)

Finley, M. K. (1984). Teachers and tracking in a comprehensive high school. *Sociology of Education, 57,* 233–243.

Finnegan, W. (1990, September 10). Out there: I. A Reporter at Large, *The New Yorker,* pp. 51–86.

Fischer, C. (1982). *Ursachenerklärung im Unterricht* [Causal attribution in the classroom]. Köln, West Germany: Böhlau Verlag.

Flavell, J. H. (1976). Metacognitive aspects of problem solving. In L. B. Resnick (Ed.), *The nature of intelligence*. Hillsdale, NJ: Erlbaum.

Flavell, J. H. (1979). Metacognition and cognitive monitoring: A new area of cognitive-developmental inquiry. *American Psychologist, 34,* 906–911.

Flavell, J. H., Friedrichs, A. G., & Hoyt, J. D. (1970). Developmental changes in memorization processes. *Cognitive Psychology, 1,* 324–340.

Flavell, J. H., & Wellman, H. M. (1977). Metamemory. In R. V. Kail & J. W. Hagen (Eds.), *Perspectives on the development of memory and cognition*. Hillsdale, NJ: Erlbaum.

Folkman, S., & Lazarus, R. S. (1985). If it changes it must be a process: Study of emotion and coping during three stages of a college examination. *Journal of Personality and Social Psychology, 48,* 150–170.

Fontaine, G. (1974). Social comparison and some determinants of expected personal control and expected performance in a novel task situation. *Journal of Personality and Social Psychology, 29,* 487–496.

Ford, G. R. (1974, July 8). In defense of the competitive urge. *Sports Illustrated,* pp. 16–23.

Fordham, S., & Ogbu, J. U. (1986). Black students' school success: Coping with the burden of "acting white." *The Urban Review, 18,* 176–206.

Forrest-Pressley, D. L., MacKinnon, G. E., & Waller, T. G. (Eds.). (1985). *Metacognition, cognition, and human performance: Vol 1. Theoretical perspectives.* New York: Academic Press.

Foster, H. L. (1974). *Ribbin', jivin', and playin' the dozen: The unrecognized dilemma of inner-city schools*. Cambridge: Ballinger.

Franco, J. N. (1983). A developmental analysis of self-concept in Mexican-American and Anglo school children. *Hispanic Journal of Behavioral Sciences, 5,* 207–218.

Frankel, A., & Snyder, M. L. (1978). Poor performance following unsolvable problems: Learned helplessness or egotism? *Journal of Personality and Social Psychology, 36,* 1415–1423.

Frase, L. T. (1968). Effect of question location, pacing and mode upon retention of prose material. *Journal of Educational Psychology, 59,* 244–249.

Frase, L. T. (1970). Boundary condition for mathemagenic behaviors. *Review of Educational Research, 4,* 337–347.

Frederiksen, N. (1984). Implications of cognitive theory for instruction in problem solving. *Review of Educational Research, 54,* 363–407.

Fredriksen, N. (1989). Introduction. In N. Fredriksen, R. Glaser, A. Lesgold, & M. Shafto (Eds.), *Diagnostic monitoring of skill and knowledge acquisition* (pp. vii–xv). Hillsdale, NJ: Erlbaum.

Frederiksen, N., and J. R. Collins. (1989). A systems approach to educational testing. *Educational Researcher, 18*(9), 27–32.

Frey, D. (1978). Reactions to success and failure in public and in private conditions. *Journal of Experimental Social Psychology, 14,* 172–179.

Frey, K. S., & Ruble, D. N. (1985). What children say when the teacher is not around:

Conflicting goals in social comparison and performance assessment in the classroom. *Journal of Personality and Social Psychology, 48*, 550–562.

Friedman, S. L., Scholnick, E. K., & Cocking, R. R. (Eds.). (1986). *Blueprints for thinking: The role of planning in cognitive development.* New York: Cambridge University Press.

Friend, R. M., & Neale, J. M. (1972). Children's perceptions of success and failure: An attributional analysis of the effects of race and social class. *Developmental Psychology, 7*, 124–128.

Frieze, I. (1975). Women's expectations for and causal attributions of success and failure. In M. Mednick, S. Tangri, & L. Hoffman (Eds.), *Women and achievement: Social psychological perspectives.* New York: Holt, Rinehart & Winston.

Frieze, I. H. (1976). Causal attributions and information seeking to explain success and failure. *Journal of Research in Personality, 10*, 293–305.

Frieze, I. H., Fisher, J., Hanusa, B. H., McHugh, M. C., & Valle, V. A. (1978). Attribution of the causes of success and failure as internal and external barriers to achievement in women. In J. Sherman & F. Denmark (Eds.), *Psychology of women: Future directions of research* (pp. 519–552). New York: Psychological Dimensions.

Fyans, L. G., Maehr, M. L., Salili, F., & Desai, K. A. (1983). A cross-cultural exploration into the meaning of achievement. *Journal of Personality and Social Psychology, 44*, 1000–1013.

Fyans, L. J. (1979, July). *Test, anxiety, test comfort, and student achievement test performance.* Paper presented at the Educational Testing Service, Princeton, NJ.

Galassi, J. P., Frierson, H. T., & Sharer, R. (1981). Behavior of high, moderate, and low test anxious students during an actual test situation. *Journal of Consulting and Clinical Psychology, 49*, 51–62.

Galassi, J. P., Frierson, H. T., & Siegel, R. G. (1981). Cognitions, test anxiety, and test performance: A closer look. *Journal of Consulting and Clinical Psychology, 52*, 319–320.

Gamoran, A., & Berends, M. (1987). The effects of stratification in secondary schools: Synthesis of survey and ethnographic research. *Review of Educational Research, 57*, 415–435.

Ganzer, V. J. (1968). Effects of audience presence and test anxiety on learning and retention in a serial learning situation. *Journal of Personality and Social Psychology, 8*, 194–199.

Gardner, J. W. (1961). *Excellence: Can we be equal and excellent too?* New York: Harper & Row.

Gaskell, J., & Lazerson, M. (1980). *Between school and work: Perspectives of working class youth.* Vancouver: University of British Columbia.

Gatchel, R. J., Paulus, P. B., & Maples, C. W. (1975). Learned helplessness and self-reported affect. *Journal of Abnormal Psychology, 84*, 732–734.

Gaudry, E., & Poole, C. (1975). A further validation of the state–trait distinction in anxiety research. *Australian Journal of Psychology, 27*, 119–125.

Gaudry, E., & Spielberger, C. D. (1971). *Anxiety and educational achievement.* New York: Wiley.

Gay, G. (1986). Interaction of learner control and prior understanding in computer-assisted video instruction. *Journal of Educational Psychology, 78*, 225–227.

Georgia Department of Education. (1988). *Promotion and retention.* Atlanta, GA.

Geppert, U., & Kuster, U. (1982). The emergence of "wanting to do it oneself": A precursor of achievement motivation. *International Journal of Behavioral Development, 6*, 355–369.

Gergen, K. J. (1971). *The concept of self.* New York: Holt, Rinehart & Winston.

Getzels, J. W. (1975). Problem-finding and the inventiveness of solutions. *Journal of Creative Behavior, 9,* 12–18.

Ghiselin, B. (Ed.), (1955). *The creative process.* New York: Mentor.

Gibbs, J. T. (1985). City girls: Psychosocial adjustment of urban black adolescent females. *Sage, 2,* 28–36.

Gibran, K. (1957). *The prophet.* New York: Knopf.

Gick, M. L., & Holyoak, K. (1983). Schema induction and analogical transfer. *Cognitive Psychology, 15,* 1–38.

Gilbert, S. E., & Gay, G. (1985). Improving the success in school of poor black children. *Phi Delta Kappan, 66,* 133–137.

Giroux, H. (1983). *Theory and resistance in education.* Boston: Bergin & Garvey.

Gjesme, T. (1981). Is there any future in achievement motivation? *Motivation and Emotion, 5*(2), 115–138.

Glaser, R. (1984). Education and thinking: The role of knowledge. *American Psychologist, 39,* 93–104.

Glasser, W. (1969). *Schools without failure.* New York: Harper & Row.

Goldberg, L. R. (1965). Grades as motivants. *Psychology in the Schools, 2,* 17–24.

Goldman, R., Hudson, D., & Daharsh, B. (1973). Self-estimated task persistence as a nonlinear predictor of college success. *Journal of Educational Psychology, 65,* 216–221.

Gonzalez, H. P. (1976). *The effects of three treatment approaches on test anxiety, study habits and academic performance.* Unpublished masters thesis, University of South Florida, Tampa.

Gonzalez, H. P. (1987a). Effect of systematic desensitization, study counseling, and anxiety coping training in the treatment of test anxious students with good and poor study habits (Doctoral dissertation, University of South Florida, Tampa). *Dissertation Abstracts International, 39,* 1955B.

Gonzalez, H. P. (1987b). Systematic desensitization, study skills counseling, and anxiety coping training in the treatment of test anxiety. In C. D. Spielberger & P. R. Vagg (Eds.), *The assessment and treatment of test anxiety.* New York: McGraw-Hill.

Gottfredson, L. S. (1986). Societal consequences of the g factor in employment. *Journal of Vocational Behavior, 29,* 379–410.

Gottfredson, L. S., & Sharf, J. C. (1988). *Journal of Vocational Behavior* [Special issue], *33.* (3), 225–230.

Graham, S. (1984a). Communicating sympathy and anger to black and white children: The cognitive (attributional) consequences of affective cues. *Journal of Personality and Social Psychology, 47,* 14–28.

Graham, S. (1984b). Teacher feelings and student thoughts: An attributional approach to affect in the classroom. *The Elementary School Journal, 85,* 91–104.

Graham, S. (1988). Can attribution theory tell us something about motivation in blacks? *Educational Psychologist, 23,* 3–21.

Graham, S. (1990). The down side of help: An attributional-developmental analysis of helping behavior as a low-ability cue. *Journal of Educational Psychology, 82,* 7–14.

Graham, S., & Barker, G. P. (1990). The down side of help: An attributional-developmental analysis of helping behavior as a low-ability cue. *Journal of Educational Psychology, 82,* 7–14.

Graham, S., & Harris, K. R. (1987). Improving composition skills of inefficient learners with self-instructional strategy training. *Topics on Language Disorders, 7,* 66–77.

Grant, W. V., & Eiden, L. J. (1982). *Digest of education statistics 1982*. Washington, DC: National Center for Educational Statistics.

Greenberg, P. J. (1932). Competition in children: An experimental study. *American Journal of Psychology, 44*, 221–250.

Greenberger, E., & Steinberg, L. (1981). The workplace as a context for the socialization of youth. *Journal of Youth and Adolescence, 10*, 185–210.

Greenberger, E., & Steinberg, L. (1986). *When teenagers work*. New York: Basic Books.

Greer, M. R., & Blank, S. S. (1977). Cognitive style, conceptual tempo and problem solving: Modification through programmed instruction. *American Educational Research Journal, 45*, 295–315.

Grenis, M. (1975, November). II. Individualization, grouping, competition, and excellence. *Phi Delta Kappan, 57*, 199–200.

Griver, S. (1979, July 27). Coming close to curing leukemia. *Israel Digest, 22, 7*.

Groff, W. H. (1983). Impacts of the high technologies on vocational and technical education. *Annals of the American Academy of Political and Social Science, 470*, 81–94.

Grolnick, W. S., & Ryan, R. M. (1986). *Parent styles associated with children's school-related competence and adjustment*. Unpublished manuscript, University of Rochester.

Grubb, W. N. (1989). Preparing youth for work: The dilemmas of education and training programs. In D. Stern & D. Eichorn (Eds.), *Adolescence and work: Influences of social structure, labor markets, and culture* (pp. 13–45). Hillsdale, NJ: Erlbaum.

Grubb, W. N. (1990). Reconstructing the high school. *Educator*, The Graduate School of Education, University of California at Berkeley, *4*(3), 22–25.

Guilford, J. P. (1957). A revised structure of intellect. *Reports of the psychological laboratory, No. 19*. Los Angeles, CA: University of Southern California.

Gunderson, B., & Johnson, D. W. (1980). Building positive attitudes by using cooperative learning groups. *Foreign Language Annals, 13*, 39–46.

Haan, N. (1977). *Coping and defending: Processes of self-environment organization*. New York: Academic Press.

Hagtvet, K. A. (1974). *A generalizability study of the test anxiety construct* (Rep. No. 4 from a project concerning test anxiety). Unpublished manuscript, University of Oslo.

Hagtvet, K. A. (1980). *A domain approach to the study of test anxiety*. Paper presented at the Fourth International Symposium on Educational Testing, Antwerp, Belgium.

Hagtvet, K. A. (1983a). A construct validation study of test anxiety: A discriminant validation of fear of failure, worry and emotionality. In H. M. van der Ploeg, R. Schwarzer, & C. D. Spielberger (Eds.), *Advances in test anxiety research* (Vol. 3, pp. 15–34). Hillsdale, NJ: Erlbaum.

Hagtvet, K. A. (1983b). A measurement study of test anxiety emphasizing its evaluative context. In S. R. Irvin & J. W. Berry (Eds.), *Human assessment and cultural factors* (pp. 393–406). New York: Plenum.

Hagtvet, K. A. (1984). Fear of failure, worry and emotionality: Their suggestive causal relationships to mathematical performance and state anxiety. In H. M. van der Ploeg, R. Schwarzer, & C. D. Spielberger (Eds.), *Advances in test anxiety research* (Vol. 3, pp. 211–224). Hillsdale, NJ: Erlbaum.

Hagtvet, K. A. (1985). A three-dimensional test anxiety construct: Worry and emotionality as mediating factors between negative motivation and test behavior. In

J. J. Sanchez-Sosa (Ed.), *Health and Clinical Psychology* (pp. 109–133). Amsterdam: Elsevier (North Holland).

Hagtvet, K. A., & Min, Y. R. (1990, July). *A process analysis: The changing impact of ability, motivation and anxiety in cognitive performance.* Paper presented at the International Conference on Anxiety: Biological and Social Approach, Nieborov, Poland.

Haldeman, H. R. (1978). *The ends of power.* New York: Times Books.

Hall, J. (1971, November). Decisions. *Psychology Today, 5,* 51–54, 86, 88.

Hall, P. (1980). *Great planning disasters.* Berkeley: University of California Press.

Haller, E. P., Child, D. A., & Walberg, H. J. (1988, December). Can comprehension be taught? A quantitative synthesis of "metacognitive" studies. *Educational Researcher, 17,* 5–8.

Hallermann, B. (1980). *Anstrengungskalkulation: Bestimmungsstücke und Auswirkungen* (Calculation of effort: Determinants and consequences). Freiburg, Federal Republic of Germany: Hochschulverlag.

Hallermann, B., & Meyer, W. U. (1978). Persistenz in Abhängigkeit von wahrgenommener Begabung und Aufgabenschwierigkeit [Persistence in relation to perceived ability and task difficulty]. *Archiv für Psychologie, 130,* 335–341.

Hambleton, R. K., & Traub, R. E. (1974). The effects of item order on test performance and stress. *Journal of Experimental Education, 43,* 40–46.

Hamblin, R. L., Hathaway, C., & Wodarski, J. S. (1971). Group contingencies, peer tutoring, and accelerating academic achievement. In E. Ramp & W. Hopkins (Eds.), *A new direction for education: Behavior analysis* (pp. 41–53). Lawrence: University of Kansas.

Hamburg, D. (1986). *Toward health development in childhood and adolescence.* Charles M. & Martha Hitchcock Foundation Lectures, University of California, Berkeley.

Hamilton, J. O. (1974). Motivation and risk taking behavior: A test of Atkinson's theory. *Journal of Personality and Social Psychology, 29,* 856–864.

Hamilton, V. (1975). Socialization anxiety and information processing: A capacity model of anxiety-induced performance deficits. In I. G. Sarason & C. D. Spielberger (Eds.), *Stress and anxiety* (Vol. 2, pp. 45–68). Washington, DC: Hemisphere.

Hansen, D. A. (1989). Lesson evading and lesson dissembling: Ego strategies in the classroom. *American Journal of Education, 97,* 185–208.

Hansen, D. A., & Johnson, V. A. (1989). Classroom lesson strategies and orientations toward work. In D. Stern & D. Eichorn (Eds.), *Adolescence and work: Influences of social structure, labor markets, and culture* (pp. 75–99). Hillsdale, NJ: Erlbaum.

Hanushek, E. A. (1989). The impact of differential expenditures on school performance. *Educational Researcher, 18,* 45–51, 62.

Harackiewicz, J. M., Abrahams, S., & Wageman, R. (1987). Performance evaluation and intrinsic motivation: The effects of evaluative focus, rewards, and achievement orientation. *Journal of Personality and Social Psychology, 53,* 1015–1023.

Harackiewicz, J. M., & Manderlink, G. (1984). A process analysis of the effects of performance-contingent rewards on intrinsic motivation. *Journal of Experimental Social Psychology, 20,* 531–551.

Harari, O., & Covington, M. V. (1981). Reactions to achievement behavior from a teacher and student perspective: A developmental analysis. *American Educational Research Journal, 18,* 15–28.

Hardin, G. J. (1968). The tragedy of the commons. *Science, 162,* 1243–1248.

Hare, B. (1985). Stability and change in self-perception and achievement among black adolescents: A longitudinal study. *The Journal of Black Psychology, 11,* 29–42.

Harlow, J. F. (1953). Mice, monkeys, men, and motives. *Psychological Review, 60,* 23–32.

Harris, A. M., & Covington, M. V. (1989). *Cooperative team failure: A double threat for the low performer?* Unpublished manuscript, Department of Psychology, University of California at Berkeley.

Hart, M. (1976). *Sport in the sociocultural process* (2nd ed.). Dubuque, IA: William C. Brown.

Harter, S. (1974). Pleasure derived from cognitive challenge and mastery. *Child Development, 45,* 661–669.

Harter, S. (1981). A model of mastery motivation in children: Individual differences and developmental change. In A. Pick (Ed.), *Minnesota Symposium on Child Psychology* (Vol. 14). Hillsdale, NJ: Erlbaum.

Harvey, J. H., & Kelley, H. H. (1974). Sense of own judgmental competence as a function of temporal patterns of stability–instability in judgment. *Journal of Personality and Social Psychology, 29,* 526–538.

Hasselhorn, M., & Körkel, J. (1986). Metacognitive versus traditional reading instructions: The mediating role of domain-specific knowledge on children's text-processing. *Human Learning, 5,* 75–90.

Hayashi, T., Rim, Y., & Lynn, R. (1970). A test of McClelland's theory of achievement motivation in Britain, Japan, Ireland, and Israel. *International Journal of Psychology, 5,* 275–277.

Haycock, K. (1900, June). *Closing remarks.* Paper presented to the AAHE/College Board Conference on Mainstreaming University/School Partnerships, Chicago, IL.

Haycock, K., & Navarro, M. S. (1988, May). *Unfinished business: Fulfilling our children's promise* (Report from The Achievement Council, 1016 Castro Street, Oakland, CA 94607).

Hayes-Roth, B. (1980). *Human planning processes.* Rand Publications Series (R-2670-ONR), Santa Monica, CA.

Healey, G. W. (1970). Self-concept: A comparison of Negro-, Anglo-, and Spanish-American students across ethnic, sex, and socioeconomic variables (Doctoral dissertation, New Mexico State University, 1969). *Dissertation Abstracts International, 30,* 2849A.

Hebb, D. O. (1961). Distinctive features of learning in the higher mammal. In J. F. Delafresnaye (Ed.), *Brain mechanisms and learning.* London: Oxford University Press.

Heckhausen, H. (1977). Achievement motivation and its constructs: A cognitive model. *Motivation and Emotion, 1,* 283–329.

Heckhausen, H. (1982). Task-irrelevant cognitions during an exam: Incidence and effects. In H. W. Krohne & L. Laux (Eds.), *Achievement, stress, and anxiety* (pp. 247–274). Washington, DC: Hemisphere.

Heckhausen, H. (1984). Emergent achievement behavior: Some early developments. In J. Nicholls (Ed.), *Advances in motivation and achievement: Vol 3. The development of achievement motivation* (pp. 1–32). Greenwich, CT: JAI Press.

Heckhausen, H. (1986). Why some time out might benefit achievement motivation research. In J. H. L. van den Bercken, E. E. J. De Bruyn, & Th. C. M. Bergen (Eds.), *Achievement and task motivation* (pp. 7–39). Lisse, Netherlands: Swets & Zeitlinger.

Heckhausen, H., Schmalt, H.-D., & Schneider, K. (1985). *Achievement motivation in perspective* (M. Woodruff & R. Wicklund, Trans.). New York: Academic Press.

Heider, F. (1958). *The psychology of interpersonal relations.* New York: Wiley.

Heilman, M. E., & Stopeck, M. H. (1985). Attractiveness and corporate success:

Different causal attributions for males and females. *Journal of Applied Psychology, 70,* 379–388.

Heinrich, D. L., & Spielberger, C. D. (1982). Anxiety and complex learning. In H. W. Krohne & L. Laux (Eds.), *Achievement, stress and anxiety* (pp. 145–165). New York: Hemisphere.

Hellman, M., & Kram, D. (1978). Self-deprecating behavior in women – fixed or flexible: The effects of co-worker's sex. *Organizational Behavior and Human Performance, 22,* 497–507.

Helmke, A. (1986). Student attention during instruction and achievement. In S. E. Newstead, S. H. Irvine, & P. D. Dunn (Eds.), *Human assessment: Cognition and motivation.* Dordrecht, The Netherlands: Nijhoff.

Helmke, A. (1987). Mediating processes between children's self-concept of ability and mathematics achievement: A longitudinal study. Max Planck Institute for Psychological Research, Munich.

Helmke, A. (1988). The role of classroom context factors for the achievement-impairing effect of test anxiety. *Anxiety Research, 1,* 37–52.

Hembree, R. (1988). Correlates, causes, effects, and treatment of test anxiety. *Review of Educational Research, 58,* 47–77.

Hendricks, M., & Brickman, P. (1974). Effects of status and knowledgeability of audience on self-presentation. *Sociometry, 37,* 440–449.

Henry, J. (1957). Attitude organization in elementary school classrooms. *American Journal of Orthopsychiatry, 27,* 117–133.

Hermans, H. J. M., ter Laak, J. F., & Maes, C. J. M. (1972). Achievement motivation and fear of failure in family and school. *Developmental Psychology, 6,* 520–528.

Hernstein, R. J., Nickerson, R. S., de Sanchez, M., & Swets, J. A. (1986). Teaching thinking skills. *American Psychologist, 41,* 1279–1289.

Hess, R. D., Chang, C.-M., & McDevitt, T. M. (1987). Cultural variations in family beliefs about children's performance in mathematics: Comparisons among People's Republic of China, Chinese-American, and Caucasian-American families. *Journal of Educational Psychology, 79,* 179–188.

Hiebert, E., & Calfee, R. C. (1989). Advancing academic literacy through teachers' assessments. *Educational Leadership, 46*(7), 50–54.

Higgins, E. T. (1987). Self-discrepancy: A theory relating self and affect. *Psychological Review, 94,* 319–340.

Hill, K. T. (1977). The relation of evaluative practices to test anxiety and achievement motivation. *UCLA Educator, 19,* 15–21.

Hill, K. T. (1980). Motivation, evaluation and educational testing policy. In L. J. Fyans (Ed.), *Achievement motivation: Recent trends in theory and research.* New York: Plenum.

Hill, K. T. (1984). Debilitating motivation and testing: A major educational problem, possible solutions, and policy applications. In R. Ames & C. Ames (Eds.), *Research on motivation in education: Student motivation.* New York: Academic Press.

Hill, K. T., & Eaton, W. O. (1977). The interaction of test anxiety and success–failure experiences in determining children's arithmetic performance. *Developmental Psychology, 13,* 205–211.

Hill, K. T., & Horton, M. W. (1985). *Teaching and testing solutions to the problem of debilitating effects of test anxiety on test performance.* Unpublished manuscript, Institute for Child Behavior & Development, University of Illinois, Champaign, IL 61820.

Hill, K. T., & Sarason, S. B. (1966). The relation of test anxiety and defensiveness to test and school performance over the elementary school years. *Monographs of the Society for Research in Child Development, 31* (2, Serial No. 104).

Hill, K. T., & Wigfield, A. (1984). Test anxiety: A major educational problem and what can be done about it. *The Elementary School Journal, 85,* 105–126.

Hobfoll, S. E., Anson, O., & Bernstein, J. (1983). Anxiety reactions in two ego-threat situations of varying intensity. In H. M. van der Ploeg, R. Schwarzer, & C. D. Spielberger (Eds.), *Advances in test anxiety research* (Vol. 2, pp. 81–98). Hillsdale, NJ: Erlbaum.

Hodapp, V. (1989). Anxiety, fear of failure, and achievement: Two path-analytical models. *Anxiety Research, 1,* 301–312.

Hodapp, V., & Henneberger, A. (1983). Test anxiety, study habits, and academic performance. In H. M. van der Ploeg, R. Schwarzer, & C. D. Spielberger (Eds.), *Advances in test anxiety research* (Vol. 2, pp. 119–127). Hillsdale, NJ: Erlbaum.

Hoffman, M. L. (1982). Development of prosocial motivation: Empathy and guilt. In N. Eisenberg-Borg (Ed.), *Development of prosocial behavior* (pp. 281–313). New York: Academic Press.

Holland, J. H., Holyoak, K. J., Nisbett, R. E., & Thagard, P. R. (1986). *Induction: Processes of inference, learning, and discovery.* Cambridge: MIT Press.

Hollandsworth, J. G., Jr., Glazeski, R. C., Kirkland, K., Jones, G. E., & Van Norman, L. R. (1979). An analysis of the nature and effects of test anxiety: Cognitive, behavioral, and physiological components. *Cognitive Therapy and Research, 3,* 165–180.

Holloway, S. D. (1988). Concepts of ability and effort in Japan and the United States. *Review of Educational Research, 58,* 327–345.

Holroyd, K. A., Westbrook, T., Wolff, M., & Badhorn, E. (1978). Performance, cognition, and physiological responding in test anxiety. *Journal of Abnormal Psychology, 87,* 442–451.

Holt, J. (1964). *How children fail.* New York: Dell.

Homme, L. (1970). *How to use contingency contracting in the classroom.* Champaign, IL: Research Press.

Hoppe, F. (1930). Untersuchungen zur Handlungs – und Affektpsychologie IV [Psychological studies of action and affect IV: Success and failure]. Erfolg und Misserfolg *Psychologische Forschung, 14,* 1–63.

Hull, C. L. (1943). *Principles of behavior.* New York: Appleton-Century.

Hull, F. M., Friedman, N. S., & Rodgers, T. F. (1982). The effect of technology on alienation from work. *Sociology of Work and Occupations, 9,* 31–57.

Hullfish, G., & Smith, P. (1961). *Reflective thinking: The method of education.* New York: Dodd, Mead.

Hutt, M. L. (1947). "Consecutive" and "adaptive" testing with the revised Stanford-Binet. *Journal of Consulting Psychology, 11,* 93–104.

Hyland, M. E. (1988). Motivational control theory: An integrative framework. *Journal of Personality and Social Psychology, 55,* 642–651.

Jackson, P. W. (1968). *Life in classrooms.* New York: Holt, Rinehart & Winston.

Jaffe, A. J., & Froomkin, J. (1968). *Technology and jobs, automation in perspective.* New York: Praeger.

Jagacinski, C. M., & Nicholls, J. G. (1990). Reducing effort to protect perceived ability: They'd do it but I wouldn't. *Journal of Educational Psychology, 82,* 15–21.

Jamieson, D. W., Lydon, J. E., Stewart, G., & Zanna, M. P. (1987). Pygmalion revisited: New evidence for student expectancy effects in the classroom. *Journal of Educational Psychology, 79,* 461–466.

Jamieson, I., Miller, A., & Watts, A. G. (1988). *Mirrors of work: Work simulations in schools.* New York: Falmer.

Janis, I. L. (1982). *Groupthink* (2nd ed.). Boston: Houghton Mifflin.

Jerusalem, M. (1985). A longitudinal field study with trait worry and trait emotionality: Methodological problems. In H. M. van der Ploeg, R. Schwarzer, & C. D. Spielberger (Eds.), *Advances in test anxiety research* (Vol. 4, pp. 23–34). Lisse, Netherlands: Swets & Zeitlinger.

Jerusalem, M., Liepmann, D., & Herrmann, C. (1985). Test anxiety and achievement motivation: An analysis of causal relationships. In H. M. van der Ploeg, R. Schwarzer, & C. D. Spielberger (Eds.), *Advances in test anxiety research* (Vol. 4, pp. 135–146). Lisse, Netherlands: Swets & Zeitlinger.

Jervis, R. (1976). *Perception and misperception in international politics.* Princeton: Princeton University Press.

Jetter, J., & Davis, O. (1973). *Elementary school teachers' differential expectations of pupil achievements.* Paper presented at the annual meeting of the American Educational Research Association.

Johnson, D. W., Johnson, R. T., & Scott, L. (1978). The effects of cooperative and individualized instruction on students' attitudes and achievement. *The Journal of Social Psychology, 104,* 207–216.

Johnson, D. W., Johnson, R., Tiffany, M., & Zaidman, B. (1983). Are low achievers disliked in a cooperative situation? A test of rival theories in a mixed-ethnic situation. *Contemporary Educational Psychology, 8,* 189–200.

Johnson, D. W., Skon, L., & Johnson, R. (1980). Effects of cooperative, competitive, and individualistic conditions on children's problem-solving performance. *American Educational Research Journal, 17,* 83–93.

Johnson, R. T., Johnson, D. W., & Stanne, M. B. (1986). Comparison of computer-assisted cooperative, competitive, and individualistic learning. *American Educational Research Journal, 23,* 382–392.

Johnson, R. T., Johnson, D. W., & Stanne, M. B. (1985). Effects of cooperative, competitive, and individualistic goal structures on computer-assisted instruction. *Journal of Educational Psychology, 77,* 668–677.

Johnson, S. D. (1990). Teaching technical troubleshooting. *Educator,* The Graduate School of Education, University of California at Berkeley, *4*(3), 18–21.

Johnson, T. J., Feigenbaum, R., & Weiby, M. (1964). Some determinants and consequences of the teacher's perception of causation. *Journal of Educational Psychology, 55,* 237–246.

Jones, C. (1982, April). *High school and beyond: 1980 sophomore cohort first follow-up (1982) data file user's manual* (Report to the National Center for Educational Statistics, Contract OE 300-78-0208). Chicago: National Opinion Research Center.

Jones, E. E., & Nisbett, R. E. (1971). The actor and the observer: Divergent perceptions of the causes of behavior. In E. E. Jones, D. E. Kanouse, H. H. Kelley, R. E. Nisbett, S. Valins, & B. Weiner (Eds.), *Attribution: Perceiving the causes of behavior* (pp. 79–94). Morristown, NJ: General Learning Press.

Jussim, L. (1986). Self-fulfilling prophecies: A theoretical and integrative review. *Psychological Review, 93,* 429–445.

Juster, F. T. (1985). Preferences for work and leisure. In F. T. Juster & F. P. Stafford (Eds.), *Time, goods and well-being.* Ann Arbor: Institute for Social Research, The University of Michigan.

Kagan, S., & Knight, G. P. (1981). Social motives among Anglo-American and Mexican-American children. *Journal of Research in Personality, 15,* 93–106.

Kagan, S. (1977). Social motives and behaviors of Mexican-American and Anglo-American children. In J. D. Martinez (Ed.), *Chicano psychology*. New York: Academic Press.

Kagan, S., & Madsen, M. (1971). Cooperation and competition of Mexican, Mexican-American, and Anglo-American children of two ages under four instructional sets. *Developmental Psychology, 5,* 32–39.

Kahn, T. M. (1979, April). *A study of "strategic thinking" in high school students using the computer-based GAMEX system*. Paper presented at the annual meeting of the American Educational Research Association, San Francisco.

Kalechstein, P. B. W., Hocevar, D., & Kalechstein, M. (1988). Effects of test-wiseness training on test anxiety, locus of control and reading achievement in elementary school children. *Anxiety Research, 1,* 247–261.

Kalechstein, P., Kalechstein, M., & Doctor, R. (1981). The effects of instructions on test-taking skills in second grade black children. *Measurement and Evaluation in Guidance, 13,* 234–244.

Kanter, R. M. (1977). *Men and women of the corporation*. New York: Basic Books.

Kaplan, R. M., & Sacuzzo, D. P. (1982). *Psychological testing: Principles, applications and issues*. Monterey, CA: Brooks-Cole.

Kaplan, R. M., & Swant, S. G. (1973). Reward characteristics in appraisal of achievement behavior. *Representative Research in Social Psychology, 4,* 11–17.

Karabenick, S. A., & Heller, K. A. (1976). A developmental study of effort and ability attributions. *Developmental Psychology, 12,* 559–560.

Karabenick, S. A., & Knapp, J. R. (1988). Help seeking and the need for academic assistance. *Journal of Educational Psychology, 80,* 406–408.

Karabenick, S. A., & Youssef, Z. (1968). Performance as a function of achievement motive level and perceived difficulty. *Journal of Personality and Social Psychology, 10,* 414–419.

Katz, M. S. (1976). Two views of "teaching people to think." *Educational Theory, 26,* 158–164.

Keinan, G., & Zeidner, M. (1987). Effects of decisional control on state anxiety and achievement. *Personality and Individual Differences, 8,* 973–975.

Keller, G. (1983). *Academic strategy: The management revolution in higher education*. Baltimore: Johns Hopkins University Press.

Kelley, H. H. (1971a). *Attributions in social interactions*. Morristown, NJ: General Learning Press.

Kelley, H. H. (1971b). Causal schemata and the attribution process. In E. E. Jones et al. (Eds.), *Attribution: Perceiving the causes of behavior* (pp. 151–174).

Kelley, H. H. (1973). The processes of causal attribution. *American Psychologist, 28,* 107–128.

Kendall, P. C., & Hollon, S. P. (Eds.). (1981). *Assessment strategies for cognitive-behavioral interventions*. New York: Academic Press.

Kennedy, W. A., & Willcutt, H. C. (1964). Praise and blame as incentives. *Psychological Bulletin, 62,* 323–332.

Kestenbaum, J., & Weiner, B. (1970). Achievement performance related to achievement motivation and test anxiety. *Journal of Clinical and Consulting Psychology, 34,* 343–344.

Kirkland, K., & Hollandsworth, J. (1980). Effective test taking: Skills-acquisition versus anxiety-reduction techniques. *Journal of Counseling and Clinical Psychology, 48,* 431–439.

Kirschenbaum, H., Simon, S., & Napier, R. (1971). *Wa-ja-get? The grading game in American education*. New York: Hart.

Kirst, M. (1990, March). *Stanford Magazine,* p. 110.

Klein, D. C., Fencil-Morse, E., & Seligman, M. E. P. (1976). Learned helplessness, depression, and the attribution of failure. *Journal of Personality and Social Psychology, 33,* 508–516.

Klein, H. (1982, July 15). Pitting workers against each other often backfires, firms are finding. *Wall Street Journal,* p. 29.

Kleinfeld, J. (1972). Effective teachers of Eskimo and Indian students. *School Review, 83,* 301–344.

Knapp, R. H. (1960). Attitudes toward time and aesthetic choice. *Journal of Social Psychology, 56,* 79–87.

Knapp, R. H., & Green, H. B. (1961). The judgment of music-filled intervals and *n* achievement. *Journal of Social Psychology, 54,* 263–267.

Knight, G. P., & Kagan, S. (1977). Development of prosocial and competitive behaviors in Anglo-American and Mexican-American children. *Child Development, 48,* 1385–1394.

Knight, J. J. (1974). Instructional dysfunction and the temporary contract. *Educational Technology, 14*(4), 43–44.

Kohl, H. (1967). *36 children.* New York: New American Library.

Kohlmann, C.-W., Schumacher, A., & Streit, R. (1988). Trait anxiety and parental child-rearing behavior: Support as a moderator variable? *Anxiety Research, 1,* 53–64.

Kohn, A. (1986). *No contest: The case against competition.* Boston: Houghton-Mifflin.

Kolb, D. A. (1965). Achievement motivation training for underachieving high school boys. *Journal of Personality and Social Psychology, 2,* 783–792.

Krohne, H. W. (1980). Parental child-rearing behavior and the development of anxiety and coping strategies in children. In I. G. Sarason & C. D. Spielberger (Eds.), *Stress and anxiety* (Vol. 7, pp. 233–245). Washington, DC: Hemisphere.

Krohne, H. W. (1985). Entwicklungsbedingungen von Angstlichkeit und Angstbewältigung: Ein Zweiprozess-Modell elterlicher Erziehungswirkung [Determinants of the development of anxiousness and coping: A two-process model of child-rearing effects]. In H. W. Krohne (Ed.), *Angstbewältigung in Leistungssituationen* [Coping with anxiety in achievement contexts] (pp. 135–160). Weinheim: edition psychologie.

Krohne, H. W. (1990). Developmental conditions of anxiety and coping: A two-process model of child-rearing effects. *Mainzer Berichte zur Persönlichkeitsforschung* (No. 33). Johannes Gutenberg-Universität Mainz, Psychologisches Institut, Abteilung Persönlichkeitspsychologie, Mainz, Germany.

Krohne, H. W., Kohlmann, C.-W., & Leidig, S. (1986). Erziehungsstildeterminanten kindlicher Angstlichkeit, Kompetenzerwartungen und Kompetenzen [Effects of parenting styles on anxiousness, competence expectations, and competence in children]. *Zeitschrift für Entwicklungspsychologie und Pädagogische Psychologie, 18,* 70–88.

Kroll, M. D. (1988). Motivational orientations, views about the purpose of education, and intellectual styles. *Psychology in the Schools, 25,* 338–343.

Krumboltz, J. (1990, Jan.–Feb.). Do schools teach kids to hate learning? *Stanford Observer,* p. 10.

Kruglanski, A. W. (1975). The endogenous-exogenous partition in attribution theory. *Psychological Review, 42,* 449–496.

Kruglanski, A. W. (1978). Endogenous attribution and intrinsic motivation. In

M. Lepper & D. Greene (Eds.), *The hidden costs of reward: New perspectives on the psychology of human motivation.* Hillsdale, NJ: Erlbaum.

Kuhl, J., & Blankenship, V. (1979). Behavioral change in a constant environment: Shift to more difficult tasks with constant probability of success. *Journal of Personality and Social Psychology, 37,* 551–563.

Kukla, A. (1972). Foundation of an attributional theory of performance. *Psychological Review, 79,* 454–470.

Kulik, J. A., Kulik, C. C., & Cohen, P. A. (1979). A meta-analysis of outcome studies of Kellar's personalized system of instruction. *American Psychologist, 34,* 307–318.

Kulik, J. A., & McKeachie, W. J. (1975). The evaluation of teachers in higher education. In F. Kerlinger (Ed.), *Review of research in education* (Vol. 3, pp. 1–6). Itasca, IL: Peacock.

Kun, A. (1977). Development of the magnitude-covariation and compensation schemata in ability and effort attributions of performance. *Child Development, 48,* 862–873.

Kun, A., Parsons, J., & Ruble, D. (1974). Development of integration processes using ability and effort information to predict outcome. *Developmental Psychology, 10,* 721–732.

Kun, A., & Weiner, B. (1973). Necessary versus sufficient causal schemata for success and failure. *Journal of Research in Personality, 7,* 197–207.

Ladner, J. A. (1978). Growing up black. In J. H. Williams (Ed.), *Psychology of women: Selected writings* (pp. 212–224). New York: Norton.

Lafitte, R. G., Jr. (1984). Effects of item order on achievement test scores and students' perception of test difficulty. *Teaching of Psychology, 11,* 212–213.

Lampert, M. (1986). Knowing, doing, and teaching multiplication. *Cognition and Instruction, 3,* 305–342.

Larkin, J. H. (1982). The cognition of learning physics. *American Journal of Physics, 49,* 534–541.

Larkin, J. J., McDermott, J., Simon, D. P., & Simon, H. A. (1980). Modes of competence in solving physics problems. *Cognitive Science, 4,* 317–345.

Lasker, H. M. (1966). *Factors affecting responses to achievement motivation training in India.* Unpublished honors thesis, Harvard College.

Laux, L. (1987). A self-presentational view of test anxiety. In R. Schwarzer, H. M. van der Ploeg, & C. D. Spielberger (Eds.), *Advances in test anxiety research* (Vol. 5, pp. 31–37). Hillsdale, NJ: Erlbaum.

Laux, L., & Glanzmann, P. (1987). A self-presentational view of test anxiety. In R. Schwarzer, H. M. van der Ploeg, & C. D. Spielberger (Eds.), *Advances in test anxiety research* (Vol. 5, pp. 31–37). Hillsdale, NJ: Erlbaum.

Lave, J. (1988). *Cognition in practice.* New York: Cambridge University Press.

Lazarus, R. S. (1966). *Psychological stress and the coping process.* New York: McGraw-Hill.

Lazarus, R. S. (1982). Thoughts on the relations between emotion and cognition. *American Psychologist, 37,* 1019–1024.

Lazarus, R. S. (1983). The costs and benefits of denial. In S. Breznitz (Ed.), *The denial of stress* (pp. 1–30). New York: International Universities Press.

Lazarus, R. S. (1984). On the primacy of cognition. *American Psychologist, 39,* 124–129.

Lefevre, C. A. (1964). *Linguistics and the teaching of reading.* New York: McGraw-Hill.

Lefkowitz, J., & Fraser, A. (1980). Assessment of achievement and power motivation of blacks and whites, using a black and white TAT, with black and white administrators. *Journal of Applied Psychology, 65,* 685–696.

Leinhardt, G., & Greeno, J. G. (1986). The cognitive skill of teaching. *Journal of Educational Psychology, 78,* 75–95.

Lekarczyk, D. T., & Hill, K. T. (1969). Self-esteem, test anxiety, and verbal learning. *Developmental Psychology, 1,* 147–154.

Lens, W. (1983). Fear of failure and ability test performance. In J. Helmick & S. B. Anderson (Eds.), *On educational testing: Intelligence, performance standards, test anxiety and latent traits.* San Francisco: Jossey-Bass.

Lens, W., & De Volder, M. (1980). Achievement motivation and intelligence test scores: A test of the Yerkes-Dodson hypothesis. *Psychologia Belgica, 20,* 49–59.

Leonard, G. B. (1968). *Education and ecstasy.* New York: Delacorte.

Leonard, W. H. (1980). Using the extended discretion approach in biology laboratory investigations. *The American Biology Teacher, 42,* 338–348.

Leonard, W. H., Cavana, G. R., & Lowery, L. F. (1981). An experimental test of an extended discretion approach for high school biology laboratory investigations. *Journal of Research in Science Teaching, 18,* 497–504.

Lepper, M. R. (1981). Intrinsic and extrinsic motivation in children: Detrimental effects of superfluous social controls. In W. A. Collins (Ed.), *Minnesota Symposia on Child Psychology* (Vol. 14, pp. 145–214). Hillsdale, NJ: Erlbaum.

Lepper, M. R. (1988). Motivational considerations in the study of instruction. *Cognition and Instruction, 5*(4), 289–309.

Lepper, M. R., & Greene, D. (Eds.). (1978). *The hidden costs of reward: New perspectives on the psychology of human motivation.* Hillsdale, NJ: Erlbaum.

Lepper, M. R., Greene, D., & Nisbett, R. E. (1973). Undermining children's intrinsic interest with extrinsic rewards: A test of the "overjustification" hypothesis. *Journal of Personality and Social Psychology, 28,* 129–137.

Leppin, A., Schwarzer, R., Belz, D., Jerusalem, M., & Quast, H.-H. (1987). Causal attribution patterns of high and low test-anxious students. In R. Schwarzer, H. M. van der Ploeg, & C. D. Spielberger (Eds.), *Advances in test anxiety research* (Vol. 5, pp. 67–86). Hillsdale, NJ: Erlbaum.

Levin, B. B. (1990). *Portfolio assessment: Implications for the communication of effort and ability in alternative forms of assessment.* Unpublished paper, School of Education, University of California at Berkeley.

Levin, H., & Rumberger, R. (1983). The low-skill future of high-tech. *Technology Review, 86,* 18–21.

Levin, H. M. (1986). *Educational reform for disadvantaged students: An emerging crisis.* West Haven, CT: NEA Professional Library.

Levin, H. M. (1988, April). *Structuring schools for greater effectiveness with educationally disadvantaged or at-risk students.* Paper presented at the American Educational Research Association Annual Meeting, New Orleans.

Levin, J. (1983, May). When winning takes all. *Ms.,* 92–94, 138–139.

Levine, R., Reis, H. T., Sue, E., & Turner, G. (1976). Fear of failure in males: A more salient factor than fear of success in females? *Sex Roles, 2,* 389–398.

Lewin, K. (Ed.). (1948). *Resolving social conflicts. Selected papers on group dynamics.* New York: Harper & Brothers.

Lewin, K., Dembo, T., Festinger, L., & Sears, P. (1944). Level of aspiration. In J. McV. Hunt (Ed.), *Personality and the behavior disorders* (Vol. 1). New York: Ronald.

Lewin-Epstein, N. (1981). *Youth employment during high school.* Washington, DC: National Center for Education Statistics.

Lewinsohn, P. H., & Libet, J. M. (1972). Pleasant events, activity schedules and depression. *Journal of Abnormal Psychology, 79,* 291–295.

Lewis, M. A., & Cooney, J. B. (1986, April). *Attributional and performance effects of competitive and individualistic feedback in computer assisted mathematics instruction.* Paper presented at the Annual Meeting of the American Educational Research Association, San Francisco.

Lewis, M. V., Gardner, J. S., & Seitz, P. (1983). *High school work experience and its effects.* Columbus, OH: National Center for Research in Vocational Education, Ohio State University.

Licht, B. G., Kistner, J. A., Ozkaragoz, T., Shapiro, S., & Clausen, L. (1985). Causal attributions of learning disabled children: Individual differences and their implications for persistence. *Journal of Educational Psychology, 77,* 208–216.

Liebert, R. M., & Morris, L. W. (1967). Cognitive and emotional components of test anxiety: A distinction and some initial data. *Psychological Reports, 20,* 975–978.

Lin, Y.-G., & McKeachie, W. J. (1970). Aptitude, anxiety, study habits, and academic achievement. *Journal of Counseling Psychology, 17,* 306–309.

Linkskold, S. (1978). Trust development, the GRIT proposal, and the effects of conciliatory acts on conflict and cooperation. *Psychological Bulletin, 85,* 772–793.

Lipman, M. (1976). Philosophy for children. *Metaphilosophy, 7,* 17–39.

Lipman, M. (1985). Thinking skills fostered by the middle-school Philosophy for Children Program. In J. Segal, S. Chipman, & R. Glaser (Eds.), *Thinking and learning skills. Vol. 1: Relating instruction to basic research* (pp. 83–107). Hillsdale, NJ: Erlbaum.

Lipman, M., Sharp, A. M., & Oscanyan, F. S. (1977). *Ethical inquiry: Instructional manual to accompany Lisa.* Upper Montclair, NJ: IAPC.

Litwin, G. H., & Ciarlo, J. A. (1961). Achievement motivation and risk-taking in a business setting (Technical Report). New York: General Electric Company, Behavioral Research Service.

Locke, E. A. (1968). Toward a theory of task motivation and incentives. *Organizational Behavior and Human Performance, 3,* 157–189.

Locke, E. A., & Latham, G. P. (1984). *Goal setting: A motivational technique that works!* Englewood Cliffs, NJ: Prentice-Hall.

Lodico, M. G., Ghatala, E. S., Levin, J. R., Pressley, M., & Bell, J. A. (1983). Effects of meta-memory training on children's use of effective learning strategies. *Journal of Experimental Child Psychology, 35,* 263–277.

Loper, A. B., & Murphy, D. M. (1985). Cognitive self-regulatory training for underachieving children. In D. L. Forrest-Pressley, G. E. MacKinnon, & T. G. Waller (Eds.), *Metacognition, cognition, and human performance* (Vol. 2, pp. 223–265). New York: Academic Press.

Lundgren, U. P. (1977). *Model analysis of pedagogical processes.* Stockholm, Sweden: Stockholm Institute of Education.

Lutkenhaus, P., Bullock, M., & Geppert, U. (1984). Toddler's actions, knowledge, control, and the self. In F. Halish & J. Kuhl (Eds.), *Motivation, intention, and volition* (pp. 145–161). Berlin: Springer-Verlag.

MacKinnon, D. W. (1962). The nature and nurture of creative talent. *American Psychologist, 17,* 484–495.

Madsen, M. C. (1967). Cooperative and competitive behavior of children in three Mexican subcultures. *Psychological Reports, 20,* 1307–1320.

Madsen, M. C., & Shapira, A. (1970). Cooperative and competitive behavior of urban Afro-American, Mexican-American, and Mexican village children. *Developmental Psychology, 3,* 16–20.

Maehr, M. (1974). *Sociocultural origins of achievement.* Monterey, CA: Brooks/Cole.

Maehr, M. (1976). Continuing motivation: An analysis of seldom considered educational outcome. *Review of Educational Research, 46,* 443–462.

Maehr, M. L. (1989). Thoughts about motivation. In C. Ames & R. Ames (Eds.), *Research on motivation in education* (Vol. 3). New York: Academic Press.

Maehr, M. L. (1991). The "psychological environment" of the school: A focus for school leadership. In P. Thurston & P. Zodhiates (Eds.), *Advances in educational administration* (pp. 51–81). Greenwich, CT: JAI Press.

Maehr, M. L., & Braskamp, L. A. (1986). *The motivation factor: A theory of personal investment.* Lexington, MA: D. C. Heath & Co.

Maehr, M. L., & Midgley, C. (in press). Enhancing student motivation: A school-wide approach. *Educational Psychologist.*

Maehr, M. L., & Nicholls, C. (1980). Culture and achievement motivation: A second look. In N. Warren (Ed.), *Studies in cross-cultural psychology* (Vol. 2, pp. 221–267). New York: Academic Press.

Maehr, M. L., & Stallings, W. M. (1972). Freedom from external evaluation. *Child Development, 43,* 177–185.

Maller, J. B. (1929). Cooperation and competition: An experimental study in motivation. New York: Teachers' College, Columbia University.

Malone, T. W. (1981a). Toward a theory of intrinsically motivating instruction. *Cognitive Science, 4,* 333–369.

Malone, T. W. (1981b, April). *What makes things fun to learn? A study of intrinsically motivating computer games.* Paper presented at the American Education Research Association Annual Meeting, Los Angeles, California.

Man, F., Blahus, P., & Spielberger, C. D. (1989). The relationship of test anxiety to intelligence and academic performance. In F. Halisch & H. H. L. Van Den Bercken (Eds.), *International perspectives on achievement and task motivation* (pp. 183–191). Amsterdam: Swets & Zeitlinger.

Man, F., & Hrabal, V. (1988). Self-concept of ability, social consequences anxiety, and attribution as correlates of action control. In F. Halisch & J. H. L. van den Bercken (Eds.), *Achievement and task motivation.* Lisse, The Netherlands: Swets & Zeitlinger/Erlbaum.

Manchester, W. (1983). *The last lion: Winston Spencer Churchill.* Boston: Little, Brown.

Mandler, G., & Sarason, S. (1952). A study of anxiety and learning. *Journal of Abnormal and Social Psychology, 47,* 166–173.

Mansfield, R. S., Busse, T. V., & Krepelka, E. J. (1978). The effectiveness of creativity training. *Review of Educational Research, 48,* 517–536.

Marchant, G. J. (1990, April). *Intrinsic motivation, self-perception, and their effects on black urban elementary students.* Paper presented at the American Educational Research Association Annual Meeting, Boston, MA.

Marecek, J., & Mettee, D. R. (1972). Avoidance of continued success as a function of self-esteem, level of esteem certainty, and responsibility for success. *Journal of Personality and Social Psychology, 22,* 98–107.

Markus, H. (1977). Self-schemata and processing information about the self. *Journal of Personality and Social Psychology, 35,* 63–78.

Marshall, H. H. (1988, December). Work or learning: Implications of classroom metaphors. *Educational Researcher, 9,* 9–16.

Marshall, H. H., & Weinstein, R. S. (1984). Classroom factors affecting students' self-evaluations: An interactional model. *Review of Educational Research, 54,* 301–325.

Marston, A. R. (1968). Dealing with low self-confidence. *Educational Research* (Great Britain), *10,* 134–138.

Martire, J. G. (1956). Relationships between the self-concept and differences in the strength and generality of achievement motivation. *Journal of Personality, 24,* 364–375.

Maslow, A. H. (1970). *Religions, values, and peak-experiences.* New York: Viking.

Maugh, T. (1987, March 4). Gifted reported dropping out. *San Francisco Chronicle,* p. F7.

Mayer, R. E. (1989). Models for understanding. *Review of Educational Research, 59,* 43–64.

McCaslin, M., & Good, T. (1990, November). *Motivational effects of classroom management.* Paper presented at Hard Work and Higher Expectations: A Conference on Student Motivation, sponsored by the U.S. Department of Education Office of Educational Research and Improvement, Arlington, VA.

McClellan, J. (1978). What is a futurist? *Futures Information Exchange, 2,* 1–2.

McClelland, D. C. (1955). Some social consequences of achievement motivation. In M. R. Jones (Ed.), *Nebraska symposium on motivation* (Vol. 3, pp. 41–65). Lincoln: University of Nebraska Press.

McClelland, D. C. (1958a). Methods of measuring human motivation. In J. W. Atkinson (Ed.), *Motives in fantasy, action, and society* (pp. 7–42). Princeton, NJ: Van Nostrand.

McCelland, D. C. (1958b). The importance of early learning in the formation of motives. In J. W. Atkinson (Ed.), *Motives in fantasy, action, and society* (pp. 437–452). Princeton, NJ: Van Nostrand.

McClelland, D. C. (1961). *The achieving society.* Princeton, NJ: Van Nostrand.

McClelland, D. C. (1965). Toward a theory of motive acquisition. *American Psychologist, 20,* 321–333.

McClelland, D. C. (1972). What is the effect of achievement motivation training in the schools? *Teachers College Record, 74,* 129–145.

McClelland, D. C. (1980). Motive dispositions: The merits of operant and respondent measures. In L. Wheeler (Ed.), *Review of personality and social psychology* (Vol. 1, pp. 10–41). Beverly Hills, CA: Sage.

McClelland, D. C. (1985). How motives, skills, and values determine what people do. *American Psychologist, 40,* 812–825.

McClelland, D. C., Atkinson, J. W., Clark, R. A., & Lowell, E. L. (1953). *The achievement motive.* New York: Appleton-Century-Crofts.

McClelland, D. C., & Winter, D. G. (1969). *Motivating economic achievement.* New York: The Free Press.

McClintock, C. G. (1974). Development of social motives in Anglo-American and Mexican-American children. *Journal of Personality and Social Psychology, 29,* 348–354.

McCombs, B. L. (1984). Process and skills underlying continuing intrinsic motivation to learn: Toward a definition of motivational skills training interventions. *Educational Psychologist, 19,* 199–218.

McCombs, B. L. (1987, April). *Issues in the measurement by standardized tests of primary motivational variables related to self-regulated learning.* Paper presented at the American Educational Research Association Annual Meeting, Washington, DC.

McCordick, S. M., Kaplan, R. M., Finn, M. E., & Smith, S. H. (1979). Cognitive behavioral modification and modeling for test anxiety. *Journal of Consulting and Clinical Psychology, 47,* 419–420.

McGraw, K. O. (1978). The detrimental effects of reward on performance: A literature review and a prediction model. In M. R. Lepper & D. Greene (Eds.), *The hidden costs of reward: New perspectives on the psychology of human motivation* (pp. 33–60). Hillsdale, NJ: Erlbaum.

McGuire, E. & Lund, L. (1984). *The role of business in precollege education.* Washington, DC: The Conference Board.

McInerney, D. M. (1988). *Cross-cultural studies of achievement motivation: Educational implications and research directions for the future.* Macarthur Institute of Higher Education, Sydney, Australia.

McKeachie, W. J., Pintrich, P. R., & Lin, Y.-G. (1985). Teaching learning strategies. *Educational Psychologist, 20,* 153–160.

McMahan, I. D. (1973). Relationships between causal attributions and expectancy of success. *Journal of Personality and Social Psychology, 28,* 108–114.

McNabb, T. (1987). *The effects of strategy and effort attribution training on the motivation of subjects differing in perceived math competence and attitude toward strategy and effort.* Unpublished manuscript, The American College Testing Program, Iowa City, IA.

McPeck, J. (1981). *Critical thinking and education.* New York: St. Martin's.

Mecca, A. M., Smelser, N. J., & Vasconcellos, J. (Eds.). (1989). *The social importance of self-esteem.* Berkeley: University of California Press.

Meece, J., Wigfield, A., & Eccles, J. S. (1990). Predictors of math anxiety and its influence on young adolescents' course enrollment intentions and performance in mathematics. *Journal of Educational Psychology, 82,* 60–70.

Mergendoller, J., Marchman, V., Mitman, A., & Packer, M. (1988). Task demands and accountability in middle-grade science classes. *Elementary School Journal, 88,* 251–265.

Merton, R. K. (1949). *Social theory and social structure.* Glencoe, IL: Free Press.

Mettee, D. R. (1971). Rejection of unexpected success as a function of the negative consequences of accepting success. *Journal of Personality and Social Psychology, 17,* 332–341.

Metz, M. H. (1978). *Classrooms and corridors.* Berkeley: University of California Press.

Mueller, D. J. (1976). Mastery learning: Partly boon, partly boondoggle. *Teachers College Record, 78,* 41–52.

Meunier, C., & Rule, B. G. (1967). Anxiety, confidence and conformity. *Journal of Personality, 35,* 498–504.

Meyer, J. P. (1980). Causal attribution for success and failure: A multivariate investigation of dimensionality, formation and consequences. *Journal of Personality and Social Psychology, 38,* 704–718.

Meyer, W.-U. (1970). *Selbstverantwortlichkeit und leistungs.* Unpublished doctoral dissertation, Ruhr Universität, Bochum, Germany.

Meyer, W.-U., Bachmann, M., Biermann, U., Hempelmann, M., Plöger, F. O., & Spiller, H. (1979). The informational value of evaluative behavior: Influences of praise and blame on perceptions of ability. *Journal of Educational Psychology, 71,* 259–268.

Meyer, W.-U., Folkes, V., & Weiner, B. (1976). The perceived informational value and affective consequences of choice behavior and intermediate difficulty task selection. *Journal of Research in Personality, 10,* 410–423.

Michaels, J. W. (1977). Classroom reward structure and academic performance. *Review of Educational Research, 47*, 87–98.

Midgley, C., & Feldlaufer, H. (1987). Students' and teachers' decision-making fit before and after the transition to junior high school. *Journal of Early Adolescence, 7*, 225–241.

Midgley, C., Feldlaufer, H., & Eccles, J. S. (1988). The transition to junior high school: Beliefs of pre- and post-transition teachers. *Journal of Youth and Adolescence, 17*, 543–562.

Miller, A. T. (1986). A developmental study of the cognitive basis of performance impairment after failure. *Journal of Personality and Social Psychology, 49*, 529–538.

Miller, D. T. (1978). What constitutes a self-serving attributional bias? A reply to Bradley. *Journal of Personality and Social Psychology, 36*, 1221–1223.

Miller, D. T., & Ross, M. (1975). Self-serving biases in the attribution of causality: Fact or fiction? *Psychological Bulletin, 82*, 213–225.

Miller, I. W., III, & Norman, W. H. (1979). Learned helplessness in humans: A review and attribution-theory model. *Psychological Bulletin, 86*, 93–118.

Miller, L. K., & Hamblin, R. L. (1963). Interdependence, differential rewarding, and productivity. *American Sociological Review, 28*, 768–778.

Miller, R. L., Brickman, P., & Bolen, D. (1975). Attribution versus persuasion as a means for modifying behavior. *Journal of Personality and Social Psychology, 31*, 430–441.

Millroy, W. L. (1991). An ethnographic study of the mathematical ideas of a group of carpenters. *Learning and Individual Differences, 3*, 1–25.

Mincer, J. (1989, May). Human capital and the labor market: A review of current research. *Educational Researcher, 18*, 27–34.

Mineka, S., & Henderson, R. W. (1985). Controllability and predictability in acquired motivation. *Annual Review of Psychology, 36*, 495–529.

Mineka, S., & Kihlstrom, J. F. (1978). Unpredictable and uncontrollable events: A new perspective on experimental neurosis. *Journal of Abnormal Psychology, 87*, 256–271.

Mischel, W. (1960). *Delay of gratification, need for achievement and acquiescence in another culture.* Unpublished paper. Cambridge: Harvard University.

Mischel, W., & Liebert, R. M. (1966). Effects of discrepancies between observed and imposed reward criteria on their acquisition and transmission. *Journal of Personality and Social Psychology, 3*, 45–53.

Mitchell, D., & Spady, W. (1978). Organizational contexts for implementing outcome based education. *Educational Researcher, 7*, 9–17.

Mitchell, K. R., & Eng, K. T. (1972). Effects of group counseling and behavior therapy on the academic achievement of test-anxious students. *Journal of Counseling Psychology, 19*, 491–497.

Mitchell, K. R., Hall, R. F., & Piatkowska, O. E. (1975). A group program for the treatment of failing college students. *Behavioral Therapy, 6*, 324–336.

Mizokawa, D. T., & Ryckman, D. B. (1988, April). *Attributions of academic success and failure to effort or ability: A comparison of six Asian American ethnic groups.* Paper presented at the annual meeting of the American Educational Research Association, New Orleans.

Moerk, E. (1974). Age and epogenic influences on aspirations of minority group children. *Journal of Counseling Psychology, 21*, 294–298.

Monte, C. F., & Fish, J. M. (1989). The fear-of-failure personality and academic cheating. In R. Schwarzer, H. M. van der Ploeg, & C. D. Spielberger (Eds.),

Advances in test anxiety research (Vol. 6, pp. 87–103). Lisse, Netherlands: Swets & Zeitlinger.

Moore, J. W., Hauck, W. E., & Gagne, E. D. (1973). Acquisition, retention, and transfer in an individualized college physics course. *Journal of Educational Psychology, 64,* 335–340.

Moran, J. D., III, McCullers, J. C., & Fabes, R. A. (1984). Developmental analysis of the effects of reward on selected Wechsler subscales. *American Journal of Psychology, 97,* 205–214.

Moreno, J. M., & Hogan, J. D. (1976). The influence of race and social-class level on the training of creative thinking and problem-solving abilities. *Journal of Educational Research, 70,* 91–95.

Morgan, M. (1984). Reward-induced decrements and increments in intrinsic motivation. *Review of Educational Research, 54,* 5–30.

Morris, L. W., Brown, N. R., & Halbert, B. (1977). Effects of symbolic modeling on the arousal of cognitive and affective components of anxiety in preschool children. In C. D. Spielberger & I. G. Sarason (Eds.), *Stress and anxiety* (Vol. 4). Washington, DC: Hemisphere.

Morris, L. W., Davis, M. A., & Hutchings, C. H. (1981). Cognitive and emotional components of anxiety: Literature review and a revised worry-emotionality scale. *Journal of Educational Psychology, 73,* 541–555.

Morris, L. W., & Engle, W. B. (1981). Assessing various coping strategies and their effects on test performance and anxiety. *Journal of Clinical Psychology, 37,* 165–171.

Morris, L. W., Finkelstein, C. S., & Fisher, W. R. (1976). Components of school anxiety: Developmental trends and sex differences. *Journal of Genetic Psychology, 128,* 49–57.

Morris, L. W., & Fulmer, R. S. (1976). Test anxiety (worry and emotionality) changes during academic testing as a function of feedback and test importance. *Journal of Educational Psychology, 68,* 817–824.

Morris, L. W., Harris, E. W., & Rovins, D. S. (1981). Interactive effects of generalized and situational expectancies on the arousal of cognitive and emotional components of social anxiety. *Journal of Research in Personality, 15,* 302–311.

Morris, L. W., Kellaway, D. S., & Smith, D. H. (1978). The Mathematics Anxiety Rating Scale: Predicting anxiety experiences and academic performance in two groups of students. *Journal of Educational Psychology, 70,* 589–594.

Morris, L. W., & Liebert, R. M. (1973). Effects of negative feedback, threat of shock, and level of trait anxiety on the arousal of two components of anxiety. *Journal of Counseling Psychology, 20,* 321–326.

Morris, L. W., & Perez, T. L. (1972). Effects of interruption on emotional expression and performance in a testing situation. *Psychological Reports, 31,* 559–564.

Morris, R. (1977). *Increasing participation through the use of normative interventions.* Unpublished doctoral dissertation, Stanford University.

Moulton, R. W. (1965). Effects of success and failure on level of aspiration as related to achievement motives. *Journal of Personality and Social Psychology, 1,* 399–406.

Mullis, I. V. S. (1980). *Using the primary trait system for evaluating writing. National Assessment of Educational Progress Report.* Denver, CO: Education Commission of the States.

Murlidharan, R., & Topa, V. (1970). Need for achievement and independence training. *Indian Journal of Psychology, 45,* 1–21.

Murray, H. A. (1943). *Thematic Apperception Test Manual*. Cambridge: Harvard University Press.

Mussen, P. T. (1953). Differences between TAT responses of Negro and white boys. *Journal of Consulting Psychology, 17*, 373–376.

National Academy of Sciences, Panel on Secondary School Education for the Changing Workplace (1984). *High school and the changing workplace, the employer's view*. Washington, DC: National Academy Press.

National Assessment of Educational Progress (1979). *Changes in mathematical achievement, 1973–78*. Denver: NAEP.

National Assessment of Educational Progress (1981). *Reading, thinking and writing: Results from the 1979–80 national assessment of reading and literature*. Denver: NAEP.

National Commission on Excellence in Education (1983). *A nation at risk: The imperative for educational reform*. Washington, DC: U.S. Department of Education.

National Council of Teachers of Mathematics (1980). *An agenda for action: Recommendations for school mathematics of the 1980's*. Reston, VA: NCTM.

National Research Council (1979). *The state of school science*. Washington, DC: Commission on Human Resources.

Naveh-Benjamin, M. (1985). *A comparison of training programs intended for different types of test-anxious students*. Paper presented at symposium on information processing and motivation, American Psychological Association, Los Angeles.

Naveh-Benjamin, M., McKeachie, W. J., & Lin, Y. G. (1987). Two types of test-anxious students: Support for an information processing model. *Journal of Educational Psychology, 79*, 131–136.

Neimark, E., Slotnick, N. S., & Ulrich, T. (1971). The development of memorization strategies. *Developmental Psychology, 5*, 427–432.

Nelson, L. L., & Kagan, S. (1972, September). Competition: The star-spangled scramble. *Psychology Today*, pp. 53–56, 90–91.

Nelson-Le Gall, S. (1985). Help-seeking behavior in learning. In E. W. Gordon (Ed.), *Review of research in education* (Vol. 12, pp. 55–90). Washington, DC: American Educational Research Association.

Nevin, A., Johnson, D. W., & Johnson, R. (1982). Effects of group and individual contingencies on academic performance and social relations of special needs students. *Journal of Social Psychology, 116*, 41–59.

Newell, A., & Simon, H. A. (1972). *Human problem solving*. Englewood Cliffs, NJ: Prentice-Hall.

Newman, R. S. (1990). Children's help-seeking in the classroom: The role of motivational factors and attitudes. *Journal of Educational Psychology, 82*, 71–80.

Newman, R. S., & Goldin, L. (1990). Children's reluctance to seek help with schoolwork. *Journal of Educational Psychology, 82*, 92–100.

Nicholls, J. G. (1972). Creativity in the person who will never produce anything original and useful: The concept of creative as a normally distributed trait. *American Psychologist, 27*, 717–727.

Nicholls, J. G. (1975). Causal attributions and other achievement-related cognitions: Effects of task outcome, attainment values, and sex. *Journal of Personality and Social Psychology, 31*, 379–389.

Nicholls, J. G. (1976a). Effort is virtuous, but it's better to have ability: Evaluative responses to perceptions of ability and effort. *Journal of Research in Personality, 10*, 306–315.

Nicholls, J. G. (1976b). When a scale measures more than its name denotes: The case of the Test Anxiety Scale for Children. *Journal of Consulting and Clinical Psychology, 44,* 976–985.

Nicholls, J. G. (1978). The development of the conceptions of effort and ability, perception of academic attainment, and the understanding that difficult tasks require more ability. *Child Development, 49,* 800–814.

Nicholls, J. G. (1984). Achievement motivation: Concepts of ability, subjective experience, task choice, and performance. *Psychological Review, 91,* 328–346.

Nicholls, J. G. (1989). *The competitive ethos and democratic education.* Cambridge: Harvard University Press.

Nicholls, J. G., Patashnick, M., & Nolen, S. B. (1985). Adolescents' theories of education. *Journal of Educational Psychology, 77,* 683–692.

Nickerson, R., Perkins, D. N., & Smith, E. C. (1985). *The teaching of thinking.* Hillsdale, NJ: Erlbaum.

Nixon, R. M. (1962). *Six crises.* Garden City, NY: Doubleday.

Nobles, W. W., & Traver, S. (1976). Black parental involvement in education: The African connection. In *Child welfare and child development: Alton M. Childs Series* (pp. 23–36). Atlanta: Atlanta University School of Social Work.

Nolen, S. B. (1987, April). *The hows and whys of studying: The relationship of goals to strategies.* Paper presented at the annual meeting of the American Educational Research Association, Washington, DC.

Nolen, S. B. (1988). Reasons for studying: Motivational orientations and study strategies. *Cognition and Instruction, 5*(4), 269–287.

Noll, J. O. (1955). An investigation of the relation of anxiety to learning and retention. *Dissertation Abstracts, 15,* 1916A.

Nouwen, H. (1975). Reaching out, the three movements of the spiritual life. New York: Doubleday.

Nuttin, J. (1984). *Motivation, planning and action: A relational theory of behavior dynamics.* Hillsdale, NJ: Erlbaum.

Nuttin, J., & Lens, W. (1985). *Future time perspective and motivation: Theory and research method.* Hillsdale, NJ: Erlbaum.

Oakes, J. (1985). *Keeping track: How schools structure inequality.* New Haven, CT: Yale University Press.

Oakes, J. (1987, October). *Improving inner-city schools: Current directions in urban district reform.* New Brunswick: The State University of New Jersey–Rutgers and The Rand Corporation.

Ogbu, J. U. (1974). *The next generation: An ethnography of education in an urban neighborhood.* New York: Academic Press.

Ogbu, J. U. (1978). *Minority education and caste: The American system in cross-cultural perspective.* New York: Academic Press.

Oka, E. R., & Paris, S. G. (1987). Patterns of motivation and reading skills in underachieving children. In S. J. Ceci (Ed.), *Handbook of cognitive, social, and neuropsychological aspects of learning disabilities* (Vol. 2, pp. 115–145). Hillsdale, NJ: Erlbaum.

Okebukola, P., & Ogunniyi, M. (1984). Cooperative, competitive and individualistic science laboratory interactions patterns – Effects on students' achievement and acquisition of practical skills. *Journal of Research in Science Teaching, 21,* 875–884.

Olsen, C. (1991). *Achievement orientation and context effects on intensive motivation for learning a task.* Unpublished doctoral dissertation, University of California at Berkeley.

Olton, R. M., & Crutchfield, R. S. (1969). Developing the skills of productive thinking. In P. Mussen, J. Langer, & M. V. Covington (Eds.), *Trends and issues in developmental psychology* (pp. 68–91). New York: Holt, Rinehart & Winston.

Olton, R. M., Wardrop, J. L., Covington, M. V., Goodwin, W. L., Crutchfield, R. S., Klausmeier, H. J., & Ronda, T. (1967). *The development of productive thinking skills in fifth-grade children* (Tech. Rep.). Madison, WI: The University of Wisconsin, Research and Development Center for Cognitive Learning.

Omelich, C. L. (1974). *Attribution and achievement in the classroom: The self-fulfilling prophecy*. Paper presented at the meeting of the California Personnel and Guidance Association, San Francisco.

Orlick, T. (1982). *The second cooperative sports & games book*. New York: Pantheon.

Ornstein, R., & Ehrlich, P. (1989). *New world new mind*. New York: Doubleday.

Osterman, P. (1989). The job market for adolescents. In D. Stern & D. Eichorn (Eds.), *Adolescence and work: Influences and social structure, labor markets, and culture* (pp. 235–256). Hillsdale, NJ: Erlbaum.

Palermo, D. S., Castaneda, A., & McCandless, B. R. (1956). The relationship of anxiety in children to performance in a complex learning task. *Child Development, 27*, 333–337.

Paris, S. G., & Byrnes, J. P. (1989). The constructivist approach to self-regulation and learning in the classroom. In B. Zimmerman & D. Schunk (Eds.), *Self-regulated learning and academic achievement: Theory, research, and practice*. New York: Springer-Verlag.

Paris, S. G., Cross, D. R., & Lipson, M. Y. (1984). Informed strategies for learning: A program to improve children's reading awareness and comprehension. *Journal of Educational Psychology, 76*, 1239–1252.

Paris, S. G., Lipson, M. Y., & Wixson, K. K. (1983). Becoming a strategic reader. *Contemporary Educational Psychology, 8*, 293–316.

Paris, S. G., & Oka, E. R. (1986). Children's reading strategies, metacognition, and motivation. *Developmental Review, 6*, 25–56.

Parsons, J., & Ruble, D. (1977). The development of achievement-related expectancies. *Child Development, 48*, 1075–1079.

Parsons, J. E., Meece, J. L., Adler, T. F., & Kaczala, C. M. (1982). Sex differences in attributions and learned helplessness. *Sex Roles, 8*, 421–432.

Paterson, D. (1956). *The conservation of human talent*. Walter Van Dyke Bingham Lecture, Ohio State University, Columbus.

Patterson, J. (1987). *1987 and beyond: Choices for the future*. The Center for Educational Planning, Santa Clara County Office of Education, 100 Skyport Drive, San Jose, CA 95115.

Paulman, R. G., & Kennelly, K. J. (1984). Test anxiety and ineffective test taking: Different names, same construct. *Journal of Educational Psychology, 76*, 279–288.

Payne, B. D., Smith, J. E., & Payne, D. A. (1983). Sex and ethnic differences in relationships of test anxiety to performance in science examinations by fourth and eighth grade students: Implications for valid interpretations of achievement test scores. *Educational and Psychological Measurement, 43*, 267–270.

Pekrun, R. (1984). An expectancy-value model of anxiety. In H. M. van der Ploeg, R. Schwarzer, & C. D. Spielberger (Eds.), *Advances in test anxiety research* (Vol. 3, pp. 53–72). Hillsdale, NJ: Erlbaum.

Pekrun, R. (1988). Anxiety and motivation in achievement settings: Towards a system-theoretical approach. *International Journal of Educational Research* [Special issue], 307–323.

Pedhazur, E. J. (1982). *Multiple regression in behavioral research: Explanation and prediction* (2nd ed.). New York: Holt, Rinehart & Winston.

Pepitone, E. A. (1972). Comparison behavior in elementary school children. *American Educational Research Journal, 9,* 45–63.

Perkins, D. N. (1982). General cognitive skills: Why not? In S. Chipman, J. Segal, & R. Glaser (Eds.), *Thinking and learning skills: Current research and open questions.* Hillsdale, NJ: Erlbaum.

Perkins, D. N., & Salomon, G. (1987). Transfer and teaching thinking. In D. Perkins, J. Lockhead, & J. Bishop (Eds.), *Thinking: The Second International Conference* (pp. 285–303). Hillsdale, NJ: Erlbaum.

Perkins, D. N., & Salomon, G. (1988). Teaching for transfer. *Educational Leadership, 46*(1), 22–32.

Perkins, D. N., & Salomon, G. (1989, Jan.–Feb.). Are cognitive skills context-bound? *Educational Researcher,* pp. 16–25.

Perry, R. P. (1981). *Educational seduction: Some implications for teaching evaluation and improvement* (Rep. No. 7). Vancouver, British Columbia, Canada: University of British Columbia, Center for Improving Teaching and Evaluation.

Perry, R. P., & Dickens, W. J. (1984). Perceived control in the college classroom: Response-outcome contingency training and instructor expressiveness effects on student achievement and causal attributions. *Journal of Educational Psychology, 76,* 966–981.

Perry, R. P., & Magnusson, J.-L. (1987). Effective instruction and students' perceptions of control in the college classroom: Multiple-lectures effect. *Journal of Educational Psychology, 79,* 453–460.

Phase, E. J. (1976). *Locus of control in personality.* Morristown, NJ: General Learning Press.

Philips, S. U. (1972). Participant structure and communicative competence: Warm springs children in community and classroom. In C. Cazden, D. Hymes, & W. J. John (Eds.), *Functions of language in the classroom* (pp. 370–394). New York: Teachers College Press.

Phye, G. D., & Andre, T. (Eds.). (1986). *Educational psychology: Vol. 3. Cognitive classroom learning: Understanding, thinking, and problem solving.* New York: Academic Press.

Piaget, J. (1950). *The psychology of intelligence.* London: Routledge & Kegan Paul.

Pintrich, P. R. (1988). A process-oriented view of student motivation and cognition. In J. S. Stark & L. Mets (Eds.), *Improving teaching and learning through research: New directions for institutional research, 57* (pp. 55–70). San Francisco: Jossey-Bass.

Pintrich, P. R. (1989). The dynamic interplay of student motivation and cognition in the college classroom. In C. Ames & M. Maehr (Eds.), *Advances in motivation and achievement* (Vol. 6, pp. 117–160). Greenwich, CT: JAI Press.

Pintrich, P. R., & De Groot, E. V. (1990). Motivational and self-regulated learning components of classroom academic performance. *Journal of Educational Psychology, 82,* 33–40.

Pittman, T. S., Boggiano, A. K., & Ruble, D. N. (1983). Intrinsic and extrinsic motivational orientations: Interactive effect of reward, competence feedback, and task complexity. In J. Levine & M. Wang (Eds.), *Teacher and student perceptions: Implications for learning* (pp. 319–340). Hillsdale, NJ: Erlbaum.

Plass, J. A., & Hill, K. T. (1986). Children's achievement strategies and test performance: The role of time pressure, evaluation anxiety, and sex. *Developmental Psychology, 22,* 31–36.

Polson, P. G., & Jeffries, R. (1985). Instruction in general problem-solving skills: An evaluation. In J. Segal, S. Chipman, & R. Glaser (Eds.), *Thinking and learning skills: Relating instruction to basic research* (pp. 417–455). Hillsdale, NJ: Erlbaum.

Porter, A. (1989). A curriculum out of balance: The case of elementary school mathematics. *Educational Researcher, 18,* 9–15.

Postman, L. (1975). Test of the generality of the principle of encoding specificity. *Memory and Cognition, 6,* 663–672.

Powell, A. G., Farrar, E., & Cohen, D. K. (1985). *The shopping mall high school: Winners and losers in the educational marketplace.* Boston: Houghton Mifflin.

Pratte, R. (1988). *The civic imperative: Examining the need for civic education.* New York: Teachers College Press.

Prendergast, W. F. (1986). Terminology of problem solving. *Teaching Thinking & Problem Solving, 8*(2), 1–3, 6–7.

President's Newsletter (1986, April). Dream No Small Dreams, *Phi Delta Kappan,* No. 5.

Pressley, M., Borkowski, J. G., & O'Sullivan, J. T. (1984). Memory strategy instruction is made of this: Metamemory and durable strategy use. *Educational Psychologist, 19,* 94–107.

Pressley, M., Borkowski, J. G., & O'Sullivan, J. T. (1985). Children's metamemory and the teaching of memory strategies. In D. L. Forrest-Pressley, G. E. MacKinnon, & T. G. Waller (Eds.), *Metacognition, cognition, and human performance* (pp. 111–153). New York: Academic Press.

Rainwater, L. (1975). *Behind the ghetto walls: Black families in a federal slum.* Chicago: Aldine.

Ramirez, M., & Castaneda, A. (1974). *Cultural democracy, biocognitive development, and education.* New York: Academic Press.

Ramirez, M., III, & Price-Williams, D. R. (1976). Achievement motivation in children of three ethnic groups in the United States. *Journal of Cross-Cultural Psychology, 7,* 49–61.

Rand, P., Lens, W., & Decock, B. (1991). Negative motivation is half the story: Achievement motivation combines positive and negative motivation. *Scandinavian Journal of Educational Research, 35,* 13–30.

Raven, B. H., & Eachus, T. M. (1963). Cooperation and competition in means-independent triads. *Journal of Abnormal and Social Psychology, 28.* 768–778.

Raynor, J. O. (1969). Future orientation and motivation of immediate activity: An elaboration of the theory of achievement motivation. *Psychological Review, 76,* 606–610.

Raynor, J. O. (1970). Relationships between achievement-related motives, future orientation, and academic performance. *Journal of Personality and Social Psychology, 15,* 28–33.

Raynor, J. O. (1982). Motivational determinants of music-related behavior: Psychological careers of student, teacher, performer, and listener. In J. O. Raynor & E. E. Entin (Eds.), *Motivation, career striving, and aging* (pp. 309–329). Washington, DC: Hemisphere.

Raynor, J. O., & Entin, E. E. (1982). *Motivation, career striving, and aging.* Washington, DC: Hemisphere.

Reagan, D. (1990, November). Personal communication.

Reasoner, R. W. (1973). A matter of priority. *California School Boards, 32,* 24–28.

Reasoner, R. W. (1986). *Building self-esteem.* Consulting Psychologists Press, 557 College Ave., Palo Alto, CA 94306.

Reich, R. B. (1983). *The next American frontier*. New York: Times Books.

Reich, R. B. (1989, January). Must new economic vigor mean making do with less? *NEA Today*, 13–19.

Reiss, S., & Sunshinsky, L. W. (1975). Overjustification, competing responses, and the acquisition of intrinsic interest. *Journal of Personality and Social Psychology, 31*, 1116–1125.

Resnick, D. P., & Resnick, L. B. (1985). The nature of literacy: An historical exploration. *Harvard Educational Review, 48*, 370–385.

Resnick, L. (1987). *Education and learning to think*. Washington, DC: National Research Council, National Academy Press.

Resnick, L. B., & Glaser, R. (1976). Problem solving and intelligence. In L. B. Resnick (Ed.), *The nature of intelligence*. Hillsdale, NJ: Erlbaum.

Rest, S., Nierenberg, R., Weiner, B., & Heckhausen, H. (1973). Further evidence concerning the effects of perceptions of effort and ability on achievement evaluation. *Journal of Personality and Social Psychology, 28*, 187–191.

Reuman, D. A. (1988). *How social comparison mediates effects of ability grouping in mathematics on achievement expectancies*. Paper presented at the Annual Meeting of the American Education Research Association, New Orleans, LA.

Reuman, D. A., MacIver, D., Eccles, J., & Wigfield, A. (1987, April). *Changes in students' math motivation and behavior at the transition to junior high school*. Paper presented at the annual meeting of the American Educational Research Association, Washington, DC.

Reusser, K. (1987, March). Problem solving beyond the logic of things. Cited in A. H. Schoenfeld, *On mathematics as sense making: An informal attack on the unfortunate divorce of formal and informal mathematics*. Paper presented at OERI/LRCD Conference on Informal Reasoning and Education, Pittsburgh, PA.

Riessman, F. (1988, Summer). Transforming the schools: A new paradigm. *Social Policy*, pp. 2–4.

Richmond, B. O., & Weiner, G. P. (1973). Cooperation and competition among young children as a function of ethnic grouping, grade, sex, and reward condition. *Journal of Educational Psychology, 64*, 329–334.

Ripple, R. E., & Darcey, J. (1967). The facilitation of problem solving and verbal creativity by exposure to programmed instruction. *Psychology in the Schools, 4*, 240–245.

Rist, R. C. (1970). Student social class and teacher expectations: The self-fulfilling prophecy in ghetto education. *Harvard Educational Review, 40*, 411–450.

Roberts, B., & Covington, M. V. (1991). *The myth of Hermes*. Unpublished manuscript, Institute of Personality Assessment and Research, University of California, Berkeley.

Rocklin, T., & O'Donnell, A. M. (1986, August). *Self-adapted testing: A performance-improving variant of computerized adaptive testing*. Paper presented as a poster at the annual meeting of the American Psychological Association, Washington, DC.

Rogan, J. (1988). Development of a conceptual framework of heat. *Science Education, 72*, 103–113.

Rohrkemper, M., & Bershon, B. (1984). The quality of student task engagement: Elementary school students' reports of the causes and effects of problem difficulty. *Elementary School Journal, 88*, 299–312.

Rohwer, W. D., Jr. (1984). An invitation to a developmental psychology of studying. In F. J. Morrison, C. A. Lord, & D. P. Keating (Eds.), *Advances in applied developmental psychology* (Vol. 1, pp. 75–114). New York: Academic Press.

Rolheiser-Bennett, N. (1986). *Four models of teaching: A meta-analysis of student outcomes.* Unpublished doctoral dissertation, University of Oregon, Eugene. (University Microfilms No. 87-05887)

Rosen, B. C., & D'Andrade, R. (1959). The psychosocial origins of achievement motivation. *Sociometry, 22,* 185–218.

Rosen, R. (1959). Race, ethnicity, and the achievement syndrome. *American Sociological Review, 24,* 47–60.

Rosenbaum, J. E. (1976). *Making inequality: The hidden curriculum of high school tracking.* New York: Wiley.

Rosenbaum, J. E. (1980). Track misperceptions and frustrated college plans: An analysis of the effects of tracks and track perceptions in the National Longitudinal Survey. *Sociology of Education, 53,* 74–88.

Rosenbaum, M. E. (1980). Cooperation and competition. In P. B. Paulus (Ed.), *Psychology of group influence* (pp. 291–326). Hillsdale, NJ: Erlbaum.

Rosenbaum, R. M. (1972). *A dimensional analysis of the perceived causes of success and failure.* Unpublished doctoral dissertation, University of California, Los Angeles.

Rosenberg, J. (1965). *Society and the adolescent self-image.* Princeton, NJ: Princeton University Press.

Rosenberg, M., & Simmons, R. G. (1973). *Black and white self-esteem: The urban school child.* Washington, DC: American Sociological Association.

Rosenfield, D., & Stephan, W. G. (1978). Sex differences in attributions for sex-typed tasks. *Journal of Personality, 46,* 244–259.

Rosenholz, R. S., & Rosenholz, S. J. (1981). Classroom organization and the perception of ability. *Sociology of Education, 54,* 132–140.

Rosenholz, S. J., & Simpson, C. (1984a). Classroom organization and student stratification. *Elementary School Journal, 85,* 1–17.

Rosenholz, S. J., & Simpson, C. (1984b). The formation of ability conceptions: Developmental trend or social construction? *Review of Educational Research, 54,* 31–64.

Rosenholz, S. J., & Wilson, B. (1980). The effect of classroom structure on shared perceptions of ability. *American Educational Research Journal, 17,* 75–82.

Rosenthal, R. (1987). Pygmalion effects: Existence, magnitude, and social importance. *Educational Researcher, 16*(9), 37–41.

Rosenthal, R., & Jacobson, L. (1968). *Pygmalion in the classroom: Teacher expectation and pupils' intellectual development.* New York: Holt, Rinehart & Winston.

Ross, M., Karniol, R., & Rothstein, M. (1976). Reward contingency and intrinsic motivation in children: A test of the delay of gratification hypothesis. *Journal of Personality and Social Psychology, 33,* 442–447.

Rothblum, E. D., Solomon, L. J., & Murakami, J. (1986). Affective, cognitive and behavioral differences between high and low procrastinators. *Journal of Counseling Psychology, 33,* 387–394.

Rowe, M. (1972). *Wait-time and rewards as instructional variables: Their influence on language, logic, and fate-control.* Paper presented at the meeting of the National Association for Research in Science Teaching.

Rubin, H. L. (1980). *Competing: Understanding and winning the strategic games we all play.* New York: Lippincott & Crowell.

Ruble, D., Parsons, J., & Ross, J. (1976). Self-evaluative responses of children in an achievement setting. *Child Development, 47,* 990–997.

Rumberger, R,. & Daymont, T. (1984). The economic value of academic and vocational training acquired in high school. In M. Borus (Ed.), *Youth and the labor market: Analyses of the national longitudinal survey* (pp. 157–192). Kalamazoo, MI: W. E. Upjohn Institute for Employment Research.

Russell, W. J. (1988, March). Editorial: Presidential campaigns and educational policy. *Educational Researcher, 17*(2), 4, 12.

Rustemeyer, R. (1984). Selbsteinschätzung eigener Fähigkeit – vermittelt durch die Emotionen anderer Personen. *Zeitschrift für Entwicklungspsychologie und Pädagogische Psychologie, 16,* 149–161.

Ryals, K. R. (1969). *An experimental study of achievement motivation training as a function of the moral maturity of trainees.* Unpublished doctoral dissertation, Washington University, St. Louis, MO.

Sadler, W. A., Jr. (1976). Competition out of bounds: Sport in American life. In M. Hart (Ed.), *Sport in the sociocultural process* (2nd ed.). Dubuque, IA: William C. Brown.

Sagotsky, G., Wood-Schneider, M., & Konop, M. (1981). Learning to cooperate: Effects of modeling and direct instruction. *Child Development, 52,* 1037–1042.

Salamé, R. (1984). Test anxiety: Its determinants, manifestations and consequences. In H. M. van der Ploeg, R. Schwarzer, & C. D. Spielberger (Eds.), *Advances in test anxiety research* (Vol. 3, pp. 83–119). Hillsdale, NJ: Erlbaum.

Sanders, M., Scholz, J. P., & Kagan, S. (1976). Three social motives and field independence-dependence in Anglo-American and Mexican-American children. *Journal of Cross-Cultural Psychology, 7,* 451–461.

Sapp, G. L. (1971). *The application of contingency management systems to the classroom behavior of Negro adolescents.* Paper presented at the meeting of the American Personnel and Guidance Association, Atlantic City.

Sarason, I. G. (1961). The effects of anxiety and threat on the solution of a difficult task. *Journal of Abnormal and Social Psychology, 62,* 165–168.

Sarason, I. G. (1988). Anxiety, self-preoccupation and attention. *Anxiety Research, 1,* 3–7.

Sarason, I. G., & Potter, E. H., III. (1983, December 12). Self-monitoring: Cognitive processes and performance. Technical Report prepared for Office of Naval Research, 800 North Quincy St., Arlington, VA 22217.

Sarason, S. B., Lighthall, F. F., Davidson, K. S., Waite, R. R., & Ruebush, B. K. (1960). *Anxiety in elementary school children.* New York: Wiley.

Sarnacki, F. E. (1979). An examination of test-wiseness in the cognitive test domain. *Review of Educational Research, 4,* 252–279.

Saxe, G. B. (1988). Candy selling and math learning. *Educational Researcher, 17,* 14–21.

Schachter, S., & Singer, J. E. (1962). Cognitive, social and physiological determinants of emotional state. *Psychological Review, 69,* 379–399.

Schlenker, B. (1975). Self-presentation: Managing the impression of consistency when reality interferes with self-enhancement. *Journal of Personality and Social Psychology, 32,* 1030–1037.

Schmalt, H. D. (1982). Two concepts of fear of failure motivation. In R. Schwarzer, H. M. van der Ploeg, & C. D. Spielberger (Eds.), *Advances in test anxiety research* (Vol. 1, pp. 45–52). Lisse, The Netherlands: Swets & Zeitlinger.

Schneider, D. J. (1969). Tactical self-presentation after success and failure. *Journal of Personality and Social Psychology, 13,* 262–268.

Schneider, S. H. (1989). *Global warming.* San Francisco: Sierra Club Books.

Schnur, A. E. (1981). *The assessment of academic self-management skills in adolescents.* Unpublished Ph.D. dissertation, University of California, Berkeley.

Schoenfeld, A. H. (1985). *Mathematical problem solving.* New York: Academic Press.

Schoenfeld, A. H. (1987). What's all the fuss about metacognition? In A. H. Schoenfeld (Ed.), *Cognitive Science and Mathematics Education* (pp. 189–215). Hillsdale, NJ: Erlbaum.

Schoenfeld, A. H. (1989). *Reflections on doing and teaching mathematics.* Paper presented at a conference, Mathematical Thinking and Problem Solving, Berkeley, CA.

Schoenfeld, A. H. (1991). On mathematics as sense-making: An informal attack on the unfortunate divorce of formal and informal mathematics. In J. Voss, D. N. Perkins, & J. Segal (Eds.), *Informal reasoning and education* (pp. 311–343). Hillsdale, NJ: Erlbaum.

Schönpflug, W. (1982). Aspiration level and causal attribution under noise stimulation. In H. W. Krohne & L. Laux (Eds.), *Achievement, stress, and anxiety* (pp. 291–314). Washington, DC: Hemisphere.

Schönpflug, W. (1985). Goal-directed behavior as a source of stress: Psychological origins and consequences of inefficiency. In M. Frese & J. Sabini (Eds.), *Goal-directed behavior: The concept of action in psychology.* Hillsdale, NJ: Erlbaum.

Schönpflug, W. (1986). Effort regulation and individual differences in effort expenditure. In G. R. J. Hockey, A. W. K. Gaillard, & M. G. H. Coles (Eds.), *Energetics and human information processing* (pp. 271–285). Dordrecht, The Netherlands: Nighoff.

Schorr, L. B. (1988). *Within our reach: Breaking the cycle of disadvantage.* New York: Anchor/Doubleday.

Schulenberg, J. E., Asp, C. E., & Petersen, A. C. (1984). School from the young adolescent's perspective: A descriptive report. *Journal of Early Adolescence, 4,* 107–130.

Schuman, H., Walsh, E., Olson, C., & Etheridge, B. (1985). Effort and reward: The assumption that college grades are affected by quantity of study. *Social Forces, 63,* 945–966.

Schunk, D. H. (1983). Ability versus effort attributional feedback: Differential effects on self-efficacy and achievement. *Journal of Educational Psychology, 74,* 548–556.

Schunk, D. H. (1984). Self-efficacy perspective on achievement behavior. *Educational Psychologist, 19,* 48–58.

Schwarzer, R., & Cherkes-Julkowski, M. (1982). Determinants of test anxiety and helplessness. In R. Schwarzer, H. M. van der Ploeg, & C. D. Spielberger (Eds.), *Advances in test anxiety research* (Vol. 1, pp. 33–43). Hillsdale, NJ: Erlbaum.

Schwarzer, R., Jerusalem, M., & Schwarzer, C. (1983). Self-related and situation-related cognitions in test anxiety and helplessness: A longitudinal analysis with structural equations. In H. M. van der Ploeg, R. Schwarzer, & C. D. Spielberger (Eds.), *Advances in test anxiety research* (Vol. 2, pp. 35–43). Hillsdale, NJ: Erlbaum.

Schwarzer, R., Jerusalem, M., & Stiksrud, A. (1984). The developmental relationship between test anxiety and helplessness. In H. M. van der Ploeg, R. Schwarzer, and C. D. Spielberger (Eds.), *Advances in test anxiety research* (Vol. 3, pp. 73–79). Hillsdale, NJ: Erlbaum.

Schwarzer, R., Seipp, B., & Schwarzer, C. (1989). Mathematics performance and anxiety: A meta-analysis. In R. Schwarzer, H. M. van der Ploeg, & C. D. Spielberger (Eds.), *Advances in test anxiety research* (Vol. 6, pp. 105–119). Lisse, Netherlands: Swets & Zeitlinger.

Scribner, S. (1984). Studying working intelligence. In B. Rogoff & J. Lave (Eds.), *Everyday cognition: Its development in social context* (pp. 9–40). Cambridge: Harvard University Press.

Sears, P. S. (1940). Levels of aspiration in academically successful and unsuccessful children. *Journal of Abnormal and Social Psychology, 35*, 498–536.

Secord, P. F., & Backman, C. W. (1961). Personality theory and the problem of stability and change in individual behavior: An interpersonal approach. *Psychological Review, 68*, 21–32.

Secord, P. F., & Backman, C. W. (1965). An interpersonal approach to personality. In B. A. Maher (Ed.), *Progress in experimental personality research* (Vol. 1). New York: Academic Press.

Segal, J., Chipman, S., & Glaser, R. (Eds.). (1984). *Thinking and learning skills. Vol. 1: Relating instruction to basic research.* Hillsdale, NJ: Erlbaum.

Seipp, B. (1991). Anxiety and academic performance: A meta-analysis of findings. *Anxiety Journal, 4*, 27–42.

Seipp, B., & Schwarzer, C. (1990, July). *Anxiety and academic achievement: A meta-analysis of findings.* Paper presented at the 11th International Conference of the Society for Test Anxiety Research (STAR), Berlin.

Seligman, M. E. P. (1975). *Helplessness: On depression, development, and death.* San Francisco: Freeman.

Seligman, M. E. P., Maier, S. F., & Geer, J. (1968). The alleviation of learned helplessness in the dog. *Journal of Abnormal Psychology, 73*, 256–262.

Seligman, M. E. P., Maier, S. F., & Solomon, R. L. (1971). Unpredictable and uncontrollable aversive events. In F. R. Brush (Ed.), *Aversive conditioning and learning.* New York: Academic Press.

Shade, B. (1987). Ecological correlates of the educative style of Afro-American children. *Journal of Negro Education, 56*, 88–89.

Shanker, A. (1988, July). *State of our union.* Speech presented to American Federation of Teachers Convention, San Francisco, CA.

Shapira, A., & Madsen, M. C. (1969). Cooperative and competitive behavior of kibbutz and urban children in Israel. *Child Development, 40*, 609–617.

Shapiro, G. (1986). *A skeleton in the darkroom: Stories of serendipity in science.* New York: Harper & Row.

Sharan, Y., & Sharan, S. (Dec. 1989–Jan. 1990). Group investigation expands cooperative learning. *Educational Leadership*, pp. 17–21.

Shaw, M. E. (1958). Some motivational factors in cooperation and competition. *Journal of Personality, 26*, 155–169.

Shelton, J., & Hill, J. (1969). Effects on cheating of achievement anxiety and knowledge of peer performance. *Developmental Psychology, 1*, 449–455.

Shepard, L. A. (1989). Why we need better assessment. *Educational Leadership, 46*(7), 4–9.

Sherman, L. W., & Thomas, M. (1986). Mathematics achievement in cooperative versus individualistic goal-structured high school classrooms. *Journal of Educational Research, 79*, 169–172.

Shirts, R. (1969). *STARPOWER: Director's instructions.* Western Behavioral Science Institute, 1150 Silverado, La Jolla, CA 92037.

Shively, J. E., Feldhusen, J. F., & Treffinger, D. J. (1972). Developing creativity and related attitudes. *Journal of Experimental Education, 41*, 63–69.

Shuell, T. J. (1986). Cognitive conceptions of learning. *Review of Educational Research, 56*, 411–436.

Sigall, H., & Gould, R. (1977). The effects of self-esteem and evaluator demanding-ness of effort expenditure. *Journal of Personality and Social Psychology, 35,* 12–20.

Silberman, C. E. (1970). *Crisis in the classroom: The remaking of American education.* New York: Vintage.

Silver, M., & Sabini, J. (1981). Procrastinating. *Journal for the Theory of Social Behavior, 11,* 207–221.

Silver, M., & Sabini, J. (1982, January). When it's not really procrastination. *Psychology Today, 16,* 39–42.

Silverstein, B., & Krate, R. (1975). *Children of the dark ghetto: A developmental psychology.* New York: Praeger.

Simon, H. A. (1972). The heuristic compiler. In H. A. Simon & L. Siklossy (Eds.), *Representation and meaning.* Englewood Cliffs, NJ: Prentice-Hall.

Simon, H. A. (1973). The structure of ill-structured problems. *Artificial Intelligence, 4,* 181–202.

Simon, H. A. (1980). Problem solving and education. In D. T. Tuma & F. Reif (Eds.), *Problem solving and education.* Hillsdale, NJ: Erlbaum.

Simpson, C. (1981). Classroom structure and the organization of ability. *Sociology of Education, 54,* 120–132.

Singh, S. (1977). Achievement motivation and economic growth. *Indian Psychological Review, 14,* 52–56.

Skaalvik, E. M. (1990). Attribution of perceived academic results and relations with self-esteem in senior high school students. *Scandinavian Journal of Educational Research, 34,* 259–269.

Skaalvik, E. M., & Hagtvet, K. A. (1990). Academic achievement and self-concept: An analysis of causal predominance in a developmental perspective. *Journal of Personality and Social Psychology, 58,* 292–307.

Skinner, E. A., Wellborn, J. G., & Connell, J. P. (1990). What it takes to do well in school and whether I've got it: A process model of perceived control and children's engagement and achievement in school. *Journal of Educational Psychology, 82,* 22–32.

Skon, L., Johnson, D. W., & Johnson, R. T. (1981). Cooperative peer interaction versus individual competition and individualistic efforts: Effects on the acquisition of cognitive reasoning strategies. *Journal of Educational Psychology, 73,* 83–92.

Slavin, R. E. (1978). Student teams and comparison among equals: Effects on academic performance and student attitudes. *Journal of Educational Psychology, 70,* 532–538.

Slavin, R. E. (1983). When does cooperative learning increase student achievement? *Psychological Bulletin, 94,* 429–445.

Slavin, R. E. (1984). Students motivating students to excel: Cooperative incentives, cooperative tasks, and student achievement. *The Elementary School Journal, 85,* 53–64.

Slavin, R. E. (1987a). Ability grouping and student achievement in elementary schools: A best-evidence synthesis. *Review of Educational Research, 57,* 293–336.

Slavin, R. E. (1987b). Mastery learning reconsidered. *Review of Educational Research, 57,* 175–213.

Slavin, R. E., Leavey, M. B., & Madden, N. A. (1984). Combining cooperative learning and individualized instruction: Effects on student mathematics achievement, attitudes, and behaviors. *Elementary School Journal, 84,* 409–422.

Slavin, R. E., Madden, N. A., & Leavey, M. B. (1984). Effects of team assisted individualization on the mathematics achievement of academically handicapped and non-handicapped students. *Journal of Educational Psychology, 76,* 813–819.

Slavin, R., & Oickle, E. (1981). Effects of cooperative learning teams on student achievement and race relations: Treatment by race interactions. *Sociology of Education, 54,* 174–180.

Slavin, R. E., & Tanner, A. M. (1979). Effects of cooperative reward structures and individual accountability on productivity and learning. *Journal of Educational Research, 72,* 294–298.

Smith, C. A., & Morris, L. W. (1976). Effects of stimulative and sedative music on two components of test anxiety. *Psychological Reports, 38,* 1187–1193.

Smith, C. P. (1963). *Situational determinants of the expression of achievement motivation in thematic apperception.* Unpublished doctoral dissertation, University of Michigan.

Smith, E. (1982). The black female adolescent: A review of the educational career and psychological literature. *Psychology of Women Quarterly, 6,* 261–288.

Smith, M. B. (1969). *Social psychology and human values.* Chicago: Aldine.

Smith, T. W., Snyder, C. R., & Handelsman, M. M. (1982). On the self-serving function of an academic wooden leg: Test anxiety as a self-handicapping strategy. *Journal of Personality and Social Psychology, 42,* 314–321.

Smits, B., & Meyer, W.-U (1985). Lehrerreaktionen auf Erfolg und Misserfolg bei für begabt und unbegabt gehaltenen Schülern [Teachers' responses to success and failure of students believed to be gifted or not gifted]. Katholieke Universiteit, Nijmegen, Netherlands.

Snyder, C. R. (1984, September). Excuses, excuses: They sometimes actually work – to relieve the burden of blame. *Psychology Today, 18,* 50–55.

Snyder, M. L., Stephan, W. G., & Rosenfeld, C. (1976). Egotism and attribution. *Journal of Personality and Social Psychology, 33,* 435–441.

Sofia, J. P. (1978). *The influence of specific goal setting conferences on achievement, attributional patterns and goal setting behavior of elementary school boys.* Unpublished doctoral dissertation, School of Education, University of California at Berkeley.

Sohn, D. (1977). Affect-generating powers of effort and ability self-attributions of academic success and failure. *Journal of Educational Psychology, 69,* 500–505.

Solomon, L. J., & Rothblum, E. D. (1984). Academic procrastination: Frequency and cognitive-behavioral correlates. *Journal of Counseling Psychology, 31,* 503–509.

Sowder, L. (1987, June). *Searching for affect in the solution of story problems in mathematics.* Paper presented at the annual meeting of the American Educational Research Association, San Diego.

Spady, W. G. (1977). Competency based education: A bandwagon in search of a definition. *Educational Researcher, 6,* 9–14.

Spady, W. G. (1978). The concept and implications of competency based education. *Educational Leadership, 36,* 16–22.

Spady, W. G. (1982). Outcome-based instructional management: A sociological perspective. *The Australian Journal of Education, 26,* 123–143.

Spence, J. T., & Helmreich, R. L. (1983). Achievement-related motives and behaviors. In J. T. Spence (Ed.), *Achievement and achievement motives* (pp. 7–74). San Francisco: Freeman.

Spence, K. W. (1964). Anxiety (drive) level and performance in eyelid conditioning. *Psychological Bulletin, 61,* 129–139.

Spence, K. W., & Spence, J. (1966). The motivational components of manifest anxiety: Drive and drive stimuli. In C. D. Spielberger (Ed.), *Anxiety and behavior* (pp. 291–326). New York: Academic Press.

Spence, K. W., & Taylor, J. A. (1951). Anxiety and strength of the US as determiners of the amount of eyelid conditioning. *Journal of Experimental Psychology, 42,* 183–188.

Spencer, M. B. (1985). Cultural cognition and social cognition as identity: Correlates of black children's personal-social development. In M. Spencer, G. K. Brookins, & W. Allen (Eds.), *Beginnings: The social and affective development of black children* (pp. 215–300). Hillsdale, NJ: Erlbaum.

Spencer, R. M., & Weisberg, R. W. (1986). Context-dependent effects on analogical transfer. *Memory and Cognition, 14,* 442–449.

Spenner, K. I. (1985). The upgrading and downgrading of occupations: Issues, evidence, and implications for education. *Review of Educational Research, 55,* 125–154.

Spiegler, M. D., Morris, L. W., & Liebert, R. M. (1968). Cognitive and emotional components of test anxiety: Temporal factors. *Psychological Reports, 22,* 451–456.

Spielberger, C. D. (1966). Theory and research on anxiety. In C. D. Spielberger (Ed.), *Anxiety and behavior.* New York: Academic Press.

Spielberger, C. D. (1972). Anxiety as an emotional state. In C. D. Spielberger (Ed.), *Anxiety: Current trends in theory and research* (Vol. 1, pp. 23–49). New York: Academic Press.

Spielberger, C. D. (1980). *Test Anxiety Inventory: Preliminary professional manual.* Palo Alto, CA: Consulting Psychologists Press.

Spielberger, C. D., Anton, W., & Bedell, J. (1976). The nature and treatment of test anxiety. In M. Zuckerman & C. D. Spielberger (Eds.), *Emotion and anxiety: New concepts, methods, and applications* (pp. 317–345). Hillsdale, NJ: Erlbaum.

Spielberger, C. D., Gorsuch, R. L., & Lushene, R. E. (1970). *Manual for the state-trait anxiety inventory.* Palo Alto, CA: Consulting Psychologists Press.

Spielberger, C. D., & Vagg, P. R. (1987). The treatment of test anxiety: A transactional process model. In R. Schwarzer, H. M. van der Ploeg, & C. D. Spielberger (Eds.), *Advances in test anxiety research* (Vol. 5, pp. 179–186). Hillsdale, NJ: Erlbaum.

Stack, C. B. (1974). *All our kin: Strategies for survival in a black community.* New York: Harper & Row.

Stake, R., & Easley, J. (1978). *Case studies in science education* (Vols. 1 & 2). Urbana: Center for Instructional Research and Curriculum Evaluation and Committee on Culture and Cognition, University of Illinois at Urbana-Champagne.

State Task Force on Gangs and Drugs (1989, January). Final Report, California Council on Criminal Justice.

Steele, C. M. (1988). The psychology of self-affirmation: Sustaining the integrity of the self. In L. Berkowitz (Ed.), *Advances in experimental social psychology* (Vol. 21, pp. 261–302). New York: Academic Press.

Steele, S. (1989a). Being black and feeling blue. *The American Scholar, 58,* 497–508.

Steele, S. (1989b, February). The recoloring of campus life. *Harper's Magazine,* pp. 47–55.

Steinberg, L. D., Greenberger, E., Garduque, L., & McAuliff, S. (1982). High school students in the labor force: Some costs and benefits to schooling and learning. *Educational Evaluation and Policy Analysis, 4,* 363–372.

Steiner, R., Wiener, M., & Cromer, W. (1971). Comprehension training and identification for poor and good readers. *Journal of Educational Psychology, 62,* 506–513.

Stephan, C., Kennedy, J. C., & Aronson, E. (1977). The effects of friendship and outcome on task attribution. *Sociometry, 40,* 107–111.

Stephan, W. G., Rosenfield, D., & Stephan, C. (1976). Egotism in males and females. *Journal of Personality and Social Psychology, 34,* 1161–1167.

Stern, D. (1990). Continual learning on the job. *Educator,* The Graduate School of Education, University of California at Berkeley, *4*(3), 12–16.

Stern, D. (1984). School-based enterprise and the quality of work experience: A study of high school students. *Youth and Society, 15,* 401–427.

Stern, D., Hoachlander, E. G., Choy, S., & Benson, C. (1986, March). *One million hours a day: Vocational education in California public secondary schools* (Policy Paper #PP86-3-2). Berkeley, CA: University of California, PACE, School of Education.

Stern, P. (1983). *A multimethod analysis of student perceptions of causal dimensions.* Unpublished doctoral dissertation, University of California, Los Angeles.

Sternberg, R. J. (1985). Instrumental and componential approaches to the nature and training of intelligence. In S. Chipman, J. Segal, & R. Glaser (Eds.), *Thinking and learning skills: Current research and open questions.* Hillsdale, NJ: Erlbaum.

Sternberg, R. J., & Kastoor, B. (1986). Synthesis of research on the effectiveness of intellectual skills programs: Snake oil remedies or miracle cures? *Educational Leadership, 44*(2), 60–67.

Sternberg, R. M. (1987). A unified theory of intellectual exceptionality. In J. C. Day & J. G. Borkowski (Eds.), *Intelligence and exceptionality: New directions for theory, assessment, and instructional practices* (pp. 135–172). Norwood, NJ: Ablex.

Stevenson, H., & Flanagan, C. (1990, October). *A comparative study of Chinese and Japanese high school students.* Paper presented at National Science Foundation Education and Human Resources Directorate Research in Teaching and Learning, Project Directors Meeting, Washington, DC.

Stevenson, J. A. (1921). *The project method of teaching.* New York: Macmillan.

Stipek, D. (1981). Children's perceptions of their own and their classmates' ability. *Journal of Educational Psychology, 73,* 404–410.

Stipek, D. (1984). The development of achievement motivation. In R. Ames & C. Ames (Eds.), *Research on motivation in education* (Vol. 1, pp. 145–176). New York: Academic Press.

Stipek, D. J. (1988). *Motivation to learn: From theory to practice.* Englewood Cliffs, NJ: Prentice-Hall.

Stipek, D. J., & Weisz, J. R. (1981). Perceived personal control and academic achievement. *Review of Educational Research, 51,* 101–137.

Streufert, S., & Streufert, S. C. (1969). Effects of conceptual structure, failure, and success on attribution of causality and interpersonal attitudes. *Journal of Personality and Social Psychology, 11,* 138–247.

Strick, A. (1978). *Injustice for all.* New York: Penguin.

Strober, M. (1987, Spring). The scope of microeconomics: Implications for economic education. *Journal of Economic Education, 18,* 135–149.

Strober, M. (1990, Jan.–Feb.). Kindling students' passion for economics. *Stanford Observer.*

Strodtbeck, F. L. (1958). Family interaction, values and achievement. In D. D. McClelland, A. L. Baldwin, U. Bronfenbrenner, & F. L. Strodtbeck (Eds.), *Talent and society* (pp. 259–266). Princeton, NJ: Van Nostrand.

Strodtbeck, F. L., McDonald, M. R., & Rosen, B. (1957). Evaluations of occupations: A reflection of Jewish and Italian mobility differences. *American Sociological Review, 22,* 546–553.

Stulac, J. (1975). *The self-fulfilling prophecy: Modifying the effects of a unidimensional perception of academic competence in task-oriented groups.* Unpublished doctoral dissertation, Stanford University.

Suarez-Orozco, M. M. (1989). *Central American refugees and U.S. high schools: A psychological study of motivation and achievement.* Stanford: Stanford University Press.

Suls, J. M., & Miller, R. L. (Eds.). (1977). *Social comparison processes: Theoretical and empirical perspectives.* Washington, DC: Hemisphere.

Sweeney, P. D., Anderson, K., & Bailey, S. (1986). Attributional style in depression: A meta-analytic review. *Journal of Personality and Social Psychology, 50,* 974–991.

Taynor, J., & Deaux, K. (1973). When women are more deserving than men: Equity, attributions, and perceived sex differences. *Journal of Personality and Social Psychology, 28,* 360–367.

Taylor, J. A. (1951). The relationship of anxiety to the conditioned eyelid response. *Journal of Experimental Psychology, 41,* 81–82.

Taylor, J. A. (1953). A personality scale of manifest anxiety. *Journal of Abnormal and Social Psychology, 48,* 285–290.

Taylor, J. A. (1956). Drive theory and manifest anxiety. *Psychological Bulletin, 53,* 303–320.

Taylor, S. E., & Huesmann, L. R. (1974). Expectancy confirmed again: A computer investigation of expectancy theory. *Journal of Experimental Social Psychology, 10,* 497–501.

Teevan, R. C., & Fischer, R. (1967). *Hostile press and childhood reinforcement patterns: A replication.* Unpublished manuscript, Bucknell University, Lewisburg, PA.

Tennen, H., & Eller, S. J. (1977). Attributional components of learned helplessness and facilitation. *Journal of Personality and Social Psychology, 35,* 265–271.

Tetlock, P. E. (1985). Toward an intuitive politician model of attribution process. In B. R. Schlenker (Ed.), *The self in social life.* Hillsdale, NJ: Erlbaum.

Tetlock, P. E., & Levi, A. (1982). Attribution bias: On the inconclusiveness of the cognition-motivation debate. *Journal of Experimental Social Psychology, 18,* 68–88.

Thomas, J. W. (1980). Agency and achievement: Self-management and self-regard. *Review of Educational Research, 50,* 213–240.

Thomas, J. W. (1988). Proficiency at academic studying. *Contemporary Educational Psychology, 13,* 265–275.

Thomas, J. W., & Rohwer, W. D., Jr. (1986). Academic studying: The role of learning strategies. *Educational Psychologist, 21,* 19–41.

Thurow, L. C. (1975). *Generating inequality: Mechanisms of distribution in the U.S. economy.* New York: Basic Books.

Tjosvold, D., Johnson, D. W., & Johnson, R. (1984). Influence strategy, perspective-taking, and relationships between high- and low-power individuals in cooperative and competitive contexts. *The Journal of Psychology, 116,* 187–202.

Tobias, S. (1980). Anxiety and instruction. In I. G. Sarason (Ed.), *Test anxiety: Theory, research and applications* (pp. 289–309). Hillsdale, NJ: Erlbaum.

Tobias, S. (1985). Test anxiety: Interference, defective skills, and cognitive capacity. *Educational Psychologist, 20,* 135–142.

Tobias, S. (1986). Anxiety and cognitive processing of instruction. In R. Schwarzer (Ed.), *Self-related cognitions in anxiety and motivation* (pp. 35–54). Hillsdale, NJ: Erlbaum.

Tobias, S. (1989, September). Tracked to fail. *Psychology Today, 23,* 54–58, 60.

Toffler, A. (1970). *Future shock.* New York: Random House.

Tolman, E. C. (1932). *Purposive behavior in animals and men.* New York: Appleton-Century-Crofts.

Topman, R. M., & Jansen, T. (1984). "I really can't do it, anyway": The treatment of test anxiety. In H. M. van der Ploeg, R. Schwarzer, & C. D. Spielberger (Eds.), *Advances in test anxiety research* (Vol. 3, pp. 243–251). Hillsdale, NJ: Erlbaum.

Torrance, E. P. (1965). *Rewarding creative behavior: Experiments in classroom creativity.* Englewood Cliffs, NJ: Prentice-Hall.

Torrance, E. P. (1972). Can we teach children to think creatively? *Journal of Creative Behavior, 6,* 114–143.

Toufexis, A. (1989, May 1). Report cards can hurt you. *Time,* p. 75.

Toulmin, S. E., Reike, R., & Janik, A. (1979). *An introduction to reasoning.* New York: Macmillan.

Treffinger, D. J. (1971). *Improving children's creative problem solving ability: Effects of distribution of training, teacher involvement, and teacher's divergent thinking ability on instruction* (Final Report, Office of Education, Bureau Number BR-8-A-042, Grant Number OEG-5-70-0029 (509)). West Lafayette, IN: Purdue University. (ERIC Document Reproduction Service No. ED 063 268)

Treffinger, D. J., & Ripple, R. E. (1970). *Programmed instruction in creative problem solving: An interpretation of recent research findings.* Mimeographed. Lafayette, IN: Purdue University.

Treisman, P. U. (1985). A study of the mathematics performance of black students at the University of California. Unpublished doctoral dissertation, University of California, Berkeley.

Trimble, K., & Sinclair, R. L. (1986, April). *Ability grouping and differing conditions for learning: An analysis of content and instruction in ability-grouped classes.* Paper presented at the annual meeting of the American Educational Research Association, San Francisco.

Trope, Y., & Brickman, P. (1975). Difficulty and diagnosticity as determinants of choice among tasks. *Journal of Personality and Social Psychology, 31,* 918–926.

Tryon, G. (1980). The measurement and treatment of test anxiety. *Review of Educational Research, 50,* 353–372.

Tucker, J. A., Vuchinich, R. E., & Sobell, M. B. (1981). Alcohol consumption as a self-handicapping strategy. *Journal of Abnormal Psychology, 90,* 220–230.

Tulving, E., & Thomson, D. M. (1973). Encoding specificity and retrieval processes in episodic memory. *Psychological Review, 80,* 352–373.

Tyack, D., & Hansot, E. (1982). Hard times, hard choices. *Phi Delta Kappan, 3,* 511.

Vagg, P. R., & Papsdorf, J. (1987). Cognitive therapy, biofeedback and study skills in the treatment of test anxiety. In C. D. Spielberger & P. R. Vagg (Eds.), *The assessment and treatment of test anxiety.* New York: McGraw-Hill.

Valle, V. A. (1974). *Attributions of stability as a mediator in the changing of expectations.* Unpublished doctoral dissertation, University of Pittsburgh.

van der Ploeg-Stapert, J. D., & van der Ploeg, H. M. (1985). A multifaceted behavioral treatment program of test anxiety. In H. M. van der Ploeg, R. Schwarzer, & C. D. Spielberger (Eds.), *Advances in test anxiety research* (Vol. 4, pp. 43–52). Lisse, The Netherlands: Swets & Zeitlinger.

van der Ploeg-Stapert, J. D., & van der Ploeg, H. M. (1987). The evaluation and follow-up of a behavioral group treatment of test anxious adolescents. In R. Schwarzer, H. M. van der Ploeg, & C. D. Spielberger (Eds.), *Advances in test anxiety research* (Vol. 5, pp. 187–194). Hillsdale, NJ: Erlbaum.

Veroff, J. (1969). Social comparison and the development of achievement motivation. In C. P. Smith (Ed.), *Achievement-related motives in children*. New York: Sage.

Veroff, J., & Veroff, J. B. (1972). Reconsideration of a measure of power motivation. *Psychological Bulletin, 78*, 279–291.

Vroom, V. H. (1964). *Work and motivation*. New York: Wiley.

Wahba, N. A., & Bridwell, L. G. (1976). Maslow reconsidered: A review of research on the need of hierarchy theory. *Organizational Behavior and Human Performance, 15*, 212–240.

Wakefield, J. (1988). Problem finding in the arts and sciences. *Questioning Exchange, 2*, 133–140.

Wallace, P. A. (1974). *Pathways to work: Unemployment among black teenage females*. Lexington, MA: Lexington Books.

Wang, M. C., & Stiles, B. (1976). An investigation of children's concept of self-responsibility for their school learning. *American Educational Research Journal, 13*, 159–179.

Weaver, D., & Brickman, P. (1974). Expectancy, feedback and disconfirmation as independent factors in outcome satisfaction. *Journal of Personality and Social Psychology, 30*, 420–428.

Weil, M. M., Rosen, L. D., & Sears, D. C. (1987). The computerphobia reduction program: Year 1. Program development and preliminary results. *Behavior Research Methods, Instruments, and Computers, 19*(2), 1980–1984.

Weiner, B. (1972). *Theories of motivation: From mechanism to cognition*. Chicago: Markham.

Weiner, B. (1974). *Achievement motivation and attribution theory*. Morristown, NJ: General Learning Press.

Weiner, B. (1977). An attributional model for educational psychology. In L. Shulman (Ed.), *Review of research in education* (Vol. 4). Itasca, IL: Peacock.

Weiner, B. (1979). A theory of motivation for some classroom experiences. *Journal of Educational Psychology, 71*, 3–25.

Weiner, B. (1983). Some methodological pitfalls in attributional research. *Journal of Educational Psychology, 74*, 530–543.

Weiner, B. (1985). An attributional theory of achievement motivation and emotion. *Psychological Review, 92*, 548–573.

Weiner, B., & Brown, J. (1984). All's well that ends. *Journal of Educational Psychology, 76*, 169–171.

Weiner, B., Frieze, L., Kukla, A., Reed, L., Rest, S., & Rosenbaum, R. (1971). Perceiving the causes of success and failure. In E. E. Jones, D. E. Kanouse, H. H. Kelley, R. E. Nisbett, S. Valins, & B. Weiner (Eds.), *Attribution: Perceiving the causes of behavior* (pp. 95–121). Morristown, NJ: General Learning Press.

Weiner, B., Heckhausen, H., Meyer, W., & Cook, R. (1972). Causal ascriptions and achievement behavior: A conceptual analysis of effect and reanalysis of locus of control. *Journal of Personality and Social Psychology, 21*, 239–248.

Weiner, B., & Kukla, A. (1970). An attributional analysis of achievement motivation. *Journal of Personality and Social Psychology, 15*, 1–20.

Weiner, B., & Sierad, J. (1975). Misattribution for failure and enhancement of achievement strivings. *Journal of Personality and Social Psychology, 31*, 415–421.

Weinert, F. E., & Kluwe, R. H. (Eds.). (1978). *Metacognition, motivation, and understanding*. Hillsdale, NJ: Erlbaum.

Weinstein, C. E., Cubberly, W. E., & Richardson, F. C. (1982). The effects of test anxiety on learning at superficial and deep levels of processing. *Contemporary Educational Psychology, 7*, 107–112.

Weinstein, C. E., & Mayer, R. E. (1986). The teaching of learning strategies. In M. C. Wittrock (Ed.), *Handbook of research on teaching* (3rd ed., pp. 315–325). New York: Collier Macmillan.

Weinstein, R. (1976). Reading group membership in first grade: Teacher behaviors and pupil experience over time. *Journal of Educational Psychology, 68,* 103–116.

Weinstein, R. S. (1981, April). Student perspectives on achievement in varied classroom environments. In P. Blumenfeld (Chair), *Student perspectives and the study of the classroom.* Symposium conducted at the meeting of the American Educational Research Association, Los Angeles.

Weinstein, R. S. (1983). Student perceptions of schooling. *Elementary School Journal, 83,* 289–312.

Weinstein, R. S. (1985). Student mediation of classroom expectancy effects. In J. B. Dusek, V. C. Hall, & W. J. Meyer (Eds.), *Teacher expectancies* (pp. 329–349). Hillsdale, NJ: Erlbaum.

Weinstein, R. S. (1986). The teaching of reading and children's awareness of teacher expectations. In T. E. Raphael (Ed.), *The contents of school-based literacy.* New York: Random House.

Weinstein, R. (1989). Perception of classroom processes and student motivation: Children's views of self-fulfilling prophecies. In R. E. Ames & C. Ames (Eds.), *Research on motivation in education* (Vol. 3). New York: Academic Press.

Weinstein, R. S., Marshall, H. H., Sharp, L., & Botkin, M. (1987). Pygmalion and the student: Age and classroom differences in children's awareness of teacher expectations. *Child Development, 58,* 1079–1093.

Weinstein, R. S., & Middlestadt, S. E. (1979). Student perceptions of teacher interactions with male high and low achievers. *Journal of Educational Psychology, 71,* 421–431.

Weiss, D. J. (1983). *New horizons in testing: Latent trait test theory and computerized adaptive testing.* New York: Academic Press.

Welles, J. F. (1988). *The story of stupidity: A history of Western idiocy from the days of Greece to the moment you saw this book.* Orient, NY: Mount Pleasant Press.

Wertheimer, M. (1959). *Productive thinking.* New York: Harper & Row.

West, C. K., Fish, J. A., & Stevens, R. J. (1980). General self-concept, self-concept of academic ability and school achievement: Implications for "causes" of self-concept. *Australian Journal of Education, 24,* 194–213.

Whitley, B. E., Jr., & Frieze, I. H. (1985). Children's causal attributions for success and failure in achievement settings: A meta-analysis. *Journal of Experimental Psychology, 77,* 608–616.

White, R. W. (1959). Motivation reconsidered: The concept of competence. *Psychological Review, 66,* 297–333.

Whitehead, A. N. (1929). *The aims of education.* New York: New American Library.

Wicker, F. W., Payne, G. C., & Morgan, R. D. (1983). Participant descriptions of guilt and shame. *Motivation and Emotion, 7,* 25–39.

Wieland-Eckelmann, R., Bösel, R., & Dadorrek, W. (1987). *Coping styles, temporal patterns of states, and performance.* Paper presented at the 8th International Conference of the Society for Test Anxiety Research, Bergen, Norway.

Wigfield, A., Eccles, J. S., Midgley, C., Iver, D. M., & Reuman, D. (1987). *Changes in children's self-concept of ability, achievement values, and general self-esteem at early adolescence.* Paper presented at the annual meeting of the American Education Research Association, Washington, DC.

Wiggins, G. (1989, May). A true test: Toward more authentic and equitable assessment. *Phi Delta Kappan,* 703–713.

Willig, A. C., Harnisch, D. L., Hill, K. T., & Maehr, M. L. (1983). Sociocultural and educational correlates of success–failure attributions and evaluation anxiety in the school setting for Black, Hispanic, and Anglo children.

Wilson, T. D., & Linville, P. W. (1985). Improving the performance of college freshmen with attributional techniques. *Journal of Personality and Social Psychology, 49*, 287–293.

Wimer, S., & Kelley, H. H. (1982). An investigation of the dimensions of causal analysis. *Journal of Personality and Social Psychology, 43*, 1142–1162.

Wine, J. (1971). Test anxiety and direction of attention. *Psychological Bulletin, 76*, 92–104.

Wine, J. (1973). *Cognitive-attentional approaches to test anxiety modification.* Paper presented to Anxiety and Instruction Symposium at the annual meetings of the American Psychological Association, Montreal.

Wine, J. D. (1980). Cognitive-attentional theory of test anxiety. In I. G. Sarason (Ed.), *Test anxiety: Theory, research, and applications* (pp. 349–385). Hillsdale, NJ: Erlbaum.

Wineburg, S. S. (1987a). Does research count in the lives of behavioral scientists? *Educational Researcher, 16*(9), 42–44.

Wineburg, S. S. (1987b). The self-fulfillment of the self-fulfilling prophecy. *Educational Research, 16*(9), 28–37.

Winograd, P. (1984). Strategic difficulties in summarizing texts. *Reading Research Quarterly, 19*, 404–425.

Winter, D. G. (1973). *The power motive.* New York: The Free Press.

Winter, D. G. (1987). Leader appeal, leader performance, and the motive profiles of leaders and followers: A study of American presidents and elections. *Journal of Personality and Social Psychology, 52*, 196–202.

Winter, D. G., & Carlson, L. A. (1988). Using motive scores in the psychobiographical study of an individual: The case of Richard Nixon. *Journal of Personality, 56*, 75–103.

Winterbottom, M. R. (1953). The relation of need for achievement to learning experiences in independence and mastery. In J. Atkinson (Ed.), *Motives in fantasy, action, and society* (pp. 453–478). Princeton, NJ: Van Nostrand.

Wittmaier, B. (1972). Test anxiety and study habits. *Journal of Educational Research, 65*, 852–854.

Wolf, D. P. (1989). Portfolio assessment: Sampling student work. *Educational Leadership, 46*(7), 35–40.

Wolff, R. P. (1969). *The ideal of the university.* Boston: Beacon.

Wolosin, R. J., Sherman, S. J., & Till, A. (1973). Effects of cooperation and competition on responsibility attribution after success and failure. *Journal of Personality and Social Psychology, 15*, 1–20.

Wolpe, J. (1973). *The practice of behavior therapy* (2nd ed.). New York: Pergamon.

Wong, P. T. P., & Weiner, B. (1981). When people ask "why" questions and the heuristics of attributional search. *Journal of Personality and Social Psychology, 40*, 650–663.

Woodson, C. E. (1975). *Motivational effects of two-stage testing.* Unpublished manuscript, Institute of Human Learning, University of California, Berkeley.

Woodworth, R. S. (1918). *Dynamic psychology.* New York: Columbia University Press.

Wurman, R. S. (1989). *Information anxiety.* New York: Doubleday.

Wylie, R. (1979). *The self-concept: Theory and research on selected topics* (Vol. 2). Lincoln: University of Nebraska Press.

Yerkes, R. M., & Dodson, J. D. (1908). The relation of strength of stimulus to rapidity of habit formation. *Journal of Comparative Neurology, 18,* 459–482.

Young, V. H. (1974). A black American socialization pattern. *American Ethnologist, 1,* 415–431.

Yussen, S. R. (1985). The role of metacognition in contemporary theories of cognitive development. In D. L. Forrest-Pressley, G. E. MacKinnon, & T. G. Waller (Eds.), *Metacognition, cognition, and human performance: Vol. 1. Theoretical perspectives* (pp. 253–283). New York: Academic Press.

Yussen, S. R., & Levy, V. (1975). Developmental changes in predicting one's own span of short-term memory. *Journal of Experimental Child Psychology, 19,* 502–508.

Zajonc, R. B. (1984). On the primacy of affect. *American Psychologist, 39,* 117–123.

Zajonc, R. B., & Brickman, P. (1969). Expectancy and feedback as independent factors in task performance. *Journal of Personality and Social Psychology, 11,* 148–156.

Zatz, S., & Chassin, L. (1983). *Journal of Consulting and Clinical Psychology, 51,* 526–534.

Zeidner, M., Klingman, A., & Papko, O. (1987, June). *Enhancing students' test coping skills: Report of a psychological health education program.* Paper presented at the meeting of the Society for Test Research, Bergen, Norway.

Zimmer, J. W., Meinke, D. L., & Hocevar, D. J. (1989). *Effects of massed versus distributed practice on achievement and test anxiety.* Paper presented at the Tenth International Meeting of the Society for Test Anxiety Research, Amsterdam, Netherlands.

Zimmerman, B. J. (1970). The relationship between teacher classroom behavior and student school anxiety levels. *Psychology in the Schools, 7,* 89–93.

Zimmerman, B. J. (1989). Models of self-regulated learning and academic achievement. In B. J. Zimmerman & D. H. Schunk (Eds.), *Self-regulated learning and academic achievement: Theory, research, and practice* (pp. 1–25). New York: Springer Verlag.

Zoeller, C., Mahoney, G., & Weiner, B. (1983). Effects of attribution training on the assembly task performance of mentally retarded adults. *American Journal of Mental Deficiency, 88,* 109–112.

Zuckerman, M. (1979). Attribution of success and failure revisited, or: The motivational bias is alive and well in attribution theory. *Journal of Personality, 47,* 245–287.

Zytkoskee, A., & Strickland, B. (1971). Delay of gratification and internal versus external control among adolescents of low socioeconomic status. *Developmental Psychology, 4,* 93–98.

Author index

Subject Index

ability: as attributions, 169; as capacity, 38, 168–9; developmental conceptions of, 81–3; effort as a cue for, 74–6, 78–9, 82–3; entity views of, 22–3, 55, 82, 137, 142, 169; help seeking as a cue for, 137, 178; incremental view of, 22–3, 82, 142, 169, 197; multidimensional nature of, 154, 169, 279; perceived importance of, 23, 29, 74–5, 79–83, 89, 151; as resource, 22, 197; school as ability game, 136–9, 271; self-perceptions of, 74–5, 98–9, 102, 113, 118, 121, 125, 128, 136–9, 142, 159, 167, 168–9, 265, 271, 272, 279, 280; as strategy, 169–216, 196–8; stratification by ability, 138–9, 154, 258; tracking (grouping) by ability, 138–9, 145, 153; *see also* minority achievement dynamics, unidimensional classrooms
ability attributions, 53–5, 60, 62, 75
absent audience, 135
absolute standards, 163, 271
academic cheating, 91
academic standards, 39, 69, 117–19, 200–3
academic study, 39, 200–3
academic wooden leg, 88–9
acting white, 94
active avoiders, 124
amount vs. quality of effort, 68, 96, 201, 203
anxiety: anxious defensive, 32; appraisal stage of, 114, 114f, 116f, 117, 127; arousal (drive), 104, 106–10, 111, 112, 198; competition and, 128; excitability, level of, 106; failure avoidance and, 115–18, 120, 128; failure

of self, 105, 112–21, 128; hierarchy of anxiety, 122; limited capacity model of, 111; reduction of, 124–5, 126–7; retrieval deficit view, 110, 114f, 118, 120, 123; school performance and, 104–5, 118–19, 121–2; skill deficit view, 105, 110–12, 114f, 117, 119–20,123; success orientation and, 128; Taylor Manifest Anxiety Scale, 32; Test Anxiety Scale for Children, 113; test-preparation stage of, 114, 114f, 116f, 117, 127; test-taking stage of, 114, 114f, 116f, 117–18, 124–7; testwiseness, 123; trait-state theory of, 107–9, 156; untimed testing, 126–7; variation of test item order, 124–5; worry, 105, 109–110, 112, 113, 117; Yerkes-Dodson Law, 106, 111; *see also* drive theory, reduction of anxiety
anxious defensive persons, 32
approach–avoidance, 15, 28–9, 32–3, 41, 47, 52, 118, 121
Atkinson's theory of achievement motivation, *see* need achievement theory of motivation
attractiveness of goals, 33, 39
attribution retraining, 49, 67–8; *see also* motivation training
attributions: as ability, 169; ability attributions, 53–5, 60, 62, 75; controllability, 54, 65; critique and analysis of, 59–60, 68–71; educational implications of, 62–8; effort attributions, 53–5, 62–5, 70–1; ethnic differences, 61–2; Heider's causal matrix, 53–5; human development and, 55; intentionality, 54; learned helplessness, 48, 65–7, *see also* personal helplessness;

343